IRAN UNDER AHMADINEJAD
The politics of confrontation

ALI M. ANSARI

ADELPHI PAPER 393

The International Institute for Strategic Studies
Arundel House | 13–15 Arundel Street | Temple Place | London | WC2R 3DX | UK

ADELPHI PAPER 393

First published December 2007 by **Routledge**
4 Park Square, Milton Park, Abingdon, Oxon, OX14 4RN

for **The International Institute for Strategic Studies**
Arundel House, 13–15 Arundel Street, Temple Place, London, WC2R 3DX, UK
www.iiss.org

Simultaneously published in the USA and Canada by **Routledge**
270 Madison Ave., New York, NY 10016

Routledge is an imprint of Taylor & Francis, an Informa Business

DIRECTOR-GENERAL AND CHIEF EXECUTIVE John Chipman
EDITOR Patrick Cronin
MANAGER FOR EDITORIAL SERVICES Ayse Abdullah
ASSISTANT EDITOR Katharine Fletcher
PRODUCTION John Buck
COVER IMAGE Getty

Printed and bound in Great Britain by Bell & Bain Ltd, Thornliebank, Glasgow

British Library Cataloguing in Publication Data
A catalogue record for this book is available from the British Library

Library of Congress Cataloging in Publication Data

ISBN 978-0-415-45486-5
ISSN 0567-932X

Contents

Introduction **5**
A totalitarian presidency? 6
A note on information-gathering on Iran 7

Part I: The Background to Ahmadinejad's Rise

Chapter One **The Rafsanjani and Khatami Presidencies** **11**
'The era of reconstruction' 11
The ascent of the reform movement 16
Borrowing from the West: 'left' and 'right' and the 'neo-conservative' reaction 19

Chapter Two **The Triumph of the Authoritarians** **23**
Populism and other strategies 24
The mayor of Tehran 28
The Majlis elections 30
The election of Ahmadinejad 32
Ahmadinejad: policies and presentation 37

Part II: The 'Third Islamic Revolution'

Chapter Three **The Ahmadinejad Presidency: Image and Foreign Policy** **41**
The cult of the president 42
Sanctifying the nation 44
The revolution in foreign policy 45
The nuclear imbroglio 47
Israel 51
'The Socrates of the age' 53
The turn east 54
Towards the UNSC 58
Iraq 58
2006: uranium enrichment and Lebanon 62

Chapter Four **The Ahmadinejad Presidency: Domestic Policy** **67**
The economy, part one: 'economics is for donkeys' 68
The iconoclast 70
A new elite and its opponents 72
Repression 76
Vulgar nationalism 77
The economy, part two: oil and excess 79
Imperial overstretch 83
Economic crisis 83
The critics convene 85
Defeat? 87

Conclusion **91**

Notes **97**

INTRODUCTION

The election of Mahmoud Ahmadinejad to the presidency of the Islamic Republic of Iran in the summer of 2005 thrust Iran into the international limelight in a way that few would have predicted. Robust, confrontational and given to bombastic rhetoric, Ahmadinejad drew condemnation from the West and praise from the Middle Eastern street in almost equal measure. This paper looks at the details of his political rise and assesses his presidency to date within the context of the dynamics of Iranian politics. It also measures his achievements against his own goals as outlined in 2005.

Analysing key events and trends during his presidency, the study will assess the effectiveness of Ahmadinejad's policies, and the consequences of his populism, in particular his use of nationalism and the cult of the Twelfth Imam.[1] The study will argue that Ahmadinejad, far from retrenching the conservative values of the early revolution, is very much a product of the social and political changes which have occurred since the end of the Iran–Iraq War; that his populism in both politics and economics, along with the maintenance of a confrontational posture abroad, represents an ad hoc, and somewhat incoherent, attempt to disguise the growing contradictions that afflict the Islamic Republic, and the conservative vision of an unaccountable Islamic autocracy faced with growing dissatisfaction, especially among key sections of the elite.

Above all, the paper will show that, far from reconciling the Islamic Republic's many contradictions, Ahmadinejad's policies have resulted in the exacerbation of tensions, and inaugurated a depreciating cycle of crisis and repression, increasingly driven and determined by its own self-justifying logic. The internal coherence of this logic drives the faithful and maintains a momentum of certainty among the president and his allies. However, powerful ideological conviction will not be sufficient to overcome the very real institutional and economic weaknesses of the Islamic Republic – weaknesses to which the president's faction itself contributed by undermining those in power when it was in the political wilderness. In particular, the continuing failure to provide a systematic plan for the economic regeneration of the country may ultimately prove to be Ahmadinejad's undoing.

The focus of this paper is the nature of the contemporary Iranian state under the management of Ahmadinejad and his allies. The paper seeks to present an interpretative framework for understanding this state, its development to date and its possible future trajectories in light of the changes that have occurred since 2005. It does not intend to be an exhaustive account of the presidency of Mahmoud Ahmadinejad, but instead will take a thematic approach highlighting those key events, ideas and developments that have most impacted the progress of the Islamic Republic of Iran.

A totalitarian presidency?

Much has been made of the radicalisation of Iranian politics under Ahmadinejad, and the dramatic swing to the extremes his presidency appears to represent. Partly as a result of his own rhetoric, but also in large measure as a consequence of our own tendency to understand phenomena through analogy, Ahmadinejad has been described as Iran's answer to both Hitler and Stalin, or sometimes as a radical socialist populist in the same vein as Hugo Chávez, with whom he has formed a cordial relationship. The problem with these analogies, echoed by pundits within Iran, is that they tend to obfuscate as much as illuminate the real nature of Ahmadinejad's power and his ideas. They depend in order to work on structural and cultural similarities which simply do not exist. One could certainly make an interesting case for parallels between the failure of the democratic movement under Ahmadinejad's predecessor, Mohammad Khatami, and that of the democratic movement in the Weimar Republic. But for all the superficial similarity in their political climates, Iran in 2007 is not the Germany of the interwar years, either in terms of political culture or economic structure. Most importantly perhaps, Iran is not an industrial society as understood in the West. Industry of course exists, but the social organisation, structures and discipline that characterise a classic industrial society are largely absent from Iran, where informal networks and trade relationships dominate the political culture. The aspirant totalitarian ruler would therefore find his options severely constrained by the shifting realities of power in Iran.

One might respond that sheer political will and the determination to dominate could overcome these obstacles, and, as this paper will show, attempts have been made to construct a charisma for the president to help him consolidate his personal power. But the construction of a charisma conflicts with the Islamic orthodoxy of the state, and, crucially, does not have the approval of the vested interests that surround the president. Moreover, partly as a consequence of the actions of the hardliners themselves (of whom Ahmadinejad is one), large sections of the population remain too cynical, disillusioned and disengaged to be easily swayed by the charismatic claims of the president. Those that remain engaged find the reality of the economy at odds with the aspirations articulated by the president. Notwithstanding the characteristics that we find familiar, in order to understand Ahmadinejad, it is important to appreciate the environment that has produced him. It is an environment characterised more by mercantile interests and traditional networks than by industry and order, and, in consequence, it sets particular limits on the kind of president he can be.

A note on information-gathering on Iran

Despite the undoubted repression to which it has been subject since at least 2004, Iranian society remains diverse and politically plural. There are of course red lines that writers and commentators may not cross, for instance, no criticism of the Supreme Leader is permitted. The current government is enthusiastically adding more red lines, most of which are loosely defined in terms of protecting national security. It is not permitted, for example, to openly argue that Iran should cease enrichment of uranium. This is general accepted to be a 'sovereign right' and to argue against it would be tantamount to treason. Such discussions as exist are therefore broad and allusive, and readers need to be able to recognise the implicit meaning of texts that treat these issues. Writers, especially those who oppose government policy or the regime in general, tend to resort to metaphor and analogy to convey their arguments; this tactic has a long pedigree in Iran. An understanding of the myths and motifs being used is therefore necessary when dealing with written sources from Iran, and care must be taken when interpreting them.

The print media is no longer the primary repository of political discussion, and newspapers and journals tend towards self-censorship for fear of being suspended or closed down. But technological change has resulted in a shift of focus. Much of the dynamism that characterised what was probably the most radical press in the Middle East at the turn of the new century has now relocated to the web. Iran has one of the most active web communities in the world, and for a country that in economic terms remains part of the developing world, the growth of its Internet services and the blogging community in particular has been dramatic.

While the authorities have sought to restrict access, this has proved difficult, and many senior members of the elite have taken to inaugurating their own web-based news services, sometimes complete with an English-language site as well. Among the most popular of such sites is Baztab,[2] which is owned and run by the former head of the Iranian Revolutionary Guard Corps (IRGC), Mohsen Rezai, who now sits on the Expediency Council, the powerful arbitration council chaired by former president Hashemi Rafsanjani. Rezai is by background and ideological inclination a conservative, but it is indicative of the pluralism mentioned above that though his reading of conservatism is very much at odds with that espoused by the current president, he has generally been in a position where he is able to meet Ahmadinejad's attempts to filter and/or restrict Baztab with barely disguised contempt. Baztab is testament to the realisation among members of the Iranian political elite that some attempt at objectivity in news dissemination is necessary for the purposes of credibility and, ultimately, for the exercise of influence. Perhaps because of the status of its owner, Baztab has been one of the most successful of the news sites in pushing the frontiers of political acceptability. But sites that disseminate news from a wide range of sources have proliferated in recent years, and the avid surfer can find sites related to all the political factions current in Iran, from reformists all the way through to those who stand somewhere to the right of the president.

Given the quantity of potential sources, it serves the reader to be discerning, especially where opinion columns are concerned. Opinion pages are useful in that they illustrate particular ideological persuasions, but they are frequently little more than outlets for idle gossip and conspiracy theories. The Raja News website,[3] administered by Fatemeh Rajabi, the wife of the official government spokesman, Gholamhossein Elham, is a good example of this. Rajabi has a well-earned reputation as an intemperate voice of the extreme right, a reputation for which there is strong competition.[4]

It is of course true that web-based news resources are less accessible to the general population than are the more traditional mediums, because of the country's limited telecommunications infrastructure, and this may account for the greater latitude they have been afforded. But while the majority of the country may not have access to, or simply not be interested in, the more arcane political discussions that take place on the web, the Internet has a wider influence too, in that important pieces of news are often posted first on the web, and then downloaded and disseminated through another technological medium, usually the favourite tool of youth culture in Iran, the mobile phone. As will be seen, the mobile phone has proved to be an extremely important campaigning tool in elections, and it is also used more broadly as a means of creating community and of criticising the president. In the aftermath of the sudden announcement of petrol rationing in the middle of 2007, Iran's main mobile network reportedly crashed, such was the torrent of abuse and jokes being circulated. Mobile phones have also facilitated the increased dissemination of videos and pictures of incidents the government would prefer were not shown, and these have emerged with alarming frequency, from the point of view of the regime, on websites such as YouTube. Technology provides observers with a window on the undercurrents of Iranian political culture, and reminds us that for all the government's repressiveness, a thriving Iranian underground persists.

Part I: The Background to Ahmadinejad's Rise

CHAPTER ONE

The Rafsanjani and Khatami Presidencies

In his presidential election campaign in 2005, Ahmadinejad made great play of the fact that he sought to inaugurate the 'third Islamic revolution', and return the country to the purity of the early days of revolutionary fervour. The first revolution had come with the departure of the Shah and the return of Ayatollah Khomeini in 1979, and the second, Ahmadinejad argued, with the seizure of the US embassy on 4 November of the same year, a defining moment, he claimed, for the international dimension of the revolution. Then came the 'Holy Defence', the war against Iraq; a war which had been 'imposed' by foreign powers and in which Iranians had nobly, and by relying on their faith, seen off the invader. For many Iranians, the war had indeed been the expression of wider international hostility, and few doubted that the West, most obviously the United States, had been the prime mover behind Saddam Hussein's invasion. In 1989, the year after the end of the war, Khomeini died, and Hashemi Rafsanjani was inaugurated as president. Rafsanjani was to serve for two terms in what became known as the 'era of reconstruction', to be followed by eight years of 'reform' under Khatami. For Ahmadinejad and his supporters, the period from 1989 onwards marked the great betrayal of the revolution – unsurprisingly, his repeated comments to this effect went down badly with his predecessors.

'The era of reconstruction'

At the core of Ahmadinejad's view was opposition to the political and economic arrangements put in place by Rafsanjani in the aftermath of the war, his 'political settlement'.[1] The onset of the war with Iraq in 1980 had effectively stalled attempts at finding a stable political settlement, or long-term way of doing (government) business, and forced the leadership to prioritise enacting emergency measures to put the Pahlavi state it had taken over onto a war footing. Serious economic decisions with long-term consequences needed to be deferred in the face of the urgency of war. By and large the new elites managed their complex inheritance competently, such that Iran emerged from the war with negligible financial debt (an achievement that was aided, ironically, by the extensive arms embargo). But a major reason why such an eclectic collection of revolutionaries was able to operate together effectively was the charismatic presence of the founder of the revolution, Ayatollah Khomeini. While never master of all he surveyed, Khomeini was nonetheless the essential steady hand on the tiller, and when he died a potentially dangerous vacuum was left at the heart of the Islamic Republic. Fortunately for the republic, a shrewd political operator of moderate conservative bent by the name of Ali Akbar Hashemi Rafsanjani was on hand to manage the transition, albeit not in a way of which all his contemporaries approved.

He did so with the help of Khomeini's son, Ahmad Khomeini, and the then president, Ayatollah Sayyid Ali Khamenei. The latter, having reportedly been nominated for the position by Khomeini himself, was made Supreme Leader of the Revolution (a promotion that dismayed many of the ulema,[2] who viewed him as academically underqualified for the job), while Rafsanjani became president, his mandate strengthened by a change in the constitution that saw the abolition of the post of prime minister. Although in time the transfer of the prime minister's executive responsibilities to the office of the president would have the unforeseen consequence of further exalting the role of the Supreme Leader, partly as a counter to the empowered presidency, in 1989, Rafsanjani appeared to have successfully concentrated executive power in his own hands. All the more so because Khamenei, the obsequious eulogising of the official media notwithstanding, lacked a distinct constituency and appeared if anything to be politically reliant on Rafsanjani, who did have a constituency.

The mercantile elites based in the traditional bazaar were to be the source of much of Rafsanjani's power and wealth. The alliance with the *bazaaris* was not a difficult one for the new president to make, since, for all his clerical training, he was equally if not more at home with the merchant community as with the scholarly one, having made most of his money in business prior to the revolution, and still maintaining a commanding stake in the pistachio trade. Rafsanjani's arrangement with the merchants, his 'political settlement', was a prudent one, though it was also to prove flawed. Acutely aware that the Shah had undermined himself by failing to anchor himself to a social base, Rafsanjani determined to bind his own presidency and power to that of the mercantile classes whose wealth had enabled them effectively to fund the revolution.

This settlement was to be more than a temporary alliance, and it arguably represented a return to a traditional socio-economic relationship that had existed for centuries, though this time with considerably more resources at stake, and with no qualifying authority to intervene or moderate. There was no secular aristocracy or monarch to oversee relations as there had been in the past, and Khamenei was too weak to have much influence.

In simple terms, the relationship was one whereby the mercantile elites effectively funded the state, mostly through informal and often dubious business arrangements with individual members of the elite and clerical institutions, and in return the state, in the image of President Rafsanjani, supplied an economic environment in which they could make money. Under Rafsanjani, the wartime era of austerity was declared to be over and the era of 'reconstruction' was to begin; Iran was open for business. In the first few years of the Rafsanjani presidency, Iran appeared to make a sudden return to the international marketplace. Oil-rich and hungry for goods, it became a country where substantial sums of money were to be made from imports. Businessmen from around the world flocked to Tehran. But if they had anticipated a return to the halcyon days before 1979, they were to be rudely disappointed. There was money to be had to be sure, but this was an economy that was being driven by trade, not investment, and for all the talk of 'free markets' and 'privatisation', it was quite clear that definitions differed. When Iranian merchants talked of the free market, they meant an economic system that was free from state control, but very much in their own hands. Politics and money went hand-in-hand, and there was little chance that the new economic elite was about to risk divesting itself of the bonanza Rafsanjani was offering them by allowing free trade in a Western sense. There was some justification for the retention of protectionist measures – Iran's post-war economy was not in a position to contend with open competition from Western economies – but it became increasingly apparent that politics, rather than economics, was driving the agenda. Western businessmen interested in investing in oil and other industries came to discover that Iran was ill suited to strategic investment over the long term. Alongside fears about long-term stability were anxieties over the lack of transparency and accountability within the system. But an opaque and unaccountable business environment was actively preferred by Iran's mercantile elite, enthusiastic as they were to make money quickly and with minimal intrusion.

The mercantilism that gradually came to permeate all aspects of Iranian society affected the country in ways that were wholly unproductive. It was not simply the fact that many organisations that were little suited to or inclined towards business were either encouraged or tempted to investigate the possibilities (or compelled to do so by circumstance: one consequence of cutting down the size of government as Rafsanjani had done as part of his wooing of the merchants was that public institutions now needed to raise their own money, without government subsidy, and individuals employed by those institutions often had to pursue trade in order to supplement their increasingly meagre incomes), but that the mentality popularised by this socialised mercantilism had damaging effects. While transparency and accountability in the marketplace were shunned, along with any sort of legal system of regulation, volatility and short-termism predominated. This atmosphere of impunity resulted in the establishment of informal networks and cartels of business associates, unregulated and avaricious in the extreme. Many ordinary Iranians deplored the growing disparity in wealth as a new 'thousand families' emerged who indulged in a good deal more conspicuous consumption than had been exhibited by the elites under the Shah.

But of more concern to Rafsanjani and his allies was the dissension that was emerging from the early 1990s onwards among the political elites. Rafsanjani had intended that the mercantile–clerical alliance, with himself the crucial bridge between the two, would be sufficient to ensure his preponderant power while he managed the system and kept the people happy with the occasional populist policy. Where populism failed, there was always religion to keep the faithful content with their lot, and, for a time, this strategy worked. The righteous rich looked down upon the mass of the poor safe in the knowledge that religion would protect them from opposition.

But despite, or more likely because of, the huge amounts of money being made, tensions among the powerful inevitably intensified. Rafsanjani was keen to maintain at least a facade of liberalism and political change, knowing that prudence dictated that the intelligentsia be regularly placated. But those on the right, resenting the control Rafsanjani retained through his relationship with the *bazaaris*, saw no reason to indulge in exercises in populism and certainly not reform, and instead rallied to an increasingly authoritarian version of Islam, moving to enhance the position of the Supreme Leader as their standard-bearer. While Rafsanjani toyed with the idea of liberalisation, and at times ventured to turn it into a partial reality, his hardline opponents argued that democracy was an unnecessary fiction that should be discarded. Khomeini, they argued, had never intended to establish a republic. The idea had been imposed on him by liberal intellectuals, and in any case was only a means to an end. This end was an authoritarian Islamic state under the guardianship of the Supreme Leader, who, following a constitutional amendment in 1989, was now formally designated as 'absolute' (*motlaqe*).[3]

Rafsanjani sought to manage the increasingly authoritarian conservative faction by compromising on issues such as social and religious morality, and, most importantly, the makeup and functions of the judiciary. By his second term (1993–97), Rafsanjani was very much a president under siege. Already under attack from the left for his enthusiasm for mercantile capitalism and the concentrated accrual of vast wealth, he now came under further criticism for the blind eye he turned towards the excesses of the right in their strongholds of the judiciary, the Interior Ministry and various associated agencies; excesses which were to come to horrifying light during the Khatami presidency, with revelations about the murder of intellectuals.

Yet as the struggle between the pragmatic and authoritarian right took an attritional turn, the real challenge was coming from elsewhere. During the revolution and the war, the left[4] in Iranian politics had suffered enormously from purges and other repressive measures, and had been much weakened as a result. By the end of the war, it had begun to redefine itself in Islamic terms, largely in order to survive, and its ranks were soon swelled by the masses of unemployed war veterans who looked on the 'era of reconstruction' and its self-proclaimed 'commander' Rafsanjani with incredulity, and sometimes disgust. For these people, the revolution and war were not fought so that a few could enrich themselves. While some veterans turned to the politics of the right, where there undoubtedly were ample opportunities to gain from the informal economy that was associated with conservative politicians under Rafsanjani's settlement, a great many more argued that they had fought for an Islamic republic in which all the people were represented. For the veterans, supported by intellectuals and student movements, Rafsanjani and his hardline critics were simply extensions of each other, equal in greed and corruption, and nothing represented this corruption better than the increasingly notorious Foundation of the Oppressed (Bonyad-e Mostazafan), a huge conglomerate of businesses whose function had originally been to redistribute wealth to the poor. Critics remarked that if Rafsanjani was serious about his (somewhat improbable) proclaimed desire to create an accountable republic, then the first thing he would do would be to tackle the foundation, which seemed to be nothing more than an enormous laundering operation for the ill-gotten gains of the elite. By the mid 1990s, the Iranian press were openly ridiculing the organisation's importation of Mercedes limousines, noting sarcastically that they were clearly intended for the 'oppressed'.

A beleaguered Rafsanjani increasingly began to ingratiate himself with the emerging reformist movement. There seems to have been little ideological basis for this realignment: Rafsanjani, to the chagrin of some of his supporters, is a politician motivated by self-interest and the desire to protect his own power above all. This particular move of his was, accordingly, partly a consequence of the personal bitterness that had come about between conservative former allies, with Rafsanjani viewing the reform movement as a stick with which to beat his detractors, but it is also likely that he recognised that an authoritarian retrenchment would not facilitate the sort of economic reconstruction he still envisaged for the country. In 1997, after some months of overtures, he threw in his lot definitively with the reform movement, now led by his former culture minister, Mohammad Khatami.

The ascent of the reform movement

The argument of Ahmadinejad and other hardliners that the revolution had lost its way with the election of Rafsanjani in 1989 was based on the idea that Rafsanjani had polluted a spiritual (and ethical) revolution with the corruption of materialism. This view betrays a highly idealised understanding of the revolution and an overestimation of Rafsanjani's influence; furthermore, as the latter could well point out, many of his hardline critics were quite happy to enjoy the fruits of the mercantilism he had encouraged. This blatant contradiction between the hardliners' austere principles and their enjoyment of the riches of mercantilism was later to be resolved with a quasi-doctrinal division of the country into, effectively, the 'elect' and the rest (though it was never formally designated in this way), but in 1997 this was still far away, and the election of the liberally minded Khatami presented a far more serious threat to the aspirations of the hardline conservatives than Rafsanjani had ever done.

It is regularly argued that Ahmadinejad is the antithesis of Khatami, and there can be little doubt that, in terms of their philosophies, the two men are poles apart. Yet it also needs to be borne in mind that hardline conservatives like Ahmadinejad are haunted by Khatami and what he achieved. Ahmadinejad's much-remarked populism is a direct response to the genuine popularity Khatami generated and continues in some measure to hold among the people, and many of Ahmadinejad's performances (notably his notorious attempts at philosophising at the UN) are direct attempts to imitate and if possible surpass Khatami's successes on the world stage. Partly, this is motivated by personal jealousy, but the broader aim of the conservative faction is to show that one of their own can do better; to shatter the bond between the reform movement and the populace and forge a new bond between the people and their own ideology. Ahmadinejad was to be the hardline conservative populist who would capture the public imagination.

In order to be able to fully appreciate the hardliners' response to the reform movement, and why many on the right considered it such a threat to their interests, we need to understand the movement and what it aimed to achieve. Reformism emerged during the 1990s out of a coalition of interests dissatisfied with the Rafsanjani government and its apparent inability to deal with the myriad problems facing the country. These difficulties were both economic and political, and while Rafsanjani and his conservative pragmatists tended to argue that economic progress would itself yield political reform, their critics argued that both needed to be undertaken in tandem, and that the Rafsanjani settlement itself, with its corruption and instances of repression, had shown precisely why reform needed to be undertaken as well as money-making. Both groups held the view that the Islamic Republic had not yet achieved the goals of the revolution, though there were clear differences between them over how these might be achieved. In this respect, both Rafsanjani and his reformist critics differed from the hardline conservatives, who argued that the Khomeini era had been the Golden Age of the revolution. Reformists argued that the war had distracted from the process of political reform and had effectively deferred it. This aspect of the revolution now had to be attended to, and the reformists saw it largely in terms of strengthening the aspects of the constitution that provided for electoral freedoms and that held the state to account, changes that were anathema to the hardliners.

In political terms there was much that Rafsanjani and the reformists could agree on. It was on matters of the economy that differences emerged. Reformists argued that Iran was in need of proper foreign investment in order to regenerate its oil sector and make the most of its natural gas resources. This was critical to providing enough funds to invest in a diversification of the economy and create jobs for a baby-boomer generation that was coming of age. Khomeini had encouraged

Iranians to procreate, and although in the early 1990s extensive and rather ruthless steps were successfully taken to curb population growth, the energetic efforts of Iranians in the previous decade had ensured that Iran's economic planners now faced a youthful population which was almost double that faced by their predecessors. This demographic time bomb posed an immediate challenge, and drove many of the debates on the economy. As we have seen, the reality of the Rafsanjani presidency was that foreign investors simply did not find Iran an attractive option. While this was partly due to the economic sanctions imposed by the United States (executive orders in 1995, the Iran–Libya Sanctions Act in 1996), investors were almost unanimous in arguing that the fault lay mostly with Iran itself. The absence of transparency and accountability (most companies had no accounts, and no auditing procedure) – a clear consequence of the dominant mercantile mentality – and an acute nationalist fear of being misled by foreigners meant that any business negotiations were at best a tortuous affair, and at worst, a waste of everyone's time. So while international trade relationships continued, meaningful investment was absent. Even when Rafsanjani took the dangerously political decision of awarding a contract to a US oil company (Conoco, 1995), the Clinton administration was reluctant to engage, indicating just how difficult the situation had become.

The solution to these economic difficulties, according to the reformists, was to begin the process of democratisation in earnest, concentrating in particular on the development of aspects of civil society, and to initiate a wholesale restructuring of the economy. This ambitious project alienated Rafsanjani from the movement and, when a triumphant reform movement seized the Majlis (parliament) in the 2000 elections, the fears of many conservatives, moderate and hardline alike, appeared to be realised. With the legislative branch as well as the presidency now under their control, the reformists could initiate a root-and-branch reform of the economy, beginning with an anti-corruption drive.

Yet the gradual demise of the reform movement as a serious political force can in fact be traced to this moment of triumph, and its failure to capitalise on it. With little access to the key institutions of coercive power, the reformists' political strength largely resided in their mass appeal and an ability to connect with the people. By 2003, the popular connection had almost been severed, the movement having wasted much of the intervening three years on internal bickering and indecision in the leadership. This critical disconnection was to make the movement increasingly vulnerable to the attacks of its opponents.[5]

Meanwhile in 2000, still on the margins at this point, Iran's conservatives, faced with a new challenge, were seeking to redefine themselves and their agenda.

Borrowing from the West: 'left' and 'right' and the 'neo-conservative' reaction

Commentators have long noted the imitative quality of Iranian society and politics, and it has never been more in evidence than in our increasingly communicative and globalised world. Iranians, while also learning from their own experience of politics, tend also to avidly scour the international arena for examples and models. For example, for many Iranians (including many members of the ulema), the Islamic Revolution is firmly ensconced within a European narrative of revolution, and a common topic of intellectual discussion has typically been a comparison between the French, and to a lesser extent Russian, and Iranian revolutions.[6] It might seem odd that a revolution whose ideology appears so determinedly anti-Western should chose to situate itself within a distinctly Western framework, but it reveals much about Iranian psychology. During the 1990s, Iranian intellectuals and students devoured theoretical treatises from the West, arguing for a synthesis of ideas that would legitimate Western thought within an Iranian framework. Against those critics who argued that everything from the West was alien and should be shunned, they responded that this was clearly what the Islamic *Republic* was all about; a uniquely Iranian synthesis, the term 'republic' being a wholly Western contribution. Probably the most intriguing intellectual development in this period was the appropriation of Tocqueville's thesis of American democracy as the union of religion and democracy to the cause of Islamic democracy in Iran. Khatami himself gave the most visible expression to this idea, extending the comparison to point to a fundamental similarity between American and Iranian political aspirations in an interview with CNN in 1998.[7]

The emergence of ideas such as these was in many ways an extraordinary process, and one which proved immensely attractive to the country's youth, especially as it seemed to offer a reconciliation of the many contradictions of the Islamic Republic, particularly in its relations with the West. The eminent lay religious philosopher Abdolkarim Soroush even went so far as to argue that Western ideas were among the three great inheritances of Iran (along with pre-Islamic and Islamic thought), at a stroke legitimising their appropriation and adoption.[8]

If many in the West were oblivious to this intellectual revolution, it did not go unnoticed by the hardline critics of reformism. It is one of the striking features of Khatami's presidency that it was at this time that hardline cleric Ayatollah Misbah-Yazdi began sending his pupils to the West in order to dissect and understand its ideas. Misbah-Yazdi's purpose was of course very different from that of pro-Western thinkers; nevertheless, any encounter usually results in a measure of appropriation, as indeed the hardline rejectionists argued. But this was a new type of conservatism that was emerging, which argued that wholesale rejectionism was not an option. There was a solid pedigree to this of course; Khomeini himself had taught Western philosophy in order to debunk it, and his critique of Marxist materialism had led to the appropriation – and Islamisation – of Marxist terms for use in the Iranian context. Khomeini's division of the world into the oppressors and the oppressed would be familiar to any reader of the *Communist Manifesto*; and the phrase 'Great Satan', for example, can be seen in terms of the Islamisation of the Marxist contention that capitalism corrupts and will inevitably collapse under the weight of its own contradictions (such motifs were to be enthusiastically taken up by Ahmadinejad and applied to Zionism). Borrowing from or imitating the West, therefore, whatever the purpose, was not new, and, in view of this, it may be useful and appropriate to use the term 'neo-conservative' to denote the new conservatism that was emerging in the Khatami era, particularly as the movement was in many ways inspired by developments in 'conservatism' overseas.

It is worth reflecting for a moment on the origins of the political nomenclature that has become common in contemporary Iran. During Khomeini's lifetime, the notion of contending parties, of 'left' and 'right' for example, was frowned upon. To begin with, there was only one party that was worth joining, and that was the Islamic Republican Party. Then, following the stabilisation of the regime, this party was summarily disbanded by Khomeini as redundant. The only party now worth belonging to was 'Islam' (some interpreted this as meaning they should form a 'party of God' (Hizbullah)). But during the Rafsanjani administration, the enthusiasm for 'normalisation', or to appear 'normal' politically to the rest of the world, resulted in the application – albeit often clumsy – of the language of 'left' and 'right' to Iranian politics. Such language was rarely equal to the complexity of Iran's fractious politics, which remained highly personal, and its use regularly resulted in confusion, especially among foreign commentators. But the usage stuck. It is interesting to note that 'left' and 'right' were tentatively adopted by Iranian politicians partly in an attempt to emulate the political set-up in the United Kingdom, which, it was felt, for all its perfidy, still understood politics better than anyone else.

Ironically, the term 'conservative' (*mohafezeh-kar*) was actually popularised within Iran by the BBC's Persian service.

So, by the time of Khatami's presidency, the reformists tended to be seen as occupying the position of the 'left', while Rafsanjani and his supporters were situated somewhere in the middle of the spectrum, and were labelled 'moderate conservatives'. Within this frame of reference, Iranian politics became understood by Iranians themselves as a contest between left and right, and the gridlock that stalled Khatami's presidency from 2000 onwards was explained by some analysts as the result of the failure of the traditional left and traditional right to work together for the future of the country. Analogies were drawn with the Democrats and Republicans in the United States.

But while there were many reasons why the reformists reached a political dead end not long after they gained the Majlis, and while they themselves must take a share of the blame for failing to properly manage the political situation, it is fair to point out as well that the political opposition they faced was not normal, in Western democratic terms. Not many governments in the West faced oppositions that harassed, imprisoned and attempted to kill them. The determination of many Iranians to make their country politically 'normal' continued to encourage thinkers to look for solutions to their problems abroad. In the UK's Tony Blair, they found a politician who argued that left and right were meaningless in the modern age, and that what was needed was a synthesis. The 'Third Way' was music to many Iranian ears, and its main theoretician, Anthony Giddens, was very popular among Iranian intellectuals and university students (in 2004, plans were made to invite him to speak at Tehran University).

Meanwhile, the more conservatively inclined were seeking their own third way, aiming to renew themselves intellectually and redefine themselves in popular terms. To date, conservatives had been seen too much as the establishment faction; wealthy, aloof and with little connection to the youth of the country. But from the turn of the new century onwards, they were to define themselves through a heady mix of radical Islam, nationalism and, where necessary, socialism (or egalitarianism, which was very much part of the Islamic ethos). In many ways, they were seeking to take ideas that had helped to galvanise the reform movement, in particular about national pride and the use of populist leadership, and make them their own. One of the ways in which they differed from the reformists, however, was in their pugnacious approach. Recognising the growing disenchantment due to the gridlock in government and the apparent inability of Khatami in particular to overcome the multiple obstacles facing his government, they argued for a forceful and action-orientated politics. In doing this, they were drawing direct inspiration from what they understood to be the neo-conservative movement in the US, having noted the unfavourable comparisons many Iranians had made between Iran's leadership and the energetic, can-do attitude of the American 'neo-cons'.

CHAPTER TWO

The Triumph of the Authoritarians

The man in charge of this intellectual and political revitalisation of the hardline conservatives was senior cleric Ayatollah Misbah-Yazdi. Misbah undertook his project with energy and strategic foresight. The heresy of reform – for such he understood it to be – could not be removed overnight. This was a process that would take time, and it would begin with the education of his own supporters, who would then be placed in key state institutions, in particular the judiciary and the Ministry of Intelligence. The latter had effectively been purged by Khatami after the uncovering in 1998 of a particularly brutal sequence of murders of intellectuals by agents of the ministry during the Rafsanjani era, known as the 'chain murders'.[1] But Misbah was determined to use his power and influence as a wealthy cleric to repopulate the ministry, filling key positions with true believers convinced not only of the religious merits of the authoritarian position, but also of the intellectual coherence of its arguments. In order for this intellectual solidity to be achieved, Misbah's acolytes would spend time abroad, learning the ways of the West (mainly philosophy and politics) in order to be able successfully to counter them. The reformists had always believed that while the conservatives might dominate in the use of coercion – unleashing vigilantes when necessary – they themselves would always win the argument. Misbah wanted both to retain control over the streets and win the argument.

Thus was cultivated a new generation of articulate conservatives who would present the case for authoritarianism. The failure of reform, the case ran, was not caused by the violent obstruction of conservatives, as reformists charged, but by the failure and inadequacy of the very idea of democracy, an idea, it was argued, which was ill-suited to Iran, at least in its present circumstances. The notion that all could participate in politics was nonsense. The new conservatives used a particular interpretation of Islam to underpin the idea that politics was the preserve of a select few, that they themselves were the elect, uniquely qualified to rule. This was not a new idea, and would have been familiar to the Shah, but it was articulated in dramatically new terms by authoritarians seeking among other things to further enhance the position of the Supreme Leader to the point where he would, in contrast to the revolution's anti-monarchical ideals, effectively become something like a king.

In the context of the impasses and inefficiencies in the government from 2000 onwards, the authoritarians' argument began to resonate with an increasingly disillusioned public.[2] Even those who had no sympathy with the ideology of the right reluctantly conceded that perhaps Iran was simply not ready for democracy. That the hardline conservatives, with the support of the Supreme Leader, had themselves played a major role in the suffocation of the democracy movement was either overlooked or concealed. The idea was that this was a problem that went to the heart of what it meant to be Iranian. Put simply, you couldn't have democracy without democrats, and Iranians were genetically ill suited to being democrats. In many ways, this attitude that Iran's 'neo-cons' were seeding could be viewed as an internalisation of traditional Orientalism, making them in this particular respect the opposite of their namesakes in the US.

Populism and other strategies

While this view could gather widespread sympathy as a rather generalised notion, its core supporters were conviction politicians who believed firmly in the primacy of the Islamic state over any sort of democracy and in their particular interpretation of Islam over any suggestion of pluralism, and who argued, in effect, that it was better for their own inner circle to govern, via the institution of the Supreme Leader, than to allow any type of government that involved the participation of those who did not adhere to or 'understand' the faith. This was a highly elitist philosophy that went against one of the central myths of the Islamic revolution: that of its inherent popularity and mass base. There were three ways in which the ideologues of the neo-conservatives sought to overcome, or blur, this crucial contradiction. Firstly, they tried to distract attention from it by exploiting the disenchantment with the reformist regime. This strategy was of limited use, however, as on its own it would only succeed in depoliticising the public, and would not bring about the enthusiastic support the 'neo-cons' were determined to build.

Secondly, they indulged in populist rhetoric to excite the masses. This took two forms, both of which were rooted in the desire to appropriate the reformists' erstwhile success in appealing to popular patriotism and memories of the war against Iraq. In the first instance, the conservatives took to championing the spirit of the war, arguing that, far from being a trauma, the war in fact represented the halcyon days of the revolution, when faith sustained the nation and materialism was nowhere to be seen. War 'martyrs' were to be commemorated, and veterans honoured. This discourse had the desired effect of pulling in support from disaffected veterans, originally disenchanted by the materialism of Rafsanjani, and now disappointed by the lack of progress under Khatami. In stark contrast to the reformists, who seemed preoccupied with interminable legislative battles in the Majlis, the conservatives also made sure to be seen to actually spend some money, hiring unemployed veterans in ad hoc jobs. Thus they came to be seen as doing something, rather than just talking about it. The cultivation of the war myth and celebration of the heroism of the veterans was in time expanded to encompass the families of martyrs and even the 'oppressed' in general, and a sense of there being reward for the travails of the poor and suffering waiting just around the corner – whether in this life or the next – was strongly encouraged.

The danger of such myth-making was that it could, and did, create a tendency to look to the war as a period of spiritual cleansing, and even as such as a desirable event, rather than, as it had traditionally been seen, an 'imposed war', forced on Iran by outside powers. In this mythology, furthermore, the cataclysm of war was almost an essential precursor to utopia: in sum, the new conservative discourse contained seeds of millenarianism.

These Islamic motifs of jihad and sacrifice were then compounded for the benefit of the less religious constituency within the country by powerful, and vulgar, nationalist myths. This nationalism was not founded on pride in Iranian cultural achievements and respectful interaction with the world, but on a sense of victimhood and unjust treatment at the hands of a treacherous and uncomprehending world. Such paranoia about the outside world and its effects on Iran was central to the worldview of hard-line conservatives, but it also had a receptive audience among war veterans, who had their own reasons for being suspicious of the outside world, and, more worryingly, among reformists. Many reformists concurred with the conservatives' assessment of Iran's problems as, in their view, the demise of the reform movement had much to do with the failure of the West to engage with Khatami. This renewal of distrust of the West among otherwise sympathetic reformists began with the US State of the Union speech of 2002 in which President George W. Bush situated Iran, Iraq and North Korea on an 'axis of evil'. The impact of this speech on Iranians can barely be underestimated, and it would be fair to say that in the aftermath of the 11 September attacks and the war in Afghanistan, in which Iranian help was crucial in the overthrow of the Taliban, many reformists felt betrayed. They were mocked by conservatives for their naivety in trusting the West, and for a number of them, this sense of betrayal turned into an avowed, almost pathological distrust. They proved willing recruits to the revitalised revolutionary ideology. Their distrust of the West would later be reinforced by the occupation of Iraq and its consequences, and by the Western reaction to the Majlis election of 2004, of which more later.

The nationalist myth that Iran was singularly important in the world and singularly unjustly treated in it largely served the conservatives' practical purpose of perpetuating an atmosphere of international crisis in order to deflect attention from their own contradictions and to suppress dissent. Though not yet in the presidency or even dominating the Majlis, the faction had considerable power in several organs of state, notably the judiciary, and this mythologising helped them to silence critics of their tactics of harassment of and violence towards their reformist opponents.

Their final strategy for securing power for their brand of elitism and authoritarianism was to find, if at all possible, an individual who could effectively encapsulate these ideas, popularise them further and capture the public imagination for the new conservatives; to be, in effect, the conservatives' Khatami. This appeared to be the hardest of the three strategies to achieve, for the simple reason that a suitable candidate was not immediately forthcoming. The conservatives were keenly aware of just how much Khatami, for all the disillusionment of the public with reform and the resonance of the conservatives' myth-making, had remained personally popular for most of his presidency. One of the contradictions the neo-conservatives had struggled with as they tried to build mass popularity for themselves was that a high turnout at the polls had tended to favour Khatami, and therefore the only way they could win an election and get their people into office was by ensuring a low turnout so that their own loyal constituency would have a decisive impact. The other possible method, cheating by barring opponents from running and stuffing ballot boxes, was initially considered to be counter-productive. The aim was, after all, to present an image of popularity and, if at all possible, to become genuinely popular. But for the first few years of the Khatami presidency, this proved an impossible goal. Despite his opponents' best efforts, Khatami won a landslide in both 1997 and 2001, while the reformists organised effectively for victory in the Majlis elections of 2000. Energised and dynamic at this point, the reformists had calculated that there would be official obstruction and vetting of candidates, and planned accordingly.

Ruthless attempts at subverting the reformist regime on the part of the authoritarian conservative faction (as well as their propaganda drives and the reformists' own failings) undoubtedly contributed to its demise. In the aftermath of the reformists' success in 2000, hardline conservatives, supported by the Supreme Leader, who took the unprecedented step of intervening to prevent the ratification of a new, more liberal, press law, moved to block any progress by the reformist Majlis and present it to the public as an ineffective talking shop. They also sought to decapitate the movement through harassment, imprisonment and assassination. In March 2000, the architect of the Majlis victory, reformist strategist Saeed Hajarian, was gunned down outside his offices. The shots, fired at point-blank range, failed to kill him, but, in an apt metaphor for the reform movement as a whole, he was left crippled. Key Khatami lieutenants were forced to resign, or else impeached by a judiciary increasingly dominated by hardliners in accordance with Misbah's plans. State television, at the time run by hardliner Ali Larijani, spared no effort in portraying the reformists as incompetent, screening nightly broadcasts throughout 2002 and 2003 of the proceedings of the reformist-controlled Tehran municipal council in such a way as to point up infighting and the apparent chaos the council was in.

In 1999, Khatami had introduced nationwide municipal elections as part of his drive towards the development of civil society and an electoral culture. Khatami was convinced that a democratic culture could only be inculcated from the ground up, and that ordinary people had to feel involved. The first municipal elections had been hailed as a success, but the second, scheduled for 2003, were announced at a time when the public was growing increasingly disillusioned, and this disillusion was thought likely to translate into a low turnout, especially in municipal elections, which, in spite of Khatami's democratising moves, few considered important. The elections were therefore regarded by hardliners as a valuable window of opportunity – though, as the repeated ridicule of the reformists on state television indicated, they were taking no chances. If they gained control of Tehran city council, they would be able to nominate the mayor of the capital, an enormously influential role and one that traditionally brought with it a seat in the cabinet. Even more importantly, control of the council would enable the neo-conservatives to build a loyal constituency in the city. It is often said that the neo-conservatives had a natural constituency among the poor and devout, including in the capital. But this was not the case before 2003, when the devout poor by and large voted for the reformists, who were considered to oppose the rich elites – and Khatami was after all a 'Sayyid', a lineal descendant of the Prophet (as indicated by his black turban). In 2003, however, after careful preparation, and on a low turnout of 15%, the neo-conservatives won control of Tehran city council, with Mahmoud Ahmadinejad elected as the new mayor, and with it influence over a large number of the reformists' traditional constituency. Typically, the development went largely unnoticed among reformists, although one or two of the movement's more astute strategists did view it as a worrying consequence of their neglect of their core constituents in favour of inward-looking factionalism.

The mayor of Tehran

Ahmadinejad himself was generally considered to be a political lightweight with strangely unorthodox religious ideas. He succeeded in part precisely because his reputation for ineptitude and eccentricity meant that he was not taken particularly seriously, and many reformists believed that this ineptitude meant he would not be in post for long. Significantly, this was a view shared by many conservatives, even hardliners, who regarded Ahmadinejad's track record as largely unimpressive and his obsession with the Twelfth Imam unhealthy. Perhaps the only person who did register concern was Khatami himself, who summarily refused to accord him the customary seat in the cabinet. This was regarded by some as unchivalrous, but Khatami wanted to distance himself from someone he clearly considered his philosophical antithesis, and whom he considered to be dangerous for the country.

For all his idiosyncrasies, Ahmadinejad proved to be an adept public relations man, and he was quick to present himself as a man of the people, and, importantly, a straight-talking, simple veteran, with simple if firm beliefs. He soon acquired a reputation as a good man-manager, someone with a deft personal touch, if not a good manager in the general sense. Indeed, for all his common touch, the civil servants who managed metropolitan Tehran considered their new mayor to be somewhat quixotic. One recalled briefing the new mayor on the problems of traffic in the city (a perennial cause for complaint), only to be quizzed at the end of his lengthy presentation on why the women in his office did not wear proper hijab.[3] Other critics commented that Ahmadinejad's understanding of management was weak, despite his stint as governor of Ardebil province, which his supporters unsurprisingly presented as an unmitigated success. Some feared that he would 'Islamise' the city, although in the two years of his term, little appeared to change; not, it would appear, for want of his trying, but due to the simple reality that Ahmadinejad failed to appreciate that issuing a decree in itself rarely resulted in action.

A reported exchange between the then president and Tehran's mayor nicely encapsulates Ahmadinejad's attitude at this time: running late for a meeting, Khatami is reported to have joked about the extent of the traffic and wondered what the mayor was doing about it. To which Ahmadinejad is said to have retorted, damningly, that had the president actually lived in the city rather than in the (affluent) north, he would have got to his meeting on time. The remark went down well with the public. The resonance of this comment reveals how far public perception had shifted by this point, such that the reformists were now considered by many to have been corrupted by power and to have become part of the establishment.

Two policies stand out from Ahmadinejad's time as mayor of Tehran. Both were widely ridiculed at the time, but both were – successfully – calculated to cultivate support among core constituents. The first was the policy of re-interring the remains of war martyrs in key public locations throughout the city so that citizens could be reminded of and duly commemorate the sacrifices of the people during the war. This extraordinary idea, sensational and media-grabbing, stunned the more refined citizens and many members of the political elite, who publicly baulked at the idea that Tehran should be turned into an ad hoc cemetery. But it played well with the majority of the Basij militia[4] and hardliners throughout the country, who felt that the sacrifices of the war had been forgotten in the rush towards materialism. Veterans who may not have liked the idea in practice nonetheless concluded that Ahmadinejad had cleverly raised public awareness of their experiences by suggesting it. Despite objections from senior reformists, Ahmadinejad went ahead with the project, and interred remains within the grounds of select universities (those considered to be centres of reformist agitation) and some public parks, though he was careful to deny that he had intended to populate Tehran's public thoroughfares with graves. The fact that Ahmadinejad implemented his policy in the face of stiff protest bolstered his credibility as an action-orientated man of the people who cared little for his popularity, and was genuine concerned for the ignored and the dispossessed.[5]

Intimately associated with these themes of dispossession and neglect was the promise of salvation. Ahmadinejad was widely known to be obsessed with the 'imminent' return of the Twelfth, or 'Hidden', Imam, and he claimed to know where, if not exactly when, his return would occur ('imminent' having the benefit of raising anticipation without specifying a time). He claimed that the imam would appear from a well south of Tehran in the small town of Jamkaran, and made it a policy priority to keep the shrine there well supplied with refreshments and amenities to encourage pilgrimages.[6]

The appeal of ideas like these, limited though it was, was nevertheless substantial in key sections of the population who had been disenfranchised by social and economic change and who were overwhelmed and bewildered by what had afflicted them.[7] Members of the political and intellectual elite, including many senior clergy in Qom,[8] dismissed Ahmadinejad's Jamkaran cult as superstitious nonsense. Other commentators viewed this and other beliefs with a mixture of shock and amazement. But the reality was and is that the development of cults such as these is very often not only a sign of devoutness, but also a consequence of desperation. What some commentators observed with concern at the time was that the cultivation and maintenance of such chiliastic myths paradoxically required that Ahmadinejad *encourage* a sense of desperation and crisis, thus setting in motion a self-perpetuating cycle that, hindsight now tells us, was eventually to come close to severely damaging the state itself.

This, however, lay still very much in the future, and few people took the prospect of the further rise of Ahmadinejad seriously. Even to the most zealous neo-conservatives, the mayor's religious idiosyncrasies seemed to militate against any such development, and reformists along with many conservatives simply did not regard Ahmadinejad as anything other than marginal to mainstream politics. Throughout 2003 and towards the pivotal Majlis elections of 2004, even neo-conservative eyes were elsewhere.

The Majlis elections

Ever since the reformist landslide in the Majlis elections of 2000, conservatives of all political hues had been determined to exact their revenge, and with Iran's nuclear negotiations apparently moving towards a mutually satisfactory resolution following the Tehran Agreement in October 2003, conservatives were buoyant and confident. It was they, after all, under the leadership of the then secretary of the National Security Council, Hassan Rowhani, who had secured this agreement and achieved what looked as if it might be a resolution to the ongoing crisis. Even Iran's European interlocutors appeared more comfortable dealing with these (moderate) conservatives, who at least could get things done, than with the rather more shambolic reformists. Behind the scenes, however, both these moderate conservatives (essentially those in Rafsanjani's corner) and their European negotiating partners were about to be outmanoeuvred by the neo-conservatives. One of the unspoken aspects of the deal signed in October, in which Iran agreed to sign and provisionally implement the Additional Protocol to the Nuclear Non-Proliferation Treaty (NPT) and to commence ratification procedures, was a reassurance from Europe, wisely given from the point of view of the negotiations themselves, that it would not interfere in Iran's domestic politics. However, few could have anticipated the sheer scale of the manipulation that was about to take place during the race for the Majlis, and Europe's subsequent silence in the face of what was a monumental exercise in electoral fraud was to damn them in the eyes of many Iranians.[9]

Unlike in the municipal elections, Iran's neo-conservatives could not rely on a low turnout to triumph in the Majlis. As in most countries, parliamentary elections are considered important in Iran, and turnout is regularly at least 60%. Few expected that the reformists would be returned with an extensive majority, and many argued that they would lose their overall majority. But the hardliners who dominated the Guardian Council, the powerful body charged with checking that legislation conforms to Islamic law and with vetting candidates for election, were taking no chances. They barred over 3,000 candidates from running, many of them sitting deputies, in a process that took place entirely behind closed doors; barred candidates were not told the reasons for their disqualification, other than a sudden assessment that they were 'un-Islamic'. They also mobilised an enormous election management team of some 40,000 personnel to monitor voting stations. This monitoring was traditionally and indeed legally the responsibility of the Ministry of the Interior, but the Guardian Council contended, with no hint of irony, that the ministry had become politicised and was biased in favour of the reformists. The vetting in particular caused an outcry, and as the reformist leadership, including Khatami, vacillated and prevaricated over what to do, thereby losing what sympathy they might have retained in the electorate, appeals were sent to the Supreme Leader to arbitrate. Khamenei responded by asking the Guardian Council to review the process, which it duly did, restoring no more than a handful of candidates to the list. The Council calculated that the public was fed up with the internecine squabbling of politicians and would not take to the streets in protest at what one reformist politician called a 'parliamentary coup'.[10]

It was right. With no hint of protest from the EU or anyone else, the process took its course, resulting in a dramatic landslide victory for the new conservatives. One European diplomat epitomised the more cynical type of Western response at the time when he noted that '[there are various issues] that we have to deal with security people on – in other words the conservatives ... The reformists have never been in the loop on these kinds of things. Having conservatives running everything may not be a reflection of the will of the Iranian public, but it will probably make our job as diplomats trying to deal with the people that matter much easier.'[11]

Yet the conservatives who had come to dominate the Majlis were not the moderates and pragmatists epitomised by Rowhani; those with whom the West could do business. They were not traditional conservatives, but *osulgaran*, literally 'principlists'; the Persian translation and reinterpretation of the English term 'fundamentalist'. This semantic change itself shows how far this group had come, that they had succeeded in turning what had been a term of abuse into a positive epithet for themselves.[12] The new parliament immediately announced that it would not be ratifying the Additional Protocol to the NPT, and berated Rowhani and his team for being too soft in their negotiations with the West.

The political turnaround was almost complete. Not only had the reformists been driven from power, but the traditional conservatives had also been outmanoeuvred, without a hint of protest on the streets or from abroad. Hardline clerics gloated, one even remarking with undisguised conceit that the successful candidates had been named by the Hidden Imam himself in a message to the Supreme Leader, an astounding claim that Ayatollah Khamenei did not consider it necessary to rebuff.[13]

The election of Ahmadinejad

It has become commonplace to view the election of Ahmadinejad in 2005 as the turning point in recent Iranian domestic politics. But, as we have seen, Ahmadinejad was only one part of a broader hardline conservative attempt to seize power in Iran, and until the presidential elections, he was not regarded as anything other than a marginal or supporting figure.

In early 2005, buoyed by the results of the municipal and Majlis elections, and the ease with which they had ended the reformist supremacy (and outwitted Rafsanjani), Iran's newly ascendant 'principlist' faction enthusiastically contemplated the possibility of seizing the presidency. But their first choice of candidate was not Ahmadinejad, and the outcome of the election was by no means a foregone conclusion. If the reformists were unlikely to be able to field a serious candidate, a strong contender was still likely to emerge from among the traditional conservatives. In any case, it was generally acknowledged that, for all his faults, had Khatami been allowed to run for a third term (the constitution allowed only two consecutive terms), he would have stood a very good chance of winning again. Many of the problems facing the principlists with regard to popular support remained, particularly as no one had been fooled by the machinations of 2004 – indeed even the most traditional conservatives had viewed the exercise with some distaste. A real concern for the principlists was that the reformists would rally, and they knew that they could not simply rely on the fact that their strongest competitor was barred from running. The faction's more astute tacticians recognised that, though they had got away with it in 2004, the exercise had not looked good. What they needed on this occasion was a genuine win; or at least an outcome that resembled one.

Much to the conservatives' gratification, the reformists failed, as anticipated, to put up a serious presidential candidate. Mostafa Moin, the former minister of education, had initially been barred from running by the Guardian Council, but was later among the few candidates to be summarily reinstated following Khamenei's intervention; conservatives on the Council banking on Moin's lack of charisma being a sufficient barrier to his success. Khatami was always going to be a hard act to follow, and Moin indeed proved himself a clumsy prospective successor, uncomfortable in public and unable to engage with the electorate. The other explicitly reformist candidate, Mehdi Karrubi, the former speaker of the Majlis, was regarded by many, despite his outspoken manner, as being very much part of the establishment. Karrubi nonetheless managed to energise his campaign by offering explicit bribes, literally handing out large quantities of IOUs for the sum of 500,000 rials with his name on them, to be redeemed on his election. (As the documents closely resembled banknotes, some electors managed to 'spend' them before the election, to the subsequent fury of a number of shopkeepers.)

Four candidates came from the conservative camp, though two, Mohsen Rezai and Mohammad Baqer Qalibaf, ran on a very moderate ticket, borrowing heavily from reformist policies. The two other candidates were regarded as the principlists; former director of state television Ali Larijani, who could best be described as a tactical principlist, and the hardline mayor and conviction principlist Mahmoud Ahmadinejad.

One major challenge to the hardline conservatives was the long-anticipated delayed candidacy of former president Hashemi Rafsanjani. Rafsanjani entered the race very much in the belief that he was the only realistic candidate in a period of domestic political gridlock and international crisis, and, although he waited till very late in the day to announce his candidacy, preparations had been long in gestation. Rafsanjani had been situating his supporters in key positions in the government and the diplomatic service for some time with a view to getting the networks in place that would enable him to regain the presidency and move quickly to tackle Iran's various crises, most obviously the lingeringly poisonous relationship with the US. Rafsanjani had long been viewed as a supporter of better relations with the US, and rumours abounded of his intention to put relations on a more constructive footing, although publicly his statements remained ambiguous and the province of readers of the political runes. In private, a number of his supporters were adamant that his first move in office would be to act to deal with the burgeoning international crisis. He may not be popular, his supporters argued, but he is the only man for the job; the only man with the political authority to move things forward.

However, by casting himself as the only possible option and the country's undoubted saviour, Rafsanjani managed to give offence to both left and right, and, more importantly, believing himself to be the only real choice, he neglected to campaign rigorously. Being the only rational option did not make him the popular choice. Furthermore, Rafsanjani's campaign appeared more preoccupied with convincing the Western media of his value than it did the Iranian electorate, and his cultivation of the youth vote through the extensive use of pretty female campaigners did little to counter the widespread perception of Rafsanjani as a rich man disconnected from reality. His apparent unwillingness to campaign in person – justified on the grounds of excessive security costs – only compounded the aloof image.

Nevertheless, the former president was a substantial candidate, and his entry altered the shape of the contest. For one thing, it damaged the reformist cause by further dividing the moderate vote and providing an ample target for any anti-establishment candidate to run against. In 2000, when distaste for him was at its peak, Rafsanjani had acted as a lightening rod for the reformist vote, his presence in the race ensuring a high turnout for reformist candidates. In 2005, in the context of widespread disenchantment with the reformists, his presence had an altogether different effect. With Moin largely irrelevant, garnering little support in any case, Rafsanjani drew support away not only from Mehdi Karrubi but also from more centrist candidates, in particular Mohammad Baqer Qalibaf. Mohsen Rezai withdrew from the contest shortly before the first-round voting in order to allow for a more coherent conservative front in the belief, shared by many, that either Qalibaf or Larijani could then win sufficient votes to go into the second round. With Larijani, who was openly backed by the Supreme Leader, finding his popularity waning, conservative eyes turned to Qalibaf.

Qalibaf had an excellent conservative pedigree, having served as commander of Iran's Law Enforcement Forces. He was also respected for his very practical management style, and seen as a pragmatist: he had famously been scolded by hardliners for announcing that alcohol smuggling across the Azeri border was problem of high demand, not supply. Qalibaf appears to have had the support of several conservative factions, and his entry into the race was characterised by enthusiasm and panache, as he reinvented himself as a man of action who would not have been out of place on the set of *Top Gun*. His campaign literature certainly put across a film-star image: by some accounts, his press campaign packs included bottles of his own name-brand eau de cologne. So carried away did Qalibaf become about his prospects at one point in the campaign that he reportedly rather rashly announced his intention to be the 'Reza Khan' of the Islamic Republic.[14]

This provoked consternation among some key backers. Reza Khan, the founder of the Pahlavi dynasty, was certainly a quintessential 'man of action', and his popularity had been growing among Iranians, but this popularity was due as much to his attitude towards the ulema (deeply antagonistic) as it was to his reputation for getting things done, an association that did not play well with many of Qalibaf's fellow conservatives. Moreover, Reza Khan had taken power through a military coup, and many members of the establishment were perennially conscious of the danger of a coup. In invoking Reza Khan's name, Qalibaf recklessly excited suspicion about ambitions he may not have had. That said, had Qalibaf's campaign managed to galvanise the popular vote in favour of the conservatives, he might still have retained the support of the key financial backers. As it was, despite his efforts and the hopes invested in him, polls indicated that he was not posing a realistic challenge to Rafsanjani. Early assessments indicated that Rafsanjani and Karrubi would occupy the first and second slots in the first round of voting, leading to a runoff between the avowed pragmatist centrist and the pragmatist reformist. Some conservatives complained that this would not make for a dynamic and properly popular election. Others observed gloomily that yet again the conservatives were to be locked out of a presidency they felt was rightfully theirs (for many, Rafsanjani barely counted as a conservative). Some urgent rethinking of strategy was required.

It is important to recollect that, as late as a week before the second-round voting, Ahmadinejad barely registered on the electoral radar. The latest polls had shown him trailing the other candidates. However, it was also becoming increasingly clear that he had a loyal if small following and, more importantly, that he appeared to possess a deft personal touch and a campaign that was distinctive enough to seem to offer a real difference to the electorate. At a meeting of the five leading pillars of the hardline establishment, on the reported prompting of Mojtaba Khamenei (a younger son of the Leader), the decision was taken to switch logistical support from Qalibaf to Ahmadinejad (Larijani had long been regarded as incapable of winning). This bold decision instantly provided the hitherto low-profile mayor of Tehran with a nationwide campaign organisation. The decision's importance can barely be underestimated, and it should lay to rest the myth of Ahmadinejad's untainted popular election. There is little doubt that Ahmadinejad, in successfully running an innovative and original campaign on limited funds, made the best of the opportunities afforded to him, but the evidence suggests that without this late switch in support, he would not have made it into the second round.

Ahmadinejad's inventive campaign certainly stood out against the well-financed and somewhat pretentious campaigns of his rivals, but equally, in this first round, the IRGC command and the Basij Militia were effectively operating as ad hoc party activists; turning out voters, monitoring election stations, and at times simply buying and selling votes. On at least one occasion, the total votes for a district surpassed the number of registered voters, and on a number of occasions, dead people were said to have cast ballots. As in the Majlis elections, the Guardian Council and the Ministry of the Interior clashed over the management of the elections, and there were disagreements about recorded turnouts and 'electoral inconsistencies'.

When the results of the first round were finally revealed, Rafsanjani was put in pole position, but he was being closely chased by Ahmadinejad, with some 5.5 million votes. Ahmadinejad had beaten Karrubi by approximately 500,000 votes, a relatively small margin and one that could easily have been the result of 'creative' election management. Whatever the truth, Rafsanjani, Qalibaf and Karrubi all bitterly protested the result. Karrubi took the unprecedented step of writing to the Leader and accusing his son of intervening in the election, and all three considered withdrawing from the election altogether. While Ahmadinejad deftly dismissed the protests as the unfortunate ranting of sore losers, a serious constitutional crisis genuinely loomed. While a couple of withdrawals might have just about been tolerable, had the front-running former president also withdrawn, the entire process would have collapsed. He was, however, persuaded to remain in the race for a showdown with Ahmadinejad in the second round.[15]

Ahmadinejad: policies and presentation

For all the 'logistical support' he received, it is nevertheless still true that much of the credit for Ahmadinejad's success in 2005 must be ascribed to the skilful way in which his campaign spoke to popular discontent. This was in spite of the fact that Ahmadinejad had not always done well in those constituencies that had experience of him. He may have enjoyed the support of many of the particularly religious poor, but not all poor people supported him by any means, and in Ardebil province, where he had been governor, he came fifth out of six candidates in the first round.[16] His supporters were certainly loyal, but they represented rather a specific constituency, and to succeed in the second round, he needed to broaden his base considerably. This broadening of Ahmadinejad's appeal was achieved with a mixture of well-managed logistics, a populist campaign message and the judicious presentation of the candidate's background, character and policies. This last was helped by Ahmadinejad's own scrupulous attention to presentation, which included taking care to avoid being seen as playing up to the image which was building around him. On the question of image, he was also aided substantially by the stark negative contrast of his opponent.

Rafsanjani, as we have seen, represented the establishment. With no reformist candidate left in the race for dissatisfied electors to kick against, Rafsanjani's presence functioned much as it had in 2000; ensuring that his opponent would benefit from the distaste that he had accrued among liberals and conservatives alike. For reformists on this occasion the situation was tricky; the reformist press had spent much of the previous weeks highlighting Rafsanjani's faults and weaknesses and now, in an abrupt and desperate volte-face, they were driven to calling for a pragmatic vote to prevent Ahmadinejad from winning. Some made comparisons with the French presidential election in which Chirac had faced Le Pen, describing Ahmadinejad in terms that were even less sympathetic than equivalent discussions of the French extremist. In some ways, this worked in Ahmadinejad's favour: he was able to turn the vituperative and contemptuous criticism he received from his opponents to his advantage; as commentators routinely described him in terms that betrayed the worst type of class prejudice, Ahmadinejad's dignified response raised his stock among undecided voters, who simply could not accept that he was as bad as his opponents sought to portray him as being. His opponents' dismissal of him as a low-class unsophisticate who had trouble washing – who was 'no better than a baboon', in the words of one taunt – did nothing to dent Ahmadinejad's popularity among the poor, who began increasingly to empathise with the 'persecuted' candidate. Ahmadinejad began to be seen as the epitome of all that was oppressed; thus Rafsanjani, who was known to live in palatial luxury, represented the oppressors. Ahmadinejad used his class background to communicate to voters that he was one of the pure revolutionary poor, and uncorrupted by power.

His campaign drew heavily on Khatami's 1997 campaign, which had also presented the candidate as a simple man of the people. Indeed one of the more striking aspects of Ahmadinejad's campaign in 2005 is just how similar it was in terms of presentation, if not in substance, to Khatami's campaign in 1997, both men employing the crucial tactic of seeming to be anti-establishment. Ahmadinejad not only presented himself as a humble man, an erstwhile teacher in a Basij militia college, but he also took pains to listen to people, most noticeably through his website, which regularly asked visitors to register their views on a number of issues.

For all the critical sloganeering of his opponents, there was very little actual scrutiny of Ahmadinejad's policies, enabling him to largely get away with presenting a series of somewhat ambiguous promises and assurances that things would get better. Strikingly, in policy terms, the emphasis of his campaign was almost wholly on the economy and the consequences of political corruption, while religion, Ahmadinejad's personal hobby horse, was left out, largely because of the embarrassment potential of his more peculiar beliefs. Particular focuses of the campaign were the mafia cartels and, especially, the abuse of oil wealth. Echoing his hero, Ayatollah Khomeini, Ahmadinejad promised to put the country's oil wealth on people's dinner tables, arguing that since 1989, the few had acquired oil wealth at the expense of the many. Such claims, targeted squarely at Rafsanjani and his family, were of course bitterly resented in the former president's camp, but in the unaccountable political and economic atmosphere he had helped create, Rafsanjani found it difficult to convince people they were wrong. He had lost the trust of the people, and while Ahmadinejad may have been an unknown quantity for the majority of the electorate, many conjectured that he simply could not be any worse.

Ahmadinejad worked hard to convince electors that he actively *could* be trusted. Not only would be shake up the economy and bring justice for all, but as someone who had stayed faithful to the revolution and not been tempted by materialism, he could empathise with the suffering of ordinary people. Positive stories were circulated about him: his father had been a humble blacksmith; he had bravely served with distinction in the war, moreover in the special forces, and behind enemy lines; he had been an enormously successful governor; he had been judged one of the most successful mayors of 2005. These latter two claims were unquestioningly repeated despite the fact that he had done very badly in the first-round elections in Ardebil and that his mayoral achievements were generally agreed to have been unspectacular. The 'World Mayor Contest' in which he was ranked in the top ten, which furnished the basis for the latter claim, could hardly be considered decisive given that the total number of votes registered worldwide for 'mayor of the year' was a modest 87,100.[17] The claims had the desired effect nevertheless, persuading the more sober-minded Iranians who were less likely to be swayed by emotional appeals to class and war glory that Ahmadinejad was at the very least a competent manager. If there were concerns about his extreme religious zeal, then these too were effectively dismissed by the campaign as the slanders of bankrupt opponents. In a tactic common to election campaigns worldwide, they were framed as personal attacks and derided as poor substitutes for policy alternatives. It mattered little that Ahmadinejad had not provided a detailed policy blueprint, the fact was that he was new, and he promised a revolution in government.[18]

Part II: The 'Third Islamic Revolution'

CHAPTER THREE

The Ahmadinejad Presidency: Image and Foreign Policy

In the summer of 2005, Rafsanjani suffered the second serious electoral humiliation of his career, one that many at the time believed marked its definitive end. As the reality of Ahmadinejad's election began to sink in, despondency was felt in some quarters, particularly among the political establishment. Although Ahmadinejad and his supporters were keen to sell their victory as a miraculous triumph of the people against a corrupt establishment – a third Islamic revolution – there was no sense of popular empowerment such as had accompanied the first dramatic landslide victory of Mohammad Khatami. On the contrary, the outcome had given rise to a rather bitter atmosphere in the country, as, remembering the principlists' ruthless and repressive tactics, many people who had voted for Ahmadinejad viewed the president their protest votes had let in with some discomfort. The post-election atmosphere was so negative, in fact, that Khamenei decided to refuse Ahmadinejad permission to publicly celebrate his victory. A show of modesty was to be the order of the day, and, in stark contrast to 1997, it proved difficult to find people who would admit to having voted for Ahmadinejad. This is not to deny his undoubted, if partly engineered, electoral victory over Rafsanjani, but the general embarrassment showed that not only was Ahmadinejad's overall level of support lower than the results might indicate but, where it did exist, it was often quite shallow. Put simply, many who eventually voted for him did so without enthusiasm. For the new president and his supporters, however, this mattered little. What was important was the appearance of an electoral, *legitimate* political triumph for their faction, and if doubters persisted, with oil revenue at record highs, Ahmadinejad and the principlists were in a good position to be able to convert them, and consolidate their own power. Ahmadinejad's function was to use his populist touch to erase the heresy of reform from popular consciousness and convert people to the principlists' particular brand of Islamism, with its authoritarian, rather than democratic, theory of political development and its confrontational approach to international relations. The distinct historical narrative of the revolution and its betrayal that Ahmadinejad had communicated during the campaign – now culminating in his own 'miraculous' triumph – was, of course, part of this process. Ahmadinejad took to explaining his victory in providential terms, which not only appealed to his religiously minded core constituents, but also had the added advantage of disguising the electoral chicanery that had helped his election along. Indeed at times it was as if electoral fraud was itself an act of God.[1]

The cult of the president

The principlists' strategy for hegemony – and it is important not to forget that the faction aimed to definitively dominate the domestic political landscape – had three main components: political and economic populism, repression and the sustenance of crisis in foreign relations. These three strands of policy, carefully managed, were to ensure a consolidation of hardliner power and the ultimate elimination of any realistic opposition. But, as we have seen, there was a fundamental contradiction between the notion of the revolution's mass base and such a concentrated hold on power. However, the two could be reconciled, it was thought, and the latter legitimised, if the ruling faction had a focus of mass popularity. Thus, in order to secure the group's hegemony, members of the principlist faction developed a fourth strand to their strategy, which was perhaps the most controversial of all, even amongst the president's allies. This was the Ahmadinejad personality cult.[2]

This has progressed in fits and starts, and has usually made use of the president's (still much ridiculed) obsession with the imminent return of the Hidden Imam. Iranian leaders have always had a tendency towards the mystical – even the last Shah related dreams in which he encountered Shia imams – but in Ahmadinejad, the tendency has reached startling proportions, a central theme of his mysticism often being the special role of Ahmadinejad himself. The president's own statements and those of his most dedicated followers have from time to time conflated the idea of the Hidden Imam with that of the president's own particular importance.

Take for example the now famous incident from early in his presidency, when Ahmadinejad proclaimed that, during a speech to the UN General Assembly, his supporters could see a green light hovering behind him.[3] It is unclear from his account whether the light represented the supportive presence of the Hidden Imam, or whether he was suggesting that the imam was actually speaking through him. Several of his supporters have concluded the latter, making overexcited claims about the president's close relationship with the Hidden Imam. In this instance, it seems that the cult was taken too far: the public response to this revelation was not what the president's supporters had hoped for, and Ahmadinejad's meeting with a distinguished cleric in which he related the story to him was not a success, the elderly ayatollah being, by all accounts, singularly unimpressed.

The construction of such charisma is nevertheless an important element in the presidential political arsenal; a means of further justifying and legitimating the 'third revolution'. Efforts to bolster it increase in times of difficulty. In the president's ideal world, everyone would be convinced of his righteousness, and there would be no need to repress dissident or critical voices. But as Ahmadinejad's populist economic policies falter, a certain amount of selective repression is required to keep the resulting dissatisfactions under control, and this can then be justified with reference to the charismatic qualities of the president; a leader whose vision is so profound that it simply cannot be comprehended by those uninitiated into his inner circle.[4] The more limited this inner circle of believers becomes, the more convinced its members become of the righteousness of the task before them, and of the ignorance of those outside. The more their hegemony and legitimacy seem to be challenged, the more determined become their attempts to reinforce them; the less persuasive the case they make, the greater their resort to coercion.

Ahmadinejad's charisma interweaves religion and nationalism. Insofar as charismatic authority needs an esoteric dimension to function, the religious element is essential, though controversial. The controversy is particularly acute as, in the Islamic Republic of Iran, to presume charismatic religious authority is to pose a direct challenge to the authority of senior clerics, not least the Supreme Leader himself, who, as we have seen, is not averse to claiming (or at least having claims made on his behalf) that he is in some form of communication with the Hidden Imam. For the clerics of the rationalist branch of Islamic political and legal thought, Ahmadinejad's claims are absurd, and potentially dangerous. These clerics have remarked that encouraging a belief in the imminent return of the Hidden Imam is not only cynical, playing as it does on the desperation of the populace, and theologically spurious (as no-one can know when the imam will arrive), but it also risks creating political instability by engendering a popular feeling that the institutions of the republic are ephemeral and soon to be superseded by the new order that will arrive in the imam's wake. It is a millenarian utopianism that depends for its appeal on a belief in the utter degradation of the world, and is quite at odds with the successful image of the Islamic Republic that many would like to present. It works above all by manipulating the superstitions of the believing public. Inasmuch as senior clerics have exploited such beliefs and moods themselves, it can be argued that they have brought this upon themselves, and Ahmadinejad has turned their machinations against them. Like a good medieval millenarian, his views tend towards the anti-clerical, something which, ironically, has won him the support of some secularists.

Sanctifying the nation

Also like some millenarians of the past, he mixes in a healthy dose of nationalism of the most vulgar kind with his religious worldview, effectively synthesising Iranian-ness with his brand of radical Islam, and sacralising the Iranian nation to the point of portraying Iranians as a 'chosen people'. This view has, to be sure, its historical and ideological precedents,[5] but Ahmadinejad seems to have refined it to a pitch of intensity at which it is as intoxicating to nationalists as it is ridiculous to intellectuals of all political persuasions. In many ways, his seemingly innocuous campaign slogan, 'It's possible, and we can do it', can been seen as summing up this fever-pitch nationalism, by implying that there are no limits to what Iranians can achieve. In one of his more bizarre recorded claims, Ahmadinejad told an apparently receptive audience at a mosque that such was the genius of the Iranians, a 16-year-old schoolgirl had successfully 'discovered nuclear energy' at home using bits and pieces bought at the bazaar. The girl has since been hired by the Iranian nuclear agency and reportedly has her own chauffeur-driven car and other special privileges.[6]

Whether or not Ahmadinejad actually believes such nonsense (and great efforts were made by his supporters at the time to dismiss this particular incident as a brief excess of an idealistic president), the idea of celebrating an innate (God-given) Iranian genius on which Iranians can depend seems to be to emphasise that anyone can achieve anything. In many ways this idea has been the perfect antidote to years of state-sponsored fatalism, and the dispiriting fact that many Iranians have seen their relative economic condition stall, if not deteriorate, in the years since the revolution. The purpose of Ahmadinejad's rhetoric is to hold up the possibility of a rapid turnaround in the fortunes of the most desperate Iranians. It is feelgood politics aimed at the most receptive, because the most desperate, sectors of the population, and if doesn't make much sense, this matters little, because making sense isn't the point. It hardly signifies if Ahmadinejad's ideas suffer from profound contradictions because charisma needs no justification other than itself, and if intellectuals bemoan the inconsistencies in the president's thinking, it is because impure (Western) knowledge has corrupted their understanding. These are after all the decadent intellectuals who brought Iranians the discredited 'reform movement'. Their criticism should not only not come as a surprise, but should in fact be seen as a vindication of Ahmadinejad's 'truth'. Such naysayers should, in 'truth', be removed. Unsurprisingly, intellectuals have been a primary target of the Ahmadinejad government's repressive measures.[7]

The revolution in foreign policy

The enemy abroad is a crucial tool for reshaping domestic politics to Ahmadinejad's purposes. This component of the principlist strategy is crucial in that it offers an apparently reasonable justification for establishing the faction's hegemony throughout the country. Resisting the foreign oppressor is so central to Iranian nationalist mythology, and so broad in its appeal, that Ahmadinejad has been able to use it to project an inclusivity which his other approaches deny him. People may disagree with his religious views, or criticise his economic mismanagement, but these weaknesses pale into insignificance when compared with his staunch defence of the 'fatherland', and, in a development familiar the world over, dissent and criticism can quickly be characterised as unpatriotic. The maintenance of the foreign-relations crisis has thus facilitated the tightening of authoritarian rule at home, while the country's worsening economic condition means that its leaders increasingly depend on the foreign threat in order to keep attention focused abroad. But the international crisis, though sustaining relatively high oil prices, has itself, under the management of Ahmadinejad, ensured that the economy has not been able to stabilise; thus ironically reinforcing the problems that the government continually attempts to alleviate by turning up the heat abroad.

It is of course not difficult to blame the West for Iran's ills, as in truth the West has not handled its relations with Iran well. Yet the government of Mahmoud Ahmadinejad has enjoyed advantages that could have enabled it to reliably strengthen its domestic position without needing to rely nearly as heavily as it has on the perception of a foreign threat for popular support. It is estimated that Ahmadinejad has enjoyed more oil revenue in the first two years of his administration that Rafsanjani did in his entire eight years as president.[8] This revenue was widely expected to have been the financial cement that would consolidate the principlist hegemony. It has at least acted as a cushion against greater economic difficulties, but it is an inheritance that Ahmadinejad has largely wasted; meanwhile the paradoxical fact remains that the charismatic incoherence on which he depends to maintain his power is also his greatest weakness, and lies behind his failure to consolidate this power. Rather than effectively exploiting his 'charisma' to stabilise his position (while destabilising his enemies), Ahmadinejad appears to have used it to lock himself into a depreciating cycle of instability and, crucially, damage to the economy that could have been his greatest asset, negatively reacting to events while keeping up a pretence of mastering them. His approach to foreign policy exemplifies this self-defeating approach.

At the heart of the foreign policy of the principlists is a move away from dialogue, as championed by the reformists under Khatami, and an increasingly insistence on a robust and confrontational attitude towards the West.[9] Indeed a central pillar of their worldview is the idea that Iran and its Islamic revolution are inherently incompatible with the notion of international integration and collaboration, because these can only dilute the purity of the revolution. Confrontation must be the norm. While some hardline conservatives before the Ahmadinejad administration took the view that a robust posture was a tactical necessity, the only means by which Iran could effectively negotiate with the West, the principlists led by Ahmadinejad took the confrontation idea a step further and argued that it was a constant reality, rather than a means to an end. They drew on popular consciousness of the trauma of the Iran–Iraq War in support of the message that, essentially, knuckling down to a long and thankless fight was Iran's heroic destiny in a hostile world. But this worldview is by no means espoused by the majority of veterans, indeed the most active promoters of 'war nostalgia' (as distinct from simple commemoration of the war) are treated with suspicion by veterans, who often question what they actually did in the war. Ahmadinejad himself has come in for significant criticism from veterans, who point sceptically to the absence of pictures of Ahmadinejad in uniform, and the fact that, unusually, there appear not to have been any war martyrs in his family. Ahmadinejad's allies have defended his record by celebrating his time in the special forces; however, those who knew and commanded him have been less than flattering about his performance. His first experience of active service seems to have been towards the end of the war, in 1987, and in Kurdistan, rather than in the real heat of battle in the south. Ahmadinejad's enthusiastic invocation of the war era in the service of a pugnacious foreign policy therefore sits rather uneasily with a war record that is considerably less active than that of many of his compatriots.

The nuclear imbroglio

The principlists' primary criticism of the Khatami administration's nuclear negotiating teams and chief nuclear negotiator Hassan Rowhani was that they had been far too soft on the West, indeed that they were more than happy, cynically or naively, to sell Iran's interests in return for Western favour: 'diamonds for chocolates', as Rowhani's successor, Ali Larijani, famously said.[10] It must be added that, in painting a picture of the West as essentially the enemy, the principlists were ably assisted by the West itself, and the US in particular, which very publicly humiliated Khatami with the 'axis of evil' speech in 2002, making a mockery of his ambition to build bridges with the West. From that point on, negotiations on Iran's nuclear programme had proved more difficult, and, some thought, futile, as mutual distrust mounted and positions polarised. The one real opportunity for a negotiated solution that was represented by the Tehran Agreement of October 2003 was lost in February the following year, when the principlists won control of the Majlis, a change which, as we saw earlier, the West at first welcomed, believing that business-minded conservatives were back in control. Iran's much-heralded agreement to suspend its uranium-enrichment activity and sign and ratify the Additional Protocol to the NPT was dismissed by the new Majlis as irresponsible and an irrelevance. The protocol was not ratified, and a new and dangerous front was opened up against any further agreements. If the Europeans felt undermined by their American backseat driver, similarly, throughout 2004, Iran's negotiators found themselves being undermined and derailed by a Majlis which considered them to be traitorously incompetent, as the political landscape in Iran shifted away from the reformists and moderate conservatives and towards the principlists, the latter buoyant following their two successive electoral triumphs.

As Iran's nuclear negotiators found themselves under increasing attack at home, the situation of the European negotiators was no less critical. Having assured the US that they would be able to secure a diplomatic solution to the nuclear crisis, the 'European Three' (E3) of the UK, France and Germany now had to contend with the reality that the changes in Iran had effectively set back progress by nearly a year. For the better part of 2004, the Europeans were anxiously seeking to make up lost ground in an environment that was decidedly worse. There was even less room for compromise, and the Europeans struggled to formulate an agreement that would satisfy hardliners in both Iran and the US. More often than not, it was the latter that was uppermost in the minds of the Europeans, with the effect that offers they drew up that might have been attractive to the Iranians tended to be buried under so much bureaucratic verbiage that both Americans and Iranians were deterred in almost equal measure.

By the time of the run-up to the Iranian presidential elections in the summer of 2005, the negotiating situation had become extremely tense. A rather elaborate Iranian offer, made in the spring, that sought to 'contextualise' a proposed compromise by requesting acquiescence in a raft of other measures as well, was to all intents and purposes dismissed out of hand by the Europeans, exasperated by the breadth of the demands. This rejection was so badly received by the Iranian negotiators that they effectively turned their backs on the Europeans, protesting as they had done before that only negotiations with the US were of any value, as the Europeans were clearly incapable of delivering a solution. Privately, some in Iran were arguing that the only thing to be done now was to wait for a Rafsanjani victory in the forthcoming elections and a return to negotiations with a clean slate and within a new political framework.

This disconsolate mood was shared by the European negotiators, who nonetheless set to work formulating an offer of their own. Unfortunately, the atmosphere in Tehran was about to take a decided turn for the worst with the election of Ahmadinejad. This European offer, constructed during the presidency of Mohammad Khatami, was to receive its answer from Mahmoud Ahmadinejad. This was particularly galling since, for all their stubborn resistance to the earlier Iranian compromise, the Europeans had now made an important, if unheralded, concession.

The talks that had appeared promising in 2003 had faltered in 2004 in part over the interpretation of two concepts: 'objective guarantees' (that the nuclear process had a purely peaceful purpose) and 'suspension'. The Europeans and the Americans behind them had insisted on a fairly rigid interpretation of 'objective guarantees', which at times appeared to the Iranians to mean the complete dismantling of Iran's nuclear energy programme. Iranian negotiators complained that the West looked on Iran as a defeated enemy and sought to treat it as it had Iraq after 1991. The Europeans and Americans came to recast their articulation of this point as it became clear that it would not in fact be legal to compel Iran to dismantle its nuclear infrastructure, since the NPT guaranteed its signatories the right to a civil nuclear programme, and to do so would have resulted in a breakdown of the international consensus on the issue. The Europeans – and the Russians – convinced the Americans to publicly register acceptance of Iran's civil programme, which Bush duly did in September 2005, but, it is fair to point out, they did so without enthusiasm. Indeed from the Iranian perspective, the repeated US insistence that Iran follow Libya's path to international salvation by renouncing its uranium enrichment project confirmed the suspicion, enthusiastically encouraged by hardliners in the regime, that the West's real agenda in denying it the right to make its own reactor fuel was to deny Iran a civil nuclear programme. Lingering ambiguity at the negotiating tables on this point made it easy for hardline critics of the negotiations to argue that the West did in fact seek to end Iran's civil nuclear programme, that Iran's negotiators were blind to this, and that this was first and foremost a matter of national rights and dignity.

'Suspension' was even more problematic and contentious. At issue was the definition of suspension of uranium enrichment and the length of the period of suspension, and, while the Iranians were willing to voluntarily suspend enrichment as defined by the International Atomic Energy Agency (IAEA) in order to create a climate of goodwill, there was throughout the first half of 2004 growing frustration that this was not matched by any reciprocal show of goodwill from the European side. On the contrary, the negotiations were appearing to become even more prolonged and pedantic, as Western terms became, by Iranian accounts, ever more rigid and obscure. Then, in the summer, the Iranian concern that the 'temporary suspension' that the E3 was insisting on as a condition for continuing the negotiations and not reporting the issue to the Security Council was suspiciously indefinite was vindicated when became clear that permanent suspension was indeed what the Europeans were continuing to seek. This demand, though it had some merit as negotiating tool, had very little merit in diplomatic terms. No Iranian negotiator could concede the permanent suspension of an activity that not only was the source of such national pride, but was also enshrined in the NPT as an inalienable national right.[11] While the Europeans argued over details of international law and Iran's legal obligations, the Iranians were able to present the entire process as a battle for Iran's rights, with the West trying to prevent the Iranians from benefiting from technological progress. Europe and Iran were arguing at different levels, to different constituents. The weakness of the European position with respect to Iranian public opinion, which the E3 barely addressed, was exemplified by the fact that even the Iranian diaspora in the West stood full square behind Iran's nuclear programme (and some diaspora Iranian positions were even more hardline than the official Iranian one).[12]

But then, a year later in the summer of 2005, the E3 quietly dropped the demand for permanent suspension, in favour of temporary suspension for a minimum of ten years.[13] Unfortunately, the change was so quiet and so deeply (and deliberately) buried in the eurocratic language of the offer, and Iran's preoccupation with its own internal issues so pronounced at this point, that the noise of Ahmadinejad's election easily drowned it out. The Europeans had to wait for a considerable period of time while the changeover in Tehran took effect before negotiations could properly resume, and, when they did, Ahmadinejad made it clear from the outset that the good times were over and that henceforth Iranian interests would be resolutely defended on his terms. The new secretary of the National Security Council and chief nuclear negotiator Ali Larijani barely attempted to disguise his contempt for his predecessor, and the animosity of the new negotiating team towards their European counterparts soon proved mutual. The first Iranian response to the E3 offer was an extraordinarily blunt letter demanding an apology for the affront the Europeans had made to Iran's dignity. Apparently typical of the new team's perspective and assumed to be of their writing, it now seems as if the letter was in fact a parting shot from the previous team. Neverthless, Larijani made no attempt to distance himself or his team from the message, and it set the tone for what was to become an increasingly hopeless negotiating process.

As the outgoing team reflected on their successes and failures, considerable Western attention was focused on a review by Hassan Rowhani of his time as chief negotiator in which he tried to justify his position to his hardline critics by suggesting that the prolonged nature of the talks had at least allowed Iran to further its nuclear programme and had provided Iran with some diplomatic leverage – justifications which horrified hardline critics of the European negotiations in the US. Much less attention, however, was paid to Rowhani's statement that he believed that the West had never been interested in helping Iran and was inherently untrustworthy.[14] If this had been the unspoken assumption of negotiators like Rowhani, under Ahmadinejad, the assumption was made explicit. What had been a diplomatic exercise with increasingly political overtones now became pure political theatre, packed with symbolism. For Ahmadinejad, the nuclear crisis was a means to a domestic political end, nothing more, nothing less, and he spent his first few months in office lambasting both the previous government and the West, while presenting himself as a latter-day – more devout – Mosaddeq, a champion of Iran's national interests in the face of extraordinary odds, odds that his political will and revolutionary faith would overcome.[15] Even for those Iranians who were bored of politics, Ahmadinejad was making life dangerously interesting.

Israel

Western proponents of engagement with Iran had already suffered a serious setback in the crushing of the reform movement. The last semblance of rationality in Iranian politics appeared to have gone with Khatami, and in his place was an individual who seemed to relish international attention whatever the consequences. Ahmadinejad was no 'Iranian Chávez'; his radical politics featured an obsessive religiosity and, notably, a special animosity towards Israel, which his Latin American counterpart did not have. Opponents of Iran's nuclear programme no longer had to point to worrying trends; in Ahmadinejad, the problem was clear, and immediate. Two public statements early on in his presidency drew international attention to the president's extreme worldview and confirmed the worst fears of his opponents. Not only did Ahmadinejad apparently consider himself divinely guided (as shown by the 'green light' incident at the UN in 2005), but his statements were often incendiary: at a conference entitled 'A World Without Zionism' held in Tehran in the same year, the president triumphantly announced that the world could look forward to a time when Israel would be erased from the pages of history. Later in the year, on one of his many tours of Iran's provinces, he articulated his view that the Holocaust was a 'myth'[16] put about in order to justify the creation of the state of Israel.

These two statements had more of an impact on the nuclear negotiations than any amount of diplomatic engagement, and they have coloured the process ever since. They underscored the general feeling that the negotiations were no longer a diplomatic process, but a distinctly political one. It was to Iran's detriment that the man most responsible for generating this feeling seemed to have little idea of the consequences of his comments in terms of deepening distrust of Iran internationally, and little if any will to extricate the country from the diplomatic mess it was in.

Considerable amounts of ink have been spilt over what exactly Ahmadinejad meant by his remarks, with both sides often dealing in exaggeration. With respect to the remarks about the future of the state of Israel, it is important to point out that such attitudes are not unique to Ahmadinejad, and that they do not represent a return to 'revolutionary values', as some have claimed. The view that the state of Israel is illegitimate and should not exist is broadly held among the political elite of the Islamic Republic, and indeed across the Muslim world. Moreover, the view that Israel is doomed to disappear, as all 'unjust' creations are bound to do in time, can be viewed as no more than an Islamic adaptation of the idea that capitalism or communism will in time collapse under the weight of their internal contradictions.[17] Indeed references to the imminent demise of the US made in the same speech betray Ahmadinejad's debt to the Marxist view of capitalism as inherently incoherent, illogical and bound eventually to be superseded by revolution. Israel, like apartheid South Africa before it, will inevitably be defeated by the forces of 'justice'. This is classic millenarian politics, and as such not unusual in the Middle East; however, Ahmadinejad has undoubtedly marked himself out with the sheer intensity and fervour with which he communicates such ideas, and he has been criticised as reckless for encouraging his constituency to anticipate these and other events as 'imminent'.[18] That Ahmadinejad and his more zealous supporters would indeed like to work towards the end of vanquishing Israel is clear, but it should also be borne in mind that 'erasing' refers to the state of Israel as a political and administrative system, and not to the people of the country. Israeli contentions that Ahmadinejad is promoting genocide are therefore wide of the mark.

The focus on this remark about Israel has in fact distracted attention from the more significant statement made by Ahmadinejad in this speech; that America is a declining power, and that a world without the US may not be far away. This statement reveals far more about Ahmadinejad's foreign-policy perspective; specifically his rather reckless contempt for American military power,[19] a contempt which the war in Iraq and the conflict in Lebanon in 2006 were only to reinforce.

His comments on the Holocaust were, however, more distinctive, representing a departure from conventional anti-Israel rhetoric in the Islamic Republic. The Holocaust is discussed in Iran usually only insofar as it relates to the idea that the Palestinians have been punished for the sins of another continent, a popular view in the Islamic world in general, and it is certainly the case that there is a strain of thought in Iran that treats the issue rather dismissively. But in questioning the actual truth of the events themselves, which he justified on the supposedly scholarly grounds that all historical events should be rigorously questioned, researched and discussed, Ahmadinejad went considerably further even than this.[20] While on the theme of Israel's eventual and inevitable demise Ahmadinejad could cite the rhetoric of others, including Ayatollah Khomeini, in support of his view, on this, he was very much on his own, and the frailty of his reasoning and the intellectual incoherence of his position stood clearly exposed.[21] This did not, however, discourage him from repeating on a number of occasions, most notoriously at a conference hosted by the Iranian Foreign Ministry in December 2006, his view that the standard portrayal of the Holocaust was a fraud invented to justify the creation of the state of Israel (a poor grasp of history leading him, among other, much larger, errors, to overlook the fact that Zionism as a political movement predated the Holocaust). Ahmadinejad's sense of injustice extended not only to the Palestinians who had suffered indignities on the back of the Holocaust 'hoax', but to the people of Germany, who, he has said, had been needlessly made to feel guilty by their opponents in the West for too long.[22]

Just how delusory this imagined universe of the president's was was revealed when the organiser of the now-notorious Tehran conference, an old friend of Ahmadinejad's called Mohammad Ali Ramin, told an incredulous Iranian journalist – having first remarked that he could not see what all the fuss was about (regarding the ethics of holding such a conference) and outlined his rather tortured understanding of European history – that Ahmadinejad's plans for the establishment in Tehran of a 'Holocaust Institute' for the purposes of debunking the 'myth' were only temporary, as he was earnestly looking forward to the establishment of the institute's headquarters in Berlin.[23] Ahmadinejad's obsession with the Holocaust is seen by many Iranians as being at best rather peculiar, and at worst not only morally wrong, but dangerously ill advised and destructive of Iran's international image. One cleric berated him for attracting the support of neo-Nazis. The popular success of the drama serial *Zero-Degree Turn,* based on the true story of Iranian diplomats in occupied Paris who saved French Jews during the Second World War, is a good indication of the divergence of Ahmadinejad's views from those of the general public. It is also worth bearing in mind that such a programme, with its sympathetic portrayal of Jews, would not have been made elsewhere in the Islamic Middle East.

'The Socrates of the age'

Attempts to situate his wild revisionism within a scholarly framework have further exposed Ahmadinejad's intellectual naivety, such as when he argued, most recently at Columbia University in New York in September 2007, that there were no absolutes in knowledge and everything was subject to continual reinterpretation. This address saw Ahmadinejad at his performative best, trying to outshine his predecessor as a philosopher-president and to show that he was as comfortable with issues of epistemology and hermeneutics as any intellectual.

Intellectual legitimacy is an important element of a leader's credibility in Iran, and, historically, Iran's most popular leaders have always had philosophical tendencies. They have either been famous for their learning or have shown an openness to metaphysical discussion which has set them apart. Ayatollahs Khomeini and Khamenei are both portrayed as serious, if unorthodox, intellectuals. By contrast, the last Shah had a difficult relationship with the country's intellectuals, and sought to counter their influence by disparaging them and representing himself as wise and scholarly. Similarly, knowing full well that Iran's intellectuals do not accept him as an equal, Ahmadinejad is dismissive of the intelligentsia, often using the (populist) language of inverse snobbery, and strives to surpass it intellectually, typically responding to criticism from intellectual quarters with the retort that the critics do not understand his 'genius'.

The high stock of intellect and scholarliness in Iranian life helps to explain much of the jealousy that has been directed towards Khatami, who, unlike the many members of the political elite who inflate their postgraduate qualifications, actually did study philosophy and was comfortable, and probably happiest, when discussing it. (Such a reputation can have negative effects as well: Khatami's scholarliness was also invoked to imply that he was politically naive and unworldly.) Determined to surpass his predecessors' intellectual reputations, therefore, Ahmadinejad constantly reiterates that he is a simple teacher and an educator, and the lengths to which his office will go to ensure this hallowed yet humble status have frequently resulted in widespread mockery. In one incident, the presidential office proceeded with the establishment of a 'publication committee for the president's thought' without actually consulting the prospective members.[24] The mildest criticism of this project was that it was rather premature, given that the president's first term had yet to conclude. Most recently, his supporters have taken to describing him as 'the Socrates of the age'.[25] His remark at Columbia that knowledge is not absolute was an attempt to reinforce this impression of philosophical sophistication. However, by invoking a radical postmodernism – there are no facts, only interpretations – to argue that the Holocaust never happened, Ahmadinejad made the mistake of being seen to undermine the epistemological basis of Islamic doctrine, which teaches that there are certain objective truths (not least of which is God himself). Indeed, he managed effectively to position himself at the intellectual extreme of the reformist movement he so detested.

The turn east

Comments such as these, though they certainly made politics stimulating if nothing else for an Iranian public that had become bored and disillusioned,[26] unsurprisingly created enormous problems for Iran on the international stage. Not that Ahmadinejad or his supporters were much aware of or concerned about the consequences of his words, arguing that faced with someone 'speaking truth to power', it was not surprising that the 'Global Arrogance' (the US) should get upset, and that, far from causing problems, blunt criticism of Israel would reinforce Iran's popularity on the Arab street. Making a distinct break with the foreign policy of his two most recent predecessors, Ahmadinejad stated that the strategy would henceforth be, as in the early years of the revolution, to give priority to building regional relations and strength, over and above any bridge-building with the West. Not only was Ahmadinejad not interested in building bridges with the US, he also made a virtue of neglecting the Iranian diaspora, most of whom lived in the West. Although this attitude softened later in the presidency, few Iranian leaders have alienated the diaspora so effectively.[27]

As tensions with the US intensified, any pretence of shoring up relations with the EU was also abandoned. At least since 1989, Iranian foreign policy had always sought to use the EU as a counterweight to the US, but now, partly in response to the perceived failure of the nuclear negotiations and the inability of the E3 to deliver a solution to Iran's liking, this important aspect of diplomatic relations was recklessly neglected. By engaging in Holocaust revisionism and anticipating the collapse of the state of Israel, Ahmadinejad not only made engagement with Europeans in general more difficult – apart from anything else, it showed a grotesque insensitivity to European politics – but he emphatically alienated the European state whose economic and cultural links with Iran were the strongest: Germany. No German politician could realistically associate with or be seen to make excuses for a state whose leader brazenly brought the Holocaust into question.

The provocation of European sensibilities as good as ensured that the nuclear file would move swiftly from the remit of the IAEA to that of the UN Security Council (UNSC). One of the Europeans' most serious miscalculations had been to assume that Iran, for reasons of international prestige, would remain anxious to avoid being referred to the UNSC. They had used the Iranian desire to avoid the chastisement of the UNSC as leverage when they had negotiated with Rowhani's team. But with the rise of the principlists from the 2004 Majlis elections onwards, the view was increasingly expressed in Iranian political circles that the Europeans' bluff should be called, and that, furthermore, even if the matter were sent to the UNSC, Iran had little reason to care. Under Ahmadinejad, this attitude became policy, and while chief negotiator Ali Larijani considered defiance as a tactical posture, Ahmadinejad himself gave every indication that he really did not care. Underlying his attitude were two beliefs: that the pressure from the E3 and the IAEA process itself were unjust (there was a widespread view in Iran that the IAEA was being bullied by the US) and that it was therefore inevitable, and even honourable, that Iran would be referred; and that Iran would be able to rely on Chinese and Russian support in the UNSC.

Iranian foreign policy had been engaging with China and Russia for some time, but the turn east received its most definitive statement under Ahmadinejad. For the better part of the previous decade, Iranian foreign-policy analysts had been arguing that Iran needed to look eastward in terms of building alliances, in large part because the growing Chinese economy would in time be Iran's largest market for oil. During the presidency of Rafsanjani, there had been plans to build a railway as a new 'silk route' to connect China to Europe via Iran, and commentators excitedly spoke of Iran, China and India as the three 'mother civilisations' of Asia. Much time had also been spent planning a gas pipeline from Europe to the east with Iran as the hub, and while taking it all the way to China was considered impractical, reaching India via Pakistan (though some of the proposed routes avoided Pakistan) was a goal pursued with mutual enthusiasm, despite resistance from the US.

There was much to commend such approaches to eastern powers, not least the recognition of the Far East as an essential market for Iranian oil products. But the gas-pipeline strategy and other schemes were very much centred on Iran as a connecting point between east and west. Under Ahmadinejad, the Western connection was discarded altogether, and while there has been much talk during his presidency of emulating the 'Chinese model' of development (liberalising economics rather than politics), there has seemed at the same time to be little real appreciation of what precisely this model involves. In addition to enjoying the luxury of a permanent seat on the UNSC, China also, for all the friction that exists, enjoys a healthy economic relationship with the US, and with the Chinese-American population in particular. These are aspects of the Chinese position which Ahmadinejad did not factor into his equations. The Chinese, resource-hungry as they are, have been keen to develop their economic relations with Iran, but there is little doubt that the relationship has been constrained by China's relations with other countries, notably the US, as well as by the short-termist mercantile attitude of the Iranians, felt by the Chinese to militate against long-term investment. More obviously, the turn east has also been limited by the fact that for all the economic interest in China, the cultural leanings of the Iranian elite are very much towards the West.

With respect to Russia, the problems are of a slightly different nature, relating as they do more to the history of the relationship between the two countries. For a variety of reasons, the relationship between Russia and Iran became unusually close after the collapse of the Soviet Union; a product both of necessity and empathy. The Western arms embargo had driven Iran towards Russia in search of replacements for its much dilapidated military hardware in the aftermath of the Iran–Iraq War, and Iranian interest in Russian hardware was then further boosted by the sudden flight of the Iraqi air force to Iran during the first Gulf War. The Iranians, who subsequently kept the defeated air force's Russian-made equipment as 'reparations' for the Iran–Iraq War, were highly impressed with their new Russian planes, and decided to turn their attention to building an arms-dealing relationship with Russia. They found a country politically wounded by the collapse of the Soviet Union and eager to do business, even to the extent of picking up the pieces of Iran's neglected nuclear programme by agreeing to complete the construction of the Bushehr power plant, begun under the Shah and now abandoned by the Germans. But the relationship also went deeper than simple economic interest. Iran with its mercantile economic structure had found a like-minded partner in the robber-baron economic culture of Russia in the 1990s, and strong personal networks came to underpin the developing military–industrial relationship. The relationship was then cemented at state level by the resurgence of Russian autocracy under Vladimir Putin, and a mutual interest in avoiding 'velvet revolutions'. The impact of this developing relationship on the underlying direction of domestic Iranian politics should not be underestimated.

Yet many Iranians have viewed the firm alignment with Putin's Russia with trepidation. It is not only the long-standing negative association many Iranians have of Russian involvement in Iran with encouraging autocracy, but also the feeling that the Russians are inherently unreliable partners.[28] Many in Iran point to what they see as Russia's betrayal of Iran's trust over the legal status of the Caspian Sea as a particular example of Russian unreliability: the two countries had for a long time been in mutual agreement that the Caspian should be defined as a lake, rather than a sea, thereby making sure that under international law both had equal rights over its resources, until Russia, attracted by the possibilities offered by the carve-up that would result from a change in its legal status from lake to sea, reneged on the deal. More recently, Russia's apparent procrastination over the completion of the Bushehr plant is cited as another example of its untrustworthiness. On the Bushehr issue, the Russian position is that the Iranians have not paid their dues promptly, but suspicions abound that this is something of an excuse. Russia has its own interests to pursue vis-à-vis Iran, and would like to be seen in the West as a solver of the Iranian problem, rather than a facilitator of proliferation. Compounding the friction over Bushehr is also an Iranian belief that Russian standards of work and technology are not equal to those provided in the West; the spectre of Chernobyl still looms large. Russia has in recent years attempted to find a compromise that would satisfy both Iranian and Western allies on the nuclear issue by offering to enrich uranium for Iran; but, though Iran may publicly consider the idea, it does not take it seriously, given its perception of Russia as unreliable, and the current Iranian agenda of national self-sufficiency.

Towards the UNSC

Ahmadinejad may have asserted that a referral to the UNSC was of no consequence to Iran, but there was little doubt that the IAEA decision taken in early 2006 to make the referral unsettled many in Tehran, who recognised that the crisis had proceeded to a different level. Members of the old negotiating team made no secret of their dismay, and criticisms of the president began to mount. But as UN sanctions loomed, Ahmadinejad remained confident that China and Russia would prove an immovable obstacle to their imposition (confidence that was to prove misplaced, though China and Russia did play a role in softening elements of the relevant resolutions). In any case for Ahmadinejad, and indeed for many others in Iran, the apparently political nature of the West's opposition to Iran's nuclear programme fatally weakened it, the strength of Iran's legal position with regard to the NPT meaning that there was really no case to answer, and that therefore any sanctions would be slight, and certainly no worse than Iran had grown used to over the previous two decades. In part, it was the broader regional political environment that emboldened Ahmadinejad at this point, and encouraged the provocative attitude that so disillusioned Iran's friends and angered its enemies.

Iraq

Ahmadinejad's refusal to take American objections to Iran's nuclear programme seriously had less to do with his interpretation of international law and more to do with his firm belief in the decline of American power. Nowhere did this decline seem to be more apparent than in the emerging debacle of Iraq. For many Iranians, the invasion of Iraq had been a fatal mistake that exposed the increasing frailty of American military power, the revelations of Abu Ghraib confirming the moral bankruptcy of the American dream. At both a material and ideological level, American power was seen as being in decline, and, Ahmadinejad claimed, the Islamic Republic of Iran was the ideal candidate to fill the vacuum that would be created by America's inevitable departure. As fanciful as this conclusion may seem to outside observers, it nevertheless lies behind much of the decision-making of the Ahmadinejad presidency, and shows the extent to which the conviction that the US is in terminal decline drives Ahmadinejad's foreign policy. It is also important to appreciate how American mistakes and poor decision-making (rather than any positive strategy on the part of Iran itself) have strengthened Iran's regional position and thereby reinforced this belief in America's demise. Interestingly, the Iranian analysis of US capabilities is somewhat different when it comes to the possibility of an attack on Iran, which the regime had until recently talked up the probability of for the benefit of its domestic audience.

While Iranians had generally been enthusiastic supporters of the war against the Taliban, in 2003 there was considerably more ambivalence among government officials about the prospect of a US attack on Iraq. Few Iranians would shed a tear for Saddam Hussein, but there was also anxiety about the consequences for the region of an American victory; anxieties which surfaced soon enough as the Ba'athist regime collapsed with embarrassing haste. Much as some Westerners had felt about the combatants in the Iran–Iraq War, some in the Iranian government reflected that it would be better if the US were engaged in a prolonged fight. Not only would this sap its desire for any further conflict – i.e., with Iran – but it would also put Iran in the gratifying position of being able to offer to help the US extract itself from its quagmire. Broadly speaking, up until 2004, the position of the Iranian government was satisfaction at the fall of Saddam, combined with anxiety about American ambitions, a concern to prevent the emergence of a strong military power in Iraq, and caution about the next steps. Until 2004, Iran was carefully establishing community and welfare networks in both northern and, especially, southern Iraq, often with the passive acquiescence of the Coalition, who found Iranian involvement with the Shia in particular to have its uses, mainly with regard to keeping the peace. While American officials occasionally expressed rather hysterical concern about infiltration from Iranian 'agents', British officials tended to prove more sanguine, noting that an Iranian presence was in some regions actually making the occupation manageable.

At the same time, it was privately admitted that if the political situation with Iran should become more volatile, the Iranians could use their presence in Iraq to highly disruptive effect. This was particularly the case given that, along with the various Iranian NGOs and welfare organisations, IRGC networks were also being established in the country. The advantages the Iranians had over the Coalition were threefold: firstly, Iranian access to Iraqi society was facilitated by the extensive personal networks which linked the various Shia clerical families; secondly, unlike most Coalition operatives, many Iranians spoke very good Arabic, and, thirdly, the experience of the revolution, of having quickly to create systems out of chaos, gave many Iranian operatives in Iraq a greater ability than the by-and-large less experienced Americans to manoeuvre around the complexities of post-invasion Iraq. The networks they established, both civil and military, were intended to allow Iran to influence the flow of events, and effectively to back the winner by supporting as many credible currents as was feasible. This did not necessarily extend to supporting Sunni insurgents, as alleged by the US, but it did mean that Iran could and would back a multiplicity of factions. The main aim of Iranian policy throughout had been to prevent the re-emergence of an Iraqi military threat. This was to be achieved by ensuring that Iraq had a government that was friendly, politically stable and coherent, and militarily weak. The development of a strong Iraqi state allied to an antagonistic United States was not a desirable option, but nor, the Iranians calculated, was it the most likely one, as the US would eventually exhaust itself and leave.

Thus prior to the ascendancy of the principlists, the dominant Iranian policy was to keep a presence next door in Iraq, monitor the Americans, and facilitate their departure. With the accession of Ahmadinejad, this help became a good deal more proactive. In line with his repudiation of the Khatami government's approach to the West, Ahmadinejad, who loudly proclaimed his affiliation with the IRGC, gave Iranian elements in Iraq a freer hand to do as they pleased and to engage in behaviour calculated to hasten the departure of the Americans: one could almost be forgiven for thinking the 'inevitable' American decline and retreat were too slow for the new president's liking. While some foreign ministry officials argued for a more supportive approach as American fortunes in Iraq worsened, Ahmadinejad seemed eager to gloat. Not that he believed the US was thoroughly defeated yet, or that any confrontation would be a cakewalk. On the contrary, much to the consternation of the elder statesmen of the Islamic Republic, Ahmadinejad appeared to be actively pursuing a fight.[29] It was a fight he believed he could win, and one that would consolidate his power within Iran, via the extension of Iranian hegemony in the region. Ahmadinejad's predictions of an imminent US collapse and Iran's corresponding rise pandered to the nationalist constituency, which found the imminent prospect – as repeatedly promised by the president[30] – of 'great power' status intoxicating. At the same time, it is worth noting that, for all the bombast, Ahmadinejad was careful to be somewhat ambiguous about his strategy of confrontation with the US in his presentations to the Iranian public. There is little doubt that he and his inner circle at times relished the prospect of a military confrontation that they calculated they would win, and go on to establish the hegemony of an Ahmadinejad-led Iran in the region. But at the same time as he openly indulged in nationalistic tub-thumping, Ahmadinejad also reassured a curious and cautious wider public not necessarily convinced of the wisdom of extreme nationalism that it would never actually get to a fight, and that warnings of a military confrontation were simply the US indulging in a bit of psychological warfare. It was important, he argued, to counter bombast with bombast, and during the first 18 months of his presidency, despite the occasional raising of voices of concern,[31] his strategy was broadly accepted.

The worsening of the situation in Iraq served Ahmadinejad's interests, and he was keen to exploit it domestically. His desire to get the Americans out of Iraq was almost equalled by his satisfaction at seeing them bogged down and distracted, and the occupation also offered a useful example of 'freedom', American-style: the Iranian government wasted no opportunity to draw attention to the scandal of Abu Ghraib.[32] For the many Iranians who had, unlike most people in the Middle East, been broadly sympathetic to American aims in the beginning, the tragedy that the occupation was turning out to be came as a profound disappointment, and the view of the US as a sinister and chaotic power began to become widespread in Iran. Even those who were ill-disposed towards their own government increasingly feared the consequences of any American intervention in Iran (something that had been anticipated at least since the 'axis of evil' speech of 2002) more than they did Ahmadinejad. Whatever the stupidities of the president – and he would not be there forever – at least Iran had order and a measure of stability. From the end of 2003 onwards, Iranians in general were becoming more willing to tolerate the suppression of what limited political liberties they had had in order to avoid the worse development of appearing weak to the corrupt power next door, and/or succumbing to the kind of anarchy they saw in their neighbour. Thus, far from encouraging a democratic revolution in the Middle East, the example of Iraq had precisely the opposite effect.

Criticisms of Ahmadinejad's aggressive posture nevertheless persisted. Some members of the political elite privately argued that provoking an American withdrawal was unnecessary; that the Americans would eventually leave Iraq of their own accord. Moreover, if the Americans left Iraq, not only would they would no longer be preoccupied and might in time turn their attention elsewhere, but if they went in haste, Iran and others in the region would be left to pick the pieces. The problems created by a fractured Iraq could already be seen in the spillover of Arab infighting into the southeastern province of Khuzestan.

The problems in Khuzestan had a different significance for Ahmadinejad, however. He used them to exploit nationalist fears about the disintegration of the country. Iran has always been sensitive about the territorial integrity of the Iranian state and the dangers posed by separatist movements. Khuzestan, with its Arab population, was subject in the 1920s to a policy of radical Persianisation by Tehran in response to the concern that the British would encourage the formation of an Arab emirate there, as it had done elsewhere in the Gulf. As it was, the British rejected the idea once they recognised that their interests lay with the reinvigorated central government in Tehran. But suspicions die hard as far as British 'plots' against Iran are concerned, and Ahmadinejad's anti-Americanism is far outweighed by his Anglophobia. Anxieties about British political manipulation are common in Iran: a popular theory is that the Americans invaded Iraq at the behest of the British (as shown by the fact that Britain had conveniently taken control of the oil-rich south, while the Americans had been dispatched to Baghdad). The regime was easily able to exploit these anxieties to good nationalist effect by holding up the Khuzestan spillover conflict as a sign of British infiltration of the Islamic Republic.

Yet if, despite the popularity of ideas such as these, some still had doubts about the wisdom of Ahmadinejad's posturing on Iraq, events further afield were to provide the president with just the public-relations triumph he needed to convince his domestic sceptics.

2006: uranium enrichment and Lebanon

Seemingly indifferent to the criticisms of the international community, Iran continued throughout 2005 and 2006 to work towards the technological breakthrough of uranium enrichment. For Ahmadinejad, the attainment of this milestone would enhance the standing of his government and publicly affirm the notion that Iranians could indeed achieve anything if they put their minds to it. In the spring of 2006, Iran demonstrated for the first time that with a cascade of 164 centrifuge machines it was able to enrich uranium to the level necessary for fuel production (3.5%), and the president was not shy in proclaiming this to the world. Precisely how much uranium had been enriched and how well the centrifuges were working was not made clear. Sceptics continued to question the scale of the achievement, noting that Iran appeared to have skipped normal testing stages in order to be able to make the announcement. Nevertheless, both Ahmadinejad and his Western critics made much of the breakthrough, and nothing reflected the theatrical nature of Ahmadinejad's politics so aptly as the somewhat surreal song-and-dance show the president used to present Iran's accomplishment to the world. Never one to spurn display, Ahmadinejad decided to celebrate the national triumph with a stage show in which actors dressed in various ethnic costumes – presumably to indicate national unity – paraded mock tubes of enriched uranium, along with doves symbolising Iran's peaceful intentions.[33]

As critics of European policy bewailed the lack of determination that had allowed Iran to ignore warnings against moving forward with enrichment, most Western officials were at a loss as to how to respond to this particular piece of showmanship. The more sober observers concluded that the spectacle was in fact an attempt at disguising the fact that progress had been patchy at best, but whatever the technical realities, Ahmadinejad's performance helped to raise the political tempo. This was a good example of how political rhetoric on both sides was losing touch with the realities on the ground. Responses to events in Lebanon over the summer were to perpetuate this trend.

Following Iran's proclaimed achievement, which seemed to many to make a mockery of the West's red lines, the diplomatic process continued ponderously on, to the UNSC and the delivery of a presidential statement, followed on 6 June by a resolution (UNSCR 1696) demanding that Iran cease uranium enrichment by 31 August, and holding out the prospect of sanctions in the event of a refusal. Rumours abounded that Larijani, who at this point was in protracted talks with EU Special Representative Javier Solana, was, for all his hardline credentials, keen to come to some sort of resolution – especially if he could take the credit for it – and had been favourably disposed towards the latest E3 offer. But Ahmadinejad was significantly less attracted to any deal that involved the suspension of uranium enrichment, however brief. A deal at this stage would have interrupted the narrative of success that Ahmadinejad had been presenting to the Iranian public. It would, he calculated, be seen by Iranians as an unnecessary compromise. But perhaps more than anything, the president was motivated by a concern to prevent Larijani benefiting from any deal. Domestic political rivalries, after all, always take precedence over foreign policy considerations. This divergence of perspectives within the Iranian conservative elite itself was indicative of how polarised the situation had become.[34] On the one hand, Europe was still anxious to keep the crisis under control. On the other, Ahmadinejad was effectively arguing that the nuclear file was closed, and that his policy, and Iran, stood triumphant. Meanwhile, events were about to take a turn that few had predicted. The events of the summer of 2006 would reinforce Ahmadinejad's worldview of Iran as a victim of Western plots and slanders, and point up the ever-increasing contrast between the different narratives about the Middle East in Iran and the West.

In early July, Larijani was on his way home from another round of talks with Solana, during which the latter had apparently pulled no punches and explained firmly that European patience was wearing thin, as Ahmadinejad took several deliberately provocative months to respond to the latest E3 offer. On the way back, Larijani stopped off in Damascus to brief the Syrians on the latest stage of talks. The next day, Hizbullah launched a raid into northern Israel and captured two Israeli soldiers. Israel's dramatic response of bombarding Lebanon took Hizbullah, Lebanon and most of the region by surprise. In the US, the blame for the Second Lebanon War, as it would soon become, was rapidly allocated to Iran, with Larijani's stopover in Damascus offered as proof that Iran had instructed Hizbullah to take action in order to divert attention away from the nuclear crisis.

This theory may have served the interests of the White House and Tel Aviv in providing Israel with a casus belli equal to the vehemence of its offensive, but it bore little relation to events as seen from Iran. The notion that Iran would provoke a war in Lebanon to distract attention from its own difficulties was not borne out in Iran itself where Ahmadinejad, as we have seen, was portraying the nuclear impasse as a triumph for his policy and for the country. Furthermore, to employ such a strategy, Iran would have had to know that the Israeli response would be as dramatic as it was, and the theory also ignored the local tensions and pressures that had given rise to the soldiers' abduction. We now know from the findings of the Winograd Commission that Israel had in fact been planning for just such an engagement, because of its concerns over the consolidation of Hizbullah in southern Lebanon and repeated border violations. Hizbullah's genuine surprise at the Israeli response reflected the fact that reciprocal cross-border attacks had been a feature of life over the previous years. The timing of the group's actions on this particular occasion had probably had more to do with the emerging confrontation in Gaza between Israel and Palestinian militants than with any enticements from Tehran.

At the same time, there can be little doubt that Iran had been supporting and arming Hizbullah as a counter to Israel. In addition, affiliation with a coherent military organisation in southern Lebanon provided Iran with valuable political leverage in the Arab world. Iran's relationship with Hizbullah was founded on the idea that Israel was the Americans' Achilles heel in the Middle East, and that therefore to repulse the US, what was needed was a forward aggressive posture towards Israel, such as Hizbullah provided. Of course, much as with the forward strategy being deployed in Iraq by Iran – or by the US for that matter – this provocative deterrence tended to increase, rather than decrease, levels of insecurity and paranoia. But in spite of the belligerence of the approach, it was precisely the double use of Hizbullah to Iran, both a defence against a direct Israeli/American attack and as a possibly tool for retaliation in the event of such an attack, that made it important not to take the provocation too far and risk wasting this valuable resource in what was, as far as Iran was concerned, a premature engagement of its guerrilla ally. The war made far more sense from the Israeli point of view, as an opportunity to remove a dangerous irritant from Israel's northern border.

Whatever the immediate reasons for the war in July 2006, the decision on the part of both the US and Israel to ascribe all responsibility to Iran was to have the unforeseen consequence of substantially strengthening Ahmadinejad's hand. As the 34-day war progressed and Hizbullah's effectiveness showed no sign of waning, Iran was only too pleased to accept the responsibility assigned to it. The Lebanon War of 2006 is a prime example of Israeli and Western defeat snatched from the jaws of victory. Whatever the material losses suffered by Hizbullah – and these were certainly substantial – the standard for victory Israel set itself in declaring the goal of obliterating Hizbullah was so high as to more or less ensure its defeat. Hizbullah simply had to survive to be able to declare victory, a victory given all the more power because enacted on the television screens of the world as a successful confrontation with the most powerful armed forces in the Middle East. On a political and ideological level, this was a catastrophe for Israel, and Ahmadinejad knew it, and gloated. Furthermore, it was not only Hizbullah's victory, but that of Iran, and its rumbustious president. In the autumn of 2006, Ahmadinejad's position seemed unassailable, both at home and abroad.

CHAPTER FOUR

The Ahmadinejad Presidency: Domestic Policy

For all the importance of international affairs to the Ahmadinejad presidency, it should be kept in mind that the central consideration was always the establishment of domestic hegemony. The international stage was an arena in which domestic political rivalries could be played out – a reality frequently overlooked by observers in the West – as well as the vital means for consolidating domestic control. The atmosphere of heightening crisis that dramas abroad brought about allowed Ahmadinejad to play the role of glorious leader and enabled the government to get away with being more repressive. The ongoing happy coincidence of a high oil price also helped the president along by financing populist economic policies. It is worth emphasising just how much the strategy of accentuating confrontation abroad paid dividends in terms of the president's standing at home. The greater the confrontation, the wider and more powerful the array of enemies, the greater the lustre and glory to be attained by defeating them. Ahmadinejad appeared to enjoy an unshakeable, and somewhat infectious, conviction that victory was indeed within reach. At the conclusion of the Lebanon War, Ahmadinejad felt able to answer his domestic critics and largely to dissolve the doubt among the elite to swell the ranks of the faithful.

Yet this sense of triumph was to prove all too ephemeral, as before the end of 2006, Ahmadinejad and his faction had suffered two dramatic electoral defeats; in the same municipal elections that in 2003 had signalled his rise to national prominence, and, more ominously from his personal point of view, in the elections to the Assembly of Experts, the body charged with electing the Supreme Leader. That this should have been the case in the same year as what were generally felt to be successes on the international stage was due to the president's extraordinary mishandling of the domestic political and economic situation. As Iranian economists had privately argued in 2005, it seemed that it was the economy that would prove in time to be Ahmadinejad's undoing.

The economy, part one: 'economics is for donkeys'

Of the four aspects of the principlist strategy for securing domestic hegemony – the maintenance of a 'managed' international crisis; political and economic populism; the creation of a charisma around the person of the president; and a gradual increase in political repression – in theory the last ought not to be needed, as the other strategies should be able to secure power without it. Economic populism ought to have been one of the most straightforward. As reformists had lamented at the time, Ahmadinejad entered office in 2005 with oil at around US$60 per barrel. This was far in excess of the prices under his two predecessors; indeed, when Khatami had entered office in 1997, oil was nearer US$10 per barrel. Even the most incoherent economic strategy, it was thought, would yield results. Salaries could be doubled, and jobs created through investment in vast infrastructural projects – the population could if necessary be effectively bribed into supporting the government, while Western powers would lose much of their economic leverage. If Khatami had had to impose a measure of financial discipline, Ahmadinejad could spend the fruits of the previous eight years' austerities. He could also begin to realise his ambitions for Iranian self-sufficiency, free from the conditionality of foreign loans and investment. For the principlists and Ahmadinejad, the timing of this windfall was, literally, divinely inspired.

Both the Rafsanjani and Khatami administrations had – admittedly with patchy success – tried to wean Iran off its dependence on oil revenue and move towards diversifying the manufacturing base. This was always going to be difficult, given the dominance of mercantile interests and the lack of industrial investment, especially from overseas companies with the technical expertise needed to upgrade and modernise Iran's somewhat dilapidated industrial base. Rafsanjani sought initially to spend and then borrow his way through reconstruction, arguing when Iran faced the first serious prospect of defaulting on its overseas debts that by borrowing from the West, Iran was getting 'investment' by the back door and thus ensuring an ongoing Western commitment to its economic growth.

Not everyone was convinced of the wisdom of this argument, and under Khatami the emphasis shifted to developing the industrial base through using constructive international relations to attract proper investment. The drive to modernise Iran's 'diseased' and structurally flawed economy had to come from within, Khatami argued, and be a deliberate commitment in itself, rather than part of a strategy to secure outside help. Many economists felt that the collapse of the oil price in the 1990s had been a blessing in disguise, as it had meant that Iranians could no longer be complacent – necessity would be the mother of invention, and Iranians were nothing if not creative under pressure. Economists pointed out at the time that the greatest growth in the Iranian economy had in fact occurred before the dramatic oil-price rises of 1973.

But neither Rafsanjani's nor Khatami's route to modernisation appealed to the principlists, as economic integration implied dependency. As we have seen, their dominant narrative was that the revolution had lost its way with the presidency of Rafsanjani and the pollution of revolutionary values through the introduction of rampant materialism and the corruption which accompanied it. Looking back nostalgically at the economy that had seen Iran emerge from the war in 1988 with a balanced budget and minimal debts, they viewed with disapproval what they regarded as Rafsanjani's reckless spending and accumulation of debt. The argument that was made in response, that it is necessary to engage with wider markets and other economic actors at least to some degree in order to be able to make money, cut little ice with the prophets of national self-sufficiency. Khatami's economic prescriptions, too, they viewed unfavourably, not only because of the danger of dependence on outsiders and the political implications of economic reform, but also because extensive foreign investment could threaten Iran's mercantile political economy and the vested interests it supplied and supported. The principlists thought the answer was to increase domestic investment instead, essentially by channelling oil revenue through their own organisations and networks into various business and industry projects, often of dubious viability. The favoured political elite would manage and oversee investment in the economy via non-state organs of their own, diverting money away from government ministries (which were officially accountable to parliament) and towards revolutionary and religious institutes and foundations. Especially vulnerable to the vagaries of this haphazard and unaccountable system was the oil reserve fund that Khatami had painstakingly built up for times when the oil price dipped below budget forecasts. Not long into Ahmadinejad's presidency, the economists of the 'government of the faithful' were looking as if they had taken Khomeini's much-quoted aphorism that 'economics is for donkeys' to heart to an extent that shocked even hardened conservatives, and it began to become apparent to some that the new regime might be about to squander the country's rather golden economic opportunity.

The iconoclast

Other indications of trouble ahead came in the first few months of Ahmadinejad's presidency, with his nominations to cabinet posts. Appointing the cabinet had proved a tortuous affair during the Rafsanjani and Khatami eras since the Majlis, which was usually dominated by rival factions, saw it as an opportunity to flex their political muscles and vie for the promotion of their men. On this occasion, however, both the dominant faction in the Majlis and the president came from the same political faction, so it was initially assumed that all would go smoothly. The first shock for many, both elites and indeed ordinary voters who had thought this kind of politics to be relegated to Iran's past, came with Ahmadinejad's nominations to the key portfolios of interior and intelligence minister of Mostafa Pourmohammadi and Gholamhossein Mohseni-Ejei respectively, followed by his suggested candidates for other key administration posts, including Gholamhossein Elham for official government spokesman. Probably the most disgraceful eventual appointment was the promotion of Tehran's notorious chief prosecutor, Saeed Mortazavi – a man implicated in the murder of Canadian-Iranian journalist Zahra Kazemi – to the post of UN human rights envoy.

Many Iranians were appalled that individuals associated with the worst excesses of revolutionary justice and human-rights abuses were being proposed for senior ministerial posts from which their records should surely disqualify them. The appointments, which almost all went through in part thanks to the conservative dominance of the Majlis, reflected the rise within the new administration of those elements within the IRGC establishment whose remit, like that of Ahmadinejad himself, had previously been domestic security and logistics.[1] The dominance of this particular element of the national military–security apparatus was in many ways to be more damaging than the ascendancy of the IRGC proper that many had originally dreaded would come about. But while these appointments failed to rankle with members of the Majlis, who on the whole excused any past excesses with reference to nominees' impeccable revolutionary credentials, Ahmadinejad's choice to head the all-important Oil Ministry did pose a problem to them, and it was at this point that the political tensions became most dramatic.

It is worth noting at this stage that it was Ahmadinejad's cavalier approach, and not always his policies, which most often raised the hackles of his political cohorts and erstwhile allies. It was not long into his term that Ahmadinejad's exaggerated self-belief got the better of what limited political judgement he had, and he quickly alienated some supporters by dismissing the practical support that had helped to catapult him to power in favour of more dramatic charismatic/religious explanations for his success. Ahmadinejad allowed his vanity to be the master of him sooner than most, giving in quickly to the enticements that went with power in Iran. Intoxicated by the sudden increase in attention and curiosity about him, internationally as well as at home, and surrounded by the traditional coterie of sycophants, Ahmadinejad appeared to move from being a genuine, unsophisticated 'man of the people' to a self-indulgent, decadent man of politics with rather startling alacrity. He had always sought to make a virtue of his rough, down-to-earth manners, styling himself as a rejuvenating working-class presence in politics, a *sans-culotte* ready to restore the revolution. But many felt that he took the brisk demeanour too far; treating friend and foe with equal vulgarity, and appearing disdainful of all people and organisations that did not answer to or believe in his particular utopia. In a political system defined by personal networks and a rigorous, often pedantic system of social etiquette, Ahmadinejad's overt determination to pursue a policy of anti-establishment populism against the interests of many of those around him came as something of a shock to many of his allies. Thus the Majlis felt that this particular wayward son was in need of a rebuke, and accordingly it rejected three of Ahmadinejad's nominees for the Oil Ministry job on the grounds of inexperience and/or a lack of relevant qualifications.

Indeed, now that he was in power, Ahmadinejad did seem more interested in appointing friends and ideological bedfellows to key ministries than the competent managers he had suggested during his election campaign – merit for Ahmadinejad was defined more in terms of political loyalty than by ability to do the job. Eventually, on his fourth attempt, with no resolution of the dispute in sight, the president had to settle for a caretaker oil minister drawn from the cabinet of his predecessor. This was seen by many as a promising sign of continuity, and as an indication of the ongoing dominance of the oil interests (led by Rafsanjani) whom Ahmadinejad had sworn to remove. But while it was undoubtedly a setback for the president, the reasons behind the defeat had more to do with Ahmadinejad's lack of tact than with any major concerns about the capabilities of his nominees to this particularly important ministry. Ultimately, in spite of its reservations about his style of governing, parliament supported the president, and, as we have seen, was happy to ratify the appointment of two controversial figures in key interior and intelligence positions. The fact that Ahmadinejad had to settle for a hangover from the Khatami cabinet at the Oil Ministry reflected more the president's own tendency to misjudge how to handle his allies than the strength of his opponents.

A new elite and its opponents

With the new cabinet finalised by the end of the summer of 2005, measures were put in place to begin to purge the ministries considered to have become strongholds of reformist thinking. One of the arguments that hardliners had made for the extraordinary influence over and intervention in the presidential election by the Guardian Council had been that the Ministry of the Interior had been infiltrated by reformists to such an extent that it effectively operated as a political party. Accusations of endemic bias in the civil service were of course not new: a similar charge was made by reformists against the conservative establishment in the 1990s. But by 2005, the roles were reversed and Iranian politics was witness to the peculiar spectacle of a radicalised conservative establishment – the principlists – presenting themselves as anti-establishment purifiers of a political system corrupted by liberalism. Interestingly, the wide scope of the removals did in fact demonstrate that the Khatami administration had influenced the character of government in Iran quite considerably. The principlist purges of 2005 and later showed that, far from being a mere ineffectual intellectual, Mohammad Khatami had managed to push through some far-reaching changes during his period in office.

The pace of change in the makeup and activities of the ministries should not, however, be exaggerated. Ahmadinejad's priority, if not preoccupation, in the first 18 months of his administration was the management of the international crisis, and he did not want to needlessly provoke the population by immediately moving to tighten up restrictions on social life or impose Islamic mores. He had been eager to emphasise during the election campaign that he had far more serious issues to deal with than whether Iranian women were properly dressed, and argued – convincingly to many – that his opponents were slandering him with scare stories about the draconian measures he would implement. And indeed, once in power, Ahmadinejad talked the language of Islamic purity, but did little to enforce it. This approach beguiled the public, and lent support to his claim that his target was the elite, not ordinary people. Even as he targeted the elite by purging the ministries, he was selective about his targets, continuing as much as possible a conservative strategy which sought to avoid a dangerous reaction by exploiting the self-interest of individuals and factions to gain converts to the hardline project, as well as simply removing the old guard. To the vast majority of ordinary Iranians, the spectacle of the elite turning on itself was either an irrelevance, or else just part of the entertainment of Iranian politics. For those in the lower ranks of the governing structure, Ahmadinejad's attack on the old elite promised new opportunities, and there was a genuine sense among many junior officials, who largely did not share Ahmadinejad's political and religious outlook, that his iconoclastic attack on a complacent and corrupt elite that had essentially rotated in and out of power over the last two decades, rather than ever relinquishing it, was a much-needed and good thing.

The reality was that Ahmadinejad did not exclusively target the corrupt and complacent, but primarily those who did not share his very particular views. Significantly, the most prominent casualties were in the Foreign Ministry, where a string of senior ambassadors were retired, recalled or allowed to go on sabbatical. In many cases these replacements were not forced. While some officials were able to make the transition from reformist to principlist, arguing with some justification that the politics of the president should not affect their service to their country, others were less sanguine about the prospect of serving under a president whose international perspective ran contrary to everything they had sought to achieve over the past 15 years. In quantitative terms, the replacements were not as extensive as some had feared, but there can be little doubt that the qualitative impact was significant. The ambassadors who were removed had by and large been based in Europe, where they had spent their time cultivating relationships and generally presenting an image of Iran as coherent and amenable, an approach that was viewed with suspicion by the new team in Tehran. Their abrupt replacement interrupted enormously valuable channels of communication at a time when Iran could ill afford to disrupt any positive processes in its international relations. The officials who took their place not only operated under a strict confrontation-only policy, but were also for the most part less apt or able than their predecessors to act on their own initiative. Europe found to its frustration that Iran's new representatives stuck dogmatically to the Tehran line, and the diplomatic rapport and networks that had been developed with their predecessors were absent, and showing no signs of re-emerging. Iran's new government had in effect quarantined its diplomatic wing.[2]

This applied too to the nuclear negotiating team, headed as of August 2005 by Ali Larijani. Larijani himself was to mellow over the course of his extended round of negotiations with Javier Solana, but his public statements were intransigent, and he was consistently scathing about his predecessor's achievements. His criticisms did not go unanswered, and opposition to Larijani's position within Iran strengthened as Ahmadinejad's strategy of confrontation resulted in the UNSC referral in 2006. A number of individuals who had been 'retired' were to become serious thorns in the president's side; revealing not only the limitations of the purge as a tactic for consolidating control, but also the deep resentment the principlists had incurred in their rise to power and through their attempts at politicising the civil service. Herein lay a fundamental weakness of Ahmadinejad's administration: for all its aspirations to popular legitimacy, it had gained power to a large degree on the back of voter apathy and protest voting, and the faction's ruthless treatment of its opponents. While both the electorate and the civil service were undoubtedly disillusioned by the failures of the reform movement, and there was a feeling among many to begin with that a change was needed and, for a time, welcome, it did not follow that a majority respected or liked the new regime as the months drew on.

One of the many purposes of Ahmadinejad's populism was to show a sceptical technocratic elite that he and the movement he represented were simply too popular and successful to be dismissed. In many ways, the principlists were confident about the capacity of the population at large to be repeatedly won over by populist policies, and about the extent to which the effective and occasionally ruthless exercise of power would act as a reminder of authority. But if the population in general was regarded as malleable, especially when presented with a display of patriotic defiance abroad, the political elites were noticeably less forgiving. Ahmadinejad's initial strategy had been to treat them as an irrelevance, part of the discredited establishment that he had come to overthrow (a dangerous posture in Iran's highly sensitive system of social etiquette and deference[3]). Complacency and conceit soon tempted him and his allies, however, to make open attacks on their opponents' abilities and integrity. If political conventions and discretion prevented these opponents from responding immediately, there was little doubt that the insults rankled, and if to begin with the expression of grievances against the new rulers among the elites was restricted to private circles – which to Ahmadinejad's irritation often included foreign friends and contacts – this was partly because the elites believed that it was only a matter of very little time before the Ahmadinejad honeymoon ended in economic disaster.

Ahmadinejad's opponents were also guilty of complacency in believing that he could not last, that his extraordinary ego and sheer economic incompetence would bring his government to a quick and ignominious end. If he survived, they argued, it would be as a result of the international crisis fuelled by foreign hardliners, who had their own reasons for wanting to keep Ahmadinejad in power. There was truth in this view to the extent that the ongoing sense of international crisis did much to constrain political life and debate in Iran (and had done ever since the US 'axis of evil' speech in 2002), but it also reflected a prejudiced and cynical tendency among Iranian politicians to exaggerate the influence of the West in Iranian politics, which rather conveniently justified inaction by locating responsibility elsewhere. Domestic critics of Ahmadinejad often complained that the West did little to undermine Ahmadinejad's power, while at the same time urging caution on the West lest criticisms from abroad fuel his populist appeal. This confused approach reflected the fact that few within Iran actually understood Ahmadinejad, and that in trying to make sense of this self-proclaimed charismatic national saviour, several of his opponents fell victim to his greatest political asset: an extraordinary and protean charismatic personality cult that defies attempts to understand it and successfully mystifies its subject to outsiders. It acts as its own validation; as long as the initiated, the believers, understand, it hardly matters, indeed is positively a good thing, if everyone else does not.[4]

On the terms of the myth of Ahmadinejad, the incomprehension of the establishment was proof itself of the president's exalted and mystic status. The theme of the iconoclast who shocks and mystifies the established powers has a sound religious pedigree; but equally this failure of understanding also reflected the very real divisions in Iranian society between tradition and modernity. The fact that a traditional constituency existed that supported Ahmadinejad was an embarrassment to many of the technocratic elite whose idea of Iran did not allow for the existence of a group that represented, in their eyes at least, the persistence of superstition and ignorance. Although the Islamic Republic helped to sustain and support such a constituency, for those who believed that the Islamic Republican system was about enlightenment and modernity within an Islamic framework, the persistence of such a constituency was an anachronism – even a sign of failure – that many sought to deny. This denial of unpalatable truths was a flaw in the political perspective of this section of the elite that affected their strategy, and which Ahmadinejad was able to exploit.

At the same time, the idea, keenly argued by a number of observers both within and outside the country in the aftermath of Ahmadinejad's election victory, that this traditional constituency represented the 'real' Iran, was equally inaccurate. However, along with damage done by allegations that various of the more liberal members of the elites were colluding with Westerners, this perception seems to have functioned as an excuse for some of Ahmadinejad's opponents to remain in a political stupor, procrastinating over tackling him, for at least the first 18 months of his presidency.

Repression

The international crisis, and the way it framed and constrained political contest within Iran, was nevertheless still the primary reason for the cautious inaction of Ahmadinejad's enemies. Several factors, including the belief that Ahmadinejad would fall victim to his economic mismanagement, straight denial of his appeal and, for some, this gloomy incomprehension and suspicion that the president did in fact represent the country's traditionalist hinterland, reinforced the inertia. Another factor was repression.

Ahmadinejad's strategy of persecution tended to avoid direct confrontation with his political opponents. Despite extensive and occasionally direct threats made to the Rafsanjani family, and the widespread assumption in the aftermath of the election that it was only a matter of time before Rafsanjani's sons would be arrested on corruption charges, no such moves were initiated. On the contrary, the government decided on a more indirect approach, which nonetheless signalled a broader shift in policy towards an increased use of intimidation in politics.

In April 2006, Iranian academic Ramin Jahanbegloo was arrested at Tehran airport on his way to an international conference. Interrogated over a period of four months, Jahanbegloo reportedly revealed a vast network of academics and think tanks involved in what the government alleged was an attempt to launch a 'velvet revolution' in the country. Jahanbegloo was eventually released, but the information he provided led to the arrest and detention without trial of a number of prominent Iranian-American academics over the following year – including the director of the Middle East programme at the Woodrow Wilson International Center for Scholars, Haleh Esfandiari – all on the grounds that they supported a 'velvet' revolution. The allegations struck most observers, friends and foes alike, as palpable nonsense.[5] The televised 'confessions' of those accused that were the price of their eventual release revealed very little, other than a government that did not understand the concept of civil society. In any case, after the disappointments of the reform era, the regime's fears seemed ill founded: it seemed highly unlikely to most that Iranians had the inclination or indeed the energy to engage in popular resistance.

The obsessive fear of a 'velvet revolution' is an example of the paranoia of a government that is deeply insecure, knowing that, despite its undoubted populist appeal, it in fact enjoys little popular legitimacy.[6] The arrests may have served their purpose of warning the academic community to avoid contact with foreign and diaspora colleagues, but a wiser strategy, surely, would have been for the government to try to broaden its base by reassuring and ingratiating key intellectuals. Instead Ahmadinejad's government lost support in the population at large (though it did gain some among its core constituents) as it was seen to respond paranoiacally to the most trivial of threats.

To Ahmadinejad's closest allies, allegations against intellectuals were an easy sell to its superstitious core supporters, raised as they were on a diet of conspiracy theories about the West, and indeed they did soon generate their own sustaining momentum. The emphasis was thus kept for a time on closing down intellectual debate within the universities, and on undermining their links abroad. For Ahmadinejad, Iran's universities needed a new cultural revolution. What he disdained as 'secular' education, which had dominated Iran's universities for the better part of 150 years, had to be purged, and, much to the horror of local academics, a cleric was appointed chancellor of Tehran University.

The assault on the universities was not only to have an enormously detrimental effect on Iran's international academic reputation, as the effects on intellectual activity and debate began to be felt, but also, more immediately crucial in political terms, it alienated diaspora and foreign academia. Scholars at American universities had been at the forefront of moves towards taking a more nuanced approach to the Islamic Republic. With Iranian-American academics imprisoned in Iran, such moves were at best restricted, and at worst became impossible. In Iran itself, the regime was correct to calculate that its targeting of what were essentially third parties would mean that its political opponents would not risk their own positions, thus far largely unthreatened, to protect their academic contacts, even as the repressive measures were damaging their highly valued connections with the outside world, connections which had been encouraged by both Rafsanjani and Khatami.

Vulgar nationalism

The attack on the intellectuals was in part a consequence of the vulgar nationalism encouraged and developed by Ahmadinejad. In the nationalist view, intellectuals had not only polluted the purity of the Islamic revolution by importing strange disruptive ideas from the West; they were in effect a fifth column. The repression of intellectual activity was therefore presented as an act of national purification and made easier to swallow for the less convinced by the general atmosphere of continuing international threat. Ahmadinejad was assisted in sustaining this atmosphere by the incoherence of the messages coming out of the West and the US in particular, where a desire to protect the NPT regime and prevent nuclear proliferation was often intermingled with the rhetoric of regime change. In Iran, such messages were used to promote the view that the West represented an existential threat to Iran. This was admittedly a rather awkward position to sustain at the same time as boasting of the government's triumphs overseas and Iran's regional dominance, but it received a boost when a range of neo-conservative thinkers in the US began mooting the idea that America should encourage ethnic separatist movements in Baluchestan, Khuzestan, Azerbaijan and among the Kurds.[7] Although the US government vigorously denied pursuing such a policy, the consequent rumour that it was was enough to enable the Iranian government to exploit historically rooted nationalist fears to good effect. For the stubborn sceptics, the government held up the example of Iraq, and warned of the consequences of trusting the Americans. In such an environment, it was increasingly difficult for a critic to speak out without immediately being labelled a traitor and risk to national security.

Some of the clearest examples of the exploitation of nationalist sentiment were to be found around the nuclear crisis. Here the terms of the debate were painted in the broadest nationalist brush strokes and the argument framed exclusively in terms of national rights and dignity.[8] Uranium enrichment was not a technical process, but a right which could not be compromised. Indeed the mere mention of compromise was against the national interest and treasonous, and debate, insofar as it had existed at all on this issue, was effectively closed down. Any realistic assessment of public opinion on the nuclear programme was consequently difficult to make, especially amid all the fanfare and theatricals about Iran's 'innate genius'. Ahmadinejad was effectively selling pride to the Iranians, arguing that the route to renewed greatness lay through a self-sufficient nuclear programme. It was because the West wanted to prevent Iranian progress that it consistently obstructed the development of this programme.

Ahmadinejad also appealed to memories of the shaking off of colonialism by comparing the nuclear project to the movement for oil nationalisation against the British of the early 1950s. Indeed for a time, perhaps because, unlike the US, the UK still had an embassy in Iran, the British returned as the foreign conspirator of choice, with moves in the summer of 2007 to repossess the British embassy's summer compound in Golhak.[9] The desire among some of Ahmadinejad's supporters to recreate the atmosphere of the early days of the revolution was clear.

But one manoeuvre in relation to the British seemed to many Iranians to display Ahmadinejad's peculiarities and pretensions rather more than it did his zeal in defending the realm. While many Iranians applauded the decision to seize 15 British sailors in the Persian Gulf in the March 2007 on the grounds that they were trespassing on Iranian waters, they were perplexed by the president's handling of the situation thereafter, particularly the manner in which the sailors were released. Not only did the president 'congratulate' the captives on their enforced break from duties, but he treated them to a presidential visit and an official send-off, complete with new suits and gifts. Most controversially, Ahmadinejad made a great show of 'pardoning' them, in doing so exercising a prerogative he did not legally enjoy. Although the UK Royal Navy's decision to allow the sailors to sell their stories to the newspapers helped Ahmadinejad by transferring the focus of criticism elsewhere, in Iran, people were astonished by the regal pretensions of their president.[10] At this rate, some said, it would surely only be a matter of time before the president became the author of his own destruction.

The economy, part two: oil and excess

That that time was longer in coming than many expected has much to do with the unusually high price of oil. Ahmadinejad's political opponents looked on in awed envy at the enormous revenues he had at his disposal; far in excess of anything either Rafsanjani or Khatami had enjoyed. To some, oil at US$60 a barrel and rising meant that the principlist ascendancy was unassailable, and it was only a matter of time and some judicious spending before the hardline hegemony was firmly consolidated. The general assumption at the beginning of his presidency, as we have seen, was that Ahmadinejad would use the oil windfall to initiate an extensive programme of infrastructural projects; putting people to work, increasing salaries and rejuvenating the industrial base of the country. Most importantly, he was expected to be able to create what his predecessors had struggled towards: a diversified economy based on tax and manufacture, rather than oil revenues alone. As the man thus responsible for the resurrection of the Iranian state, Ahmadinejad's legacy would be untouchable. In light of this, and of his various campaign promises, there was a great deal of anticipation in 2005 about a new era for the economy.

This hopefulness, however, reckoned without the peculiar economic ambitions of the president's faction, outlined earlier, and the idiosyncrasies of the president himself, who, in economics as in everything else, not only tried to copy his intellectual and spiritual mentor, Ayatollah Khomeini, particularly in his autarkic ambitions and his disdain for the detail of market economics, but also sought, to a far greater extent than his mentor, to personally dominate all aspects of policymaking. It is worth noting at this point the differences between Ahmadinejad's situation in 2005 and Khomeini's in the early days of the revolution. While Khomeini might have successfully played the role of trailblazing iconoclast, he still felt able to delegate on matters of administration and policy to those who were more qualified. By contrast, Ahmadinejad's insistence on directing economic projects he did not fully understand was to cause numerous difficulties.

Furthermore, Khomeini had inherited an economy that had been growing for the past 50 years, and which possessed significant assets that could, in a worst-case scenario, always be drawn down to make savings. The imperatives of war also made life somewhat easier as far as making economic choices was concerned – the only realistic option was a state-dominated, centrally run economy. Perhaps most importantly, the spirit of the revolution was at its height in Khomeini's early years. People were willing to make sacrifices in the sincere hope of a better future. But by 2005, hope had been replaced with cynicism and a measure of desperation, as it had become clear that the revolution was failing on a number of fronts. This was of course a major reason for Ahmadinejad's election victory itself, but Ahmadinejad was to consistently fail to acknowledge the importance of the role of the country's underlying economic problems in creating and sustaining this national malaise.

While the economy he inherited did enjoy a degree of stability and a financial surplus (carefully nurtured over previous years), it was not robust, and could fairly be said to be underperforming. Certainly the industrial potential of the country as it had been identified during the reign of the Shah had not been realised, as both Khatami and to a lesser extent Rafsanjani had recognised. The great ambition of successive administrations to diversify the economy and secure foreign investment to this end had not been realised, and any belief that Iranian industry could recuperate on its own had been found to be hopelessly optimistic. Iran's economy remained firmly mercantile and vulnerable to the vagaries of the oil market. That said, Ahmadinejad did now have the opportunity to turn things around, and some commentators believed that his more reckless tendencies would be constrained by the fact that he would have to operate within the framework of the Twenty-Year Plan drawn up by the civil service, an ambitious and aspirational document which lay down broad parameters for where the Islamic Republic saw itself in 20 years' time. To be sure it was, like many such documents, strong on ideas and somewhat vague on practicalities, but it did nonetheless present a vision for what might loosely be termed the normalisation of the economy.

The debacle over the appointment of the oil minister in August 2005, however, served notice that Ahmadinejad had different ideas. The rejection of his nominees was presented by the president's camp as an attempt by the establishment to prevent Ahmadinejad from truly revolutionising the economy and freeing it from the grip of the mafias he had alluded to in his campaign. But others argued, with more justification, that the president was not appointing competent managers, but loyal political friends, some of whom had half an eye to the money that could be made in government office. Indeed it soon became apparent that the principlists led by Ahmadinejad were just as eager to plunder the resources of the state as any of their predecessors, and, if anything, were especially rapacious. Any suggestion of economic transparency, an essential prerequisite of foreign investment, was effectively abandoned, as Ahmadinejad determined to use Iran's oil wealth to concentrate on domestic investment and shun foreign investment in line with his isolationist worldview. The religious foundations and revolutionary organs, including the IRGC, to which Ahmadinejad directed resources at the expense of state ministries were mostly by tradition and/or law not accountable to parliament, but to the Supreme Leader, making the destination of the funds that entered them almost impossible to monitor.[11]

Furthermore, it soon became clear that the rather ad hoc expenditure plans that appeared to represent Ahmadinejad's economic strategy did not in fact amount to 'investment' of any kind. Awash as it was with oil money, the Iranian government appeared to be unsure what to do with it. With his lavish, unstructured expenditure,[12] Ahmadinejad seemed more like a traditional potentate than a manager of a modern state. Rafsanjani had been criticised for extravagance, but the sums available to him had been far smaller. With a total oil revenue in the first two years of Ahmadinejad's presidency of US$120bn, the administration still found it necessary to deplete Khatami's emergency oil reserve fund. What was most troubling to observers of all political hues was that it was unclear where all the money was going. A considerable amount seems to have gone in cash handouts to the poor, distributed with great fanfare on the president's many tours of the country. Substantial funds went to various revolutionary and religious institutions as noted above, and it also appeared that funds were used to massively subsidise additional religious and other foundations that had traditionally been eligible for (hitherto much more modest) state subsidy.

It is worth bearing in mind that this spending was taking place at a time when economic events outside Iran, primarily the weakening of the US dollar, were setting some limits on the uses of the oil windfall. Unable to purchase goods in the US as a result of US sanctions, Iran found its costs rising in Europe and the Far East. In addition, the increasing pressure of sanctions meant that there were fewer and fewer destinations for Iranian revenue. This was especially the case once banking sanctions came into effect in late 2006 and 2007, and Iranian businesses for the most part closed their European bank accounts. Iran might have managed this situation with a carefully structured programme of domestic investment combined with reserves of income to be drawn on at a later stage if necessary. But the former was not forthcoming and the latter increasingly depleted.

The much criticised presidential policy of periodically decreeing that interest rates be lowered in order to enable more loans to small businesses compounded problems with the twin effects of creating capital flight and encouraging one of the most dramatic injections of liquidity into the Iranian economy since the Shah's 'Great Civilisation' initiative in the 1970s. The money leaving the country resulted in a further depression of the already weak rial against other currencies, and, as those who decided not to send their money abroad invested in housing, property prices were forced upwards. The rise in property prices, which was especially marked in Tehran, and the concomitant increase in rentier income, further encouraged growing income inequalities, but it also allowed optimists to argue that the economy was in fact robust. And for those ordinary people on the receiving end of presidential cash handouts, it did indeed seem for a while as if the good times had finally arrived. It is not difficult to see how this policy alone, which appears to have affected considerable numbers of people, bankrolled as it was by the high oil price, could have enabled Ahmadinejad's popularity to initially soar, even as the economic troubles were building. The president's opponents saw the wisdom in sitting out this honeymoon period and allowing him to enjoy the plaudits his indiscriminate generosity, attacks on the establishment and provocative posturing towards the international community won him: soon, surely, he would need to explain the economic bust that would follow.

The honeymoon continued, however, throughout the first 18 months of his presidency. Even critics of the president were being swayed by his apparent success on the international stage, as the nuclear programme looked to be proceeding apace with little that the international community could do about it. The US, bogged down in the quagmire of Iraq, seemed clearly to be a busted flush, and, ironically perhaps (and in striking contrast to the emollient but, Iranians felt, ultimately uncooperative international reception of Khatami), it appeared as if Ahmadinejad's confrontational approach was actually winning him and the country the kind of international attention that some thought could even have the potential to regain a degree of influence for Iran. With traditional Iranian fatalism, some began to conclude that perhaps Ahmadinejad just knew what he was doing – maybe the most charismatic recent Iranian leader really did have access to some esoteric masterplan. More sober observers remained convinced otherwise, but, for the time being, they kept their own counsel.

Imperial overstretch

At the end of the summer of 2006, Ahmadinejad was at the pinnacle of his power. Not only did he appear domestically secure, but his politics of confrontation seemed to have given Iran a dominant role in the region as Israel, its great regional rival, stood badly wounded, and Iran's manipulation of the events in Lebanon had won it the ideological leadership of the Arab world. Yet at the end of the same year, the fragility of Ahmadinejad's power, both domestically and internationally, began to be exposed, as the weakness of his domestic base became more evident. The relative ease with which Iran was able to exercise its regional power had had the effect of intoxicating its leadership even further, encouraging more *folies de grandeur*, both at home at abroad, which weakened what had seemed even a few months earlier to be an unassailable position. For all the talk of national rejuvenation, Iran's regional influence was fragile, having, as we have seen, more to do with the incompetence of its opponents than with any internal strength. Ahmadinejad's successful use of a tense international environment to disguise, perhaps even to himself, the fissures opening beneath his feet, seemed to be coming to an end, and his opponents began to see their chance to tackle him.

Economic crisis

For all the temptation to attack him on his religious heterodoxy and claims to divine inspiration, the president's opponents chose to focus their criticism on the more practical aspects of his administration, principally his handling of the economy. By the end of 2006, it had become clear that the president's promises were not being fulfilled and that, far from bringing the country's oil revenue to its people's dinner tables, the immediate consequence of his lavish spending was inflation. This did not only affect luxury goods, but everyday necessities. The dramatic increase in liquidity and reckless government spending had not been matched by any increase in available goods or domestic production, and consequently the price of what were very finite goods went up. Official figures put inflation at around 20%, but it appears that the figure was substantially higher. Moreover, this was combined with a deeply unfavourable international climate, as sanctions and the threat of further sanctions gradually tightened the noose around Iran's mercantile economy. A trade-based economy like Iran's requires networks and cannot function in an environment of growing isolation. The view of Ahmadinejad and some others that the country had survived the war and sanctions, and could survive again, missed the fundamental points that the economy was not as strong as it had been in the 1980s, and, more importantly, that the mercantile system built up under Rafsanjani in the 1990s would not work in isolation.[13] Indeed the joke throughout the 1990s had been that Iranian merchants had an unerring capacity to establish international networks and roots despite US attempts to isolate Iran. Now, however, with his antagonism towards the EU – Iran's one serious ballast against the US – Ahmadinejad appeared to be doing America's work for it, and furthering the isolation. The turn east could only be a long-term project, and it would not eradicate the need for Europe or European markets overnight.

The reality in late 2006 was that business in Iran was coming to a standstill and Ahmadinejad was fast losing the support, not only of the mercantile elite (which had in any case been lukewarm), but also now of many of the poor whom he had championed.[14] As strikes and lay-offs mounted, employment could only be kept stable through subsidies to vast swathes of the economy, which in turn fuelled the black economy, as goods were thereby made even more expensive.[15] Ahmadinejad pointed to the fact that the economy was still growing, but others noted that it was not growing fast enough to produce the jobs needed. His defenders might argue that such problems had afflicted the president's predecessors, but the retort was that they had not enjoyed the enormous oil revenues at his disposal.

Throughout these severe difficulties, Ahmadinejad's flippant attitude towards his critics, most obviously those in the Majlis, whose constitutional duty it was to scrutinise the government's budgets and economic policy, was also a cause for concern. Ahmadinejad's arrogant attitude remained even as the facts moved against him and prudence dictated that he secure his alliances. He would frequently refuse to turn up for question time in the Majlis, and, in one notorious encounter, while he was presenting the budget, he taunted a heckling deputy with the jibe that if he found the price of tomatoes too expensive, he should shop in Ahmadinejad's local grocers, where the prices remained eminently reasonable.[16] This was particularly badly received as it demonstrated the extent to which he failed to take the problem of inflation seriously. Majlis deputies also repeatedly criticised the president for his failure to acknowledge that the price of oil would not stay high forever. One of the reasons why the Islamic Republic had been able to weather a variety of political storms over the course of its existence had been that, in spite of appearances, the management of the economy had on the whole been conservative and cautious. Particular care was taken with predicting the price of oil, with a tendency to err on the low side so as to be prepared for any fall and ensure that economy would be able absorb an oil-price shock. Ahmadinejad, however, was having none of this, and argued that a maximalist approach should be always be adopted. Majlis deputies and independent economists consistently warned that a drop in the oil price could have ruinous effects. So far, of course, Ahmadinejad has been correct in predicting a high price, but his reckless spending has ensured that Iran is now more dangerously dependent on this oil income than ever before.[17]

The critics convene

In late 2006, criticisms of the president were beginning to take hold, and Ahmadinejad was losing the support of key allies, even within the IRGC and the Basij militia. The clear effect of his policies was to make the poor worse off and, for all his protestations that everything was going well, that criticisms were the propaganda of his opponents, or even that his policies were being obstructed by the 'mafia' establishment, the electorate increasingly was not to be mollified, as shown by ongoing criticism on the Internet and in the press, along with some street protests. Furthermore, serious divisions began to emerge within the principlist camp itself.[18] Ahmadinejad's populism and his repeated attacks on the elite, and the mercantile elite in particular, did not go down well with conservative merchants who had expected him to serve their interests. He had indeed done so, up to a point, but the overall decline in business activity was detrimental to all merchants, regardless of their politics, and combined with their disapproval of his increasingly unorthodox religious claims (which also raised eyebrows among the senior ulema), this prompted many to distance themselves from Ahmadinejad. The president demanded total loyalty, but by the time of two significant elections scheduled for the same day in December 2006, the mercantile arm of the principlist faction had made it clear that they were willing to offer nothing more than 'partnership'. The principlists were divided just in time for the elections.

Both the municipal elections and the elections to the Assembly of Experts were, for different reasons, regarded by most as rather peripheral to the political life of the country. But it had been the low turnout in the municipal elections in 2003 that had ensured Ahmadinejad's election as mayor of Tehran, and for this reason, activists saw in these elections their first chance to register formal dissent.

The Assembly of Experts might best be likened to a college of cardinals. It is comprised of 86 senior clerics, whose main function is to elect the Supreme Leader. Elected every eight years, the assembly had before 2006 distinguished itself by doing very little in the long intervals between Leader elections; hence the lack of public interest. Its other constitutional function, to hold the Leader to account (with the ultimate prerogative of impeachment), was little mentioned and largely unknown to the wider public. The assembly's chairman, the aged Ayatollah Meshkini, filled his time by periodically praising the Leader for his insight and divine inspiration – most notoriously so during the wholesale vetting of candidates that preceded the Majlis elections in 2004, when Meshkini informed an incredulous public that an angel had been sent by the Hidden Imam to the Leader with the names of the winning candidates.[19]

Now, however, the elections to this rather arcane assembly mattered. Not only was Meshkini an old man, and likely to retire soon, but the Leader himself was ill. Khamenei's illness came to widespread public attention not long before the December elections, with the announcement that the Leader's absences from a number of public occasions were due to a bad bout of flu. However, it was generally acknowledged, if unconfirmed, that flu had exacerbated a more serious ailment, rumoured to be prostate cancer. How far developed Khamenei's illness was is unclear, but nevertheless the signal of his mortality prompted thoughts about succession, and it is this great unknown that has shaped Iranian political life over the past year or so. With the news of the Leader's illness, the Assembly of Experts elections of 2006 suddenly became especially important and politically sensitive, as it was the new assembly that would elect Khamenei's successor. Like the other factions, the principlists hoped to win control of the assembly and thus the direction of the Leadership. If they succeeded in this, they would gain control over all the elected offices of the Islamic Republic, and there was much anxiety that, once again, the faction would use illegal methods to get the result they wanted.

However, as noted above, on this occasion, the principlists presented a divided field. By contrast, their opponents were determined to show a degree of unity unknown since 1997. This unity was symbolically represented by a remarkable rapprochement between Mohammad Khatami and Hashemi Rafsanjani, an alliance between reformists and traditional conservatives that represented, in essence, the centre ground of Iranian politics. It was hoped that the skills of the one would offset the weaknesses of the other: Khatami was regarded as popular but ineffectual, while Rafsanjani remained unpopular, but was widely acknowledged as a master political operator.

What was most striking about this new coalition was its electoral strategy in the face of increasingly repressive government measures. Ahmadinejad had his list of candidates, entitled 'The Scent of Service', and felt confident that with the government's resources behind him, he could if necessary force the results he wanted. Restrictions on campaigning were imposed, and so his opponents had to find increasingly indirect methods of reaching the public. One singularly successful strategy they adopted was that of building networks using private contacts and mobile-phone text messaging. Text messaging had long been a favourite tool of student political organisations for coordinating demonstrations, its effectiveness shown by the fact that the government would shut down the mobile networks whenever they feared an event was being planned. Now these methods were applied to electoral mobilisation, modified to prevent sudden 'power cuts' through the use of local networks and connections between individuals, thus avoiding any centralised organisation that could be vulnerable to shutdown. Campaigners adapted the methods used by pyramid sellers, with individuals forwarding campaign messages to an ever-increasing number of recipients in an extended anonymous chain. This proved to be a highly effective way of circumventing the state machinery to achieve an overwhelming electoral victory over not only Ahmadinejad's list, but the principlist faction as a whole.

Defeat?

In a dramatic sweep, principlists lost control of every municipal council they had in the country, with traditional conservatives asserting themselves in all the major cities. Contrary to expectations, the reformists also secured a fair number of seats, giving the lie to the notion that they were a spent force. But the undoubted victors were the traditional conservatives, winning control of the all-important Tehran city council and triumphing in the Assembly of Experts, where Rafsanjani topped the list with almost twice as many votes as his nearest competitor. The principlists' chief ideologue, Ayatollah Misbah-Yazdi, and the extremely hardline secretary of the Guardian Council, Ayatollah Jannati, though both winning a respectable number of votes, were placed well down the list. The government sought to put a brave face on the result, with the minister of the interior arguing that the elections had proved once again the popularity of the Islamic system, and promising that of course the government would take note of any popular grievances. Despite the fact that the results rather dramatically revealed the principlists' strategy for the consolidation of their power to have failed, they were essentially interpreted by the government as no more than a mid-term blip.[20]

The immediate practical significance of the results was twofold: firstly, Mohammad Baqer Qalibaf, a loser in the 2005 presidential elections and a staunch opponent of the president, was confirmed as mayor of Tehran. He determined to use his position to build up his power base in the city in preparation for a possible candidacy in the presidential elections of 2009 and to seek out evidence of financial malpractice on the part of his predecessor. Secondly, in position at the head of the list of nominees to the Assembly of Experts, Rafsanjani was now the frontrunner to take the position of chairman when Meshkini retired, putting him in all likelihood in the position of kingmaker once the time came to elect a successor to Khamenei. Rafsanjani, who was known to want a leadership council to be created to replace the office of Supreme Leader, categorically stated that his election would give new life to the assembly.[21] It seemed that the days of inactivity in the anti-principlist camp were well and truly over, and when Rafsanjani became chairman of the assembly on Meshkini's death in the summer of 2007, the latent tensions between himself and Khamenei spilled over into public recrimination.[22]

The election results prompted a sudden reinvigoration of political life in Iran, as if, all of a sudden, all the suppressed anger had been allowed to surface. Journalists and intellectuals started to comment on the presidency in an unprecedented manner, roundly criticising Ahmadinejad for his mishandling of the economy and international affairs.[23] Commentators observed that, despite repeated reassurances from the government, the nuclear file was far from closed and was still resulting in UNSC sanctions. Ahmadinejad's dismissive retort that the UN resolutions were mere scraps of paper earned him, it was reported, a veiled reprimand from the Supreme Leader, a story which gave his critics further encouragement.[24] Criticism of the president, whether of his economics or his foreign policy, focused primarily on his judgement, in particular his boast that he was guided by instinct rather than logic. Normally deferential journalists took to irreverently probing the president's thinking, and expressing their disbelief at the excesses of his allies and friends, as in the case of the reporter who openly showed his incredulity at the claim, mentioned above, of the organiser of the Holocaust (denial) conference hosted that winter by the Foreign Ministry's think tank that he anticipated the creation of a similarly themed 'Holocaust institute' in Berlin.

Through January 2007, it appeared as if the forces of opposition were gaining while Ahmadinejad weakened by the day.[25] The Majlis even touted the idea that the following year's parliamentary elections should, 'for efficiency's sake', be combined with the presidential elections; thereby bringing the date of the presidential elections forward a year, and potentially reducing Ahmadinejad's term. When Ayatollah Khamenei appointed key figures from the pragmatic conservative camp to the Expediency Council[26] (chaired by Rafsanjani), the noose appeared to tighten yet further. Yet shortly afterwards, in an example of the balance-of-power manoeuvres that define Iranian politics, Khamenei moved to bolster Ahmadinejad's support in the Council with a number of principlist appointments.[27] This reinforced Ahmadinejad's base at a critical time, giving his supporters a second wind and encouraging polarisation. For Khamenei, feeling the heat after Rafsanjani's election success, it was an understandable response. But for a country facing a mounting international crisis and even possible military confrontation, this tactical move lacked strategic foresight.

Ahmadinejad moved quickly to make up lost ground. Cocooning himself in an increasingly hermetic state of denial, he moved swiftly to silence his academic critics[28] with draconian measures that further isolated Iran's academic establishments and prevented students from studying abroad.[29] He sought to galvanise public opinion by attacking British 'perfidy', encouraging not only direct action against the British embassy[30] but also attacks on those with connections to the British. Most dramatically, he responded vigorously to the challenge posed by Rafsanjani by attacking one of the senior nuclear negotiators of Rafsanjani's presidency, Hussein Musavian. Musavian was a wealthy businessman and a member of the governing elite. To pursue him, arrest him, and charge with him spying on behalf of 'foreign powers' (later named as British), as Ahmadinejad did in April 2007, was therefore extraordinarily bold. To many the attack on Musavian represented a reckless escalation of the political contest, especially since the penalty for espionage was death, and it seemed highly unlikely in the frenzied Anglophobic climate Ahmadinejad had generated that a pardon could be expected.[31] At the time of writing, the charges had been dismissed by the judiciary (not known as a bastion of liberalism), but Ahmadinejad and his intelligence minister, Gholamhossein Mohseni-Ejei, are persisting with the claims and have asked for tapes to be released which they claimed corroborate their story.

Meanwhile, with the economy continuing to deteriorate and tensions with the US over Iranian involvement in the insurgency in Iraq looking as if the confrontation policy could be getting dangerous, the domestic criticism of Ahmadinejad shows little sign of ebbing.[32] There was particular anger over the decision to introduce petrol rationing in the summer of 2007.[33] Lauded as a bold and long overdue decision by his hardline supporters, the announcement and the paucity of time it allowed for planning and preparation left the country dumbstruck. So abrupt was the announcement that many Iranians were stranded in their cars, unable to acquire enough petrol to drive to their destinations. As in many other sectors of the economy, the black market soon stepped into the breach and, in the words of one Iranian wit, the usual two local petrol stations miraculously became 40.[34]

Though Ahmadinejad cannot be held responsible for structural weaknesses in the Iranian economy, the lack of oil-refining capacity that was the immediate cause of this particular crisis can only be addressed through a programme of investment, a programme which the president had never shown any desire to undertake. Few images sit more awkwardly with Ahmadinejad's vision of a resurgent Iran than that of a country replete with oil and gas resources forced to ration its domestic petrol consumption.[35]

CONCLUSION

At the end of October 2007, Ali Larijani resigned from his position as senior nuclear negotiator. A staunch hardliner, Larijani had been one of the most ardent proponents of Ahmadinejad's tough policy towards the West. But Larijani, like others before him, had discovered that his president did not like to share the limelight, and certainly was not prepared to allow others to take credit for any successes, and he turned away from Ahmadinejad in consequence.[1] Reformists had long claimed that the chief motivator of their hardline critics was envy. They were jealous of Khatami's achievements and profile on the international stage and their stubbornness over the nuclear issue would, reformists claimed, last only as long as a way did not present itself for them to take credit for resolving the crisis. Larijani fits this characterisation rather well: a tactical hardliner who ultimately favoured his own ambition to be hailed as a saviour of Iran's international standing over ideological consistency. In Ahmadinejad, he had encountered an individual whose self-regard exceeded even his own, and Larijani's concern for his reputation had led him to abandon his president to indulge his vanities alone.

Larijani was the latest in a succession of senior officials to resign their posts. Ahmadinejad had presented most of these resignations as sackings for inadequate performance during a cabinet reshuffle over the summer, but there are indications that the reshuffle itself was undertaken in part because of the criticism that was increasingly emerging from within the cabinet, and the desire of a number of its members to leave. It was no coincidence that most of the officials who left were responsible either for the economy or for oil. Although government spokesmen tried to put a positive spin on the departures, the ill feeling was clearly apparent as, typically, the official presentation of events only served to raise tensions further and highlight the dissension within government about the direction of policy.[2] Ahmadinejad has since signalled his intention to bring economic policy and planning under his sole control, with the abrupt abolition of the Management and Planning Organisation, an important arm of the civil service.

The loss of important supporters such as Larijani seems to have had no chastening effect on the president. On the contrary, their departures appear to have reinforced his self-confidence to such an extent that senior establishment figures have been moved to call on him to tolerate and listen to criticism, largely in vain. When the head of the judiciary, Ayatollah Shahrudi – not a noted liberal – voiced his concerns that the government was not doing enough to address social and economic problems, the response was swift and unprecedented. A government spokesman urged the judiciary to stay out of the affairs of the executive in uncharacteristically blunt terms, and the attitude of the president's allies and the accusations they levelled at the eminent cleric shocked observers. Critics of the government – who now include Iran's most senior judge – were branded as anti-Islamic and servants of the US, extraordinary allegations that seemed to be indications of a contracting circle of loyalists and 'revolutionary' purists.[3]

In the past year, as the pressures on him have mounted, both abroad and at home, the president has become ever more certain of his convictions and bolder in his assertions.[4] If high-profile critics have been branded heretics, then those at the lower end of the political spectrum have been treated with a ruthlessness unseen since the early days of the revolution. A campaign against 'thugs and hooligans' has resulted in a dramatic increase in summary public executions, intended both to establish the government's commitment to the maintenance of order and to send a clear signal that social and political agitation will not be tolerated.[5] Few developments better express the crisis in confidence between state and society.

Even more shocking perhaps was the Supreme Court's decision in April 2007 to uphold a decision to exonerate murderers in Kerman province on grounds that they had genuinely suspected their victims to have been acting immorally. This judgement (if it ultimately stands – one last appeal remains) effectively makes the Islamic Republic the only modern state to forfeit its monopoly on violence, a situation the prosecuting lawyer in the case viewed with incredulity.[6]

Convinced of his popularity and his mission, Ahmadinejad has sought to extend his cult of personality abroad, seeking international success as a justification for monopolising power at home. Consequently, he continues to appeal to the Arab street over the heads of the rulers of the Arab nations; thereby alienating neighbouring governments as their concern over Iranian and Shia dominance in the region grows. Relations with Saudi Arabia have continued to deteriorate, and the Iraqi government has expressed concern at Ahmadinejad's boast that Iran would fill the vacuum left by a US departure. While evidence suggests that Iran's military support for the Shia militias in Iraq decreased over the summer of 2007, the Iranian presence in the country remains extensive. On the nuclear front, Ahmadinejad remains uncompromising, continuing to showcase various technical 'leaps forward' in the most elaborate theatrical style.

Broadly speaking, the Iranian public does not oppose what are presented as the president's moves to defend national security and encourage scientific development in themselves. What it does increasingly oppose is the reckless and self-perpetuating policy of international confrontation apparently for its own sake; clearly damaging economic policies; and, perhaps most importantly, the attitude of a president who brooks no criticism and whose ego has crossed the threshold of acceptability. Though few in Iran applauded Columbia University's strikingly ungracious reception of Ahmadinejad in September 2007, neither did many accept the line of his supporters that the event represented a 'metaphysical battle' in which the president triumphantly defended the national honour. Much to the embarrassment of commentators in Iran, the president's allies even argued that Ahmadinejad's speech at the university was a greater achievement than the celebrated capture of the Fao Peninsula during the Iran–Iraq War.[7] This extraordinary statement gives the lie to the respect for war veterans that Ahmadinejad has often claimed. Furthermore, the view that his religious beliefs, which have always provoked ridicule in some circles, are simply too eccentric, is becoming more widespread. One staunch principlist complained in June 2007 that the real legacy of Ahmadinejad's presidency would be the spread of atheism through Iranian society.[8]

Ahmadinejad's power has rested in part on the support he has retained from key members of the conservative establishment determined to rid themselves once and for all of the heresy of reform and political pluralism. In this regard, the support of the Supreme Leader, Ayatollah Khamenei, has been crucial. Yet Ahmadinejad has also benefited from the caution of his opponents, the inertia of the political system in general and the luxury of high oil prices resulting from a continuing international crisis in which the incoherence of his foreign opponents has complemented and in some measure encouraged the inaction of the domestic opposition. The US government's National Intelligence Estimate issued in December 2007 that concluded, apparently against much US policy of the months leading up to it, that Iran's nuclear weapons programme had been suspended since 2003, is an interesting example of how the vicissitudes of Western postures towards Iran are used by Ahmadinejad for rather crude domestic gain. The president has not only declared himself exonerated by the Estimate, and victorious over his Western critics, but he has also used the document to cast doubt on the honesty of the reformists, during whose political tenure, it judges, a weapons programme did exist.

Yet it is a reflection of the depth of discontent in Iran that even the president's celebration of this 'international triumph' has been plausibly spun by his opponents as a rash and premature declaration that betrays the president's failure to properly understand the international situation. Indeed, it seems possible that the domestic situation has become so critical for Ahmadinejad that only the most dramatic and unambiguous international success could positively affect his popularity at home. Certainly, in the absence of widespread manipulation, the expectation is that the principlists will lose control of the Majlis in the elections in March 2008.[9]

When Ahmadinejad was elected in 2005, there were some who argued that the reformist experiment had been an exercise in wishful thinking that had not reflected the reality of Iran, and that, with Ahmadinejad's election, the real, raw Iran had finally come to the foreground. This view is now a rarity, and, crucially, the president's stock within his own faction is falling. Despite the extraordinary advantage afforded to him by high oil prices, Ahmadinejad has failed to achieve the defining goal of his presidency, to which all other principlist strategies had been subordinated: the establishment of the domestic hegemony of hardline conservatism. The populist had been invited to turn the faction's particular agenda into a national one – to restore the revolution to its true path. But Iran's revolutionary president has proved to be an anachronism, unwilling to recognise the changes that have transformed Iranian society. And it is these social transformations, which long predate Ahmadinejad's rise, that will ultimately determine the direction the country will take in the future.

As his problems mount, Ahmadinejad will increasingly rely on the assets he and his supporters place the most faith in: his charisma and the cult of personality. Ahmadinejad still speaks the language of the poor and dispossessed, and his promises of utopia around the corner still have their power. Not for him a dialogue of civilisations, or talk of economic growth, but a complete solution to a total problem. Ahmadinejad can be interpreted as a consequence of the continuing crisis in Iran's mercantile capitalist system. He was a short-term solution to a long-term problem, but he may well prove more damaging to the very foundations of the Islamic Republic than his backers could ever have imagined.

NOTES

Introduction

1 The Twelfth, or Hidden, Imam is descended from the Prophet through the Prophet's son-in-law, the first Shia imam, Ali. He is believed by adherents of the sect of Shiism dominant in Iran to have gone into 'greater occultation' in the ninth century and is expected to return to the world at the end of time to inaugurate an 'age of justice'. The belief that in occultation, the Imam remains with us, though in a different dimension, has enabled some to claim communication with him. Millenarian movements claiming esoteric links with the Hidden Imam are not unusual in Iran and build on centuries, if not millennia, of a saviour tradition in the country. The last great millenarian movement in Iran occurred with the 'Bab' in the first half the nineteenth century, leading to the development of the Baha'i religion. The Bab and his followers were ruthlessly hunted down by the religious and political authorities on charges of heresy.

2 Originally at http://www.baztab.com. This site was closed down in autumn 2007, and the content subsequently moved to another site, http://www.tabnak.ir/#Group.

3 http://www.rajanews.com/. Attempts have been made by Raja News to discredit rival sites; see for example 'Iranian Conservative Website Accuses ISNA of Discrediting Government', 14 January 2007, on BBC Monitoring Online.

4 Rajabi has been heavily criticised for her extremism. See for example 'Neveshteh-ye jadid-e fatemeh rajabi: een bar khatami meihman-e estemargar pir', Noandish News, 13 November 2006, http://www.noandish.com.

Chapter One

1 For a detailed discussion of what Rafsanjani's political settlement was and how it worked, see Ali M. Ansari, *Iran, Islam and Democracy: The Politics of Managing Change* (London: Royal Institute of International Affairs, 2006).

2 'Ulema' means those who study *elm*, or science, which is generally now used to mean religious scholarship. The ulema are religious scholars, and function in the Islamic system essentially as a kind of clergy.

3 This amendment continues to be a source of enormous controversy. See Mohsen Kadivar, *Baha'ye Azadi: defa'at Mohsen Kadivar* (Tehran: Ghazal, 1378/1999–2000), pp. 149, 152.

4 See pp. 20–22 for a discussion of the usage of the terms 'left', 'right' and 'conservative' in Iranian politics.

5 For an account of the rise and fall of the reform movement in Iran, see Ansari, *Iran, Islam and Democracy: The Politics of Managing Change*.

6 See 'Octobr-ya, fevrier, bahman! Moghayeseh enqelab iran ba rusie va faranseh', Baztab.com, 18 Bahman 1385/7 February 2007.

7 President Mohammad Khatami, interview with CNN, as broadcast by the Islamic Republic of Iran Broadcasting, Tehran, 8 January 1998, in *BBC Summary of World Broadcasts, The Middle East* (SWB/ME) 3210 MED/2, 9 January 1998.

8 Abdolkarim Soroush, 'The Three Cultures', in A. Sadri and M. Sadri (eds), *Reason, Freedom and Democracy in Islam: Essential Writings of Abdolkarim Soroush* (Oxford: Oxford University Press, 2000), pp. 156–70.

Chapter Two

1 For more on these murders, see H. Kaviani, *Dar jostejoye mohafel jeneyatkaran* (Tehran: Negah-ye Emruz, 1378/1999–2000).

2 See *Yas-e No*, 19 Bahman 1382/8 February 2004, p. 1.

3 Private communication.

4 The Basij is a nationwide Islamic militia network, founded by Khomeini at the beginning of the revolution.

5 See Kasra Naji, *Ahmadinejad: The Untold Story of Iran's Radical Leader* (London: I.B. Tauris, 2007). Ahmadinejad continued the graves policy as president; see Golnaz Esfandiari, 'Iran: Students Protest Burials of War Dead on Tehran Campuses', Radio Free Europe/Radio Liberty, 15 March 2006, http://www.rferl.org/featuresarticle/2006/03/6035bfe4-0e35-4807-ad4b-cdd4fce89821.html.

6 In a bizarre recent incident, it appeared that someone had spiked some of these refreshments, causing stomach upsets among pilgrims, for reasons unknown. See 'Bastani-ye mashkook dar masched jamkaran', Baztab.com, 31 Mordad 1386/22 August 2007.

7 See Norman Cohn, *The Pursuit of the Millennium: Revolutionary Millenarians and Mystical Anarchists of the Middle Ages* [1957, revised 1970] (London: Pimlico, 2004), p. 53.

8 Qom is a city south of Tehran. It is the centre of religious activity in Iran and is currently also the intellectual centre of global Shiism.

9 See *Aftab-e Yazd*, 10 Esfand 1382/29 February 2004, p. 11.

10 See Behzad Nabavi writing in *Entekhab*, 18 Bahman 1382/7 February 2004, p. 3.

11 'Iran Conservatives to Ease Engagements', Agence France Presse, 18 February 2004.

12 For Ahmadinejad's interpretation of the word 'fundamentalist', see 'Deed gaha-ye Mahmood Ahmadi Nejad siyasi (3)' (Mahmoud Ahmadinejad's political views (3)), on the Islamic Republic News Agency (IRNA) website, 4 Tir 1384/26 June 2005, www.irna.ir.

13 See p. 86 for more on this incident.

14 Abbas Pazouki, 'The Challenges of the Military's Presence in the Election', Mardomsalari website, 2 June 2005, in *BBC Summary of World Broadcasts, The Middle East.*

15 See 'Rafsanjani Mulled Pulling out of Iran Run-Off', Iranmania.com, 20 June 2005, http://www.iranmania.com/News/ArticleView/Default.asp?NewsCode=32732&NewsKind=Current%20Affairs.

16 See election results posted on IRNA website, http://www.irna.ir, 30 Khordad 1384/20 June 2005.

17 'City Mayors', an international project for the promotion of 'strong cities and good local government' runs the contest annually. More information can be found at http://www.worldmayor.com/results05/worldmayor_methodology05.html.

18 The argument, commonly made, that it was worth voting for Ahmadinejad as a vote against Rafsanjani was expressed eloquently by reformist politician Davoud Soleymani in an interview with the Iranian Students' News Agency (ISNA), 28 Tir 1385/19 July 2005, http://www.isna.ir.

Chapter Three

1 See Fatemeh Rajabi, *Ahmadinejad: Mojeze-ye hezare-ye sevom* (Tehran: Nashr Danesh Amuz, 2005).

2 A central element in this strategy has been Ahmadinejad's frequent and extensive tours of the provinces for the purpose of being seen to reach out to the people. DVDs of the trips have been produced, prompting wry remarks from some commentators; see 'Seedee serial safarhaye ostani reseed', Baztab.com, 11 Tir 1386/2 July 2007.

3 For a video of Ahmadinejad making this claim, go to http://uk.youtube.com/watch?v=M1iqFe2nNnk.

4 It is in view of characteristics such as these that the crisis of Iranian mercantile capitalism can be interpreted as having produced a kind of fascism.

5 See Cohn, *Cosmos, Chaos and the World to Come* (New Haven and London: Yale University Press, 2001), p. 256.

6 For the speech in which he made these claims, see http://uk.youtube.com/watch?v=9cIrymEv8xI. Ahmadinejad also boasts of the extraordinary advances in stem-cell research made by Iranian scientists.

7 See 'Amin-Zanjani's One-Month Opportunity to Sacked Lecturers', *Etemad* website, 2 September 2007, on BBC Monitoring Online; Rasool Jafarian, 'Ta'aroz Amniat va elm Amoozi?', Baztab.com, 11 Khordad 1386/1 June 2007.

8 'Namayande-ye dowlat: dashteem va kharj kardeem!', Baztab.com, 10 Tir 1386/1 July 2007.

9 Iran's political and military figures typically take a defiant tone when discussing Iran's capabilities, particularly in relation to a possible attack from the US. See for example 'Defiant Iran Warns West Against Attack', Agence France Presse, 23 September 2007, http://afp.google.com/article/ALeqM5io2lohyDltkeAQ_yeCUwIST-zY-w.

10 Mohammad Ali Abtahi, 'Regarding the Dangerous Resignation of Ali Larijani', Webnevesht (Abtahi's blog), http://webneveshteha.com/en/weblog/?page=2&cat=&search=.

11 For an articulate defence of the Iranian position in the negotiations, see Javad Zarif, 'An Unnecessary Crisis: Setting the Record Straight about Iran's Nuclear Program', *New York Times*, 18 November 2005.

12 A good example of a typical diaspora view is that of the Shah's foreign minister and an original signatory to the NPT, Ardeshir Zahedi. See Zahedi, 'Vazir Kharejeh-ye Shah: Enerji-ye hastehi haq Iran ast', Baztab.com, 13 Ordibehesht 1385/3 May 2006.

13 The 5 August 2005 E3 proposal for a framework for a long-term agreement called for Iran to make a binding commitment not to pursue fuel-cycle activities other than building reactors, but provided for a mechanism to review this commitment every ten years.

14 Rowhani's final report to President Khatami can be found on the ISNA website, http://www.isna.ir, dated 31 July 2005.

15 Some principlists also tried to claim Mosaddeq's achievements for the clerics of the time, arguing that the religious leader of Mosaddeq's political movement, Ayatollah Kashani, had in fact been the prime mover behind the nationalisation of oil, rather than the prime minister himself. See Hosseinian, 'Nagofethaye Nezhat melli sanat naft', Baztab.com, 26 Esfand 1385/17 March 2006.

16 Doubts have been expressed by some as to whether Ahmadinejad meant 'myth' in its dismissive sense, but the Persian word he used was *afsaneh*, which means 'myth' as in a fiction, rather than 'myth' as it is used by social scientists, leaving little doubt on this point.

17 The view that Israel will collapse in this way is laid out in Ali Yusefpur, 'The Day of Islam–Heresy Confrontation', *Siyasat-e Ruz*, 6 October 2007, on BBC Monitoring Online.

18 For an excellent discussion of this issue, see Jafarian, 'Alajab kol alajab, bein jamadi va rajab!', Baztab.com, 30 Khordad 1386/20 June 2007.

19 Similar views have been expressed by Ayatollah Khamenei; see 'Iranian Leader Says US Sinking into the Abyss', Iranian Radio, 19 August 2007, on BBC Monitoring Online.

20 See interview with Ahmadinejad: 'Defa az baz khani-e holokaust', Baztab.com, 4 Farvardin 1386/24 March 2007, in which he reiterates this justification.

21 Though several of Ahmadinejad's allies have also been clear about denying the Holocaust, see in particular the editorial in Iranian daily *Keyhan* 'Een Mikh va an taboot', 28 January 2007.

22 In 2006, Ahmadinejad chose to make observations to this effect to the German chancellor. See 'Text of Ahmadinejad Letter to Merkel' posted on Jihad Watch website, 28 August 2006, http://www.jihadwatch.org/archives/2006_08.php.

23 Interview with Mohammad Ali Ramin, Baztab.com, 'Bazkhani-ye Holokaust dar Iran', 6 Dey 1385/27 December 2006.

24 Entesab-e shoraye be-sabegheh bedoon etela-ye ozaye asli', Baztab.com, 20 Khordad 1386/10 June 2007.

25 'Nahad Riyasat Jumhuri: Ahmadinejad soghrat-e zaman ast', Baztab.com, 28 Shahrivar 1386/19 September 2007.

26 In line with their elitist ideology, the principlists had been more than happy to encourage apathy and depoliticisation in the general population, enthusiasm for populist nationalism and other cults aside.

27 See Rafsanjani's warning against alienating Iranians abroad, 'Rafsanjani: daneshmandan-e Irani shayad ba ma mokhalef bashand ama ba Iran mokhalef neestand', Baztab.com, 7 Khordad 1386/28 May 2007.

28 See 'Zende kardan khatereh taqsim iran bein rus va inglis, beh naf rusieh neest', Baztab.com, 23 Esfand 1385/14 March 2007.

29 See 'Pasokh-e Talo'ehe Hashemi beh ezharat-e Ahmadinejad', Baztab.com, 4 Bahman 1385/24 January 2007, in which Rafsanjani discusses a confrontation with Ahmadinejad over what he calls Ahmadinejad's 'complacency' about foreign threats, and claims that Ayatollah Khamenei agreed with Rafsanjani and not the president.

30 See interview with Ahmadinejad on ISNA website, 24 January 2007, http://www.isna.ir, for an example of such promises.

31 For example Mohsen Rezai, 'Ghatar-e hastei ham tormuz darad ham rannande', Baztab.com, 3 Khordad 1386/24 May 2007.

32 See for example Ayatollah Khamenei's New Year speech, 21 March 2007, on BBC Monitoring Online.

33 For details of similar theatrics in the following year, see 'Hashiyeh-ha az ain elam khabar khosh hasteyi', Fars News Agency, 28 May 2007.

34 See also Rowhani's comments cited in 'Former Top Nuclear Negotiator Comments on Draft Resolution Against Iran', IRNA, 1 November 2006, on BBC Monitoring Online, and Larijani's account of the Solana talks, 'Iran's Nuclear

Negotiator on Failure of Western Policy', Mehr News Agency, 18 October 2006, on BBC Monitoring Online, for further examples of profound disagreements among the conservatives on the nuclear issue.

Chapter Four

1 It is important to draw a distinction between these IRGC men and the war veterans, who were just as likely to have devoted their time to reformist politics as to the ideas of Ahmadinejad, and many of whom looked with disdain on the machinations of those promoted under Ahmadinejad, who seemed more concerned with making money than with defending the revolution.

2 See Bill Samii, 'No Welcome for President's New Elite', Radio Free Europe, 24 February 2006.

3 See Rafsanjani's warning to Ahmadinejad not to alienate the political establishment, 'Rafsanjani: nagozareem neerohaye vafadar beh enqelab delsard shavand', Baztab.com, 11 Tir 1386/2 July 2007.

4 For examples of some of the more extravagant statements about the president from Ahmadinejad's inner circle, see 'Mesbah-Yazdi Supporters Liken Ahmadinezhad to 1st Shia Imam', *Aftab*, 1 November 2007, on BBC Monitoring Online. One principlist politician, Sadeq Mahsuli, declared that the reason few could understand Ahmadinejad was because he 'moved with the speed of a fighter jet': 'Sadeq Mahsuli: sorat Ahmadinejad manand yek jet *Phantom* ast', Advar News, 30 Mordad 1386/21 August 2007, http://www.advarnews.us/politic/print/5609.aspx.

5 See 'Jumhuri Eslami beh koja reseedeh ast?', Baztab.com, 28 Tir 1386/19 July 2007; 'Jumhuri Eslami ra zaif jelo nadaheed', Baztab.com, 31 Tir 136/22 July 2007.

6 See interview with the intelligence minister, Mohseni-Ejei, ISNA, 7 February 2006, http://www.isna.ir. See also the comments made by his predecessor Ali Yunessi, 'Iranian People's Discontent Far Greater Threat Than Foreign One, Ex-Minister', ISNA 16 February 2007, on BBC Monitoring Online.

7 See Mahdi Darius Nazemroaya, 'Plans for Redrawing the Middle East: The Project for "A New Middle East"', Centre for Research on Globalisation, 18 November 2006, http://globalresearch.ca/index.php?context=va&aid=3882, for a related discussion. See also Edward Luttwak, 'The Scariest Prospect of All: Iran with the Bomb', *Daily Telegraph*, 23 January 2005, http://www.telegraph.co.uk/opinion/main.jhtml?xml=/opinion/2005/01/23/do2301.xml, for an example of the kind of American writing about the ethnic makeup of Iran that was apt to excite defensive nationalist feeling. See also 'Ahmadi Moghadam: Hemayat Amrika va Inglis az Jundullah', Baztab.com, 11 Tir 1386/2 July 2007; 'Khansi shodan amaliat terroristi dar Khuzestan', Baztab.com, 16 Mordad 1386/7 August 2007.

8 For a useful critique of Ahmadinejad's approach to the nuclear issue, see 'Former MPs Review Nuclear Case', *Etemad-e Melli*, 27 January 2007, BBC Monitoring Online; see also a damning indictment from Mohsen Rezai, 'Residan beh cheshm andaz bedoon tahavol emkan pazir neest', Baztab.com, 12 Esfand 1385/3 March 2007.

9 A website was even established dedicated to the project of seizing the compound; http://www.baghegholhak.ir. An interesting account of the British ambassador's reaction to plans to assault the embassy claims that he retorted with a letter stating that Islamic centres in the UK would be closed down and

repossessed if any moves were made on Golhak; see 'Safir Inglis va elam bahai bagh gholhak', Baztab.com, 30 Khordad 1386/20 June 2007. The British embassy denied any such message was ever sent.

10 See Masih Mohajeri, 'Ta'adol mahor basheed, lotfan!', Baztab.com, 26 Ordibehesht 1386/16 May 2007.

11 See Farid Modarresi, 'Ahmadinezhad, Proponent of State Sponsorship for Seminaries', *Etemad,* 10 May 2007, on BBC Monitoring Online, for an example of the view, held by some, that this shift of resources was part of an attempt by the president to control the seminaries.

12 See 'Former Minister Criticises Government's Budget Bill', *Etemad,* 22 January 2007, on BBC Monitoring Online.

13 Ahmadinejad's apparent lack of concern about the situation drew widespread criticism; see for example 'Mr President, We Wish it May Be So', editorial in *Etemad,* 25 January 2007, on BBC Monitoring Online.

14 For thorough critiques of government economic policy, see 'The Second Warning of Economists to the Administration: The Full Text of the Letter of 57 Experts and University Professors to [Mahmud] Ahmadinezhad', *Etemad,* 12 June 2007, on BBC Monitoring Online; Said Leylaz, 'Warning', *Ayande-ye Now,* 21 January 2007, on BBC Monitoring Online.

15 An indication of the country's economic difficulties is given by the high number of departures from Iran of well-qualified and able young people; see Frances Harrison, 'Huge Cost of Iranian Brain Drain', BBC News Online, 8 January 2007, http://news.bbc.co.uk/1/hi/world/middle_east/6240287.stm.

16 A point Ahmadinejad repeated in an interview with Iranian television, IRTV2, Tehran, 23 January 2007, available on BBC Monitoring Online.

17 'Sait-e Tavakoli: Afzayeh-e vabastegi-ye budjeh beh naft', Baztab.com,12 Shahrivar 1386/3 September 2007.

18 For an example of dissent within the ranks, see 'We are Against the Creative Principle-ist Faction: Interview with Ahmad Tavakkoli', *Ayandeh No,* 24 January 2007, in BBC Monitoring Online.

19 See ISNA, 22 Khordad 1383/13 June 2004, code 8303–09201, www.isna.ir. Meshkini claimed that an angel had brought a list of candidates to Khamenei to sign some seven months before the elections.

20 See the report of an Interior Ministry press conference, 'Dowlat payam natayej entekhabat ra sheneed', Baztab.com, 29 Azar 1385/20 December 2006.

21 'Rafsanjani: dore-ye jadidi dar khobergan aghaz shud', BBCPersian.com, 8 September 2007.

22 See 'Posht-e Sahneh-ye Entkhab rais majlis khobregan', Baztab.com, 13 Shahrivar 1386/4 September 2007.

23 In an indication of how much journalistic attitudes were shifting, one television interview in particular, conducted in January 2007, in which the president outlined his policies and worldview, was roundly criticised by journalists in Iran for being too soft on its subject; see 'Interview with President Ahmadinejad', IRTV2, 23 January 2007, BBC Monitoring Online. For an example of the criticisms of the interview and the president, see Hamid Reza Shokuhi, 'Analysis of the President's Interview Broadcast by TV Channel Two: Twenty Other Questions for the President', Mardom-salari website, 25 January 2007, on BBC Monitoring Online.

24 Nazila Fathi, 'Iran's President Criticised over Nuclear Issue', *New York Times,* 18 January 2007.

25 See Bill Weinberg, 'Iran: Move to Impeach Ahmadinejad', World War Four Report, 12 January 2007, http://ww4report.com/node/3031. The move to impeach, organised by a group of reformists, was more symbolic than real, since it was known to be unlikely that enough deputies would sign up to the motion, and indeed they did not. For criticisms of Ahmadinejad from this time, see also 'Payam-e soferhaye khali baraye Ahmadinejad', Baztab.com, 4 Bahman

1385/24 January 2007; 'Jenab-e rais jomhur, lotfan kami negaran basheed', Baztab.com, 4 Bahman 1385/24 January 2007.

26 The Expediency Council, set up by Khomeini, mediates disputes between the Majlis and the Guardian Council.

27 'Iranian Leader Designates Members of the Expediency Council for Five-Year Term', Iranian Radio, 27 February 2007, on BBC Monitoring Online.

28 See Hassan Rowhani, 'Nabayad zaban-e gorohaye mokhtalef ra bast', ISNA, 30 January 2007, http://www.isna.ir, for an attack on Ahmadinejad for his response to his critics and to intellectuals in general; see also 'Hoshdar namayandegan be Ahmadinejad aleye barkhord ba resaneh-ha', BBCPersian.com, 24 July 2007.

29 Reza Ansari, 'The Intelligence Minister's Warning Should be Taken Seriously', *Etemad-e Melli*, 1 September 2007, on BBC Monitoring Online. See also Jafarian, 'Ta'aroz amniat va elma amoozi', Baztab.com, 11 Khordad 1386/1 June 2007; Morteza Kazemian, 'Lawful Detention, Unlawful Detention', *Etemad-e Melli*, 17 July 2007, on BBC Monitoring Online; 'Eghdam be-sabegheh dar control safar asateed daneshgah', Baztab.com, 1 Shahrivar 1386/23 August 2007.

30 Among the more absurd charges made against the embassy was that a tunnel existed beneath the embassy building for ferrying in and out spies and prostitutes; see 'Hosseini: tooneli dar kar neest', Baztab.com, 22 Mordad 2007/13 August 2007.

31 Even hardliners thought the attack on Musavian a step too far: see the editorial in the hardline *Jumhuri Islami*, 'Mardom cheh gonahi karde-and', 21 November 2007, http://www.jomhourieslami.com.

32 A poll conducted by Baztab in 2007 showed the president's popularity in decline. The poll was challenged by the president's office, see 'Natayej-e Nazarsanji bozorg Baztab rajeb-e Ahmadinejad', Baztab.com,10 Tir 1386/1 July 2007.

33 Rumours that electricity would also be rationed were vigorously denied; see 'Ahmadinejad: meetavan barq ra samimehbandi kard', Baztab.com, 12 Tir 1386/3 July 2007; 'Takid rais jomhur bar sarfeh jooyee na samimeh bandi barq', Baztab.com, 12 Tir 1386/3 July 2007.

34 See 'No Accountability in Iran Petrol Rationing Black Market', Iranian Radio, 18 August 2007, on BBC Monitoring Online.

35 Ahmadinejad tried, unconvincingly, to argue that only 5% of Iranians were affected by petrol rationing, 'Had-aksar panj dar sad dar mozoo-ye benzin moshkel darand', Baztab.com, 4 Mordad 1386/26 July 2007.

Conclusion

1 Care was taken in the tense period leading up to the announcement to ensure that the relationship between the two appeared harmonious in public. See 'Ahmadinezhad, Larijani have no Differences on Nuclear Issue', *Farhang Ashti*, 5 October 2007, in BBC Monitoring Online.

2 Confusion reigned, and in its attempts to make the process look like an ordinary reshuffle, the regime inadvertently prompted further wranglings, as when the oil minister told the press he had been summarily sacked after having consistently been overriden and ignored while in post. Ahmadinejad retorted by claiming he had indeed sacked him, but for incompetence. See 'I Did Not Resign I Was Dismissed – Outgoing Iranian Oil Minister', Mehr News Agency, 19 August 2007, on BBC Monitoring Online.

3 For a critical discussion of these allegations, see 'Agar rais ghove-ye ghazai dar khat-e

amrikast, cheh kasi khodi memanad?', Baztab.com, 29 Mordad 1386/17 August 2007.

4 See 'Ba etemad-e mardom bazi nakoneed!', Baztab.com, 4 Tir 1386/25 June 2007, for a typical attack on the president's reckless confidence.

5 See Ayatollah Jannati, Friday Prayer Sermon, 27 July 2007, on BBC Monitoring Online; 'Iran to Execute Twenty Thugs', IRTV1, 10 July 2007, on BBC Monitoring Online; 'Iran Senior Judicial Official Urges Speedy Sentencing in Security-Related Cases', IRTV1, 18 August 2007, on BBC Monitoring Online.

6 Nehmat Ahmadi, 'Negahi beh parvandeh-ye ghatl-haye mahfeli-e kerman az aghaz ta konoon,' *Etemad*, 29 Farvardin 1386/18 April 2007.

7 See Abtahi, 'Martyrs of the War and Triumph of Columbia University', Webnevesht, http://webneveshteha.com/en/weblog/?page=2&cat=&search=; 'Fath alfutoo daneshgah columbia fartar az fath fao', Mizan News Agency, 26 October 2007, www.mizannews.com.

8 'Khoshchehreh: Natijeh-ye nakami Osolugarayan: laik shodan jame'eh', Baztab.com, 19 Khordad 1386/9 June 2007.

9 'Majlis-e hashtom, eidi bozorg-e mohafezeh-karan beh eslah talaban?', Baztab.com, 10 Mordad 1386/1 August 2007.

THE WORKS AND CORRESPONDENCE OF DAVID RICARDO

VOLUME XI

PLAN OF THE EDITION

VOLUME

I. Principles of Political Economy and Taxation

II. Notes on Malthus

III. Pamphlets and Papers, 1809–1811

IV. Pamphlets and Papers, 1815–1823

V. Speeches and Evidence

VI. Letters, 1810–1815

VII. Letters, 1816–1818

VIII. Letters, 1819–June 1821

IX. Letters, July 1821–1823

X. Biographical Miscellany

XI. General Index

THE WORKS
AND CORRESPONDENCE OF

David Ricardo

Edited by Piero Sraffa
with the Collaboration of M. H. Dobb

VOLUME XI

General Index

LIBERTY FUND
INDIANAPOLIS

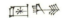

This book is published by Liberty Fund, Inc., a foundation established to encourage study of the ideal of a society of free and responsible individuals.

The cuneiform inscription that serves as our logo and as the design motif for our endpapers is the earliest-known written appearance of the word "freedom" (*amagi*), or "liberty." It is taken from a clay document written about 2300 B.C. in the Sumerian city-state of Lagash.

First published by Cambridge University Press in 1951.

This edition of *The Works and Correspondence of David Ricardo* is published by Liberty Fund, Inc., under license from the Royal Economic Society.

10 09 08 07 06 05 04 P 5 4 3 2 1

Printed in the United States of America

Library of Congress Cataloging-in-Publication Data

Ricardo, David, 1772–1823.
[Works. 2004]
The works and correspondence of David Ricardo / edited by Piero Sraffa; with the collaboration of M. H. Dobb.
p. cm.
Originally published: Cambridge: At the University Press for the Royal Economic Society, 1951–1973.
Includes bibliographical references and index.
Contents: v. 1. On the principles of political economy and taxation—
ISBN 0-86597-965-0 (pbk.: alk. paper)
1. Economics. 2. Taxation. I. Sraffa, Piero.
II. Dobb, M. H. III. Title.

HB161.R4812 2004
330.15′13′092—dc21 2002016222
ISBN 0-86597-975-8 (vol. II: pbk.: alk. paper)
ISBN 0-86597-976-6 (set: pbk.: alk. paper)

Liberty Fund, Inc.
8335 Allison Pointe Trail, Suite 300
Indianapolis, IN 46250-1684

Text and cover design by Erin Kirk New, Watkinsville, Georgia
Typography by Impressions Book and Journal Services, Inc., Madison, Wisconsin
Printed and bound by Edwards Brothers, Inc., Ann Arbor, Michigan

CONTENTS OF VOLUME XI

ADDITIONAL LETTERS

3a	Ricardo to S. Beckett	21 June 1810	*page* ix
137a	Ricardo to Joseph Hume	8 Nov. 1815	ix
197a	Malthus to Ricardo	11 January 1817	x
259a	Ricardo to Torrens	15 June 1818	xi
418a	Ricardo to Miss Bayley	30 January 1821	xii
492a	Ricardo to Thomas Booth	28 March 1822	xiii
516a	Ricardo to Wilmot Horton	19 January 1823	xv
517a	Mallet to Ricardo	24 February 1823	xvii
517b	Ricardo to Mallet	25 February 1823	xxi
531a	Townsend to Ricardo	20 July 1823	xxii
531b	Ricardo to Townsend	25 July 1823	xxiv
	Ricardo to Wright	22 August 1823	xxv
	Tooke to John Murray	8 January 1824	xxvi

ADDITIONAL NOTES

David Hume's supposed notes on the Wealth of Nations	xxvii
Changes in location of Manuscripts	xxvii
First publication of J. S. Mill's letter on his studies	xxvii
Identification of 'Piercy Ravenstone'	xxviii
Authorship of 'Life of Huskisson'	xxix
Marriage of Ricardo's grandfather	xxix
Pirated edition of 'Plan for a National Bank'	xxix
Build-up of mistakes in French editions of 'Principles'	xxix
Swift's Church of England Man	xxx
A second freak copy of 'Principles'	xxx
Authorship of 'Reply to Mr. Say'	xxx

CORRECTIONS TO VOLUMES I–X
(additional to the list in Volume X, p. 411) xxxi

INDEX

PREFATORY NOTE

THIS much delayed Index completes the edition of Ricardo's *Works.* Of the previous attempts at making an index, only one, sketched out with the help of Professor A. Heertje, proved useful for the final version. For the rest I am indebted to Mrs Barbara Lowe, who returned to Cambridge to help to complete the work begun many years ago.

P. S.

Additional Letters

3a. RICARDO TO HIS SUPERIOR OFFICER, S. BECKETT [1]

New Grove Mile end
21st June 1810

Sir

I received your letter dated the 18th inst, directed to the Commander of the St Leonard Volunteers, with instructions concerning assembling the Corps this day at 4 oClock.— I think it necessary again to acquaint you, that the Bromley St Leonard Volunteer Corps, which I had the honour to command, has been disbanded nearly six months

I am Sir
Your obedt humble Servt
DAVID RICARDO

S. Beckett Esqr

137a. RICARDO TO JOSEPH HUME [2]

Gatcomb Park
8th Novr 1815

My Dear Sir

It is with the greatest concern that I inform you I am obliged to go to London on Sunday next[3] by the Gloucester

[1] MS in Public Record Office, "H.O.42–107". I am indebted to Sir Leon Radzinowicz for calling my attention to it.

Ricardo joined the Bromley and St. Leonards Volunteers in 1803, and was commissioned as Captain in the same year. See above, X, 47 & n.

[2] Addressed: "Joseph Hume Esqr / Cheltenham".—MS, International Autographs, New York, Cat. 15, 1964, item 292.

Joseph Hume (1777–1855), from 1818 M.P. for Aberdeen. At the time of this letter he had, at Mill's suggestion, planned to bring his newly wedded wife to Gatcomb. On a previous occasion he had arrived there only to find the family away. (See above, VI, 158, 310, 313, 325.) He became later one of Ricardo's chief allies in parliament.

[3] 12 November.

Mail, and that on Saturday I am going to Gloucester to pass that day with a friend of mine to whom I had written to secure me a place in the Mail. I very much regret that I am again disappointed in not having the pleasure of seeing you here, particularly as Mrs. Ricardo and I would have been happy in the opportunity which your visit would have afforded us of becoming acquainted with Mrs. Hume. There appears to be a fatality attending our meeting in this part of the world,—I hope we shall become better acquainted in London. I am writing immediately after the receipt of your letter, but have some doubts whether I shall be in time for the Post

I am My dear Sir
Yours very truly
DAVID RICARDO

197a. MALTHUS TO RICARDO[1]

[*Reply to Letter* 197.—*Answered by* 199]

[11 Jan. 1817]

[...] I am sorry to find from what you say that you do not feel yourself able to approach nearer to those opinions, which I still continue after repeated consideration to think correct.

Everything that has occurred lately appears to favour my idea of the all powerful efficacy of demand, and to shew that is very far indeed from depending merely on supply. I quite

[1] Addressed: "D. Ricardo Esqr. / Upper Brook Street / Grosvenor Square". Incomplete, dated from postmark.

MS in the Rothschild Library, n. 1388 of the Catalogue.

Ricardo had asked Malthus for his opinion on the plan lately adopted for the relief of the poor by employing them on public works. He himself did not think it a very efficacious mode of relief, as it diverted funds from other employments. (Above, VII, 116.)

agree with you in thinking that the funds raised for the support of the poor (though perhaps necessary at the moment) essentially interfere with other employments. But this opinion appears to me to accord with my view of the subject, more than with yours. According to you and Say, if people were willing to subscribe and convert their *revenue* into *capital,* there ought to be no difficulty, if the sole want is the want of supply; but in my view of the subject there ought to be a difficulty, from the want of a proportionate demand.

I shall be most happy to visit you in Brook street the very first time I am in Town; but I have now been a truant for some time and must stay at home a little.

Mrs M joins me in kind regards to Mrs Ricardo

Ever truly Yours

T. R. Malthus

259a. RICARDO TO TORRENS [1]

London, Upper Brook St.,
15 June, 1818, 5 o'Clock

My Dear Sir,

I have this moment returned home, and find your letter[2] dated from the King's Head Inn, Rochester (13th June) on my table.

Mr. Philips[3] is in Sussex, attending his own election, and therefore he cannot be applied to attest that you are a fit and proper person to serve in Parliament,[4] in time to be of any

[1] This letter was quoted by Torrens in an election speech in 1832, and printed in full in the *Bolton Chronicle* of 17 November 1832. It was discovered by Mr B. A. Corry and published by him in *Economica,* 1957, pp. 71–2.

[2] Torrens' letter is not extant.

[3] Probably G. R. Phillips (as spelt three lines below), M.P. for Horsham.

[4] Torrens was contesting Rochester in the general election of 1818.

use to you,—but from my knowledge of Mr. Phillips opinion of you, I can attest that those are his sentiments, and if he were in town I am sure he would say that and much more in your favour. My own acquaintance with you entitles me to give it as my opinion that you would render great service to your country in the House of Commons. From your knowledge of Political Economy, your advice would be of essential use in all financial questions, and at present there appears to be a great dearth of that sort of talent amongst our legislators. It will give me great pleasure to hear of your success.

As High Sheriff for the County of Gloucester, I shall be obliged to leave town the latter end of the week, to preside at the election of members for that county.

I am sorry that I did not see your friend.

I am, most truly yours,

DAVID RICARDO

418a. RICARDO TO MISS BAYLEY[1]

London 30 Jany 1821

My Dear Miss Bayley

I shall be happy to forward your letters whenever you will favor me with them;—that which you enclosed to me this morning was immediately after I received it despatched by the 3^{d} post to its address.—I promise to do this, or any other kindness in my power for you, although I should not be flattered by the account of such favorable opinions as Mr. Corrie expressed of my arguments in favor of my own

[1] MS in the Houghton Library, here printed by permission of the Harvard College Library. I am indebted to Professor Frank W. Fetter for calling my attention to it.

Ricardo had met the Bayley sisters, Sarah, Elizabeth and Ann, at Easton Grey, the home of Thomas Smith. See above, X, 350 & n.

doctrines on the disputed points in Political Economy. In truth however I am pleased that they had some effect on him.

You will like to know what Mr. M^c^Culloch said of my notes. He thinks that I should not publish them in their present form—they are in his opinion too controversial, and although he considers them as establishing the doctrine of the effects of accumulation on the ground on which I had previously placed it, before Mr. Malthus wrote his work, he thinks I should lower my reputation if I became a commentator of every erroneous opinion which I might think I discovered in the writings of another political economist.[1]

I shall therefore I think proceed no further with the notes. They are now in the possession of Mr. Malthus and if they have any influence with him in inducing him to make corrections in his next edition they will not have been written in vain.

Pray give our united regards to Mrs. and Mr. Smith and Miss Mary Ann Bayley,[2] and accept them yourself from our family circle. I hope you will hear good accounts of your sister Anne.

Y^rs^ with great esteem
DAVID RICARDO

492a. RICARDO TO THOMAS BOOTH[3]

London 28 March 1822

Sir

I am very much obliged to you for the frank communication of your sentiments respecting the probability of

[1] See M^c^Culloch's letter of 22 Jan., above, VIII, 338–40.

[2] Probably to be identified with the "Miss Mary Ann" of Ricardo's letter of 20 April 1822, above, X, 164–6.

[3] Addressed: 'Thomas Booth Esqre / Foxteth Lodge / near / Liverpool'. MS in Sotheby's sale, 28 July 1964, lot 534.

success, if I were disposed to listen to Mr. Hodgson's suggestion of becoming a candidate to represent in Parliament the town of Liverpool.[1] With your means of information I cannot have the least doubt that the opinion you have formed is a correct one. If I were well disposed to enter into so fearful a contest, your letter would make me pause and hesitate, as on the whole it does not hold out much promise of success; but since I had the pleasure of seeing Mr. Hodgson I have given the subject the most serious consideration, the result of which is that I must give up all thoughts of commencing a contest for which I am so unfit. I should be sacrificing my peace of mind for a considerable time for an object which I should not probably after all attain. I should be exchanging a seat of comparatively little trouble for one which would require constant attention, if I were to succeed. It is true that I should have the honour, which I know how to value, of representing a very important place, but I doubt whether I could be altogether as useful in my humble line, fettered as I should be by the particular views and opinions of my constituents, as I am now.

The reflection that Mr. Hodgson and a few of his friends thought so favourably of me as to be willing to give me their aid in elevating me to the rank of a representative of Liverpool will always be a source of satisfaction to me.

I remain

Sir

Your obed[t] and humble Serv[t]

DAVID RICARDO

[1] See Ricardo's letter to David Hodgson, declining the invitation to stand for Liverpool, above, IX, 182.

516a. RICARDO TO WILMOT HORTON [1]

Widcomb House, Bath
19 Jany 1823

My dear Sir

My servant at Gatcomb Park having neglected to send my letters after me, I did not receive your note, with the pamphlets accompanying it, till this morning.

You know I am frequently reproached with being a theorist, and if those who so reproach me, mean that I am not conversant with the practical details of the subjects which have engaged my attention, they are right. The subject of the Poor-laws for instance is one intimately connected with the science of Political Economy, but nobody is so little acquainted with them, as forming a part of parish economy, as I am.

The question you refer to me relates wholly to Parish economy, and therefore I am not qualified to give a good opinion on it.

I can have very little doubt but that the plan[2] would be favorable to parishes. With the waste and extravagance of our system of poor laws an able bodied pauper must cost the parishes more than £35.[3] It is said in the "Outline"[4] that each able bodied pauper costs the parish £10 p^{r} Ann^{m}, but

[1] MS in Central Library, Derby: it was located by Mr R. N. Ghosh (*Economica,* 1963, p. 47 n.).

The letter was first printed in Wilmot Horton's pamphlet, *Causes and Remedies of Pauperism, Part I* (London, Murray, 1829), but was overlooked until Lord Robbins found it and reprinted it in *Economica,* 1956, pp. 172–3.

Robert John Wilmot Horton (1784–1841), M.P., was at the time Under-Secretary for War and the Colonies.

[2] The plan was to mortgage the poor rates in order to finance the emigration of paupers to Upper Canada.

[3] The sum calculated as necessary to get a man to Canada and keep him until he was self-supporting.

[4] *Outline of a Plan of Emigration to Upper Canada* (printed, but not published, Jan. 1823).

against this must be set the value of the work which such pauper may be made to do for the parish, and also the general saving in the wages of labour which accompany the present system. If the farmer who pays £10, saves £5 in the wages of the rest of his workmen, his real contribution is only £5, and the real saving to the parish will be only a like sum.

With every emigrant we are to divest ourselves of £35 capital. If employed at home, with that portion of capital, he could replace it with a profit, England would be a loser by the proposed plan. The enemies of the plan will say that he could do so, and if they could make that appear I would rather adopt their plan, than the one recommended.

At the present moment however we are to compare the emigration plan to the system actually existing, and I can have no doubt that it would be attended with great advantages over it. The plan would be economical; it would enable us to get rid of the most objectionable part of the poor laws, the relieving able bodied men; and what is to me by far the most important consideration, it could not fail to make the wages of labour more adequate to the support of the labourer and his family, besides giving him that as wages which is now given to him as charity.

I told you how incompetent I was to say any thing worthy of your attention on this subject and I have now convinced you of it.

Believe me
Very truly yours
DAVID RICARDO

If you wish to have the pamphlets returned I will give them to you when we meet in London.

517a. MALLET TO RICARDO [1]
[*Answered by* 517b]

Upper Gower Street
24 Feby 1823.

My dear Sir,

Mr Hume has given notice of a motion relative to Savings Banks, which has excited the attention of some of the principal Managers of these Institutions in London, and given them some anxiety. In the first place, we think that a habit of minute regulation, and of frequent Legislative interference is unfavorable to the experiment we are trying.

So far as could be collected from Newspaper Reports, Mr Hume's observations related to the rate of interest granted by Government to Depositors in Savings Banks, which he seemed to think unreasonable and wasteful. But I did not understand whether the observations were intended to apply to the rate of interest originally granted, or whether Mr Hume thought that the circumstances of the Country, or the state of the Banks, called for a reduction of the rate of interest.

On the first supposition, I should beg him to observe, that altho' the rate of interest originally granted and now enjoyed by the Banks £4.12 per cent was beneficial as compared with the rate of interest on other Public Securities, it was not materially so; the 5 per cents being then (June 1817) at 104$\frac{3}{4}$ or 105 the 3 per cent consol. 74. Then there are comparatively speaking, a few cases only in which the

[1] MS in *R.P.*—This letter was published in Ricardo's *Minor Papers*, ed. by J. H. Hollander, 1932, pp. 210–13, but was not included in the present edition. Ricardo's reply having since come to light, the two letters are now published together.

John Lewis Mallet, son of Mallet du Pan; his diaries have been frequently quoted in these volumes. On Mallet's and Ricardo's common interest in Savings Banks, see above, VII, 50 n.

Depositors receive the whole amount of the interest granted by Government; the expenses of management of the Banks being generally defrayed out of the allowance of interest. The Depositors in two of the largest Banks in London, receive a rate of interest, not exceeding £3.17 per annum, which is in fact less than the interest they would have received had they invested their money in 3 per cent consol. If it be asked why so large a deduction is made, and why Government should bear this expence, the answer is that it is incidental to the proper management and security of such Establishments in large towns; and particularly in London. It is of the greatest importance that the Persons who conduct these Institutions should be men of the greatest respectability and at the same time, men of business. I speak from long experience when I say that it is extremely difficult to find Persons of this description who can give up any part of their time and that those with whom I am acquainted, and who attend to the Saving Banks in the City and in Southampton Row, are considerable Merchants, or men engaged in active professional pursuits. Now, when it is considered, that from the year 1817 to the year 1822, 6472 accounts were opened at the Bank in Southampton Row; which accounts must be kept with the greatest regularity, checked with the Depositors Book, the interest computed, the repayments entered; when it is further considered that notices of every repayment are to be given at least a week previously to the receipt of the Money; that these notices are all entered, and contain the particulars of the name and situation of the Depositor, his place of residence, the amount of his deposit; and that they are to be compared with the original entries of the Depositor, the signature of the depositor, and the Ledgers: it may easily be conceived, that independently of the labour of the Cash transactions of the Bank, which partly occupy 2 or 3 Managers and four Clerks, twice in the week, the business of such an Establishment cannot be conducted without efficient and regular assistance; other than can be expected from the Managers themselves. But this is not all. The actuary and Clerks are necessarily entrusted to a considerable extent with the custody of Money; and we therefore require securities: their salaries are therefore necessarily higher. Again, convenient and large premises are required; both with reference to the great number of Persons who attend the Bank, and the number of Ledgers and Desks in constant use, and the propriety of decent accommodation for the Managers. Under all these circumstances, a large deduction from the rate of interest granted by Government seems unavoidable.

On the second supposition: namely that the circumstances of the country or of the Banks, or both, are so far altered, as to require a reconsideration of the rates of interest, I should say that the present state of Public Securities, affords no grounds for any change in this respect. The price of 3 per cents is the same as it was when the 57 Geo. 3^{d} Ch. 130 was passed: and in proof of the greater advantage derived from investments in Stock, I would mention that a great number of the larger Depositors in Savings Banks in London, have lately withdrawn their deposits, to place them in the funds. Our repayments for several weeks have exceeded by several hundred Pounds every week the amount of our receipts. With regard to the large accumulation of deposits in Savings Banks, amounting to several Millions; and the idea generally entertained that a portion of these deposits are received from an improper description of Persons, I beg leave to observe with reference to my former remarks, that Depositors do not at present derive, and are not likely to derive any advantage from depositing their Money in Savings Banks instead of purchasing stock; and that this is not therefore a proper time for proposing any alteration in the rate of interest granted by Government. The sacrifice made by Government has been inconsiderable; particularly with reference to the great importance of the experiment now going on, and to the excellent effects which have already resulted from the Establishment of these Institutions. I think I may safely refer to the enclosed Report in support of this opinion.

Upon the whole I cannot but conceive that the agitation of the question as to Government keeping the terms upon which the Banks have been established, cannot but be productive of harm; and that any alteration in those terms would greatly check the progress of these useful Institutions, shake confidence and embarass and discourage to a very great degree, the Persons who have devoted to them so much of their time and attention.

Convinced as I am that Mr Hume has no other object than the Public good in view, I trust that if you will have the goodness to communicate these observations to him, he will not be unmindful of the circumstances to which I have taken the liberty of requesting your attention.

Believe me my dear sir

Your's very faithfully

J. L. Mallet

517b. RICARDO TO MALLET [1]

[*Reply to* 517a]

Upper Brook Street
25 Feby 1823

My Dear Sir

Your very judicious remarks upon Savings Banks shall be communicated to Mr. Hume, and I have no doubt he will think with you that it will not be expedient to agitate the question of interest at the present moment. I heard the observations he made in the House—his objection was against the rate of interest allowed by Government, he said that a considerable loss was sustained by the public between the rate allowed, and that obtained by the Commissioners by investing the money in Stock. For the reasons you give I think the present not a favourable time to make any alteration in the rate of interest. Mr. Woodrow, the author of an annuity plan,[2] is very desirous of giving the working classes the opportunity of purchasing annuities on the lives of their children to commence after the children arrive at a certain age: I once mentioned the plan in the House. If any alteration were made in the Savings Bank Act I think I should again suggest this annuity plan.

Ever My Dear Sir
Yours very faithfully
David Ricardo

J. L. Mallet Esqr

[1] MS in Sotheby's sale of 19 Feb. 1963, part of lot 456.

[2] On Woodrow's annuity plan, see above, V, 121, 128–9.

531a. TOWNSEND TO RICARDO [1]
[*Answered by* 531b]

Figgs Marsh, Mitcham
July 20th 1823

Sir

Altho' I have not the honour of knowing you, permit me to offer you my best thanks for the manner in which you have advocated the cause of religious freedom, and the important point of free discussion, and the liberty of the Press, whenever those topics have come under the consideration of the House of Commons during the present Session: and however much I might regret that your efforts, combined with those of Mr. Hume, and Sir Francis Burdett, proved of no avail in the House, I rejoice in the assurance that they were duly appreciated by the enlightened part of the Community out of it. Your Arguments, together with those Gentlemen who delivered their Sentiments on the same side, against the folly, as well as the injustice, of punishing Men for their Opinions, were, as the Examiner justly observed, admirable, clear, powerful conclusive-convincing, and the effect arising from the impression which they must have made upon the minds of those who perused them I have no doubt will ere long be fully evinced.

To Yourself Sir, as also to the above named Gentlemen,

[1] Addressed: 'David Ricardo Esqr M.P. / Upper Brook St.' Both Townsend's and Ricardo's letters were published in Richard Carlile's paper, *The Republican,* 26 Sept. 1823, Vol. 8, pp. 369–70.

Townsend's letter is here printed from the MS in *R.P.* It differs from the published version in being dated from Figgs Marsh, Mitcham (instead of from London), and containing the postscript.

Carlile came again to the defence of Ricardo in *The Republican,* 16 Jan. 1824, pp. 65–9, in a review of a pamphlet by the Rev. William Baily Whitehead, *Prosecution of Infidel Blasphemers, briefly vindicated in a letter to David Ricardo, Esq., M.P.*

all those Individuals who know how to estimate the importance of Political and Religious liberty, cannot but feel greatly indebted, for the open and candid manner which you have shown yourselves the enemies to every species of persecution; and when I see Gentlemen of talents, fortune, and integrity, standing up and holding such just and liberal Sentiments, undismayed by the taunts of the bigot, and the frowns of the interested; I say, when I behold Gentlemen sitting in Parliament manfully contending for the rights of the people, and that too, in a strain of reasoning that cannot be refuted, I am (notwithstanding the gloom which at present obscures the political horizon) led to cherish the hope that by such exertions, I shall yet see the day when there will be a less expensive and more happy form of Government established in this Country than at present; and that in fact, when Tyranny and Superstition shall be banished from our Thresholds, and never more venture to violate our Sanctuaries.

To conclude, as one of a numerous body of Men who profess Republican principles, I cannot withhold my admiration of your conduct with respect to that much injured, and much calumniated, and misrepresented Individual, Mr Carlile; and whose Sister's Petition you so ably supported. It is in pursuing such a course as this Sir, that you secure the affections of all honest and well-meaning Men; and as you appear to be actuated by a sense of the manifest wrong, in imposing penalties for opinions expressed, either with regard to Theology, or Politics, I cannot suppose for a moment that you will relax in your endeavours to effect free toleration, or that you will permit yourself to be deterred therefrom, by any insults which the fanatic, and the placeman, may think proper to offer you; but that you will prove the Patriot, to stand by and advocate the great cause of free discussion as alone calculated to elicit truth, and that you will not fail to denounce the iniquitous and cruel proceedings which continue to be exercised towards those, who seek for the Reformation of the Government.—I am Sir

With the highest respect

Your mo. Obed.[t] Serv.

JN P. TOWNSEND

David Ricardo Esq[r] M.P.

P.S. My situation in life precludes me from openly declaring my Opinions, and therefore I write this in perfect confidence; but there are several Letters of mine in the "Republican", with no other Address than that of "London", I will, if you see no objection thereto, procure this to be inserted likewise, but certainly not without your permission.

531b. RICARDO TO TOWNSEND [1]

[*Reply to* 531a]

Gatcomb Park, Minchinhampton
July 25, 1823.

Sir,

I am happy that the sentiments which I expressed, on the occasion of the late discussion in the House of Commons on religious freedom[2] are approved by you: I trust I shall ever be found advocating the same cause, whenever it shall be submitted to the consideration of the House.

With respect to the publication of the letter, which you have done me the honour to address to me, in the Republican, you will be so good as to decide on the expediency yourself: being a friend to free discussion I leave every one

[1] The MS of Ricardo's letter is not extant. It is here reprinted from *The Republican.* See above, p. xxi n.

[2] See above, V, 324–31, and cp. 277–80.

to praise or censure my public conduct as he may think fit.

I remain, Sir, your obedient and humble Servant,

DAVID RICARDO

To Mr. John Townsend, London.

RICARDO TO WRIGHT [1]

Gatcomb Park
Minchinhampton
22 Aug. 1823

Sir

The speech on Mr. Western's motion[2] of which you wish to have a correct copy for the *Parliamentary Debates* contained a great many remarks on Mr. Western's pamphlet,[3] which besides being in my opinion very attackable on its own merits, was at variance with the frequently declared opinions of that gentleman. As I have not that pamphlet here I cannot refer to it, nor is it perhaps desirable that all those remarks should be published. I will look over the newspaper reports, and will, within the time you mention, send them back either with the printed report corrected, or with the speech written out as far as I can recollect it.

I am Sir

Your obed.t servant

DAVID RICARDO

[1] Addressed: 'J. Wright Esq.r / 112 Regent Street / London.— MS in Sotheby's sale of books 4 Nov. 1969, part of lot 274.

This letter is in reply to one (printed above, V, xxx) from John Wright, editor of *Hansard's Parliamentary Debates,* who had asked for a transcript of Ricardo's speech on Western's motion of 10 July 1823.

[2] Above, V, 309–21.

[3] *Second Address to the Landowners...*, by C. C. Western, 1822. See above, V, 317 & n. and cp. 522–8.

THOMAS TOOKE TO JOHN MURRAY[1]

Russell Square
Jan. 8, 1824

My dear Sir

Some manuscript papers of the late Mr Ricardo have by his executors been placed in the hands of my friend Mr. Mill with a view to his determining whether they are deserving of publication and if so in what form they should appear. One of these papers entitled "a plan for the establishment of a national bank"[2] is in a perfectly finished state:— It is very short but very clear and every way worthy of the Author's reputation.

Mr Mill is desirous, as you published for our late friend when living, that you should undertake this his posthumous work. I propose that he (Mr. Mill) and myself should meet if agreeable to you in Albemarle Street for the purpose of arranging the materials and the form of publication. I have accordingly to beg you that you will let me know whether it will suit you to receive Mr. Mill and me on Monday morning at a little before 10 and to devote half an hour to the object in question—With my best regards to Mrs. Murray believe me to be

Dr Sir
Most truly yrs
THO^S TOOKE

[1] MS in the possession of John Murray, the publishers. I am indebted to Professor F. W. Fetter for drawing my attention to it. A postscript dealing with a second edition of a work by Tooke himself is here omitted; Murray was at this time his publisher.

[2] Above, IV, 271–300.

Additional Notes

VOLUME I

[p. vii] DAVID HUME'S SUPPOSED NOTES on the 'WEALTH OF NATIONS'. An allusion by Professor Foxwell to the destruction of Hume's notes on the *Wealth of Nations* was quoted in the General Preface (I, vii). It should be made clear that the lost notes which Foxwell assumed to be by David Hume, the philosopher, were in fact by his nephew and namesake, a Scottish judge. See *Letters of Eminent Persons addressed to David Hume,* ed. by Hill Burton, 1849, pp. 315–17.

VOLUME VI

MARIA EDGEWORTH'S PAPERS (above, VI, xxxii–xxxiii, X, 387–8 & n.). At Mrs Harriet J. Butler's death, these papers passed to her son, the late Professor Harold Edgeworth Butler. In his will he expressed the hope that the MSS would be given to the British Museum, without, however, making it binding on his executors.

FRANCIS HORNER'S PAPERS (above, VI, xxxv). The bulk of these papers, lately in the possession of Lady Langman, have been deposited in the Library of the London School of Economics. Others, including the letters of Ricardo used for this edition, were retained by the family.

RICHARD SHARP'S PAPERS (above, VI, xxxvii). At the death of the Hon. Mrs Eustace Hills (Nina Kay-Shuttleworth), the MS of her biography of Richard Sharp was deposited in the Bodleian Library, Oxford. The papers of Sharp were dispersed, some being bought by Miss Myers, autograph dealer, of Dover Street, London.

VOLUME VIII

[p. 198 n.] J. S. MILL'S LETTER ON HIS STUDIES, FIRST PUBLICATION. J. S. Mill's boyhood letter to Sir Samuel Bentham was said (above, VIII, 198 n.) to have been published 'apparently for the first time' in A. Bain's biography of J. S. Mill, 1882. It has now been found that the letter was first printed in *The Sheffield Telegraph* of 13 Feb. 1877, and reprinted in *The Times* two days later.

VOLUME IX

[p. 45] IDENTIFICATION OF 'PIERCY RAVENSTONE, M.A.' Ricardo refers several times with interest to the book, *A few Doubts as to the Correctness of some Opinions generally entertained on the subjects of Population and Political Economy,* 'by Piercy Ravenstone, M.A.'[1] It has been generally accepted that 'Piercy Ravenstone' is a pseudonym,[2] and it is now possible to give the author's real name.

A copy of *A few Doubts* has come to light, on the title-page of which 'Piercy Ravenstone, M.A.' has been crossed out, and 'Richard Puller' written in; 'Puller on Political Economy' is lettered on the spine of the binding, which is contemporary; this may well have been the author's own copy. Another copy, which is in the Feltrinelli Library in Milan, is inscribed on the fly-leaf: 'The real author of this book was Richard Puller, brother of Sir Christopher Puller, Chief-Justice of Bengal, and uncle of Christopher Puller, member for Hertfordshire about 1858. The present head of the family is Charles Puller, of Youngsbury, Herts.'[3]

Of Richard Puller little else is known. He is mentioned in the will (dated 2 October 1789) of his grandfather, Christopher Puller (1707–89), a director of the Bank of England; on 7 February 1827 he was given the administration of the estate of his father, Richard Puller (1746–1826), of Painswick Court, Glos., a director of the South Sea Company. His signature and his address, Park Street, Grosvenor Square, appear on an affidavit, dated 10 October 1831, in

[1] London, J. Andrews, 1821. See above, IX, 45, 59–60, 62–3, 64.

[2] See Max Beer, *History of British Socialism,* Vol. 1, p. 251, and Kenneth Smith, *The Malthusian Controversy,* p. 142. Professor J. Dorfman, in his Introduction to the reprint of *A few Doubts* (A. M. Kelley, New York, 1966), has suggested that Ravenstone was the Anglican minister, Edward Edwards, but there appears to be no evidence to support this conjecture.

[3] Charles Puller inherited Youngsbury in 1885 and died in 1892—which fixes the time limits for this inscription.

connection with the will of his sister, Charlotte Louisa Puller, of Painswick Court.

[p. 270n.] AUTHORSHIP OF THE LIFE OF HUSKISSON. The author of the biography of William Huskisson prefixed to his *Speeches* is E. Leeves, and not, as stated above, IX, 270 n., John Wright, who only edited these speeches. See British Museum Catalogue of Add. MSS 1911–15, p. 230.

VOLUME X

[p. 19] MARRIAGE OF RICARDO'S GRANDFATHER. Joseph Israel Ricardo was not married twice, as said above, X, 19, but only once, to Hannah Abaz. There were, however, two marriage ceremonies, the civil, in which his wife's name is recorded as Hannah Abaz, and the Synagogue, in which it appears as Hannah Israel. (Information from the Amsterdam records supplied by Professor A. Heertje.)

[p. 367] PIRATED EDITION OF 'PLAN FOR A NATIONAL BANK', 1824. An unrecorded printing, no doubt pirated, of this pamphlet has turned up. The pagination is [i]-iv, [5]-31 with a blank page at the end; as opposed to that of the original, which is [i]-vi, [1]-32 with two unnumbered pages of advertisements at the end. The only 'signatures' shown in the pirated edition are '2' on p. 9 and '3' on p. 17, whereas the original has the regular signatures, 'A' on p. [v], 'A2' on p. [1], 'B' on p. 15, 'B2' on p. 17, and 'C' on p. 31. Although the lay-out of the title-page is the same in both editions, the depth of the type area is $6\frac{3}{8}''$ in the 'pirate', as against $5\frac{3}{8}''$ in the original. The copy in question was supplied by Mr Ambaras, antiquarian bookseller of New York, and it seems likely that this pirated edition is American.

[p. 376] FRENCH TRANSLATION OF THE 'PRINCIPLES'. A build-up of mistakes in successive French editions of Ricardo's *Principles* resulted in a total travesty of his original statement on the effects of machinery. He had written: 'the opinion entertained by the labouring class, that the employment of machinery is frequently detrimental to their interests, is not founded on prejudice and error, but is conformable to the correct principles of political economy.' (I, 392.)

The chapter on Machinery (which was added in ed. 3 of the *Principles,* 1821) was first translated into French in the Paris edition of 1847, and the above passage read as follows: 'l'opinion des classes ouvrières sur les machines qu'ils croient fatales à leurs intérêts, ne repose pas *seulement* sur l'erreur et les préjugés, mais sur les principes les plus fermes, les plus nets de l'Économie politique.'[1] (Editor's italics.)

The intrusion of the word 'seulement' made nonsense of the whole statement. The editor of the next French edition (1882) tried to put it right without referring to the original English; and taking it for granted that Ricardo must have held the orthodox view, amended the passage to read: 'l'opinion des classes ouvrières sur les machines qu'ils croient fatales à leurs intérêts, ne repose pas *seulement* sur l'erreur et les préjugés, mais sur *l'ignorance* des principes les plus fermes, les plus nets, de l'Économie politique.'[2] (Editor's italics.) Thus the revised version represented Ricardo as saying precisely the opposite of what he had actually said.

This travesty held the field for half a century. The correct version was first given in C. Debyser's translation of the *Principles,* Paris, Costes, 1933–4, p. 217.

[p. 394, line 21] The 'work in English' referred to is Swift's *Sentiments of a Church of England Man.*

[p. 403] A second freak copy of Ricardo's *Principles,* 1817, containing pp. 219–22 in both the original state and the 'cancel' state (as described above, X, 403 ff.), has been found by Professor Heertje of Amsterdam, and is now in his possession.

[p. 405] The author of the anonymous pamphlet, *A Reply to Mr. Say's Letters to Mr. Malthus* (annotated by Ricardo) is John Cazenove, who has been mentioned as the author of another anonymous pamphlet above, III, 428 n. 1. See Halkett and Laing's *Dictionary of Anonyms.*

[1] *Œuvres complètes de David Ricardo* (in *Collection des principaux économistes*), Paris, 1847, p. 367.

[2] *Œuvres complètes de David Ricardo* (in *Collection des principaux économistes*), Paris, 1882, p. 329.

Corrections to the First Printing of Volumes I–X*

(Additional to the list in Vol. X, p. 411)

VOLUME I

p. xxxviii, note 3, *for* n. 2 *read* n. 3
p. 99, n. 2, line 4, *for* 1815 *read* 1816
p. 248, n. 3, last line, *for* 40, n. 2, *read* 41, n. 1
p. 421, n. 2, col. 2, end of last line, *for* rent. *read* rent,

VOLUME II

p. 336, line 7 from bottom, *for* cause *read* causes
p. 455, col. 1, under Distribution, lines 2–3, *for* introduction *read* production

VOLUME III

p. 165, line 8, *for* 'disadvantages' [misquoted by Ricardo] *read* 'advantages'
p. 179, n. 3, line 2, *for* An II *read* An XI
p. 345, line 2 and line 6, *for* October *read* September
p. 345, n. 2, lines 1–4, *for* 'Advertisement in *Monthly Literary Advertiser,* 10 Oct. 1810: a new edition was advertised on 10 Jan. 1811' *read* 'Advt. in *The Times,* 23 Sept. 1810; and a new ed., *ib.* 13 Dec. 1810 [nos. 2 and 4 in F. W. Fetter's 'Editions of the Bullion Report', *Economica,* 1955, pp. 153–4]'

VOLUME IV

p. 45, line 20, *for* their *read* its
p. 100, n. 2, last line, *for* 1926 *read* 1826
p. 125, line 3, *for* 1814 *read* 1804
p. 126, note †, *for* p. [120] *read* p. [122]
p. 157, line 14, *for* fifty- *read* sixty- (error in *Enc. Brit.*)
p. 162, line 26, *for* 793, 343 *read* 793, 348 (misprint in *Enc. Brit.*)
p. 274, line 11, *for* 14 pages *read* 14 leaves
p. 420, in heading, *for* Editions 1–2 *read* Edition 2

VOLUME V

p. xx, n. 4, *for* 197–8 *read* 246
p. xxix, n. 2, for *Cobbett's Parliamentary Debates* read *Cobbett's Parliamentary Register*
p. 369, n. 1, for *Abbott* read *Abbot*
p. 432, no. 54, *for* as *read* has
no. 55, *for* found *read* sound

*[These corrections are reflected in the 2004 Liberty Fund Edition.]

p. 461, lines 4 and 12, *for* Catley *read* Cattley
p. 522, n. 3, *for* vol. X *read* X, 349
p. 530, col. 1, 3 lines from bottom, *for* Catley, Mr *read* Cattley, Stephen
  col. 2, line 21, *for* 491 n. *read* 492 n.
  col. 2, line 29, *for* 364, *read* 365
p. 532, col. 2, under Marcet, *for* 353–4 *read* 352–3
p. 534, col. 1, line 7, *for* Sidney *read* Sydney

VOLUME VI

p. viii, letter 103, *for* 1915 *read* 1815
p. xvi, n. 1, *for* VIII *read* VII
p. 337, 14 lines from bottom, at end of line, comma instead of full stop

VOLUME VII

p. 120, n. 3, line 2, *for* 10 *read* 410
p. 121, n. 1, *add* [But see XI, x–xi]
p. 197, n., col. 2, last line, *for* 1779 *read* 1781
p. 244, line 6, *for* difficult *read* different

VOLUME VIII

p. 116, n. 1, line 4, *for* 116 *read* 261
p. 207, n. 1, *for* I *read* II
p. 208, n. 3, *for* 22–4 *read* 122–4

VOLUME X

p. 359, entry [1*h*], line 2, *for* [12] *read* [13]. (The same correction to be made on p. 360, entry [2*c*], line 2; p. 361, entry [3*d*], line 3; and p. 366, entry [6*f*], line 2.)
p. 363, entry [5*a*], the paragraph headed *Variant* should not be under the First Edition of *Principles* but under the Third Edition on p. 364, entry [5*c*]
p. 397, line 11 from bottom, *for* 179 *read* 197
p. 400, line 11, *for Supplement,* 1811 *read Supplement,* 1810

INDEX

Abaz, Hannah (Ricardo's grandmother), X, 19, XI, xxix
Abbot, Charles, Lord Colchester, *Diary and Correspondence,* V, 369 n.
Abe, Hiroshi, X, 384
Abercomby, James, M.P. for Calne, VII, 264 & n., see also V, 351, 352, 354
Aberdeen magistracy, VII, 303 & n.
Abrahams, Dudley, on 'Jew Brokers of the City of London', X, 22 n., 57 n.
Absentees in foreign parts, petition for tax on, V, 186–8
Absolute price, I, 63; absolute revenue, III, 281–2; absolute value of money, V, 209
Absolute value and exchangeable value, papers on, IV, 357–412. See also Value, absolute
Abstract currency:
  abstract pound sterling, VIII, 32
  ledger pound, VII, 44
  imaginary currency (Blake), IX, 286
  currency without a standard (Sir James Steuart), IV, 59–62
Abundance: effect of, on price of corn, IV, 219–22, see also V, 318–20, 523, IX, 378; different effects of, on money and on commodities, V, 169–71; see also Agricultural distress
Accarias de Serionne, Jacques, *La Richesse de la Hollande,* 1778, IX, 135 n.
Accounts, public: methods of keeping, V, 67–8, 100, 115–16, 139; committee on, V, xxv–xxvi; balance-sheet form adopted at Ricardo's suggestion, V, 145
Accumulated and immediate labour, I, 34, 410, IV, 379, 386, VII, 316 n., IX, 307, 338–9, 343, 365
Accumulation: a misleading word, II, 320 n.; of capital and of produce distinguished, VI, 155, 164. See Capital
Acland, Sir Thomas Dyke, M.P. for Devonshire, V, 278
Acres, W. M., *The Bank of England from Within,* IV, 97 n.
Addington, Henry, later Lord Sidmouth, IV, 153–4, 165, VI, 261
Addison, Joseph, VI, 279
Address to the Nation...on the Doctrines lately advanced by Mr Malthus, 1815, VI, 269–70 n.
'Adjustment of property', V, 266, and cp. 21, 34–5, 126, VIII, 147 & n. See National debt, Ricardo's plan
Adler, secretary to Prince of Denmark, IX, 195
Administration of the Affairs of Great Britain, 1823 (attributed to J. S. Copley), V, 250 n., IX, 269 & n.
Agents of production (M^c^Culloch on), IX, 342–3, 356–7, 359, 367–8
Agio: on British money, III, 288, on Napoleons, IX, 224
Agiotage, VII, 352
Agricultural Committee, 1820, V, 48, 56 & n., see also xxiv
Agricultural Committee, 1821, IV, 203–4, V, xxiv–xxv
  speech on motion for, V, 81–91, VIII, 352–60
  Ricardo a member of, V, 86–7
  evidence, IV, 210–11, 221, 228 & n., 231, 241 & n., 259–60, 265, V, 214, 258, VIII, 366–7, 369–74, IX, 1, 66–7, 86–7, 106
  Report, IV, 210 n., 244–5, 249, 251–3, V, 114, 151–2, 157, IX, 1, 28
    drafted by Huskisson, V, 151 n., VIII, 390
    reviewed by M^c^Culloch, IX, 7 & n., by Senior, IX, 109 & n., 122

Agricultural Committee, 1822, IV, 203–4, V, xxv
speech on motion for, V, 129–38, IX, 163–4, 166, 175
Ricardo a member of, V, 138, 157 n., 182, 322, IX, 164, 176–7
evidence, V, 173–4, 181–3, 228
Report, IV, 245 & n., 246–50, 253, V, 148, 155, 162–4, 172, 224–5, 228–9, 235, IX, 180
speeches on, V, 151–3, 155–7, 164–86, IX, 187–8
Ricardo refuses to concur, V, 182–3; his Propositions, V, 158–9, 172–6, 180–1, 184–6, IX, 194 & n., 197
Report reviewed by McCulloch, IX, 186 & n., 188
see also Corn Laws
Agricultural distress:
speeches on, V, 47–56, 141–2, 148–54, see also 124–5
due to abundance, IV, 241–2, 258–61, 263, V, 108, 125, VIII, 371, IX, 157–8; and to corn-laws, V, 73–4, 79, 151, 170, VIII, 345, 357
not due to currency, IV, 230–1, V, 149–50, 233–4, 241–2, 315, IX, 167; nor to taxation, IV, 255–9, V, 84, 89, 124, IX, 152, 165–6, 199–200
proposed loans to parishes for, V, 129, 133, 136, see also IV, 235 n.
see also IV, 234 n., IX, 267 n., and under Labouring classes
Agricultural horses tax, V, 101, see also IV, 255
Agriculture:
no claim to pre-eminence over manufactures, I, 75, VIII, 102–3; Adam Smith controverted, I, 76–7 n., 429, and Malthus, II, 18–22, IV, 37–8; see also VI, 229–30, VII, 270–1, 279
profits of, regulate all profits, VI, 104; dispute with Malthus, VI, 117–18, 133, 139–40, 144–5, 152–5, 162–3, 167, 170, 182–3, 194
Agriculture (*cont.*)
withdrawal of capital from the land, I, 80–2, 267–71, II, 135–6, IV, 28, 248–9
see also Corn, Diminishing returns, Improvements in agriculture, Land
Aillaud, J.-P., publisher, VIII, 225 & n.
Albury, Malthus family home, his MSS at, VI, xix–xx, X, 386
Alembert, d', his correspondence with Voltaire, IX, 335, 374
Alessandria, X, 335, 337
Alexander I of Russia, X, 208
Algiers, V, 495
Ali Bey el Abbassi [pseud.], *Travels in Morocco,* 1816, VII, 189 & n.
Alien bill, V, xxii
Allardyce, Alexander, IV, 112–13; *Address to the Proprietors of the Bank of England,* 1798, IV, 106 n., 110 n., 415, VI, 242, 260, 265; *Second Address,* 1801, IV, 103 n., 112 & n., VI, 288 n.
Allen, Elizabeth, X, 45 n.
Allen, Jessie, Sismondi's wife, VIII, 25 n.
Allen, John, V, 471 n.
Allen, Mr, X, 285
Alpnach, X, 250
Althorp, Viscount, M.P. for Northamptonshire, his amendment to Ricardo's resolutions on the corn duties, V, 176–8, 184–5, IX, 197; see also V, 86
America:
Birkbeck's settlement, VII, 257, 259–60
cheap food and population, I, 409
emigration to, IX, 61
English currency in, III, 182–3 & n.
no-rent land in, I, 328, VII, 289, 297
prices of wheat and labour, VI, 232, 234, 236, 241, see also I, 15–16, 395, II, 138, 194–5, 213
relative prices of domestic and foreign commodities, II, 145–7, 156, 383, IX, 78, 83–4, 91–3, 97–100
rate of profits, VI, 129, 210, VII, 52, 57

America (*cont.*)
War of Independence, III, 251, 417, 419, V, 24, 215
see also III, 89, X, 271–2, and under Exchange
America, Spanish:
fertility of, II, 28–9, 87, 216, 341–3
day's labour in, II, 272
indolence of labourers, II, 337, 339–40, VII, 184, VIII, 216
gold and silver mines, I, 86, 195–9, III, 111, 127, 171, 362, 375, 391, V, 93 n., 391 n.
see also V, 205, 477
'Amicable arrangement' for national debt, V, 251–4. See Fundholders, gains and losses of
Amsterdam:
Ricardo's ancestors in, X, 18–19, 21
at school in, X, 3, 30–2
visit to, X, 205–12
Bank of, III, 126, 288
Exchange with, III, 73–4, VI, 97–9, 298–9
Anabaptists, Bayle's article on, X, 394
Andréadès, A., *History of the Bank of England,* X, 367–8
Angerstein, John Julius, X, 82
Anholt Mail, VI, 79 n., 80
Annales de législation et d'économie politique, 1822, IX, 245 & n.
Annales de législation et de jurisprudence, 1820, VIII, 376 n.
Annals of Philosophy, 1815, VI, 244 n.
Annual Biography, Memoir of Ricardo, I, xix n., III, 3 n., 4 n., 6 n., 9 n., IV, 273 n., X, 3 n., 14 & n.
Annual parliaments, VIII, 99, 107
Annual Register, for 1819, VIII, 111 n.; for 1822, IX, 195 n.
Annuities:
circulating, VIII, 293–5
life, V, 121, 129, XI, xxi
pensions plan and, V, 160, 191–5, 281
terminable, V, 270–1, IX, 175
see also I, 55–9, 174, III, 93–4, 341, IV, 64, 277
Antwerp, visit in 1817, VII, 160–2; in 1822, X, 191–3
Arbuthnot, Charles, Patronage Secretary, V, xvi, VII, 347
Arcot, Nabob of, VII, 243
Ardoin & Co., Ricardo's bankers in Paris, X, 99–101, 390
Arena for the employment of capital (Malthus), VI, 103 & n., 104, see also II, 140, 293
Aristocracy, political power of, V, 284–6, 496, VII, 323, IX, 86, 217
Aristocratical Conspiracy, Mill on, VIII, 106, 291, 295, 328, IX, 42
Arkwright's cotton-machine, IV, 33
Armstrong, F. E., *The Book of the Stock Exchange,* X, 129 n.
Arth, X, 245
Artificial checks to population, VII, 63, VIII, 71 & n., 80–1, IX, 62 & n.
Ashurst, William Henry, M.P. for Oxfordshire, V, 351, 366
Asiatic Journal, 1822, V, 475 n., 478 n.
Aslett, Robert, embezzler, IV, 97 n.
Aspland, Robert, Unitarian minister:
petition for free discussion of religious opinions, V, 324 n.
Ricardo attends his chapel, X, 40–1
Memoir of, by R. B. Aspland, V, 324 n., X, 40 n.
Assize of bread, V, 109
Astley, Francis Dukinfeld, X, 99
Atheists, no justification for silencing, IX, 278, see also V, 277–80, 324–31
Atkinson, Jasper, *Letter to a Member of Parliament,* 1810, X, 401
Attwood, Mathias, M.P. for Callington:
on rise in prices since 1819, V, 105, 108
speech on agricultural distress, V, 162–9
attacks Peel, V, 186
on machinery and unemployment, V, 302
'no cause for triumph' over Ricardo, IX, 265–6
Letter to Lord Archibald Hamilton, V, 321 & n.

Attwood, Thomas, evidence before Agricultural committee, 1821, VIII, 370 & n.; Tooke on its absurdity, VIII, 371; see also V, xxiv, IX, 156
Prosperity Restored, 1817, VII, 151 n.; *The Remedy,* 1817, VII, 151 n.
Auckland, Lord, letter quoted, III, 413 n.
Austin, Anthony (D.R.'s son-in-law), X, 62; on Ricardo's last illness, IX, 388–9; see also VII, 13 n., 54, 325 n., 375, X, 161–3, 261, 348, 350, 352
Austin, Edward, sen., on Fanny Ricardo's marriage, X, 161–4
Austin, Edward (D.R.'s son-in-law), X, 62, see also VII, 325, 335, 350, 375, VIII, 183, X, 161–3, 348
Austin, Fanny, see Ricardo, Fanny
Austin, Humphrey, VIII, 226
Austin, John, introduced to McCulloch, IX, 124–5, 138, 142, 148–9, 187; see also X, 162
Austin, Priscilla, see Ricardo, Priscilla
Austin, William (D.R.'s grandson), X, 54
Austria, V, 77, VIII, 363 n.
Authentic Narrative of the Westminster Election, 1819 (by J. C. Hobhouse and F. Place), VIII, 125 & n.
Automaton Chess Player, V, 368, X, 402
Autun, X, 344–5
Avallon, Ricardo sleeps in the bed of Napoleon, X, 345–6
Axon, E., *The Family of Bayley,* X, 350 n.

Babington, Thomas, M.P. for Leicester, VII, 356
Bacon, Lord, 'Of Ambition', VI, 327; see also VII, 211
Baden, X, 230–1; Grand Duke's palace, VII, 165
Bagshot, Military College, J. S. Mill attends lectures, VII, 313–14, 326
Bagshot heath, VI, 124, VII, 300, 302
Bagster, bookseller, VI, 260
Bailey, Samuel, *Critical Dissertation on Value,* 1825, I, xxi–xxii, IX, 27 n.
Baillie, Joanna, IX, 143 n.
Baillie, Mathew, M.D., VII, 90
Baillie, Mrs, VII, 265, IX, 143
Baily, Francis, VI, 270, VII, 14
Bain, Alexander, *James Mill,* I, xxi n., III, 9 n., VII, 8 n., VIII, 60 n., 84 n., 243 n., 251 n., IX, 6 n., 150 n., 159 n., 280 n., 390 n., 391 n., X, 47 n., 118 n.
J. S. Mill, VII, 313 n., VIII, 198 n., XI, xxvii
Balance of powers in government, VII, 367–9, 374, VIII, 13–14
Balance of trade, III, 54
and balance of payments distinguished, III, 101 n.
unfavourable, always due to redundant currency, III, 59–61, 64 notes, 116, 360–2, V, 394–5, VI, 25–6
see also III, 205–13
Baldwin, C., publisher, VII, 207, 210, IX, 116
Bâle, X, 233
Ballot at Bank Court, VII, 19
Ballot, plan of voting by, V, 504–12, see also V, 112, 285–6, 474, 485, VII, 261, 272–3, 299, VIII, 99, IX, 60, 119
Bangor, VI, 107, 109, 113
Bank Advances bill, V, 23
Bank notes:
circulation of, in 1805–8 and 1812–15, VI, 266 & n.; in 1799–1815, VI, 286; in 1814–15, VI, 260 & n.
country, in relation to Bank of England, notes, III, 26–7, 86–8 & n., 227–35, V, 202, 375, VI, 11–13
deposited in Exchequer, IV, 79 & n., see also 91–2 n.
depreciation of, see Depreciation
economy in use of, III, 378, IV, 109
effects of resumption of cash payments on, VIII, 35 & n., 135 n., IX, 201–2
forgery of, see Forgery

Bank notes (*cont.*)
large and small, different effects of, III, 114–15, 371–2, 395
made legal tender in 1811, V, 316, VI, 45, 68
of insolvent banks, VI, 53, and cp. III, 202 n.
quantity of, relation to price of gold, III, 123–4, V, 423, see also VI, 281 n.; to bullion price of commodities, III, 64; no relation to public deposits, IV, 78–9
Bank of Amsterdam, III, 126, 288
Bank of England:
accounts, publication advocated, IV, 110–14, V, 36, 463–4, 466, VI, 268, 335; tables of, IV, 115–35, VII, 39
an unnecessary establishment, VI, 268, IX, 325–6
balances of cash, 1799–1800, IV, 91 n., 92 n., VI, 257
bargain with Perceval in 1808, IV, 53–4, 81–3, 89–90, VI, 261, 333, 337, 347
Charter, terms of renewal in 1800, IV, 53, 87–8, 91–4, 140–1, VI, 268
proposed extension, 1822, IV, 272, 278, V, 156 & n., 193, 247
report on, 1832, IV, 100 n.
see also IV, 106 n., V, 282, 336, VIII, 35
Court of proprietors, Ricardo's speeches at, V, 461–7, VI, 335–6, 343, VII, 11, 19 & n., 21
see also III, 9, 145, IV, 90, 106, 110, 231–2 & n., VI, 242, 276–8
Directors, their ignorance of the principles of currency, I, 353–4, III, 131–3, 147, 221, 377, IV, 112, 334, V, 14, 18, 201, 207, VIII, 21; their incompetence, V, 12, 76, 134–5, 143–4, 518–19, IX, 15, 176
fearful for the safety of their establishment, III, 62, 75–6; cajoled by ministers, IV, 282, V, 15
their integrity allowed, III, 152, IV, 110, V, 134, 143, VI, 336
Remonstrance on resumption of cash payments, IV, 267–70, V, 9 & n., 14 n., VIII, 32 & n.
Resolution on resumption, V, 9 & n., VIII, 21 & n.
discounts, scale of, III, 358 & n., IV, 99, 279, 415–18, V, 12 & n.
dividend, in 1816, VII, 26
Lord King's idea to stop, while gold above mint price, VII, 262–3
reduced in 1822, VIII, 35 & n.
see also III, 95, IV, 103–6, VI, 277–8
gold, Ricardo's advice to sell, and reduce issues gradually (1819), V, 12–13, 105–6, 133; advice ignored, 207; unnecessary purchases, 76, 143–4, 199–200, IX, 140–1; issues too much restricted, IV, 231–2, V, 201, 312, see also V, 61–2
Governor of (1810), III, 193 n., 227–8; see also Dorrien, Harman, Mellish, Pearse, Samuel Thornton, John Whitmore
Grenfell's Resolutions on, 1815, IV, 76–7, 86, 136–7, VI, 242 & n., 276 & n.; his motion, 1816, IV, 51 n., VII, 22, 25–6 & n.
loans to government, V, 35–6, 60, 63, 129, 133, 143–4, VII, 252 & n., VIII, 27, 134–5 & n., see also V, 23
Mellish's Resolutions on, IV, 86–8 & n., 138–41, V, 465 n., VI, 305
moral argument against, IV, 93, VII, 5
number of clerks employed, IV, 83–4, 97, 290, VI, 276 & n., 282–3
Parliamentary papers on: 1808, IV, 54, 81, 89, 90; 1811, V, 462–3 n., VI, 281; 1815, IV, 77, 90, 91–2, VI, 257, 259–60, 266; see also Bank Restriction Act
power of forcing a circulation, III, 214–21, 336, 364, see also VI, 67
profits: calculation of, IV, 96–105, 119–35, V, 433, VI, 282–3, 285, VIII, 34–5; less than expected (1819), V, 14 & n., 62–3, VIII, 27; obligation to distribute, IV, 105–10, V, 463–4, VI, 268, 303, 313; see also V, 193

Bank of England (*cont.*)
proprietors, their timidity, VII, 15–16; kept in ignorance, IV, 113
services overpaid, IV, 76–95, V, 100, 247, VI, 313, 338
stock of, whether to invest in, VIII, 33–5, see also III, 95
Volunteer Corps, IV, 97 n.
Bank of France, IV, 234
Bank of Hamburg, III, 126, 175–6 n., 288, V, 358
Bank of Ireland, III, 370, 398, V, 70, 98–100, 143, VIII, 24
Bank of Scotland, III, 228
Bank Post Bills, III, 117, 123, VI, 259 & n., 260–1, 266 & n., 286
Bank rate, and market rate, V, 97 & n.; lowered to 4% (1822), V, 222–3
Bank reserves, not a fixed proportion of circulation, III, 312–13, 322, VI, 17
Bank Restriction Act, 1797:
report from Commons' Committee, IV, 100 n., V, 175, VI, 8 n.; from Lords' Committee, III, 33, 78 n., 163, 188–90, 238, 364 n., IV, 80 n., 119 n., 283 n., 415, V, 461–2
and depreciation of currency, III, 132, 416–18, V, 143, 217, 236–7
checks to over-issue removed by, III, 17, 78, V, 92
see also I, 368, III, 255, 367, V, 253, 313
Bank Restriction Continuance bill, 1816, IV, 51 n., V, 465, VII, 28, 30 & n., see also III, 400; in 1818, VII, 262
Lauderdale's Protest against, I, 371 n., VII, 265, 267, VIII, 3
The Bank—The Stock Exchange... An Exposé, 1821 (by J. Lancaster), X, 93–5 & notes, 123–4 & n.
Banks:
adventurers in, III, 335
compared with highways, III, 55
failures in Ireland, V, 70, 99
of credit and banks of deposit, III, 288, V, 437
Banks (*cont.*)
of issue, substitute for a gold mine, III, 54–5, 92, 215–17, 219, 376–7, provide a cheap currency, III, 55, 92 n., IV, 233–4, 276, 298, VII, 42
Scotch, III, 228, 235, 399, see also VI, xxxvii
see also Country banks
Bankes, Henry, M.P. for Corfe Castle:
on restrictions on the importation of corn, V, 176–80
on religion, V, 329 & n.
see also V, 351, IX, 176, 279
Bannister, John, X, 111
Barclay & Co., bankers, III, 373
Barclay the brewer, VII, 109
Barham, Joseph Foster, M.P., V, 189
Baring, Alexander, M.P. for Taunton:
advocates double standard, V, 45–6, 71, 74–8, 92–6, 106, VIII, 346–7, 349–50
presents merchants' petition, V, 42, VIII, 164, 183 n.; lukewarm friend of free trade, VIII, 197
criticises Ricardo on sinking fund, V, 102, and on capital tax, 265–7
moves for committee on cash payments, V, 105–8; his evidence, 93 n., 352 & n., 356, 358–9, 360–1, VIII, 18 n.; his loans to France and resumption, V, 352 n., VII, 292 n.
moves for reduction of sinking fund, V, 272–3
on law of principal and factor, V, 292
on increased output of silver, V, 391 n.
prefers no gold in circulation, V, 403 n.
see also V, xxv, 48–9, 56 n., 59, 86, 102–3, 247, 335, VI, 244, VIII, 74 n., 361, 378 n.
Baring, Sir Francis, evidence to bullion committee, III, 132, 147, 370–2, 428, X, 93
Baring, Henry, M.P., V, xxiii n.
Baring Brothers & Co., V, 352 n., 355, X, 80, 82, 93, 125

Barnard, Viscount, M.P. for Tregony, V, 185
Barnes, Anne, wife of Benjamin Ricardo, X, 59
Barnes, John, Ricardo's partner as loan-contractor, X, 79–81, 82 n., 125 n.
Barnett, L. D., *Bevis Marks Records,* X, 18 n., 26 n.
Barre, de la, affair, IX, 374
Barrett family, of Hope End, X, 267 n.; big loss in Jamaica, X, 350 & n.
Barrett, Samuel Moulton, M.P., X, 267 & n.
Barrow, John, VIII, 58
Barter, all trade finally a trade of, I, 228, II, 146, 154, VI, 109; see also I, 137, 142, IV, 214, and under Foreign Trade
Barton, C. E., *John Barton, a Memoir,* VII, 155 n.
Barton, John, letter to, VII, 155–9
  view that demand for labour depends only on circulating capital, VII, 157–9; later accepted by Ricardo, I, 395–6 n.
  see also I, lviii–lix, II, 234, 245 n.
  Observations on the Condition of the Labouring Classes, 1817, VII, 155 n., VIII, 171 n.
Basevi, George (or Joshua), sen., VII, 10 & n.
  Ricardo's oldest friend, VII, 336; early studies, X, 34–5
  his visits to Gatcomb, VI, 312, 325, VII, 306, 308, 317, 324
  projected visit to Paris with, in 1803, X, 117
  bequest to, X, 105
  see also VI, 112 n., 190, 245 n., VII, 14, X, 14–15, 50
Basevi, George, jun., architect, VI, 250 & n., IX, 104–5 & n., X, 15 n.
Basevi, Naphtali, visits Say in Paris, VI, 245 & n., 246, 250, 264, 270; see also VII, 336, 351
Bassett, Joseph Davie, VIII, 337–8 n.
  Elementary Thoughts on the Bullion Question, 1820, VIII, 337 n., IX, 135, 138–9, 156–7, 162, 164, 185, X, 400–1 n.
  Elementary Thoughts on the Principles of Currency and Wealth, 1830, VIII, 337 n.
Bath, visits to, VI, 161, VII, 15, 47, 71, 144, 307, VIII, 55, 329, IX, 101, 104, X, 7, 35–6; Malthus at, VI, 135, 139, 231, 234, 244, VII, 311, IX, 13; see also VI, 137, 157, VII, 55, 222
Bath Institution, VII, 23, 153
Bathurst, Earl, Secretary for War, V, 351, 354, 365
Battye, loan contractor, X, 82, 85
Baumstark, E., X, 377
Bautte, Jean-François, watchmaker, X, 270
Baveno, X, 291
Bayle, Pierre, *Dictionnaire historique et critique,* VII, 190, 196–7 & n., 206; extracts from, X, 393–4
  Pensées diverses, VIII, 49, X, 394
Bayley, Mary Ann, XI, xiii & n.
Bayley, Sarah, Elizabeth and Ann, VIII, 282, X, 350 & n.; letter to Miss Bayley, XI, xii
Bayley, Thomas, X, 350 n.
Beacon, newspaper, IX, 136 & n., 142, 187, 204, 207
Beattie, Dr James, VII, 277
Beaufort, Duke of: family influence in Gloucestershire, VIII, 62, 156, 162–3; hostility to Ricardo, VIII, 157 n.; see also VII, 187 n., 381–2
Beaufort, Francis, X, 167, 172, 174
Beaumont, Thomas Wentworth, M.P. for Northumberland, V, 185
Beauregard, Paul, X, 376
Bebb, Mr, V, 480
Becher, William Wrixton, M.P., V, 185
Beck and Allen, nurserymen, VII, 232
Beckett, S., letter to, XI, ix
Beer, VIII, 275, X, 198; duties on, V, 294–5, 301–2, 322, see also I, 252–4
Beer, Max, *History of British Socialism,* XI, xxviii n.
Beetroot, sugar from, IV, 248, V, 51, 91

Beggars: in Bologna, IX, 223, X, 312; in Flanders, VII, 164, much reduced in 1822, X, 184; in Ireland, VII, 175; in Leghorn, X, 321

Bellot, Pierre-François, X, 281 & n., see also IX, 220

Belsham, Thomas, Unitarian minister, VII, 171 & n.; Ricardo attends his chapel, X, 39–40; see also VII, 187, VIII, 56, 75 & n., 84

Belzoni, Giovanni, IX, 107 & n.

Benefit societies, VII, 12

Benett, John, M.P. for Wiltshire:
- presents agricultural petition, V, 148
- on import duties on corn, V, 173, 175, 181, 196 n.
- taxes on land, V, 131–2, 138, 257–8
- see also V, 129

Bennet, Henry Grey, M.P. for Shrewsbury:
- on timber imports, V, 103
- taxes and agricultural distress, V, 154
- depreciation of currency, V, 215, 216–17
- national debt reduction, V, 272–3
- wages and machinery, V, 302
- see also V, xxii, 277, IX, 165 n., 194, X, 351

Bentham, Jeremy, VI, xxviii–xxxi
- and Burdett's resolutions, V, 493
- Chrestomathic school, VI, 112, VIII, 191 n., 197–9 & notes, 212
- circulating annuities, VIII, 293–5
- on corruption, V, 507
- Ford Abbey, VI, 124–7; Ricardo's visit to, VI, 156 n., 157 & n., 161 & n.
- Benjamin Franklin's bust, IX, 228 & n.
- list of letters, IX, 393; other letters quoted, VI, 161 n., VII, 273 n.
- marginal contents, VI, 329 n.
- his political economy, III, 261 n.
- MS on profits, X, 388 n.
- Ricardo as disciple, V, xix, VI, xxviii, IX, 52, 239, 259, X, 35
- walks in Green Park, VIII, 191, in Hyde Park, VI, xxviii n., VII, 277
- see also VI, xv–xvi, xxxiii, xxxv, 48, 52, 60, 105–6, 136, 251, 264, 317, VII, 4, 14, 61, 75, 170, 182 n., 183, 192, 285, 355–6, VIII, 17 n., 57, 150, 186 n., 242, IX, 201 n., 219, 248 n., 253, 274
- *Chrestomathia,* 1816, VI, 112 n.
- *Plan of Parliamentary Reform,* 1817, VII, 261 & n., 263 & n., 270; 'Bentham made easy', 1818, VIII, 116 & n., and cp. 47
- *Table of the Springs of Action,* 1815, VI, 314 & n.
- *Tactique des assemblées législatives,* X, 399
- *Théorie des peines et des récompenses,* X, 399
- *Traité des preuves judiciaires,* 1823, X, 277 n.
- *Traités de législation,* X, 399
- *The True Alarm* (*Sur les prix*), 1810, III, 261–6, VI, 13–20; Ricardo's Notes on, III, 259–341
- *Works,* ed. J. Bowring, III, 262 n., 263 n., V, 493 n., VI, xxviii n., 106, 112 n., 161, VII, 74 n., 167 n., 273 n., VIII, 115 n., 116 n., 293–4 notes

Bentham-and-Mill school, IX, 52, 253, 259

Bentham, Sir Samuel, J. S. Mill's letter to, quoted, VII, 313 n., VIII, 198 & n., XI, xxvii; see also VI, 127

Bentinck, Lord William Henry Cavendish, M.P., motion on Sicilian affairs, V, xxii

Beranger, and Stock Exchange fraud, VI, 106

Berar and Scindia, Rajah of, VII, 243

Bergami, Bartolomeo, VIII, 304, X, 292–3 & n.

Berkeley, Colonel, VII, 221, 223–4, 335

Berkeley, George, his theory of ideas, VII, 229, 235 & n., see also 277
- *The Querist,* VIII, 353 & n., IX, 231

Berkhamstead, VI, 92

Berlin Decrees, III, 430 & n.

Bernal, Ralph, M.P. for Rochester, VIII, 157 n.

Berne, X, 261–3

Berrow, Ricardo's estate, X, 98, see also VII, 232 & n., 299 n., IX, 108, X, 105
Besterman, T., *The Publishing Firm of Cadell and Davies,* VI, 160 n.
Bex, X, 283
Biaujeaud, H., *Essai sur la théorie ricardienne de la valeur,* I, xxxviii n.
Bills of exchange:
transfer, never pay, a debt, III, 206, 246, IV, 332, VI, 80, see also III, 54
effect on prices, III, 323
and rate of exchange, I, 138–40, 146–9, VIII, 87–9
marketing of, in London, VIII, 37, 39
see also X, 29 n.
for other Bills see under Bank Post, Exchequer, Navy, Ordnance
Bimetallism, see Double standard
Binda, Giuseppe: pearls at an auction, VII, 54 n.; visits Gatcomb, VII, 56; sails to the Brazils, VII, 171–2, 276; see also VII, 114, 139, 144 n.
Bing, A., *Frankfurter Stadttheater,* X, 224 n.
Bingham Richards & Co., X, 318 n.
Binning, Lord, M.P. for Rochester, V, xxvi
Binns, Samuel Thomas, III, 345, 350
Birch, Joseph, M.P. for Nottingham, V, 185
Birkbeck, Morris: *Notes on a Journey in America,* 1818, VII, 257 & n., 259–60; *Letters from Illinois,* 1818, VII, 259 n.; see also VIII, 16 n.
Birmingham merchants' petition, V, 71
Birth control, see Artificial checks, Population, checks to, Prudential habits
Black Dwarf, VIII, 329 n.
Black, John, editor of the *Morning Chronicle,* IX, 201 & n.
Blackwood's Magazine:
on Ricardo's *Principles,* VII, 316 & n., 326, 332, 362
Blackwood's (*cont.*)
on McCulloch and the Scottish Whigs, VIII, 25 & n., 205 n., IX, 205–6 n.
Blair, Hugh, *Lectures on Rhetoric,* 1783, VI, 326 & n.
Blake, William, F.R.S., VI, 206 & n.
Observations on...the Course of Exchange, 1810, III, 173 n., 209–10, IX, 284 & n.
Observations on the Effects Produced by the Expenditure of Government, 1823, IV, 325; Ricardo's Notes on, with Blake's replies, IV, 323–52; Ricardo's unpublished review of, IV, 353–6; discussion of, IX, 271–2, 275–7, 284–7, 289, 293, see also 301 n., 312, 345, 362
letter to McCulloch, IX, 302
see also III, 11, IV, 396 n., V, 352, VII, 28–9, X, 49–50, 271, 392 n., 400 n.
Bland, Maria Teresa, X, 111
Blanqui, Jérôme Adolphe, X, 375–6, 380
Blasphemous Libels Act, V, xxii, VIII, 148 n.
Bleasdale, Lowless & Crosse, Ricardo's solicitors, V, xvii n., xviii n., VII, 306, 327, 382, X, 42, 98–9, 390
Block, Maurice, X, 376
Bloom, H. I., *Economic Activities of the Jews of Amsterdam,* X, 19 n.
Boats, at Gatcomb, VII, 51, 55–6, 68, 71, 76; Malthus's four-oar, VIII, 64
Boddington, Miss, V, 352
Boddington, Samuel, VII, 291 & n., see also V, 352, VI, xxxvi, VIII, 152 n.
Bognor, VII, 171
Bologna, X, 311–13; beggars, IX, 223, sausages, X, 303
Bolton Chronicle, XI, xi
Bonaparte, Louis, King of Holland, IX, 210
Bonaparte, Napoleon:
prevents export of corn from Russia, IV, 28; permits it from France to England, IV, 29

Bonaparte, Napoleon (*cont.*)
scheme for producing sugar from beet, V, 51, 90–1, VIII, 356
return from Elba, VI, 194 & n., 199, 229, X, 345–7, see also VI, 188, 344
Waterloo, VI, 231–2 & n., 235, 238, 280–1, X, 333
death, IX, 6, 12
anecdotes, X, 211
marks of his genius everywhere, X, 289, 299, see also IX, 221–2, 234
and *High Price of Bullion,* X, 374
see also VI, 255, VII, 267, IX, 247 n., X, 324, 335
Bonar, James, on the ingot plan, V, 369; see also II, xiv n., III, 406, IV, 415, VI, xx–xxi, 159 n., VIII, 35 n., IX, 174 n., X, 370, 371, 399
Bonazza ('Banasso'), X, 307
Bonelli, Vincenzo, his bust of Ricardo, V, 1, X, 53 & n., 318 & n.
Bonn, X, 217
Book society, VIII, 134
Bookers of Edmonton, coachmakers, VI, 131
Booth, Thomas, letter to, XI, xiii
Borghetto, X, 327, 345
Bornsteinowa, M., X, 379
Borough system, V, 509
Mallett on, VII, 254 n.
vested rights in, V, 285
boroughmongers, VIII, 74 n.
Scots burgh system, VIII, 326
Whig boroughs, VIII, 336
Borromeo, Count, X, 291
Bosanquet, Charles, *Practical Observations on the Report of the Bullion Committee,* 1810, III, 10–11, 159 & n., X, 400, ed. 2, with Supplement, III, 204 n., 247 & n.; Ricardo's *Reply to,* III, 155–256
Bosanquet, Jacob, East India Director, VII, 135–6, 139
Bossi, Giuseppe, X, 301 & n.
Bounties, I, 301–26
Adam Smith on, I, 304–10, see also VII, 100, 107–8
divert capital, I, 314, 339
Bounties (*cont.*)
drawbacks and, distinguished, IV, 243–4
on export of corn, I, 301–4, when justified, VIII, 359; on export of manufactures, I, 312–14, of Irish linen, V, 57–8 & notes
on production of corn, I, 321–5, of other commodities, 325–6
see also I, 142, 179
Bourbons, VI, 235
Bourne, William Sturges, M.P. for Christchurch:
his committee on the poor laws, VII, 209 n.
poor rates misapplication bill, V, 1, 6–7, VIII, 25, 74 n.
settlement of the poor bill, VIII, 30, 32
see also V, xxiv, 86
Bouverie and Antrobus, bankers, VI, 277 n.
Bouverie, Philip Pleydell, VI, 277 & n.
sides with Ricardo at Bank Court, IV, 106, V, 463, 466–7, VI, 335 n., 336
see also VII, 11, 15–16, 19 n.
Bow, VI, 84, VII, 80, X, 24–5, 36
Bowles, John, *Provident Institutions,* 1817, VII, 130
Bowood, VII, 191, 198 & n., 284, 311, X, 37 n.
Bowring, John, X, 58
Autobiographical Recollections, VI, xxviii, IX, 228 n., X, 73–4
see also Bentham, J., *Works*
Boyd, Benfield & Co., loan contractors, X, 75 n.
Boyd, Walter, banker, III, 364 n., VI, 9 & n.; *Letter to W. Pitt,* 1801, III, 4, 261–2 & n.
Bradford, Wilts, VI, 100 & n.
Brady, A., *William Huskisson,* III, 427 n.
Brand, T., M.P., IV, 5 n.
Brandon, Raphael, X, 25 n.
Brassage, V, 431
Bray, Miss, VII, 253
Bray, Mrs (Malthus's sister), VI, xx n., 322, VII, 265

Bray, R., VI, 322
Bray, R. A., II, xiii n., VI, xx n.
Brazils, V, 477, VII, 171–2, 276
Bread:
  early view that tax on, raises price of every commodity, III, 270; later view, I, 302; see also under Price
  demand for, not affected by price, I, 385, nor by tax, I, 237 n.
  as measure of value, X, 185
  price regulated by loaf that pays no rent, II, 42–4, IX, 171–2
Breakfast parties at Ricardo's: Maria Edgeworth, IX, 230 & n., X, 172–3; Grote, VI, xxxiv; Malthus, VI, xix, 28–9, 31, 77, VII, 35; Mill, VI, xxxiv, VII, 188; Mushet, VI, 88; Sharp, VI, xix, 28–9, 31, 77; Trower, VIII, 19, 345
Breda, gentlemanly bookseller at, X, 193–4
Brescia, X, 300–2
Brieg, X, 285, 288
Brientz, Lake of, X, 255
Bright, Henry, M.P. for Bristol, V, 306–7
Brighton, Ricardo family at, in 1795, X, 109–12; in 1810, X, 118; in 1820, VIII, 206, 213; in 1823, IX, 279–80
  see also VIII, 318, X, 336
Brinsop Court and Manor of Brinsop, Ricardo's property, VII, 217, X, 98, 105
British Press, newspaper, V, 31 n., 81 n., 93 n., 97 n., VIII, 357
British Review:
  review of Ricardo's *Principles* and Say's *Traité,* I, li, 60–1 n., VII, 219, 222, 229, 231, 235, 256, 259, 289 n.
  on Poor Law report, 1817, VII, 219, 248–9
Broad Street Buildings, family home at the time of Ricardo's birth, X, 29 & n.
Broadley, John, letters, VII, 39–44
  his Ledger pound, VII, 44
  Pandora's Box, 1801, VII, 39 n.
Brodie, John, agriculturist, IV, 260
Broglie, Duc de, IX, 242 n.
  supports Ricardo against Sismondi, IX, 218, 235, 242–3, 248, X, 277–8, 281–2, and against Bentham, III, 261 n.
  Souvenirs 1785–1870, IX, 242 n.
  see also VIII, 224, IX, 219–20, 230, 236, X, 178, 269, 351
Broglie, Duchesse de, IX, 218, 235, 243, 248, X, 277–9
Bromesberrow, Manor of, Ricardo's property, VII, 232 n., X, 97, 98, 104 & n.
Bromesberrow Place, X, 97, Osman Ricardo's residence, VIII, 48–9
  Mill prefers it to Gatcomb, VIII, 51, 231
  Ricardo papers at, I, viii, II, xv
  see also VI, xxxii, IX, 27, 37, 41, 90, 101, 104, 115 n., 263, X, 64, 386
Bromley and St Leonard Volunteers, Ricardo captain in, X, 47, XI, ix
Brook Street, see Upper Brook Street
Brooksbank, Thomas, VI, 43 n.
Brooks's club, VIII, 28 & n., 163, X, 50; *Memorials of Brooks's,* VIII, 28 n., X, 50 n.
Brougham, Henry, M.P. for Winchelsea, later Lord Brougham:
  sketch of Ricardo, V, xxxii; calls him 'an oracle', V, 40, 'dropped from the clouds', V, 56, 85
  negotiations for Ricardo's seat, V, xvi–xvii, VII, 293, 300, 304, 306–7, 355, 358–9, 362–3, 371, 373, VIII, 326–7
  on Owen's plan, V, 30, 32
  opposes Ricardo's plan for capital tax, V, 40, 268, VIII, 239
  advocates reduction of taxation, V, 124–7 & n., 132–3, 137
  on usury laws, V, 335
  on effect of agricultural taxes, IV, 239–40 & n., V, 131
  on Ricardo's resolutions on agriculture, V, 176, 177–8, 182
  Report on education of the poor, VII, 150 n., 303–4 & n., 306, X, 262 n.

Brougham, Henry (*cont.*)
model infant school, VII, 356–7 & n., 359–60, 363, 371
travels in Italy, VII, 61, 74
scandal about him, VII, 84, 86
vacillations on reform, VII, 266–7, 274, 303
his bad political economy, IX, 164, 167, 207
see also I, 269 n., V, xxiii, 86, 185, 302 n., VI, 127, 180, 280, VII, 89, 179 n., 285, 305, 382, VIII, 59, 63–4, 148, 196, 204, 289, 328, IX, 197, 265, X, 41 n., 50
Historical Sketches of Statesmen, V, xxxii–xxxiv, X, 53
Broughton, Lord, *Recollections of a Long Life,* X, 36 n., 228 n., 273 n. See Hobhouse, John Cam
Brown, James, letters, VIII, 94–104, see also X, 391 n.
Brown, Thomas, VI, 113 n.
Browne, Denis, M.P. for Kilkenny, V, 87
Brunnen, X, 245–8
Brussels, X, 187–90
Bruttini, Dr (?Butini), IX, 218, X, 271
Buchanan, David: his edition of *Wealth of Nations,* with Notes and an additional volume, 1814, VI, 159 & n.; Ricardo re-reads, VII, 101, 115, VIII, 4; Mill on, VII, 108; McCulloch on, VII, 353, IX, 206
bounties, I, 314–15
debased currency, I, 355–6, 370
rent, I, 77 n., 398–9, 400, II, 119, VII, 120
taxes on raw produce, I, 251–4, on wages, 218–20
wages and price of provisions, I, 216–18, 315, 382
see also I, 106 n., 334, II, 105, VII, 279, 316 n., X, 399
Buchanan's articles on Ricardo in *Caledonian Mercury,* IX, 206 & n.
Buckingham, Duke of, *Memoirs of George IV,* V, xxiii n.
Buckland, C. S. B., *Metternich and the British Government,* III, 432–4 notes
Budget, speeches on, (1819) V, 20; (1820) 63; (1821) 115; (1822) 220; (1823) 248
Bulky commodities and foreign trade, I, 144, II, 86, VI, 22, 27, IX, 81, 98, 285
Bullion:
its value regulated like any other commodity, VI, 24–5
effects of peace and war on price of, VI, 344
Bullion Controversy, III, 3–12, see also VII, 246
Price of Gold, Ricardo's letters on, III, 13–46
High Price of Bullion, III, 47–99
Horner's motion for committee, VI, xxxiv–xxxv, IX, 123 n., X, 8, 14–15, 92; letter to Horner, VI, 1–7
Bullion Report, 1810, III, 8, IV, 416–18; recommends reducing circulating medium, III, 142–3
Malthus's review, III, 10–12, 99–114, 120–3, VI, 50 & n., takes middle course, II, 150–1
Ricardo's *Three Letters* on, III, 129–53; his Notes on, III, 345–78
Reply to Bosanquet, III, 155–256
Mill's paper on, VI, 49–50, 60; Malthus on Mill's paper, VI, 61–2
see also III, 116, 118, 123–4, 295, 380, 385–6, 392–3, 397–401, 427–34, IV, 99, V, 461–2, VI, 43, VIII, 89 & n., 140, IX, 289, X, 399, 401
Horner's Resolutions, III, 413 & n., 414
Vansittart's Counter-resolutions, III, 413–14 & n., Ricardo's Observations on, III, 415–23
'Bullion Committee' of 1819, V, xxxii, VIII, 152 n.; see Resumption of Cash Payments
Bullion merchants, III, 71, 73, 140, 165, VI, 90
Bullion plan, Ricardo's, IV, 65–73; see Ingot plan
Bullionists, II, 150–1, VI, 328, 343–4

Buonaparte, Napoleon, IV, 28–9, V, 51, VI, 229, 235. See Bonaparte
Burdett, Sir Francis, M.P. for Westminster, VI, 181 & n.
resolutions for reform in 1818, V, 493 n., VII, 266 & n., see also VIII, 47 n.
election, 1818, VII, 269–70 & n. see also V, xxii, 169, 170, 474, 484, VII, 273 n., 274, 307 n., VIII, 6, 59, IX, 268, X, 397, XI, xxii
Burgess, H., project for an extra post, V, 148
Burke, Edmund, VIII, 385
Thoughts on the Cause of the Present Discontents, 1770, VII, 261
Works, X, 397
Burning of corn in the country, VII, 45, 49
Burton, J. Hill, *Letters of Eminent Persons to David Hume,* XI, xxvii
Bury Court, Manor of, Ricardo's property, X, 97, 104
Bury street, St Mary Axe, Ricardo's childhood home, X, 30, 36
Bushe, Charles Kendal, IX, 274
Butcher's meat, I, 424, VIII, 99, 103, see also 371–2
Butini, Dr Pierre, X, 271 n., and cp. IX, 218
Butler, Harold Edgeworth, I, xi, VI, xxxiii, VIII, 56 n., X, x, 33 n., 167, XI, xxvii
Butler, Mrs Harriet J., VI, xxxiii, IX, 203, XI, xxvii
Butterworth, Joseph, M.P. for Dover, V, 330 n.
Buxton, Thomas Fowell, M.P. for Weymouth and Melcombe Regis, defends Spitalfields Acts, V, 295, 296, 306, 307
Memoirs, 1848, X, 90 n.
Byron, Lord, his house in Venice, X, 309; see also VII, 131 n., IX, 199 n.

Cadenabbia, IX, 221, X, 292
Caff, Mr, IX, 116 & n.
Cairnes, John Elliott, I, ix, VI, xvii–xviii & n., X, 391
Calais, VII, 160, X, 182–4
Calas affair, IX, 374
Calcraft, John, M.P. for Rochester, later for Wareham, V, 84, 89, 109, VII, 252
Caledonian Mercury, IX, 206 n.
Calvert, Nicolson, M.P. for Hertford, V, 183
Cambridge: visit to Osman Ricardo at, X, 136–40; David jun. at, VIII, 284, 293, 297; see also VI, 31 & n., IX, 280 n.
Cambridge University Library, Ricardo MSS at, X, 386
Camden, Lord, X, 169
Campbell, Lord, *Life,* V, xxviii n.
Campbell, Miss, X, 272 n.
Campbell, Thomas, VIII, 152 n.
Campolongo, A., X, 355
Canada: distress in, V, 144–5; emigration to, XI, xv n.; timber trade, V, 104, 306; see also X, 395
Canals, I, 133, 152, 251, II, 368, V, 32, VIII, 155; in Venice, IX, 222, X, 309
Canard, N. F., *Principes d'économie politique,* X, 399
Cancels in first edition of *Principles,* I, xxviii–xxx, X, 403–4, XI, xxx
Candide, VII, 102
Candles, duties on, IV, 257, V, 146–7; as necessaries of labourers, I, 20, 104, 224, 234, 275, 306
Cannan, Edwin:
A Review of Economic Theory, I, xxv, xxxvi, xxxviii, xl, 20 n.
History of the Theories of Production and Distribution, VII, 3 n.
The Paper Pound of 1797–1821, III, 427
'Ricardo in Parliament', V, xxii–xxiii, 490
review of *Notes on Malthus,* II, xvi
Canning, George, M.P., President of the India Board till Jan. 1821, Foreign Secretary from Sept. 1822:
on corn bill, V, 195
reform of Parliament, V, 285–8

Canning, George (*cont.*)
in committee on resumption of cash payments, V, 350, 354, 365
his eloquence in debate, VIII, 148
resigns from Government on Queen's trial, VIII, 326 & n.
the King bars him from Cabinet, IX, 115, 120, 124
and Governorship of India, IX, 116–17 & n., 146–7, 182 n., 215
see also III, 413 n., 432, V, xix n., 197, 250 n., VII, 51 & n., 305, VIII, 20, 68 & n., IX, 270 n., X, 305
Capadose, Dr Abraham, X, 210–11 & n., *Conversion de M. Capadose,* 1837, X, 207 n.
Capadose, Dr Immanuel, X, 32, 210–11
Capital:
defined, I, 95
accumulation of, I, 131, II, 391, 417, V, 438, VIII, 102–3, see also II, 315, VI, 16–17, 164
due to productive consumption, not to non-consumption, I, 150–1 & n., II, 326–7
profit as motive for, I, 122, 290, 334, 411, II, 310–11, 331, IV, 16 n., 35, VI, 121; foreign trade as incentive to, I, 133
effects on profits, I, 126, 289–96, II, 221–2, V, 137, VI, 95, 103–5, 146–9, 162, VIII, 208–9; curious effect on rent and profits, IV, 16
limited by diminishing returns from land, I, 98, II, 302, 321, IV, 179
impeded by taxation, I, 152 & n., 160, 166, VIII, 168–70
not affected by depreciation of money, III, 273
never injurious to a country, II, 329, 365, 438, V, 118, VIII, 217; still advantageous in England, III, 274; increased in spite of war, I, 151, V, 95, VI, 94–5
and power to employ labour, I, 79, 95, 104, II, 352–3, V, 501, VI, 148, VIII, 258, 270

Capital (*cont.*)
Malthus's most objectionable chapter, VIII, 181, 185, 212, 378
agricultural capital, I, 117, 269, VI, 226; security and respectability of, IV, 38
and free import of corn, I, 269 n., IV, 32–3, 242, 248–9, V, 83–6, 88–90, 256, VIII, 108, 130
and manufacturing capital, I, 76 n.
in revulsions of trade, I, 266–71
apportionment of capital between trades, I, 88–91
arena for the employment of, II, 140, 293, VI, 103 & n., 104
circulating and fixed: distinguished, I, 31, 52 & n., 150, 207, 266; proportions of, I, 396 n.
circulating: demand for labour depends on, II, 234, see also I, 95; wages as, I, 32, 52
fixed capital: curious effect of wage-rise on products of, VII, 82–3, 98 and cp. I, 35, 43
does not reduce employment (early view), VII, 157–9; Barton's contrary view accepted, I, 395–6 n.
motives for substitution of fixed for circulating capital, VIII, 389
effect of substitution of labour for, II, 237–9
definition of fixed capital extended, IV, 312, see also 306
constant and variable, IV, 306
demand for, unlimited, VI, 301, 318, see also I, 293–4
diminution, effects of, I, 78, 165, VI, 110–11, 113–14, 116–17, 119–21, 123, 142
distribution of a country's, I, 154, 267, IV, 32, 35, V, 501, VI, 345, of world capital, I, 172
emigration of, I, 136–7, 247–8, III, 274
encouraged by high price of corn, IV, 16 n., 237, V, 33, 38, 50, by low rate of interest, VII, 171, by taxation, II, 452
in 1820–1, VIII, 152–3 n., 353, 357–8, 364–5

Capital (*cont.*)
floating capital, I, 89
whether a capital employs as much labour in foreign as in home trade, I, 350–1
labour and capital cannot both be redundant, II, 241, 339, 426–7, VIII, 181, 185, 278
Malthus's view that the proportion of capital to labour determines profits, VII, 52, 69, 77, 80, 215; opposed by Ricardo, VII, 57, 72, 78–9, 81–2
measure of capital, VI, 249, 272, 274
equal capitals and equal value of products, I, 42, 62 n., 207, IV, 307, 309–15, VII, 315 n.
difficulty of defining equal capitals, IV, 393–5, IX, 357, 359–60 & n.
mobility of, I, 134, 136–7, 191–2, 268–9 & nn., II, 87, 351, IV, 25, 28
capital not increased by increase of money, I, 143, III, 390
capital and money, proportion between, III, 54, 92–3
that pays no rent, I, 72, 74, 110, 328–9, 412–13 n., II, 73, 166–7, 172, IV, 38, 240, VI, 177, 198, VII, 372, VIII, 4, 149
proportion of, to population, V, 32; see also under Wages
of the stockholder not productive, I, 249 n.
Capital punishment, V, xxi
Capitalist, I, 90–1, 136, 424–6, II, 62, III, 165, IV, 230–1, V, 32, IX, 13, of the mine, I, 197–8
capitalists and cheap corn, IV, 35; and monopolies, II, 409
Capper, Henry, X, 55
Card, Mrs, milliner in Pall Mall, X, 145, 148, 151–3, 157–8
Carli, Tommaso, banker in Milan, IX, 224
Carlile, Mary Ann, speech for her release, V, 277–80, see also 325 n., XI, xxiii
Carlile, Richard, prosecution of, V, 325
Carlile, R. (*cont.*)
publishes Ricardo's letter in *The Republican,* XI, xxii n.
see also V, 277, 330 n.
Carlsruhe, VII, 163–5, X, 229
Caroline, Queen (till 1820 Princess of Wales):
notices Ricardo's child, X, 112
her residence on Lake Como, IX, 221, X, 292–5
her trial, V, 69, VIII, 199–200, 206, 220–1, 223, 226, 230, 237, 250, 259, 276, 284, 287–91, 314, 335, 347
barred from Coronation, IX, 30 & n.
a 'persecuted woman', VIII, 299, 303–4
popular support for, V, 469, VIII, 241–4, 295–6; higher and middle classes further separated, VIII, 308
her death and funeral, IX, 38–9, 41, 69 n., 88 & n.
see also V, 64 n., VII, 208 n., VIII, 324, 326 n., IX, 6, 12, 115
Carriages:
Malthus's low gig, VI, 130, 131, 133
low phaeton, VIII, 231–2, X, 240
carriage for the Continent, X, 177, 188–9, 197
barouche, X, 231–2
covered carriage, X, 261
charabanc, X, 250, 273
duc de Broglie's equipage, X, 281
see also I, 242, V, 148, VII, 82, 254, IX, 377, X, 208, 306, 319, 347
Carrington, Lord and Lady, X, 169–70, see also VII, 356
Carruthers, Mr, V, 477
Carrying trade, I, 293–4, 349, V, 102, 305, VI, 93
Carter, John, M.P., V, 185
Cash accounts in Scotland, I, 365–6
Cash payments bill, see Resumption of cash payments
Cassel, VII, 160, X, 183
Castlereagh, Viscount, Foreign Secretary:
in committee on resumption, V, 350, 354, 365

Castlereagh (*cont.*)
and Catholic question, VIII, 362
see also V, 17, 28, 86, 124, VIII, 374
from 1821, see Londonderry, Marquis of
Catholic emancipation, see Roman Catholics
Cato Street plot, VIII, 163 & n.
Cattle: that pay no rent, II, 70, 73; fall in value of (1822), V, 164, IX, 166; see also VIII, 371–2
Cattley, Stephen, V, 461
Cavendish, Lord George, M.P. for Derbyshire, X, 302, 305, 327
Cavendish-Bentinck, see Bentinck
Cazenove, John: *Reply to Mr Say's Letters to Mr Malthus,* 1820 (anon.), annotated by Ricardo, X, 405–10; see also X, 401 n., XI, xxx
The Evidence that WOULD *have been given by Mr* ——, 1832 (anon.), III, 428 n.
Chambers, William Cecil, evidence before bullion committee, III, 362–4, 429 n.
Chambéry, X, 340
Chamonix (Chamouny), X, 273–5
Champion, The, Torrens's newspaper, IX, 113–14 & n., 120, 122
Chancellor of the Exchequer (N. Vansittart till Jan. 1823, thereafter F. J. Robinson):
on public deposits and Bank profits, IV, 83, 87 n., 90, VI, 334
defends sinking fund, V, 5
on resumption of cash payments, V, 8, 91
denies leakage, V, 18–19
announces new loan, V, 20–2
on reduction in currency, V, 23
moves for new taxes, V, 23
on Owen's plan, V, 30
lowering of import duties, V, 57
criticised by Ricardo over Budget and sinking fund, V, 63–5, 67–8, 115–19, 138–9, 220–2, 259–65
on integrity of sinking fund, V, 79, 194
Chancellor (*cont.*)
commutation of Navy five per cents, V, 140–1
financial situation of the country, V, 248, 250 n.
new sinking fund, V, 266, 271
on condition of the people, V, 492 n.
negotiations for loans, X, 75–6, 78, 81–3, 85–90
see also II, 433, IV, 227, V, 35, 58, 61, 70, 96, 105, 108, 129, 145, 148, 156, 247, 301, 335, VI, 261, VII, 116 n., 252 n., 292 n., VIII, 29–30, 134 n., 332, IX, 291 n.
Chandler, Elizabeth, see Smith, Mrs Thomas
Chandler, Mrs, VIII, 63 n., 75
Channel of circulation, III, 148–50
Channel of currency, III, 219
Charities, I, 73 & n., VII, 248, see also VIII, 171, XI, xvi
Charlotte, Princess, VII, 207–8, 218
Charlotte, Queen, VII, 222 n., 372
Charterhouse, Osman at, X, 61; David jun. at, VI, 128 n., 239, X, 62
Chatham, Lord, VIII, 74 n.
Chaumette, L. A. de la, VI, 112 n.
Cheap currency, IV, 234, VI, 36, 41–2, VII, 42; see also Redundancy of currency
Checks, banker's, III, 237, IV, 58, whether included in money, III, 298; checks issued upon the government, V, 39
Cheltenham, visits to, VI, 135, 161, VII, 70, 358, 361; see also VIII, 243–4
Chepstow, VIII, 231, IX, 27
Chernishev, D. R., X, 382
Chesterfield, Lord, IX, 105
Chetwynd, George, M.P., IX, 181
Cheyt Sing, VII, 237
Children employed in the Manufactories, report on, 1816, VII, 146, 150
Chillon, IX, 220
Chinard, G., *Jefferson et les Idéologues,* X, 372
Chlenov, S. B., X, 383

Chrestomathic School:
Bentham's plan for, VI, xxviii–xxxi, 112 n.
subscriptions to, VI, 112–13 n.
buying ground for, VII, 184, 190, 198 & n., VIII, 191 n.
plan abandoned, VIII, 197–9 & notes
see also VI, xxxvi & n., 127, VII, 182 n., VIII, 212, IX, 58 n.
Christian VIII, IX, 195 n.; see Denmark, Crown Prince of
Christians' petition for free discussion, V, 324, XI, xxiv
Chuan Shih Li, X, 385
Church and State breed, VII, 211, see also VIII, 284
Circulating annuities, VIII, 293–5
Circulating medium, III, 74
real amount of, III, 143, IV, 58
distribution of, III, 120–2
checks and bonds not included, III, 298
see also Money
Clarendon, Lord, *History of the Rebellion,* IX, 45
Clarens, IX, 220
Clark, J. M., article on Distribution, IV, 6 n.
Classes:
higher, influence of, at elections, V, 485
rich class, existence of, ensured by rent, IX, 126
middle classes: not created by national debt, II, 444–5; their exertions justly praised, IX, 55; see also VIII, 308, 314
inferior class of tradesmen, their votes influenced by threats, V, 285
working classes: combination laws unjust to, VIII, 316; often calumniated, IX, 54–5 & n.; see also IV, 347, V, 303, 308, XI, xxi, and Labouring classes
struggle between rich and poor, IX, 42, 45
Clerk, George Russell, student of Malthus, VI, 240 & n., 291, 295, VII, 114
Clerk, Mr, VI, 240
Cleves, X, 213
Clive, E. B., V, 471
Clubs of London, The, 1828, VI, 87 n.
Clubs, Ricardo's, X, 49–51
Clutterbuck, Account of the Family of, by M. Witchell and C. Huddleston, X, 62 n.
Clutterbuck, Daniel, X, 62, 96 n., 162
Clutterbuck, Edmund, VIII, 243
Clutterbuck, Henrietta, see Ricardo, Henrietta
Clutterbuck, James, VIII, 243–4
Clutterbuck, Thomas (D.R.'s son-in-law), X, 62; buys Hardenhuish Park, X, 315–16; see also VI, 100, 219, 312, 323–5, VII, 48, 84, 110, 262, 269, 304, VIII, 56, 183, 329, IX, 44–5, 103, X, 12, 162, 261, 319, 348, 352
Coaches:
Bath and Exeter, VI, 127, 157, 320
Brighton Slap-bang, X, 110
Salisbury mail, VII, 148
Gloucester mail, XI, ix–x
London to Gatcomb, VII, 277, 331, VIII, 310
see also VI, 186, 242, 281, 285, 299, 302, VIII, 211
Coal duties, V, 275
Coal mines, I, 68, 330–2, V, 218, see also II, 22, X, 99; coal hewers, VIII, 99
Cobbett, William:
first clash with Ricardo, III, 26 & n.; dubs him the 'Oracle', V, 40–1 n.; continues attacks, VIII, 74 & n., IX, 140–1 & n., 228, 250, 266–7 & n.
dispute with Burdett, VIII, 6 & n.
on Tooke, IX, 106 & n.
defends use of machinery, V, 302–3 & n.
on gold as standard, IX, 123 & n.
the all-devouring monster (the fundholder), IV, 229 & n.
advises hoarding sovereigns, IX, 166–7 & n., 176 & n.

Cobbett, William (*cont.*)
see also II, 360 n., V, xxv, 166 n., VII, 75, VIII, 314, 317, IX, 120, 153, 265 & n., X, 185, 333 n.
Cobbett's Parliamentary Register, 1820, V, xxix n., 43 n., 48 n., 64 n.
Cobbett's Weekly Political Register, III, 26 n., IV, 229 n., V, xxvii, 41 n., 302 n., VIII, 74 n., 144 n., IX, 106 n., 123 n., 141 n., 166 n., 167 n., 176 n., 250 n.
Coblentz, VII, 165, IX, 211–12, X, 218–21
Coburg, Prince of, VIII, 347
Cochrane, Lord, and hoax on the Stock Exchange, VI, 106–7, VII, 62–3 & notes, IX, 111 & n., see also X, 41 n., 69, 124
The Trial of Lord Cochrane, 1814, X, 399
see Dundonald, Earl of
Cockburn, H., *Memorials of his Time,* VIII, 167 n., IX, 136 n., 187 n.
Cockerell, Samuel Pepys, architect employed by Ricardo, VII, 17–18 & n., X, 48
Codrington, Sir Edward, V, 352, X, 189–90
Coin:
law against exporting or melting gold coin, III, 18, 24, 25 n., 56, 60, 63, 125–6, 187–9, 415–16, V, 381, 430–1, 511–12, VI, 2; repealed in 1819, V, 490
silver coins legal tender till 1816, I, 368–9 & n., 371 n., V, 16–17 & n., VIII, 3
resumption of cash payments and gold coinage, V, 97, 206, 255, VIII, 21, 39, IX, 202
recoinage: of 1695, failure of, III, 202, see also III, 31, 69, 141, 177, V, 215, VIII, 24; of 1774, III, 32, 40, 70 n.; of 1816, V, 386–7, X, 201
see also III, 36–7, 68–9, IX, 201–2
Coke, Thomas William, M.P. for Norfolk, his Sheep Shearing, IX, 46; see also IX, 265
Cologne, VII, 160, X, 215; pont volant at, X, 216; see also IX, 209, 211
Colonial trade, I, 338–46
cannot affect rate of profits, I, 344–5, VII, 202
restrictions on, V, 144–5, 188–90, 298, IX, 130–1
see also Canada, Sugar
Colquhoun, Patrick, *Treatise on the Wealth of the British Empire,* 1814, VIII, 94
Colthurst, Sir Nicholas Conway, M.P. for Cork, V, 218
Combermere, Lord, X, 185
Combination of workmen, effect on wages, VII, 203 & n.
Combination laws, opposed by Ricardo, V, xx, 332, VIII, 313, 316, 338, IX, 55 & n., 61; see also V, 296
Commerce:
adds to utility, not to value, I, 264 n., II, 389–95, see also I, 271
profits of, regulated by profits of agriculture, IV, 23–4, VI, 167, 170
more liable to stagnation than agriculture, IV, 254–5
see also Foreign trade, Trade
Commerce, treaties of, I, 340–2
Commercial distress, 1819, speech on, V, 37–41; see also Distress
Committees, parliamentary:
on which Ricardo served, V, xxiii–xxv. See Accounts, public; Agricultural, 1821; Agricultural, 1822; Ireland, labouring poor in; Law Merchant; Poor law; Sewers; Stationery
to which he gave evidence, see Resumption of cash payments; Usury laws
other parliamentary committees, see Agricultural, 1820; Bullion; Corn laws; Corn trade; Finance; Foreign trade; Poor laws; Wine trade

Commodities:
are purchased with commodities, II, 395, see also 308 n., 393, IV, 214
whose only merit is their high cost in labour, II, 357–8
commodities generally (in general), I, 228 n., IV, 61, V, 374, IX, 79; see also Mass of commodities
Community of goods (Owen), IV, 222, V, 31, VIII, 46
Como, and Lake of, X, 292–7, see also IX, 224
Comparative costs and foreign trade, I, 133–41
Competition:
sinks prices to cost of production, I, 387, II, 24–5, 38, V, 189, VI, 24, VIII, 277, see also I, 12, 91, III, 390
domestic, and export prices, II, 153, IX, 96, 98
of capitals, and profits, III, 92, 143, 165, see also I, 62, IV, 24, VII, 69, 77
of employers for labour, I, 163, 220–1
fairest for public contracts, V, 59, for wages, I, 105, VIII, 316
see also I, 342, VI, 25, 129, 203
Complete Peerage, V, xv n.
Comte, Charles, VI, xxvii
Condorcet, *Life of Turgot,* VII, 365, 382, X, 399
Coningham, William, III, 370
Constable, Archibald, bookseller, IV, 145, VII, 316 n.
Constancio, Francisco Solano, translator of *Principles* into French, VII, 361 n., VIII, 161, 225 n., X, 374–6, 379
Constantinides, N. P., X, 355
Consumers, taxes on commodities fall on, I, 157, 159–60, 205, 252–4, 256–7, IV, 33–4 n., 240, V, 74, 136–7, VI, 173, VII, 94; see also II, 405–6
Consumption:
limited only by production, I, 151 n., II, 305–6, IV, 178, V, 435, VI, 164, VIII, 181, IX, 13; Malthus's contrary view, II, 307, VIII, 216, IX, 16, 20–1; see also V, 111, 219
effect on, of taxes on food, I, 237 n.
unproductive consumption, no more stimulating than a fire, II, 421; discussions with Malthus on, II, 421–5, 433–6, VIII, 185, 301, 311, IX, 10–11, 15–17, 19–26; by labourers, or by employers, different effects (Malthus), IX, 22; see also I, 150–1 & n., IX, 27 n.
Continental Merchant, see 'Mr ——'
Continental tour of Ricardo, with his brother in 1817, VII, 160–5, 167–8, 178, X, 343, 347; with his family in 1822, IX, 208–51, X, 175–352
Continuation, see Time bargains
Cooke, Edward, *Address to the Public,* 1819, V, 365 & n.
Cooke, W. H., *History of the County of Hereford,* X, 98
Cooper, C. H., *Annals of Cambridge,* VI, 31
Coplestone, Edward, *Second Letter to Peel,* 1819, X, 391; article 'State of the Currency', 1822, IX, 249
Copley, J. S., V, 250 n.; see *Administration of the Affairs of Great Britain*
Copper, IV, 374, VI, xxxiii n., X, 388
Coppet, visit to Duc de Broglie at, IX, 218, 235–6, 242–3, 248, X, 269, 277–80
Corn:
whether a better standard of value than gold, V, 164, 166–7, 210–13, 237–9, 313
imports of, effect on profits, II, 222, IV, 22–3, 26–7, VIII, 208–9, 357–8, on rents, I, 421 n., 427–8, IV, 35, 38–9, 41
corn that pays no rent, VII, 379, see also II, 73, 166, 182–3, IV, 240, VIII, 194
see also Agriculture, Food, Raw produce

Corn, price of:
regulated on land that pays no rent, I, 74, 110, 156, 176, 225, 329, II, 70, 73
and rate of profits, I, 113–14, 120, 132, II, 125, 217–18, IV, 26, 37, 237, V, 50, VI, 168, 194, 210, 291
price of, and value of, distinguished, IV, 235–6
real labour, or natural, value of, I, 323
natural price of, I, 301; see also under Natural price
high price, and difficulty of growing, I, 113, 145–6, 312, IV, 19, 265, V, 167, VI, 220, VIII, 209; and scarcity of fertile land, VI, 181
advantages of high price (Malthus), VI, 231, 236, 255–6; disputed, IV, 212–13, VI, 233–4, 241, 269; advantages of low price, I, 270, 424–6, II, 412–13, IV, 239
cheap corn, and ability to pay taxes, I, 8, 421–4, IV, 39–40, VII, 104; Ricardo's riddle, V, 83, 88–9
whether all prices regulated by, IV, 21 n.; see also under Price
rise in, increases the whole surplus (Malthus), VI, 185; see Surplus
at various periods, V, 167–8, 212–13, 521, see also VIII, 374 & n.
rise of, in 1814–15, IV, 40, not due to taxation, VI, 181
unnaturally low, in 1815–16, V, 318, VI, 303–4, 344, VII, 16; in 1821–2, IV, 259–61, V, 72, 89, 108, 233–4, 241, IX, 152, 157–60, 199–200
Corn laws:
true principles of, V, 256
evils of, IV, 250, V, 55, 79, 151, 170–2; diminish production, IX, 197–8; drive capital to cultivation of poorer land, IV, 247, 263; lower profits, V, 33, 38; send capital abroad, VIII, 357–8, 364–5; sudden opening of ports ruinous to home-grower, IV, 242
Corn laws (*cont.*)
withdrawal of protection proposed, IV, 263–6, V, 156–9, 172–3, 180–4, VIII, 359; countervailing duty allowed, IV, 217–19, V, 82, 87, 151–2, 159, 257–8, VIII, 356–7
Report on, 1814, IV, 3, 29 n.
corn law, 1815, IV, 3–4, 249–51, V, 48, 52; petitions and riots against, IV, 70, VI, 180 & n., 183 & n., 184; see also VI, 158, VIII, 97, 101, IX, 165 n., 176
corn law, 1822, V, xxv; speeches on, V, 155–9, 170–86, 195–7, 256–8; see Agricultural committee 1822
see also under Protecting duties, Restrictions on importation
Corn-ratio theory of profits, I, xxxi–xxxii, xlviii–xlix, VI, 204; renders theory of distribution independent of value, VIII, 194, 297, 337
Corn trade:
true principle of, V, 87–8
committee on, IV, 3
tables of quantities and prices, IV, 270–1, IX, 166 & n., 181
project of loans to speculators in, IV, 253–5, see also V, 85, 90
cost of sending corn from country to London, II, 368–9, from Poland or Prussia, VIII, 374, from interior of America, IX, 98
see also V, 101–2, and under Free trade in corn
Coronation of George IV, V, 69; a harlequinade (Mill), IX, 7; 'the mighty Corronation' (Trower), IX, 30 & n.
Correggio, price of a picture, X, 312
Corrie, Mr, XI, xii
Cossa, Luigi, X, 355
Cost of production:
made up of wages and profits, VIII, 279, IX, 75, see also II, 369, IV, 36; nearly in proportion to quantity of labour, II, 35, 79
the regulator of price, I, 73 n., II, 25, 48–9, IV, 20 n., V, 300, of value, V, 212

Cost of production (*cont.*)
cost and value distinguished, I, 47 n., II, 34–5, 101
word 'cost' used ambiguously by Malthus, II, 273, IX, 4
see also Difficulty of production, Diminishing returns, Natural price
Cost price, IX, 81, 100
Cotton:
Arkwright's machine, IV, 33
cotton goods, manufacture of, II, 153, IV, 251–2, 374; export of, II, 363
cotton-trade, V, 482
weavers, distress of, V, 68–9
see also I, 117, 317, V, 30, 31 n., 214
Coulson, Walter, VIII, 186 n., see also 10 n.
Counter-commodities, glut due to lack of (Say and Torrens), VIII, 227, 260
Countervailing duties:
principle of, VIII, 356, see also IV, 246, V, 47–8
for taxes peculiar to one commodity, IV, 243–4, 264, V, 45, 53, 82, 87, 151–2, VI, 206, IX, 8
correct view taken in Agricultural Report, 1821, IV, 251–2
on corn, Ricardo's proposal, V, 82; see under Corn laws
Country banks:
their notes and Bank of England notes, III, 87–8, 227–35, 340, V, 375–6, 384, 389–90, VIII, 85–6; guarantee for notes, IV, 72–3
their deposits in London, III, 295–6
failures in 1815, IV, 73, VI, 328, 343, see also VI, 268, VII, 16
under plan for a national bank, IV, 287–9, 292, 294–5, 300; under ingot plan, V, 380
see also III, 151, 368, V, 156 notes, VI, 116, IX, 176, 201–2
Country gentlemen:
a compact body to oppose reforms, IX, 180, 194; Ricardo a mark for, IX, 249
Country gentlemen (*cont.*)
attitudes to the poor, VIII, 43, 307, and cp. VII, 142
pursuits of (Trower on), VI, 326, VII, 173, 268, 308–9, VIII, 322, IX, 312
Ricardo not half a country gentleman, VII, 207
County meetings, see Gloucestershire, Hereford, Norfolk, Surrey
Courier, see Shuman
Courier newspaper, reports of speeches, V, 74, 76, 81, 118–20, 281, 308, VII, 283 n., VIII, 352–4, IX, 181 n.
Courtenay, Thomas Peregrine, M.P. for Totnes, IX, 198, 267 n.
Courtney, Leonard H., VI, xviii n.
Courtney, W. P., *The King of Clubs,* VI, 87 n.
'Memoir of Whishaw', VI, 66 n.
Coutts & Co., bankers, III, 380, X, 68 n.
Cowell, John, his remedy for agricultural distress, IX, 199–200
Cowell, John, jun., letter to, IX, 199–200 & n.; met on the Continent, IX, 218–19, 223, 228, X, 277 & n., 301; see also VIII, 367 n., IX, 191
Cowes, VII, 279
Cowper, Lord, IX, 94
Cox, James, of the Museum, X, 173
Craig, John, *Remarks on...Political Economy,* 1821, VIII, 378 & n.
Craufurd, Lt.-Gen. Sir Charles Gregan, letters in Ricardo Papers, X, 388
Credit: transfers, does not create, capital, V, 436–8; see also I, 249 n., 299–300 n., IV, 254–5
Crisp, theatre-manager, X, 389
Crombie, Alexander, letter to Ricardo, VII, 31–2 & n.
Letters on the Agricultural Interest, 1816, VII, 31 n.
Letter to D. Ricardo Esq., 1817, VII, 32 n., 149
see also VI, 219
Cromwell, Oliver, his head, X, 167, 172–4
Cropper, Benson & Co., IX, 182 n.

Crops: secret method of estimating, VIII, 370 & n.; alternation of good and bad, IX, 314–15; rotation of crops, I, 80
Crosse, Thomas, Ricardo's solicitor, X, 390
letters from, quoted, V, xvi n., xviii, VII, 293 n., VIII, 319 n.
see also VII, 217, 232, X, 104 n.
Crown debtors, V, 281
Cumberland, George, father of Sydney, X, 143–59
Cumberland, George, jun., X, 143, 147
Cumberland, Richard, vicar of Driffield, X, 143–4, 146–7
Cumberland, Sydney, accused of enticing Mrs Ricardo's maid, X, 143–59
Curious effect of rise of wages (lowers some prices), VII, 82–3, see also I, 61–3, II, 60
Currency:
perfect, defined, IV, 55, V, 379, see also I, 361, IV, 66
theory of price and, VI, 348
excess of, III, 56–7, 61, 92 n., 94, 142, VI, 75; criterion of, V, 448–9; use of term, III, 147–9, 228–30, 248 & n.; see also I, 354–5
void in, III, 24, 60–1
proportion between currencies and commodities of nations, VI, 40, 65, IX, 81
restoration of, to original standard, effect on taxes, III, 137–8
Western's motion on the altered state of, 1822, V, 223–31; Ricardo's speech on, 231–45; see also Resumption of cash payments
Sinclair's proposal to increase, VIII, 186, 386
see also Depreciation, Money, Redundancy
Curries, Raikes & Co., bankers, X, 277 n.
Curtis, Sir William, M.P. for the City of London, VIII, 163 & n.
Curwen, John Christian, M.P. for Cumberland:
on taxes on agriculture, V, 74
frauds in corn imports, V, 78
gluts of corn, V, 88
moves repeal of agricultural horses tax, V, 101
duties on tallow and candles, V, 146, 291
on fair protecting price for corn, V, 174
moves repeal of salt duty, V, 194–5
his notion of a countervailing duty, VIII, 356
see also I, 108 n., V, 57, 85, 87, 90, 257–8
Customs and excise, IV, 190, V, 268, 511, see also VII, 303, X, 170, 262

Da Costa, Daniel, X, 206 n.
Da Costa, Isaac, Dutch poet, X, 207–8, 211–12, see also X, 17
Da Costa, Mrs, wife of the poet, X, 211–12
Da Costa, Isaac, author of *Israel and the Gentiles,* 1850, X, 19 n.
Da Costa, Rebecca, *née* Ricardo (D.R.'s cousin), X, 19, 30, 206–7, 211–12
Daily Worker, VI, 250 n.
Dalchurst, Manor of, or Hadlow Place, bought by Ricardo, X, 96–7, 105
Dalrymple, Col. A. J., M.P. for Appleby, X, 226, 305, 317
Dalton family, VI, 35 n., VIII, 349
Damer, Hon. Mrs, V, xviii
Damiens, tortures of, VII, 319
Dansey, Dansey Richard, X, 98
Danvers, F. C., *Memorials of old Haileybury College,* VI, xix n.
Darmstadt, X, 226–7
Darn, speech by, III, 179 n.
Darton and Harvey, Map of London, 1805, X, 47 n.
Davenport, Davies, M.P. for Cheshire, V, 323
Davies, Colonel Thomas Henry, M.P. for Worcester, V, 138, 185, 274, VIII, 16 n.

Davies, Mr, project of a review, VIII, 16
Davison, T., printer, VII, 13–14
Day and New Times, newspaper, I, xix
Dead capital, proportions of, V, 177–8
Dead stock, gold as, I, 229, 232, V, 408, 434
Dearth, VII, 194, 200
Death duties, I, 153; legacy duty, V, 315; transfer of property at death, V, 291; probate duty, V, 315, X, 103
Debyser, C., X, 355, XI, xxx
De Castro, Orobio, X, 203
Decker, Sir Matthew, *Essay on the Decline of Foreign Trade,* 1744, I, 234
De Crespigny, Sir William Champion, M.P. for Southampton, his motion on Robert Owen's plan, V, 30; see also VIII, 46
Deerhurst, Lord, M.P. for Worcester, VII, 102 & n.
De Leon, Mr, X, 208
Delessert & Co., Ricardo's bankers in Paris, X, 99–101, 341–2, 390
Delessert, Benjamin, letter to Ricardo quoted, V, 466 & n.; see also IX, 144, 203–4, 236, X, 100, 351
De Lolme, J. L., *The Constitution of England,* X, 397
Del Sarto, Andrea, X, 316
Delvalle, Abigail (D.R.'s mother), see Ricardo, Abigail
Delvalle, Abraham (D.R.'s great-great-grandfather), X, 26
Delvalle, Abraham (D.R.'s grandfather), X, 21, 27–8
Delvalle, Abraham (D.R.'s uncle), X, 28–9; letter to, as wine merchant, X, 141–3
Delvalle, Daniel (D.R.'s great-great-uncle), X, 26
Delvalle, Esther (D.R.'s aunt), wife of Isaac Lindo, X, 29, 106
Delvalle, Isaac (D.R.'s great-grandfather), X, 26–7, 28
Delvalle, Isaac (D.R.'s uncle), X, 22, 28, 106
Delvalle, Joseph (D.R.'s uncle), X, 28, 106
Delvalle, Leah (D.R.'s aunt), X, 28–9, 106
Delvalle, Rebecca (D.R.'s grandmother), *née* Sequeira, X, 27
Delvalle, Rebecca (D.R.'s aunt), wife of Wilson Lowry, X, 29
Delvalle, Sarah (D.R.'s aunt), wife of Abraham Nunes, X, 29, 106
Demand:
  a desire to possess with the power of purchasing, VI, 56, 58
  where the power exists the will exists too, II, 311, 314, IV, 343–4, VI, 108; Malthus's contrary view, II, 36–7, 307, VI, 112, 123, 131–2, 155–6
  limited only by production, I, 290, II, 365, IV, 178–9, V, 435, VI, 163–4, VII, 203, VIII, 258; Malthus disagrees, II, 377–9, VI, 168, 225, 229, VII, 214, VIII, 159–60, 216, IX, 13
  lacking only if commodities are unsuitable, II, 304–5, VI, 164, IX, 26
  occasioned by accumulation as much as by consumption, VI, 133–5, 141
  effect of price on, I, 193; different for luxuries and for necessaries, VIII, 272, IX, 19, see also I, 293–4, 387; slight for bread, I, 385, great for gold and silver ware, VI, 91–2
  influence of income on, VIII, 274–5
  tax on corn, effect on demand, I, 237 & n.
  effective (effectual) demand, I, 291, II, 234, III, 25, 53, VI, 114, 120, 133, 148–9, 164, VII, 125, 131, VIII, 216, 259; Malthus, VI, 117, 131, IX, 10; Adam Smith, VI, 58, 142
  difference with Malthus on importance of, II, 370–1, VII, 57, 70, 77–8, IX, 80, XI, x–xi
  see also VI, 129, IX, 27 n.

Demand and supply:
effect on price, I, 382–5, see also I, 119–20, 164–5, II, 224–5, VIII, 272, 279, 286, 302
contingent supply and demand, VIII, 196
increase of demand linked with increase of supply, I, 130, 163
see also Price, natural and market
Demanders, whether corn raises demanders (Malthus), or demanders raise corn (Ricardo), I, 400, 405 n., 406, 409, II, 107–9, 142; discussion with Trower, VIII, 219, 235–6, 248, 255–8, 273
Denison, William Joseph, M.P. for Surrey:
advocates an 'amicable arrangement' for the public debt, V, 251
suggests taxing malt instead of beer, V, 294
see also V, 185, VII, 267
Denman, Thomas, M.P., Solicitor-General to Queen Caroline, VIII, 243–4, IX, 12
Denmark, corn imported by fraud from, V, 78
Denmark, Crown Prince of, proposed visit to Ricardo, IX, 192, 195–6
Depreciation of currency:
distinguished from diminution of value, IV, 330–1, V, 166, 203–4, 310–11, 393–4
injustice of, III, 123, 133; enriches one class at expense of another, III, 136–7, 271, IV, 229–31, VI, 233–4, IX, 72–3, 246
two tests of, III, 75
measured by excess of market over mint price of gold, III, 29, 79, 99, 175, 187, V, 392, VI, 6
no standard to judge whether gold has risen or paper fallen, II, 6–7, III, 80, V, 373–4, IX, 276
actual and relative, VIII, 92–3; real, III, 56
of paper currency from over-issue, I, 209, 371, III, 51, 63, 78, V, 143, 208–9; gradual decrease of, as
Depreciation (*cont.*)
remedy, III, 17–18, 21, 94–5, V, 2–3, VI, 44–5
no effect on rate of interest, III, 137
unfavourable foreign exchanges as proof of, III, 18, 72, 83, 199, VI, 39
effect of, on prices of taxed commodities, I, 209–10
of paper compared with debased coinage, III, 97–8, see also 74–5, 78
of money by discovery of American mines, III, 362, 376–7, see also I, 86
proposal for preventing, without depriving merchants of accommodation, VI, 67–8
money incomes and depreciation, IV, 63–4
Depression:
of agriculture, IV, 230, V, 47, 73, 89, 125, 132, X, 321
of coin or paper, III, 197 & n.
of commodities, V, 400
of the Exchange, V, 448
of price, III, 100–1, V, 399; depressed price of corn, IV, 228, V, 241
De Quincey, Thomas, 'Dialogues of Three Templars', I, xxii n.
Dermody, Thomas, Irish poet, X, 44 n.
Destutt de Tracy, A. L. C., met in Paris, IX, 248
Elémens d'idéologie, 1804–15, I, 284–5
Dick, Thomas, Edinburgh police commissioner, IX, 162–3, 164, 177
Dickinson, William, M.P. for Somerset, V, 86, VII, 232
Diehl, Karl, X, 377–8
Dietz, A., *Frankfurter Handelsgeschichte,* X, 223 n.
Difficulty of production:
or cost of production, VI, 247–8, 271
limits population, I, 373, VI, 140
raises prices, I, 191, VI, 233, 241, and wages, I, 146, 218, 296, VII, 57, 80–1

Difficulty or facility of production, regulates price, I, 73, 158, VII, 3, 250, IX, 239, and value, I, 193, 273, 277, 280–1, 363, IV, 19; see also VII, 333, IX, 94–7
see also Facility of production, and under Rent
Diminishing returns from land:
early statement, III, 287
and theory of profits, IV, 13 & n., 14, VI, 197, 204, 207, 209–10, 213–14, 216–18, 220–2, see also I, 125–6; table showing progress of rent and profits, IV, 17
and cost of production, I, 156, V, 167–8, VI, 294
and population, I, 98–9
and rent, I, 70–2, 75, 83
Disagreeables: of negotiating a seat in parliament, VII, 269; of travelling, VII, 56, X, 345
Discourses on parliamentary reform, V, 487–512, VII, 301–2
D'Israeli, Isaac, VII, 10 n.
Distress: due to reduction of circulation, 1817, VII, 151; general distress, 1819–20, V, 37–41, 133, 492 n., VIII, 103, 139, 150–1 n., 152–3 n.; see also Agricultural distress, Labouring classes, Manufacturers
Distribution:
of circulating medium, and national wealth, III, 120
good and faulty, of produce, II, 366, IX, 16–17, 24–6, 83 (Ricardo), II, 415, IX, 10, 15 (Malthus); of funds of society, I, 314; of capital (M^c^Culloch), VIII, 353
of labour, I, 132–3, 152 n.
of net income, I, 425
of produce from the land, VI, 199, 203
of property, and alterations in value of money, V, 107; results of unequal distribution of property (Sismondi), IX, 243–4
Distribution (or division) of the whole produce by proportions:
between the three classes, I, 5, 49–51, II, 195 n., VIII, 194, 278, 337; see also I, 64, 270, 347, VI, 172, 315–16, VII, 24, 71, 78, IX, 20, 22
between profits and wages, II, 194–5, 258–9, 290, 304, 344–5, IV, 366, VIII, 130, 194–5, IX, 16–17, 21, 25, on no-rent land, II, 196–7, 198 n., 278, 284, 336, the same in manufactures as in agriculture, II, 322–4, V, 177–8; see also I, 226, II, 306, 363, IV, 408
rent as share of the produce, I, 83–4 & notes, 332–4, 402–3 & notes, II, 195–8 & notes, IV, 18 & n., IX, 40, see also IV, 13
division of surplus between rent and profits, II, 223, see also VI, 203–4, 213–14
division by proportions not essentially connected with value, VIII, 194, see also 297, 337
Dividends:
on National Debt, plan to avoid disturbance to money market, IV, 74–6, VI, 286, 299, 305, 312–13, VII, 22; proposal to adjust to price of corn, I, 425–6 & notes
should be taxed directly, I, 160–1
see also Bank of England, dividend
Division of labour, I, 94, 412, II, 395, IV, 25
Dixon, S., V, 476
Docks, I, 152, VIII, 155
Doctrinaires, VIII, 224
Dolby's *Parliamentary Register*, 1819, V, xxix n.
Domodossola, IX, 221, X, 288
Dorking, VI, xvi, IX, 326, 331–3
Dorrien, George, Governor of the Bank, V, 353, 363–4
Double standard of gold and silver, V, 92, 93 n.
inconvenience of, I, 366–9, III, 65, IV, 63, V, 426–8
more variable than gold standard, V, 40, 390

Double standard (*cont.*)
Baring's proposal, 1819, V, 46, 71, 74 n., 75–8, 92–5, 105–6, VIII, 346–7, 349–50; revived in 1823, IX, 270
in France, III, 178, V, 76, 106
gold made the only legal tender from 1817, V, 16 & n., see also I, 369, 371 n., IV, 67, VIII, 3
Douglas, William Robert Keith, M.P. for Dumfries, V, 299
Dover, VII, 168, 186
Drawback on exportation, IV, 217–19, 264, of corn, IV, 243–4
Dublin, V, 219, VI, 244
Dublin Morning Post, V, 528
Dublin rioters trial, IX, 274 & n.
Duboulay, F. N., VI, 112 n.
Ducie, Lord, V, 469–70, VII, 187 n., VIII, 330, X, 187 n.
Duckworth family, X, 309
Dugdale, Dugdale Stratford, M.P. for Warwickshire, V, 71
Duguid, C., *The Story of the Stock Exchange,* X, 73 n.
Dumont, Étienne, VI, 18 & n., 19–21
his translation of Bentham's *Alarm* (*Sur les prix*), III, 259–341; discussions on, VI, 13–18
at Geneva, IX, 215–20, 242–3, 248, X, 267, 270–2
excursion to Chamonix, IX, 215–17, 244, X, 273–7
his dinner party, IX, 219–20, X, 281–2
sides with Ricardo against Sismondi, IX, 235, X, 278
his MSS at Geneva, III, 263–4, VI, 20 n.
see also III, 11 n., VI, 90, 180, VII, 74, 188, VIII, 40 n., X, 303, 399
Traité des preuves judiciaires, 1823, X, 277
'*Des présomptions anté-judiciaires*', IX, 245 & n.
Dunbar, C. F., 'Ricardo's Use of Facts', I, xx
Dundas, William, M.P. for Edinburgh, IX, 162
Dundonald, Earl of, *Autobiography of a Seaman,* VI, 107. See Cochrane, Lord
Dunn, William, letter quoted, VIII, 338 n.
Dupont de Nemours, widow of, quoted on Ricardo, VIII, 224 n.
Duval, M., singer, X, 339

East, Sir Edward Hyde, M.P. for Winchester, V, 283
East India College, Haileybury:
Malthus professor at, VI, xix, 159 n., VII, 51, 213
Ricardo's visits to, VI, 60–1, 72, 94, 135 n., 176, 211
student troubles, VI, 77 & n., 336 & n., 341, VII, 26, 119, 121, 130–2, 135–8, 251 n., IX, 251 & n.
see also VI, 240, 346, VII, 167–8 & notes, 263 n., 264
East India Company:
Ricardo's speeches at General Court, V, 475–8
directorship suggested, VIII, 250–4, 262–3, 281–2, 292
Mill's appointment at, VIII, 40 & n., 47, 162, IX, 180, 279 n., 280 & n.
exports of silver, III, 172, 173 n., 249
sales of tea, IX, 330 & n., 342
see also IV, 97 n., V, 466–7, VI, 343 n., VIII, 53, IX, 97
East India stock, IV, 115, 117, V, 301
East Indies, III, 249, V, 297, 300, VII, 109, 273 n.; muslins from, VI, 55; see also India, Sugar
Easton Grey, Thomas Smith's home, VI, 135 n., VII, 52, 139, VIII, 276, IX, 232–3, 251, XI, xii n.; conversations at, VIII, 61–3, 75
Ebel's *Manuel du voyageur en Suisse,* X, 179
Ebrington, Lord, X, 182
Eckersall, Mrs Malthus's family, VI, xix, 135 n., VII, 311, VIII, 64, IX, 9
Eckersall, George, VII, 51, 56, 68, 253
Eckersall, Lucy, VI, 322, VII, 52, 56, 71

Economic situation of the country:
stagnation after the war (1815), VI, 303–5, 328, 344–5
revival (1816–17), VII, 16–17, 174, 185–6, 192
distress (1819), VIII, 103, 129, 139
unnatural depression (1821), V, 91, VIII, 369, 371, and cp. IX, 13, 40
on the whole flourishing (1822–3), IX, 158, 160; except for agriculture, V, 321, X, 349
Économistes (physiocrats), IV, 37, 178, VI, 187
Economists, VIII, 38, 139, 321, 341, 382. See Political economists
Ede, J., *Gold and Silver Coins,* 1808, III, 183 n.
Edgeworth, Fanny, IX, 137, 295, X, 167–71, 174
Edgeworth, Harriet, IX, 137, 230, 295, X, 167–71
Edgeworth, Honora, X, 167–9
Edgeworth, Lovell, X, 167, 169
Edgeworth, Maria, VI, xxxii–xxxiii
the potatoe question in Ireland, IX, 230–2, 237–9, 252–5, 257–61
visit to Gatcomb, IX, 104, X, 167–74
advice on her investments, IX, 203–4, 261–2
list of letters, IX, 393; other letters quoted, VIII, 56 n., X, 32–3 & n.
see also VII, 312, IX, 242 n., X, 102, 179, XI, xxvii
Rosamund and the Purple Jar, X, 33 n.
Life and Letters, see Hare, Augustus
Edgeworth, Mrs, *Memoir of Maria Edgeworth,* VI, xxxii n., VIII, 56 n., X, 167
Edgeworth, Packenham, X, 167, 169
Edgeworth, Sophy, IX, 295
Edinburgh:
few converts to Ricardo in, VII, 295, 316 n.
Police bill, IX, 161–3, 179, see also 137
relief works in, VII, 116 n.
society lampooned, VIII, 112–13
see also VII, 110
Edinburgh Annual Register, II, xiv, IV, 358 n., V, 289 n., X, 39, 369
Edinburgh Magazine, 1818, IV, 306, VII, 179 n., 315–16 & n., 324, 326, 332, 338, 354, 360, 362, 376, VIII, 8, X, 397
Edinburgh Review:
early articles on political economy, VII, 246
Horner on its mercenary troops, III, 9 & n.
no rough handling of clergy, VIII, 222
number withdrawn, at news of Waterloo, VI, 280, 316
adopts Ricardo's system, VIII, 376
see also III, 434, IV, 307 n., VI, 255, 313, VII, 245 n., VIII, 17, 28 n., 44, 205 n., 242, IX, 139, 147, 150 n., 155, 206 n., 312
Edinburgh Review, articles:
1802, Thornton's *Paper Credit* (Horner), III, 64
1803, Lord King's *Restriction of Payments* (Horner), III, 73, 83
1804, Bounty on corn (Horner), I, 302, 307, 315
1808, Thomas Smith's *Essay on Money* (Mill), III, 9 n.
1809, Burdett's plan of reform (Jeffrey), X, 397
1811, Bullion (Malthus), III, 10–11, 99 & n., VI, 24–5, 38, 82 (Feb.); III, 12, VI, 31, 41, 47, 66 (Aug.)
1813, Grimm on Voltaire, IX, 375
1818, *Economical and Secure Currency* (McCulloch on), IV, 47, VII, 354, 383, VIII, 1–2, 5, 6, 10, 20, 23–4
Principles (McCulloch on), VII, 179 n., 278–9, 280–2, 285–9, 291, 295–7, 309, 316 n.
Madame de Staël (Jeffrey on), X, 397
parliamentary reform (Mackintosh), VII, 263 n.
1818, 1819, Fellenberg's school (Simond), X, 262 n.

Edinburgh Review, articles in (*cont.*)
1819, Owen's plan (Torrens), VIII, 82 n., 159, 164, 376 & n.
trade with France (McCulloch), VIII, 82, 127
1820, foreign commerce (McCulloch), VIII, 190, 197
taxation and the corn laws (McCulloch), VIII, 164–6, 168–74, 176–7
tithes (McCulloch), VIII, 203, 214, 222, 229, 237, 262
parliamentary reform (Mackintosh), VIII, 327–8 & n.
1821, Scottish juries (Cockburn), IX, 136, 142
Mushet on gains and losses to fundholders (McCulloch), VII, 93 n., VIII, 392, 396, IX, 7 n., 15
machinery (McCulloch), VIII, 325, 338, 351–2, 366, 373, 378, 383, IX, 9, 18
Godwin on population (Malthus), IX, 84, 89–90, 94, 101, 154
1822, taxes (McCulloch), IX, 160, 185
Ireland (McCulloch), IX, 186
corn laws (McCulloch), IX, 186, 188, 192, 197
1823, funding system (McCulloch), VIII, 222–3 n.
East and West India sugars (McCulloch), IX, 273, 277
periodical press (Hazlitt), V, xxvii n., VI, xxii, VII, 28 n., VIII, 186 n.
1824, combination laws (McCulloch), VIII, 313 n., 338
profits (McCulloch), IX, 179 n.
East India Company (McCulloch), IX, 330 n.
1827, taxation (McCulloch), VIII, 238 n., IX, 342, 345, 362
1830, commerce in Holland (McCulloch), IX, 135 n.
1837, life of Malthus (Empson), VI, xx, VII, 2 n., 201 n.
Edinburgh, University of: Mill at, VII, 213 n.; McCulloch and Chair at, VIII, 204–5 & n.
Education of the lower orders in the Metropolis, Report on, 1816, VII, 150 & n.
Education of the lower orders, Brougham's committee on, 1816, 1818, VII, 304 n.; report, X, 262 n.; see also Schools
Education of the poor, committee on, 1819, VII, 45 n.; see also VII, 276, 357 n.
Edwards, Mr, of Ross, VI, 13
Ehrenberg, R., *Das Haus Parish in Hamburg,* III, 431–4 notes
Ehrenbreitstein, fortifications of, IX, 211, X, 218–20
Elasticity of demand, see Demand, effect of price on
Elections:
general, 1818, VII, 264–7, 269–70, 272, 275–6, VIII, 17 n., XI, xi–xii; 1820, VIII, 156, 162–3
contested, disgusting spectacles at, V, 504–5, 508–9, VII, 272–3
triennial, VII, 261, 267, 273 & n.
see also V, 473, VIII, 164, 210–11, and under Ballot, Parliament, seat in, Westminster election
Electors' Remembrancer, V, xxii n., xxiii n., X, 267 n.
Eliason, Daniel, VI, 8–9
Eliot, F. B., *On the Fallacy of the Supposed Depreciation,* 1811, X, 401
Elizabeth, la belle batelière, X, 255
Elizabeth, Princess, X, 224
Ellenborough, Lord Chief Justice, VI, 106, VIII, 288
Ellice, Edward, M.P. for Coventry:
his amendment to Peel's bill, V, 8, 11, 206
supports colonial trade bill, V, 188
on Spitalfields Acts, V, 295–6
see also V, 222, IX, 194
Ellis, Charles Rose, M.P. for Seaford:
Bank of Ireland and Irish exchange, V, 98
protection to West India sugar, V, 297
Ellis, T. F., stockbroker, VII, 14
Ellis and Tucker, loan contractors, X, 82, 85

Ellman, John, farmer, IX, 67 & n.
Elphinstone, William, East India director, VII, 136–7
Elwin, H.: and savings banks, VII, 47–8 & n., 63, 153, 173; visits Gatcomb, IX, 46; see also VII, 155, 162, VIII, 33
Emigration:
  of artisans, restrictions on, V, xx, xxiv, 296, 332, IX, 55 & n.
  to America, VII, 257, 259–60, IX, 61
  to Canada, Horton's plan for, XI, xv–xvi
  see also V, 21, VII, 142
Employment of labour:
  relation to quantity of capital, V, 501; and to distribution of capital, I, 349, 395, IV, 35
  full employment, necessary for increase of wages, II, 412
    in 1821, IX, 13, 40
  want of employment, whether due to faulty distribution of product, IX, 10–11, 16, 20, 24–5
    in change from war to peace, I, 265
    unexampled scarcity of work, 1816, VII, 62, 66–7
    want of demand for labourers in 1817, VII, 150; labourers unemployed, VII, 194
  see also V, 113–14, 224–5, VII, 248, and under Labour, Wages
Empson, William, article on Malthus, 1837, VI, xx, VII, 2 n., 201 n.
Encyclopaedia Britannica, VIII, 66, X, 370. *Supplement* to eds. 4–6 (1814–24), IV, 145, articles in:
  Cold (John Leslie), IV, 249 n.
  Colonies (Mill), VII, 183, 195
  Corn Laws (M^c^Culloch), I, 267 n., 318, VII, 295, 337, 354, VIII, 159
  Cottage System (M^c^Culloch), VII, 295, 337
  Exchange (M^c^Culloch), VII, 384, VIII, 81, 85–93
  Funding System (Ricardo), IV, 143–200, VIII, 72, 78, 127, 144, 240, 262. See also under Ricardo
Encyclopaedia (*cont.*)
  Government (Mill), VIII, 211, 240 n., 291, IX, 154 n.
  Interest (M^c^Culloch), VIII, 313, 341
  Jurisprudence (Mill), VIII, 290, 296, IX, 5, 154
  Liberty of the Press (Mill), IX, 5, 154 & n.
  Money (M^c^Culloch), IX, 134, 149, 157, 159
  Political Economy (M^c^Culloch), IX, 206, 271, 275, includes value, VIII, 189 & n., 214, IX, 313 & n., 334 & n.
  Prison Discipline (Mill), IX, 280
  other articles projected: Lottery, IV, 147–8, National Debt, VIII, 222–3, 238, Value, VIII, 189 & n.; see also IV, 147 n.
England:
  still in the progressive state, IV, 34, VII, 17, 185–6, 192; confidence in, keeps capital at home, V, 32
  must be manufacturing as well as agricultural, V, 180
  exaggerated idea of her wealth beside the Dutch, X, 197
  as enemy of all liberal principles, IX, 217, and cp. VI, 321
  Englishmen endure abuses too long, V, 486
Ensor, George, *Population of Nations,* 1818, I, li, 100 n., VII, 334, 349
Epictetus, VI, 271–2
Equality, increase of population and of food under a system of, IX, 49–50; unequal distribution of property, IX, 243
Equilibrium:
  of currencies, I, 141–2, 145, III, 55, 170, VIII, 127
  between agriculture and manufactures, VIII, 101–2
  of imports and exports, III, 245, VII, 43
  of prices, V, 21, 304
  of profits, II, 289; between profits and wages, I, 226
Erasmus, X, 233

Erskine, Lord: *Armata: a Fragment,* 1817 (anon.), VII, 142; *Second Part of Armata,* VII, 173, X, 395; his speeches on Reform, X, 396
Espinoza, Michael d', Spinoza's father, X, 32
Essex, Lord, VIII, 28 n., X, 50, see also VII, 252 n.
Essex-street Unitarian Chapel, VII, 171 n., X, 39–40
Estcourt, T., VII, 304
Esterhazy, M., X, 383
Eton, Mortimer Ricardo at, X, 63, 389; see also VII, 138, IX, 199 n.
Eton College Tables, V, 226, 238
Euclid, V, 38
Evans, Thomas, the Spencean, VII, 307–8
Evans, William, M.P., V, 185
Evelyn, John, *Silva,* VI, 237
Everas, Ricardo's estate, X, 97
Evil, the problem of, VII, 206, 212
Examiner, X, xxii
Excess of currency defined, III, 147–9. See Currency
Exchange, Foreign, I, 146–9
  nominal and real, III, 420, IV, 336–7, 353, V, 448, VI, 23, 41, VIII, 88, 90–3, 126, 141
  principles of calculating, III, 174–5, 178–9
  par of exchange, I, 229–32, III, 109–10; with America, III, 182–3, with France, 176–80, with Hamburg, 417–18, VI, 8–10, between gold and silver currencies, III, 166–75
  real par of, III, 167–8, 185, 247, V, 391, VI, 8; whether to include expenses of transmission, III, 174, VIII, 89 & n., 92, 140–1, 178–80, 184
  unfavourable, caused by redundant currency, III, 20–1, 64 n., 75 n., 83, 100, 107, 140, 169, 194–5, 356–8, 372–3, VI, 7, VIII, 93; whether the only cause, VI, 62–5, 74–8, 82–3, 87–9, 119; whether it measures depreciation, VI, 30, 39, 83
Exchange, Foreign (*cont.*)
  whether it tends to right itself, VI, 34, 39, 75, 77, 83, VIII, 91 & n. 5
  natural limits to rise and fall of, III, 19–20, 71–2, 161, V, 448, VII, 43–4, VIII, 2
  effect of foreign subsidies on, VI, 39, 41, 73–8, 83, 89; of government foreign expenditure on, IX, 272, 276–7, 285–6, see also IV, 327–56
  in turbulent times, VI, 78–81
  effects of peace on, VI, 116, 119, 122
  recovery of, after resumption of cash payments, VIII, 44, 70, 79
  M^c^Culloch on, criticised, VIII, 85–93, 126–7, 140–1
Exchange, with America, IX, 272, 277, 301, 362, see also III, 182–3
  with Amsterdam, III, 73–4, VI, 97–9, 298–9
  with the Continent, VI, 78–9
  with Hamburg, I, 148–9, III, 80–1, 116, 118–21, 163–75, 185–6, 247, VI, 7, 86, 100–1, VIII, 91
  Irish, III, 399, V, 70, 98–100, VIII, 24
  with Jamaica, VI, 23, 28, 31–3, 35, 40–1
  between London and the country, VIII, 85–6
  with Paris, III, 164, 176–82, V, 186–7, VI, 119 n.
  with Rio de Janeiro, VIII, 92
  with Russia, VI, 79
  between Spain and her colonies, III, 171, VIII, 89, 126, 141
  with Sweden, III, 183–4
Exchangeable value, I, 11–66, IV, 361–412. See Value
Exchequer bills: not paper money, III, 290–3, 298, see also IV, 108; interest on, I, 297–9, IV, 102, V, 115, VIII, 135, IX, 262, X, 86; see also III, 233, IV, 91–2 n., 277, V, 59
Excise Duties bill, V, 23–7
Export duty on manufactures, as substitute for import duty on corn, II, 153–5

Exports:
no exports without imports, I, 263, VI, 108–9
bounties on exports, of corn, I, 301–11, of manufactures, 312–16
flourishing in 1823, V, 246
Exports and imports:
balance of, in 1810, III, 63 & n.
equilibrium of, III, 245, VII, 43
nominal and real value of, III, 133–4, 141, VI, 93
see also Balance of trade, Foreign trade
External commodities, IX, 65–6, 75–7
Extra post, V, 148
Extravagance, public, II, 307, IV, 339, VI, 120

Fabrikant, N. V., X, 381
Facility of production:
defined, VI, 292
relation of, to profits and wages, VI, 289–94, 296–7, 303–4, 319, VII, 52, 57, 69, 77–8, 80–1, VIII, 194–5, 215–16, IX, 99–101; to profits, IV, 26, VI, 140, 144–5, to wages, I, 292, VI, 224–7, VII, 80
diminishes value, adds to riches, I, 274, 281, IX, 170–1, see also IV, 407–8
see also Difficulty of production
Fair Circassian, V, 368 & n.
Fallesen, Ludvig Sophus, X, 380
Famine, I, 99, 101; in Europe, 1817, X, 184; in Ireland, 1822, V, 234–5, IX, 231–2, 254
Farmers:
profits of, regulate all profits, VI, 104. See Profits
interests of, contrasted with commercial classes, IV, 255; analogy with manufacturers, II, 200; see also IV, 229–31
mistake their own interests on protection, VIII, 337, 369–70, 374, IX, 67
distress of, V, 150, 157, 181, VII, 38, 87, X, 349
Farmers (*cont.*)
gentleman-farmers, VI, 149, 158, 279, 326, VII, 268, VIII, 109, 132, IX, 264; Ricardo as, VI, 150, VII, 170, 207, VIII, 307
Fashion, influence on price, I, 90, 119, 194, see also I, 263, VIII, 275
Fearon, H. B., *Narrative of a Journey through...America,* 1818, VIII, 16 & n.
Fellenberg, P. E. von, his school at Hofwyl, X, 262
'Fellow of University College', see West, Edward
Ferrara, X, 310–11
Ferrara, Francesco, X, 380
Ferrier, Rotterdam banker, X, 195–6
Fertility of the soil:
rent the result of diminishing, I, 69–70, 74–7, 402–4, II, 112, 116, 211, 213, VI, 292–4, 301–2
price of raw produce increases as fertility decreases, I, 72, 120, see also IV, 27
and accumulation of capital, I, 98, 126, II, 321
and profits, I, 120, 125–6, II, 132, 255, 336, 446–7, VI, 152, 162, 168, VII, 69, 78
Fetter, F. W., 'Editions of the Bullion Report', XI, xxxi
Fictitious capital, no stimulus to production, V, 445–6
Field, G., Ricardo's clerk, X, 74
Fielding, Henry, *Tom Jones,* VII, 303
Finance, Report on, 1819, IV, 193, V, 64–6; see also IV, 305 n.
Financial situation of the country, 1823, V, 248–51. See Budget
Finnerty, Peter, reporter, V, xxviii
Fire balloon at Coblentz, IX, 212, X, 218
Fisher, P. H., *Notes and Recollections of Stroud,* X, 168 n.
Fishing, at Gatcomb, VIII, 49, 283, IX, 327–8, 335; see also V, 122
Fiske, Mrs, X, 158
Fitzwilliam, Lord, VIII, 50, 111 & n., 134

Fixed capital, I, 31–2, 52, 150, 266, IV, 305–6, 311–12. See Capital, fixed, Machinery
Flogging, vote on, V, xxii
Florence, visit to, X, 312–21, see also IX, 219, 224, 247
Fluctuations in prices: injurious to farmers, IV, 238, 246, V, 88, and to landlords, IV, 266; inevitable under corn laws, IV, 240–2, 249–50
Foligny, M. de, VII, 168 & n.
Folkestone, Viscount, M.P. for Salisbury:
on raising the standard price of gold, V, 93, 254–5
proposes 'equitable adjustment', V, 322
on Mill's article 'Government', VIII, 213
a staunch reformer, IX, 268
see also V, 154 n., VI, 277 n.
Fontainebleau, X, 346–7
Fonteyraud, Alcide, French translator of Ricardo, X, 31 n., 375–6, 380
Food:
cheap food and profits, I, 119, 126, 132, 289, 296, II, 221–2, IV, 11, 22, 25–6, 347, V, 50, VI, 104
increased supply of, and increase of population, I, 292, 295, 373, II, 161, IV, 179, X, 408–9
whether food creates its own demand, I, 406, II, 111, VII, 201, VIII, 258, IX, 56–7; limit to demand for, I, 293, 387, VIII, 274–5, IX, 19
dependence on foreign food, IV, 265–6; increased production of food, during French war, VI, 94–5; see also IX, 50
consequences of cheap food in Ireland, I, 100 n., IX, 56
Adam Smith's notion that food production always yields a surplus, I, 327–9, 332–3
see also Corn, Necessaries, Potatoes
Forbach, X, 231–2
Forbes, C., V, 475, 478–9
Forced abundance of silver, low value from, I, 229; forced circulation of
Forced (*cont.*)
money, I, 231, III, 214–15, 336, 362, 364, of paper in America and France, III, 98; forced exportation of gold, III, 393, see also 220; forced value of gold coin, III, 40
Ford Abbey, Bentham's summer residence, VI, 124–7, 136, 317, VII, 76, 169; Ricardo's visit with J. B. Say, VI, 156–7, 161
Foreign Enlistment bill, V, xxii
Foreign exchange, I, 146–9. See Exchange, foreign
Foreign trade, I, 128–49
principles of, in terms of barter, I, 133–6, in terms of money, I, 137–49; finally a trade of barter, I, 228, II, 154, IV, 214, VI, 109
increases mass of commodities but not amount of value, I, 128, 319–20, II, 403, 407, V, 435, VI, 163, 167–8, 170–1, see also II, 436, III, 331, VII, 99
does not raise rate of profits, I, 128–9, 132–3, 345–6, II, 363–4, 408, IV, 25–6
and general rise or fall of home prices, I, 168–72, 228–9, 310–11, II, 154–6
between manufacturing and corn-producing countries, II, 288–91
sudden changes in channels of, I, 263–8
state of, in 1812, VI, 80; expansion of, during war, VI, 93
see also IX, 114 n., 127–8, 130, and under Commerce, Exports and imports, Trade
Foreign Trade committees, 1820: Commons', VIII, 197 & n., Lords', IX, 104 n.
Foreign vessels, reciprocity of duties, V, 305
Forgery of bank notes, IV, 292, V, 96–7, VI, 282, VIII, 350; executions for, IV, 225–7, V, 201, 279
Forster, Lubbock, & Co., Ricardo's bankers, X, 55 n., 68 & n.
Fortescue, George Mathew, X, 182 n.

Forty-shilling freeholder, V, 506
Foster, John, M.P. for County Louth, VII, 347–8, see also V, 58
Foster, John Leslie, *Essay on the Principle of Commercial Exchanges,* 1804, VII, 348 & n.
Foster, Peter le Neve, letter to, IX, 173–4
Foster, Thomas, X, 40–1
Fox, Charles James: on universal suffrage, V, 485; Mill on his India policy, VII, 238, 249; see also VIII, 6 n., X, 396–7
Fox Bourne, H. R., *English Merchants,* X, 90 n.
Foxwell, Herbert Somerton, I, vii, VI, xx n., 139 n., X, 401, XI, xxvii
France:
 in 1815, VI, 246–7, 255, 321; prosperity in 1822, X, 184; nobility miserably poor, X, 281–2
 inheritance law in, II, 386–7, see also VIII, 225, 377
 political economy in, VIII, 224–5, 227, IX, 191, 244–5, 248–9
 trade with, VIII, 82, 127, 190, 197, see also IV, 30
 visits to, in 1817, VII, 160, 164, 167–8, 178, 224; in 1822, IX, 227, 236, 244–6, 248, X, 339–52
 see also I, 134, III, 98, V, 76–7, 106, IX, 268, X, 396, and under Bonaparte, French, Paris
Franchise, extension of, V, 498–503, VII, 368–70, see also V, 112, 473, 506, VII, 273 & n.
Francis, John, *Chronicles of the Stock Exchange,* X, 58 n., 79, 123 n.
Francis, Sir Philip, X, 118; letter to, VI, 10–13
 Reflections on the Abundance of Paper in Circulation, 1810, VI, 10 n., 11 n.
Frankfort, visit in 1817, VII, 160, 164–5; in 1822, X, 222–6; theatre at, X, 223–4, 258
Franking of letters by M.P.s, VI, xxxix, 257, IX, 47 n., 163 & n., see also VI, xxxii, VII, 364, 371, 378, IX, 63, X, 261
Franklin, Benjamin, his bust, IX, 228 & n.; see also VII, 378
Free discussion of religious opinions, V, 277–80, 324–31, IX, 277–80, 288 & n., X, 397, XI, xxiv
Free trade, I, 133–4, 317–18 & n., 343, IV, 70–2, 252, V, 34, 188–90, 432, VII, 161, VIII, 228, 275, 353, 359, IX, 4, 77, 80–2
 merchants' petition for, V, 42–4, VIII, 164, 178 & n., 183
Free trade in corn:
 argument for, IV, 32–3, 36, V, 82, 87, 256, 258, VII, 271, VIII, 359, see also I, 126, 428, II, 203–5; misrepresented by Malthus, VIII, 208–9; no allowance to be made for loss of rent, VI, 173
 dangers of dependence on foreign supply considered, IV, 27–30, 264–6, V, 54–5
 increases ability to pay taxes (Ricardo's 'riddle'), V, 83, 88, and cp. I, 8, 421–4
 lowers rate of profits in exporting countries, VI, 171
 see also Corn Laws, Protecting duties, Restrictions
Freiburg, X, 232–3
French funds, VII, 230, IX, 144, 203–4, 229, 236, 256, 261–2, X, 185; loan of 1823, X, 57, 341
French Revolution, VI, 94–5, VII, 273–4, VIII, 108, 385, IX, 210, 218, 220, 274, X, 192
Frend, William, VI, xix; letter quoted, X, 34 & n.
'Friend to Bank Notes', see Trower, Hutches
'Friends of the People' (1792), VIII, 62–3
Fromowitz, Dr Wilhelm, X, 378–9
Fubini, R., X, 355
Fuchs, Major, a Swiss in the English service, X, 247–8
Fund for the maintenance of labour: and extension of market, I, 132; and immoderate savings, I, 292–3, IX, 24; and increase of money, III,

Fund for...labour (*cont.*)
302; and loss of capital, I, 222, VII, 75; and machinery, I, 286; and population, I, 78, 108–9, 218–20, 289; and price of corn, I, 270, 306; and taxation, I, 153, 196, 221–2, 225–6, V, 27; and wages, I, 164–5, 219, VIII, 258; and war, I, 265, VII, 67; see also Revenue, gross and net
Fundholders:
gains and losses of, IV, 229–31, V, 236–9, 252–3, 314, 320, VI, 178, VII, 37–8, 93 n., VIII, 396–8, IX, 39, see also I, 419–20, 425–6, II, 162–3
'landed estates mortgaged to', V, 126–7, 132, VIII, 147, see also VII, 75, IX, 267 n.
see also V, 101 n.
Funding system, IV, 143–200. See Sinking fund, and under Ricardo, David, Works
Funds:
price of, regulated by rate of interest, III, 93–4, but not a steady criterion of rate, I, 298; price of, and value of currency, V, 214–15
compared with land, as investment, VII, 187 n., 230
see also National Debt, Stocks
Fusina, X, 310

Galileo's tomb, X, 317
Gallois, J.-A. G., IX, 248
'Galovegian Stot' (M[c]Culloch), VIII, 205 n., 'Galloway Stot', IX, 205 n.
Gamage Hall, Ricardo's estate, X, 97
Ganilh, Charles: *Inquiry into the Various Systems of Political Economy,* 1812, X, 399, see also II, 16 n.; *Des systèmes d'économie politique,* ed. 2, 1821, IX, 245 n.
Garnier, Germain, his notes to the *Wealth of Nations,* VIII, 224–5, IX, 244–5, 249; *Mémoire sur la valeur des monnaies,* 1817, X, 393
Garrett, John, X, 98
Garrow, Sir William, judge, VII, 283 & n., 290, 293
Gas-lighting, V, 179, X, 56 & n.
Gaster, M., *History of the Ancient Synagogue in Bevis Marks,* X, 20 n., 27 n.
Gatcomb Park, VII, facing p. 1
purchase of, VI, 100, X, 95–6
move to, VI, 113–15, 128, 130
Ricardo on, VII, 170, 305, VIII, 231, IX, 263
Hume's description, VI, 158
Maria Edgeworth on, IX, 230, X, 167–71
visitors: George Basevi, VI, 312, 325, VII, 306, 308, 317, 324; Malthus, VII, 48, 52, 56, 361, 368–9, 370–2, VIII, 331, 334, 336; Mill, VII, 285, 292, 299, 302–3, VIII, 229, 231–2, 241, see also VI, 136–7, IX, 329, 333–4, 377, 391; Say, VI, 156–61, 273
visitors a distraction, VI, 312, 314–15, 325, 335, 340, 349, VII, 54, 262, 306, VIII, 55, 58, 77–8, IX, 328
improvements at, VIII, 282–3, 293, IX, 12, 104, 326–7
boating, VII, 55–6, 68, 71, 76; fishing, VIII, 49, IX, 327–8; riding, VI, 267, VIII, 48, 78, IX, 44–5
see also VI, 244, VIII, 230, X, 105, 295
Gatty, C. T., *Mary Davies and the Manor of Ebury,* X, 48 n.
Gaubey, Clavet, agent de change, X, 101
Gautier, Madame, IX, 236
Gelders, IX, 211, X, 213
Gell, Sir William, VIII, 276
Geneva: visit to, IX, 214–20, 234, 244 n., X, 269–73, 277–82, watchmaker, X, 270; see also VII, 61, IX, 245
Genoa: visit to, X, 328, 330–4; road from Pisa, IX, 225–6, X, 324–30; see also VII, 192
Gentleman's Magazine, V, xv, VII, 155 n., VIII, 165 n., IX, 135 n.

Gentz, Friedrich von, *Briefe,* III, 434 & n.
Geological Society of London, Ricardo a member, X, 6, 49–50; other members, VI, 90 n., 180 n., 205–6 & notes, VII, 185 n., 191 n., 269 n., 275 n., VIII, 160 n., X, 144; see also VI, xxx, VII, 119 n.
  History of, see Woodward, H. B.
George III, V, xviii, 41, VII, 218, 276; death of, VIII, 156
George IV (before 1820 see Wales, Prince of, and Regent):
  his Coronation, V, 69, IX, 6; the Queen barred from, IX, 12 n., 30 & n.
  and Canning, IX, 115
  see also V, xxiii, 28, 64 n., VIII, 200, 221 n., 230, 294, X, 111 n.
Gernsbach, X, 231
Ghent, VII, 160, IX, 211
Gibbon, Edward, his house at Lausanne, X, 264, 269; see also VI, 279
Giessbach waterfall, X, 254, 257
Gil Blas, VII, 303, X, 290
Gilchrist, Ebenezer, banker, III, 228, 231
Glasgow Herald, V, xxiv n.
Globe and Traveller, IV, 7, IX, 301 n.; see also *Traveller*
Gloucester:
  assizes, confusion at, VII, 283 & n., 290, 293; see also VII, 258–9, 277, 296, 300, 309, VIII, 56, 134, 212
  Bishop of, VI, 310
  theatre, X, 389
Gloucester, Duke of ('Silly Billy'), on Ricardo's plan, X, 187 n.; see also VI, 31 n.
Gloucestershire:
  Ricardo Sheriff of, VII, 223–4; see also under Ricardo
  clothiers, petition against corn bill, IV, 70–1 & n.; their bad wage system, VIII, 316; see also VIII, 70, X, 168–9
Gloucestershire (*cont.*)
  Commission of the Peace, Ricardo not placed on, VIII, 157 & n.
  constituency of, VIII, 156, 162–3
  county meetings: Ricardo presides at (1818), VII, 268, 272, 372, 381–2; Ricardo's speech at, for the Queen (1820), V, 469–70, VIII, 330–1
  mode of harnessing oxen, X, 231
Glut:
  general, impossible, III, 108; extreme case of, I, 292–3
    difference with Malthus on, II, 308, 312, VIII, 257, 285, 300–1, IX, 9–10, 25; with Trower, VIII, 257, 272, 289
  glut of particular commodities, IV, 178–9; from miscalculation, II, 304–5, 413, IV, 344–5; due to lack of counter-commodities (Say and Torrens), VIII, 227–8, 260–1; see also I, 89, IX, 131
  of corn, IV, 254, 263–4, 266, V, 88, 235, 304, in Europe, X, 184
  of money, III, 383
  glut in the foreign market, III, 101, VI, 38
  see also Stagnation
Godalming, VII, 23 n.
Godwin, William, VI, 158 n., VIII, 114 n.
  Of Population,…an Answer to Mr. Malthus, 1820, VIII, 291 n.; criticised by Mill, VIII, 292, by M[c]Culloch, 326, by Trower, 361–2, by Ricardo, 368, by Malthus, 376; reviewed in *Quarterly,* IX, 147, 154, in *Edinburgh Review* (by Malthus), 84, 89–90, 94, 101; see also VIII, 290, 296, 307, 323, IX, 49 n., 59–60
Gold:
  price of gold, Ricardo's letters to *Morning Chronicle* on, 1809, III, 15–46
  high price of, caused by excess of paper, VI, 1–2, 5; other causes, V, 273–4

Gold (*cont.*)
value of, in terms of goods, III, 16, 28, V, 374; in terms of corn, different in different countries, I, 144–5, 377–8, II, 86
paper, not gold, altered in value (1810), III, 80
no criterion whether gold has risen or paper fallen (1819), II, 6–7; dispute with Blake (1823), IV, 328–9, 353–5, IX, 276, 284–7, 289
value and money price of, distinguished, III, 393, VI, 5–7, see also V, 392
less required under ingot plan, V, 383, 453, IX, 123; necessary reserve estimated, V, 424
gradual reduction of price proposed (1819), V, 381–2, 439–41, 450–1
unnecessary purchases by Bank from 1819, V, 165–6, 199–200, 205, 209, 311–12, 519
below mint price in 1820, V, 61
gold as a commodity, I, 44–5, 104, 168–9, 200, 352, 376–7, III, 52, 103–4, 142, VI, 21–2, 247–8, VIII, 2
as a measure of value, IV, 371–3, 382, 386–7, 389, 400–1, 406; assumed to be invariable, I, 87 & n., II, 83; Malthus's objections to, II, 82–3, 86
picked up in a day on the sea-shore, Malthus's measure of value, II, 81, IV, 365, VIII, 343
high value of, on Continent (1822) due to England's demand, X, 192–3, 195–6, see also V, 133–4
Gold mines, I, 195–200, III, 54, 111, see also I, 86–7, III, 216–17
Gold standard: whether the effective standard, III, 41, 66–70, 85 n., 255–6, VI, 2, 5–7
inconvenience of, while other countries have silver, V, 390–1, 427–8
a variable standard, III, 391, V, 94, 212, 374, 442, 517; but the least variable known, I, 45–6, 149, III, 65 n., IV, 62–3, V, 205–6, 388, 426–7, VII, 43
Gold token, V, 92, 96
Gold and Silver:
invariability of precious metals assumed in theory of value, VI, 348–9
distributed by competition among countries, I, 137–41, 343, III, 52–4, 65, 87, VI, 74–5
free trade in, I, 229–30
value regulated by difficulty of production, I, 193, 352, V, 444
as measures of value, I, 14, 86–7, II, 29
as general medium of circulation, I, 137
natural price of, I, 86
relative value of, III, 42–5, 67–70, 84, 178, V, 75–6, 94–5, 106, 378–9, 386–7, 426–7, VI, 2–4, 6–7
their variability underrated by bullionists, IV, 62, V, 205–6, VI, 344
new uses for, if price falls, VI, 90–2
improvements in production of, no advantage to England, III, 305–6
part of capital, but yield no revenue, I, 232, III, 55, 220, IV, 276, 298
unusual demand for, 1797–8, III, 171–2
quantity coined, 1816–19, VIII, 27 & n.
see also Bullion, Coin, Double standard, Hoarding, Silver
Goldau ruins, X, 246
Goldsmid, Aaron Asher, bullion broker, III, 350, V, 462, VI, 85
Goldsmid, Abraham: evidence to Bullion committee, III, 163, 198 n., 358–9; as loan contractor, X, 80, 92–4
Goldsmid, Benjamin & Abraham, III, 395–6, X, 80, 91, 125
Goldsmid, Sir Francis Henry, *Memoir* of, IX, 277–8 notes
Goldsmid, Isaac Lyon, bullion broker, VI, 85 n.; letter to, IX, 277–8
Goldsmith, Oliver, *The Traveller*, VI, 184, 327

Goldsmiths' Library, University of London, III, 380 n., V, 128 n., 250 n., 522 n., VI, 139 n., VII, 31 n., 93 n., IX, 154 n.; Ricardo Tracts in, X, 400, 402
Gonner, E. C. K., his edition of Ricardo's *Principles,* X, 364–5, of *Essays,* 371; tables of corresponding pages in various editions, I, 443–7, III, 435–7, IV, 419–22
Gooch, Thomas Sherlock, M.P. for Suffolk, Chairman of Agricultural committee 1821, V, xxiv, 81, 86–7, 148; see also IV, 203, VII, 45
Gordon, Mrs, *'Christopher North', a Memoir of John Wilson,* VIII, 205 n.
Gordon, Robert, M.P. for Cricklade, V, 109
Gordon, Viscount, V, 351
Gorton, John, *General Biographical Dictionary,* 1826–8, X, 38 n., 39 n.
Goulburn, Henry, Chief Secretary for Ireland, V, 304, IX, 124 n.
Government, checks on, V, 495, VIII, 133; free press as, V, 497, VII, 323
Government expenditure:
effects of, I, 246, IV, 348, 355–6, VIII, 171, 174, IX, 272, 276, 287 & n., see also I, 106, 153, VIII, 155
Ricardo accused of encouraging, VII, 280–1, 286, 337–8, 353, and cp. I, 151–2 & n., 242
Malthus's peculiar opinions on, II, 433, 447, 450
see also Public expenditure, Public works
Government interference, when justified, IV, 71–2, VIII, 133
Government, opinions on, in Holland, IX, 213, in Geneva, 217
Government paper money, Say's plan, VI, 165–6
Grade, Mr, V, 186
Graham, Earl, V, 351
Graham, Sir James, *Corn and Currency,* 1827, VII, 93 n.
Grain, Lords' Report on, 1814, VI, 130, 132
Grand St Bernard, IX, 220, X, 283, 285–7
Grant, Charles, founder of the East India College, VII, 130 n.
Grant, Charles, jun., East India Director, VII, 110
Grant, James, *The Great Metropolis* and *The Newspaper Press,* V, xxvii n., xxviii n., X, 73 n.
Grant, John Peter, M.P. for Tavistock, V, 16, 110
Grant, Robert, on East India College, VII, 130–2
Granville, and house at Brighton in 1795, X, 109–10
Granville, Viscount, V, 351
Gravitation, principle of, I, 108, VI, 204; of profits, I, 120
Gray, Simon, *The Happiness of States,* 1815, VIII, 38 n. For other works see under Purves, George
Greek loan, X, 58 & n.
Greeks, defeat in 1822, X, 278, see also IX, 39
Greenland, George, bookseller, VIII, 378 n.
Greenough, George Bellas, VI, 206 n.
his geological map, VII, 118–19 & n.
Critical Examination of... Principles of Geology, 1819, VIII, 43
see also VI, xxiv, X, 49
Green Park, walks in, VIII, 191
Greffulhe, John Louis, his evidence to Bullion committee, III, 163, 178, 182, 197–8, 360–1, 429 n.
Gregory, T. E., II, xv, X, 373
Grellier, J. J., *History of the National Debt,* 1810, X, 70 n.
The Terms of all the Loans, 1812, X, 75 n.
Grenfell, Pascoe, M.P. for Great Marlow till 1820, then for Penrhyn, VI, xxxiii
resolutions on the Bank, 1815, IV, 51 n., 54, 76–7, 86, 136–7, VI, 242, 278, VII, 25–6, X, 9; other references to the Bank, V, 20, 62, 193, 247, VI, 257 n., 267–8, VII, 252 n.

Grenfell, Pascoe (*cont.*)
on Bank of Ireland, V, 70, 98
on using sinking fund to diminish borrowing, IV, 171–3, V, 4, 18, 21–2, 58, 62, 193, 243, X, 81–2, 85
and resumption of cash payments, V, 350, 352, 354, 356, VIII, 19
on proposed tax on capital, V, 270
on loan contractors, V, 4
and *Economical Currency,* IV, 45–6, 95 n., VI, 241–2, 265, 267–8, 285–6, 295, 305, 313, X, 9
Mallet on, VIII, 152 n.
list of letters, IX, 393–4
see also I, lx, IV, 82, 97 n., V, 23, 26, 37, 59 n., 65, 67, 277, VI, 284 n., VII, 15, 19 n., 22, 25 n., 189, 347, VIII, 18, 77
Speech on applying the Sinking Fund, 1817, V, 22 n., see also 4 n.
Grenside, John, IX, 166 n.
Grenville, Lord, VII, 220 & n.
letter from, VIII, 150–1
studies *Principles,* VII, 189, 220, 259
on free trade, IV, 250–1
and resumption of cash payments, V, 351–4, 356, 365, VIII, 19 & n.
see also III, 413 n., IV, 71 n., VII, 17, 262, 267, IX, 270
Grey, Earl, hollow speech on reform, VIII, 6, 8–9, Ricardo's lost paper on, 6 n., 8; see also VI, 183 n., VII, 142, VIII, 11, 68 n., 335
Griffin, C. S., editor, X, 383
Grillparzer, Franz, *Die Ahnfrau,* X, 223–4 & n., 258
Grimm, F. M., *Correspondence littéraire,* IX, 375
Grindelwald, X, 256
Grote, George, VI, xxxiii
extracts from his diary, VI, xxxiv
MS on foreign trade, VI, xxxiv
letter to, IX, 288
Question of Parliamentary Reform (anon.), 1821, VIII, 328 n.
Posthumous Papers, 1874, IX, 288 n., 301–2
Grote, Mrs, letters quoted, IX, 288 n., 301–2; *The Personal Life of George Grote,* VI, xxxii n., xxxiv, IX, 288 n.
Grote and Prescott, bankers, VI, xxxiii
Ground rent, I, 201–4
Guardian Insurance Company, IX, 104 & n.
Guido d'Arezzo, X, 312, 316
Guildford, VII, 62, 267
Guineas, I, 369–70, III, 18, 24, 32, 40–1, 69–70, 82–3, 141, 322, VI, 2, 7
Guinness, Arthur, Governor of the Bank of Ireland, V, 99
Guise, Sir B. W., M.P. for Gloucestershire, VII, 272 n., VIII, 156 n.
Gurney, Hudson, M.P. for Newton, Hants., V, 161, 202, 217–18

Haarlem, X, 204
Hadlow Place, or Dalchurst, Manor of, Ricardo's property, X, 96–7, 105
Hague, The, X, 197–203; the much-travelled waiter, IX, 213–14, X, 199–200; story of a pair of shoes, X, 32–3
Haileybury College, VI, xix. See East India College
Haldimand, William, M.P. for Ipswich, Director of Bank of England, VIII, 163 & n.
on effects of resumption, V, 198–200
his evidence, V, 352–4, VIII, 21 & n.
see also V, 185
Halévy, Elie: *La Formation du Radicalisme philosophique,* VI, 157 n., 161 n.; *History of the English People in 1815,* X, 39
Half-share tenancy in Italy, Malthus puzzled by, VIII, 377
Hall, Francis, *Travels in Canada and the United States,* 1818, X, 395
Hall, Mrs, boat-builder, VII, 51, 68, 71
Hallam, Henry, *Europe during the Middle Ages,* 1818, X, 397
Hamburg, see Bank of, Exchange with
Hamilton, Alexander, professor at East India College, VI, 66, VII, 167

Hamilton, Robert, *Inquiry concerning the National Debt,* ed. 3, 1818, IV, 149–51, 156–7, 167, 171–2, 174, 184, 199–200, 351, VII, 23 n., VIII, 61, 64, 67, 76, 78, 123–5, 320, X, 69 n., 75–8 notes

Hammersley & Co., bankers, their circular Exchange Notes, X, 192, 195, 223, 244

Hammond, George, III, 432

Hammond, William, VI, 113 n.

Hancock, C. H., stockbroker, VII, 15; letters in Ricardo Papers, X, 388; see also X, 123–4 & n., 126–8

Hand weavers' petition, V, 302; see also V, 68

Hansard's Parliamentary History, I, 107 n., X, 77 n., 396–8

Hansard, T. C., *Parliamentary Debates* (referred to as *Hansard*), V, xxix–xxxii, XI, xxv

Hansard, T. C., jun., V, xxix n.

Happiness:

- whether more in a large than in a small population, I, 349 n., Ricardo non-committal, II, 382, VII, 379
- as much from idleness as from consumption, VII, 185, see also I, 99–100 & notes, VII, 48–9, IX, 261
- depends on abundance, not value, II, 21, 203, 365, see also IV, 248–9, VI, 236
- of the people, and government, I, 99, VII, 299, 366, IX, 213; and education, VI, 264, VII, 204
- Ricardo's motto, IX, 239
- England could be the happiest country, V, 55

Hardcastle, Daniel (pseudonym of Richard Page), *Letters on the Bank Restriction,* 1819, V, 361 n., VIII, 3 n.

Hardenhuish, home of the Clutterbucks, IX, 296, X, 62, 315; Ricardo's tomb at, X, 12

Hardware, I, 134, 406, II, 390–1, IV, 251, V, 102

Hare, Augustus, *Life and Letters of Maria Edgeworth,* VI, xxxii n., VII, 264 n., IX, 143 n., 230, 295 n., X, 167

Harman, Jeremiah, Governor of the Bank of England, his evidence in 1810, III, 363, 372–7, IV, 68 n.; in 1819, V, 10 & n., 353, 363

Harrow School, VII, 138, X, 267

Harrowby, Earl of, V, 351, 354, 365, 416, 439

Hartley, David, IX, 332

Harvests, bad:

- and foreign exchange, III, 106–7, VI, 37
- and wage regulation, I, 162
- in 1816, VII, 61, 66, 87, 90
- see also Abundance

Harvey, Robert Crytoft, evidence on agriculture, IV, 210, 239–40

Hashizume, Akeo, X, 384

Hastings, Warren, VII, 237, 249

Haultain, Mr, X, 147

Haygarth, John, *Provident Institution at Bath,* 1816, VII, 130

Hazlitt, William, 'Periodical Press', in *Edinburgh Review,* 1823, V, xxvii n., VI, xxii, VII, 28 n., VIII, 185–6 n.

Heaphy, Thomas, portrait of Ricardo, VIII, facing p. 1, X, 51, 53

Heathfield, Richard, letter to, VIII, 143–5

Plan for the Liquidation of the Public Debt, 1819, VIII, 143 n.

Heidelberg, visit in 1817, VII, 160, 164, 167; in 1822, X, 227–8

Henriques de Castro, D., *De Synagoge der Portugeesch-Israelietische Gemeente,* X, 18 n.

Hereford:

- celebration for Joseph Hume (1821), IX, 113, 118–19, 121, 141 & n., Ricardo's speech at, V, 471–4, 515
- County meetings: in support of income tax (1822), IX, 247; Cobbett attacks Ricardo at (1823), IX, 266–7 & n.
- see also VII, 299, X, 98

Hertford, VI, 60–1. See East India College
Heygate, Alderman William, M.P. for Sudbury, IV, 232 n., V, 17, 61–2, 203, 295
Hibbert, X, 309, 310
Hicks, H., VII, 293, 304, 336, IX, 13
Hill, J., *Life and Writings of Hugh Blair,* 1807, VI, 326
Hills, Mrs Eustace, unpublished life of Richard Sharp, VI, xxxvi–xxxvii, VII, 291 n., XI, xxvii
Himes, N. E., 'The place of J. S. Mill and Robert Owen in Neo-Malthusianism', VIII, 72 n.
Hindus, civilisation of, VII, 223, 228, 249; metaphysics, VII, 235 n.; see also VI, 96 n.
Hitchings, James, tutor of Ricardo's children, VI, 240 & n., VII, 51, 71, 144, X, 62, 63, 389; his obituary of Ricardo, VI, xxxv
Hitzigrath, H., *Merchant Adventurers in Hamburg,* III, 430
Hoarding of gold: in banks, VI, 289, 300–1; by timid people, III, 172, 322; incitement to, by Cobbett, IX, 167 & n., 176
Hoare, P. R., *Examination of Sir John Sinclair's Observations,* 1811, X, 402; *On National Bankruptcy,* 1811, X, 400
Hoare's Bank, VI, 116
Hobhouse, Sir Benjamin, VII, 109–10, 113
Hobhouse, Edward, X, 273, 275
Hobhouse, John Cam:
  and the Westminster election, VII, 357 & n., 360, 372
  on Ricardo first reading Adam Smith, X, 36
  Mill on, VII, 363, VIII, 59
  see also V, 484, VII, 131 n., VIII, 56, 300, IX, 268, X, 58 n., 227–8, 236 and under Broughton, Lord
Hobhouse, Miss, VIII, 56, 59, 75
Hodges, John, stockbroker, VI, 112 n., X, 126–8
Hodges, William, VI, 112 n.
Hodgetts, T., engraver, X, 52
Hodgson, David, corn merchant:
  his method of forecasting crops, VIII, 370 & n., 371–2
  invites Ricardo to stand for election at Liverpool, IX, 182, XI, xiv
Hofwyl, X, 262
Holl, William, engraver, X, 52, 369
Holland:
  Ricardo's ancestors in, X, 17–21
  visits to, when young, X, 3–4, 30–3; in 1822, IX, 209–11, 213, X, 193–213
  low rate of profits and interest in, I, 290 n., IX, 160
  commerce in, article by M[c]Culloch, IX, 135 & n., 139
  see also I, 148, IV, 32, VI, 97, IX, 222, and under Amsterdam
Holland, Dr Henry, VII, 269
  Recollections of Past Life, VII, 269 n.
Holland House, VII, 54 n., 114, IX, 94, 101; Ricardo's visit, VII, 144 n.
Holland, Lady, IX, 94
  Memoir of Sydney Smith, IX, 89 n., 108 n.
Holland, Lord, VII, 54 n., VIII, 28 n., 335, IX, 94, X, 50, 396
  Memoirs of the Whig Party, 1807–21, VII, 222 n.
Holland, Swinton, supports ingot plan, V, 355–6; see also VIII, 367 n., IX, 173 n., 208
Hollander, Jacob H.:
  The Economic Library of, III, 5 n.
  David Ricardo, A Centenary Estimate, I, xxii n., IV, 203 n., X, 17 n., 18 & n., 20 & n., 21 n., 29, 37 n., 81 n.
  'Development of Ricardo's Theory of Value,' I, xxxvii, xl n.
  see also II, xv, III, 406, VII, 155 n., VIII, 136 n., X, 371–3, 387
Holroyd, Justice, VII, 293
Holte, Lady, X, 169
Homburg, X, 224–5
Hone, William, parodies of the Church Catechism, etc., 1817, prosecution for, V, 325 & n.
Hope, Mr, IX, 208

Hope, Sir Alexander, VII, 313 n.
Hopkins, T., *Bank notes,* Ricardo's comments on, X, 402
Hori, Tsuneo, X, 384
Horner, Francis, VI, xxxiv–xxxv
  and the bullion question, III, 9–10, 413–14, VI, 1–7, X, 8, 14–15, 92
  and foreign exchanges, III, 12, VI, 8–10, 78–81
  on price of corn regulating all other prices, I, 302–3
  motion for resumption of cash payments in 1816, IV, 51, VII, 28, 30
  on Locke's good temper in argument, VII, 206, 212
  his last illness, VII, 85, 89–90; tomb at Leghorn, IX, 227–8, X, 322
  letters to, VI, 1–10, 78–81; Malthus's letter to, VI, 186–8
  see also V, xiv, VI, 23, 66, 127, 159 n., VII, 193, VIII, 160, IX, 123 n., X, 49, 50, 388, XI, xxvii
  articles in *Edinburgh Review:* on Thornton's *Paper Credit,* 1802, III, 64; on Lord King's pamphlet, 1803, III, 73, 83; on a bounty on the exportation of corn, 1804, I, 302, 307, 315
  Memoirs and Correspondence, VI, 127 n.; ed. 2, III, 9–10 & n.
Horner, Leonard, VIII, 160; see also III, 10 n., VI, xxxv, 187
Horses:
  substitution of, for labour of men, I, 394–5, II, 335; and vice-versa, II, 237–9 & n.
  employed in husbandry, I, 82
  ill-treatment of horses bill, V, 122
  Lord John Russell's horse, IV, 258 & n.
  ploughing with horses in the Netherlands, X, 188
  tax on, I, 205, 242, 251, V, 101
  horses at Gatcomb, VI, 130–1, 267, VII, 361, 365, VIII, 48, 78, 231–2, IX, 44–5, X, 168; 'Old Consul', X, 348, see also 342
  on the Continent, VII, 163–4, X, 177, 183, 216, 222, 234, 237, 251, 260, 310–11, 313, 324, 343
Horton, John Robert Wilmot, letter to, XI, xv
  Outline of a Plan of Emigration to Upper Canada, 1823, and *Causes and Remedies of Pauperism,* 1829, XI, xv notes
Horwood, R., *Plan of London,* 1799, X, 29 n.
House of Commons:
  interests controlling it, V, 284, 286, 288, 470, 478, 496, VII, 49, 323, VIII, 163, 304, 330, IX, 4, 158, 198
  its ministerial compliance, V, 269
  Mill on venality of members, VI, 253, 263, 307, 310–11
  see also Parliament, Reform
Household suffrage, V, 473, 485, VII, 273 & n.
Houses, taxes on, I, 201–4; house and window duties, V, 79, 84 n.
Hudson, John, Trinity College Tutor, X, 136, 139
Hughan, T., III, 429 n.
Humboldt, Alexander von, IX, 219
  Essai Politique sur la Nouvelle Espagne, 1811, II, 28, 337–44, VII, 184, 189; English translation, X, 394; see also IX, 252, X, 293 n.
Hume, David:
  on magic effect of rise of prices, IV, 36, V, 524
  and *Wealth of Nations,* I, vii, XI, xxvii
  Essays and Treatises, VII, 197, X, 399
  Natural History of Religion, X, 395
  Political Discourses, Of Interest, III, 90, V, 12 & n.; Of Money, IV, 36–7, V, 524, VI, 34
  see also III, 163, VII, 227, 229
Hume, David, judge, XI, xxvii
Hume, Joseph, M.P. for Aberdeen and Montrose, VI, 138 & n., VIII, 209–10 & n.
  his description of Gatcomb, VI, 158
  reads *Principles,* VII, 364–5, 373
  tribute to Ricardo, V, 332
  presents petition from Mary Ann Carlile, V, 277

Hume, Joseph (*cont.*)
motion against combination laws in 1824, Ricardo's promised support for, V, xx, 332
on free discussion of religious opinions, V, 324, 330 & n., XI, xxii
sinking fund and pensions scheme, V, 161, 191–4
Spitalfields Acts, V, 295
his activity in parliament, VIII, 202, 209–10, IX, 45–6
his 'phalanx', V, xxii n.
speech in honour of, V, 471–4, IX, 141 n., see also IX, 113, 118–22, 141, 144–5
Ricardo's letter to, XI, ix, see also X, 388
see also V, 138, 185, 278 n., 281, 467, 476, VI, 107, 127, 310, 313, 325, 332, VII, 141, 303, 314, 336, 358 n., 361, 371, VIII, 8, 72, 296, 323–4, IX, 41–2, 123, 153–4, 186, 194, 228, X, 13, 58, 267 n., 388, XI, xvii, xx
Proceedings in Herefordshire, 1822, V, 471 n.
Account of the Provident Institution for Savings, 1816, VII, 34 n., 47 n.
Hume, Mrs Joseph, XI, ix n., x
Humphrey Carvick & Co., III, 430
Humphrys, Mr, VII, 327
Hunt, Henry, VII, 270 n., VIII, 66, 99, 129, IX, 120
Hunting and shooting, V, 122, VI, 300, VII, 308–9, 318–19, 335, VIII, 360 n., X, 162, 336
Huskisson, William, M.P. for Chichester, later for Liverpool, IX, 182 n., President of the Board of Trade, 1823, IX, 270 n.
his liberal principles, V, xx, 305
tribute to Ricardo, V, 332
joint author of Bullion Report, III, 413 n.
his singular argument for lowering bank rate, IV, 234 & n.
on the standard of currency, V, 198, 216–18
on unrestricted issue of paper, V, 316
Huskisson (*cont.*)
in committee on resumption of cash payments, V, 351, 353–4, 356, VIII, 19
defends sinking fund, V, 79
in agricultural committee, 1821, V, xxiv–xxv, 86, IX, 37, 197; draws up report, IV, 203, VIII, 390; declines attending 1822 committee, IX, 177
resolutions on corn importation, V, 159, 169, 172, 175, IX, 197
differs from Ricardo on desirable extent of agriculture, IX, 7–8
merchant vessels apprenticeship, V, 273, 283
East and West India sugars, V, 301
reciprocity of duties on shipping, V, 305
for repeal of Spitalfields Acts, V, 292, 308–9, IX, 318
see also V, xxi, 136, 223, 256, 282, 321, 335, 461, VII, 153, VIII, 374, IX, 176
Depreciation of our Currency, 1810, III, 11, 111–12, 171 n., 177 n., 209–10, 227, 252–4, VI, 34, IX, 270 n.; passages on which Ricardo differs, X, 400 & n.; Ricardo's lost remarks on, X, 400 n.
Speech on the State of the Finance, 1813, IV, 154, 166–7, 200
Speeches, 1831, IX, 177 n., 270 n., with biography by E. Leeves, XI, xxix
William Huskisson, by A. Brady, III, 427
Hutcheson, Archibald, *Proposal for Payment of the Publick Debts* (1714), anticipates Ricardo's plan, V, 40, 41 n., see also I, 248 n.
Hutchinson, Christopher Hely-, M.P. for Cork, V, 474
Hyamson, A. M., *The Sephardim of England,* X, 18 n., 23 n., 27 n.
Hyde, Osman Ricardo's residence, VII, 182, 186 & n., see also VII, 171, VIII, 48
Hyde Park, walks in, VI, xxviii n., VII, 277

Ice machine, IV, 249
Idleness, luxury of, VII, 70, 184–5. See Indolence
Impey, Mr, VII, 132
Import duties:
on butter, V, 218–19; candles, V, 146; cheese, V, 146; tallow, V, 146–7, 291, 294; timber, V, 102–4, 110–11; wool, V, 42
reciprocity of, V, 305–6
see also Countervailing duties, Protecting duties, Sugar
Improvements in agriculture:
two kinds of, I, 80–4
effect on profits, I, 120, II, 140–1, IV, 11 & n., 19 n., VI, 94–5, 145, 162, 339
effect on rent, I, 79–80, II, 135–6, IV, 19 n., 41, VI, 172, 190, 293–4; long and short term effects, I, 81 n., 412, II, 112–13, 118, 185, 198, VI, 302, VII, 282–3, VIII, 182, 184, 208
see also II, 161, IV, 346, V, 94, 211, VI, 104, 194, and under Leases
Inclosure bills, VII, 299, X, 98
Income, gross and net, I, 420–5
net income increased by machinery, gross income diminished, I, 388–9, see also 396
country enriched only by net income, II, 235; labouring class affected by how it is spent, I, 392–3
all taxes paid from net income, I, 178
net real income (rent and profits), I, 348
see also Revenue
Income tax:
no effect on prices, III, 241, IV, 216–17, VIII, 153
and tax on capital, I, 152–3
prying into every man's concerns, I, 160–1, and cp. VIII, 154
began 1798, VI, 282; raised to 10%, VI, 275; ended 1816, VII, 25 n.; proposed revival, 1819, VIII, 135, 190, 196
see also III, 138, IX, 246–7, and under Tax on property
India:
government of, by correspondence, VIII, 40 n.; see also IX, 116, and under Mill, James, *History of India*
labour in, IX, 305, 322, 337, 347–9
see also East India Company
India bonds, III, 291, 295, 298, IX, 262
Indies, see East Indies, West Indies
Indolence:
preferred to riches, II, 313–15, 338, VII, 70
easily obtained food and, II, 87, 334, 339–41, VII, 184–5, IX, 56; in Ireland, I, 100 n., IX, 231; in South America, II, 337, VIII, 216
'Ingenious calculator' (William Morgan), IV, 415–18; see also III, 358 n., IV, 99, 279, VI, 275
Ingliss, Stewart, IX, 184, 187, 194
Ingot plan:
paying bank notes in bullion, IV, 65–70
savings from, V, 433–4, 444–5
circulation of gold coin compatible with, V, 429–31
first suggested 1811, III, 124–7; proposed to Perceval, VI, 43–6, 70, to Tierney, VI, 67–71
submitted to 1819 committees, V, 354–64, VIII, 20–1, 23; Ricardo's evidence: Commons', V, 379–90, 405–6, 409–15, Lords', 422–33, 439–44, 450–6; his speech, V, 9–17
supported by Baring, V, 91–2, 352 n., 356, 358–61, by the Governor of the Bank, V, 363–4; as a temporary measure, by Tooke, V, 361–2, by Samuel Thornton, V, 363
opposed by Rothschild, V, 357, by Harman, V, 363
adopted till 1823, V, 7–8 & n., 367–8; with deviations, VIII, 26–7, 31–2, 35–7, 39; whether to be made permanent, V, 40, 46, 70, 92, 135
danger of forgery of small notes, V, 96–7

Ingot plan (*cont.*)
Grenfell on, VI, 286; Malthus, VI, 41 & n., 298–9; McCulloch, VIII, 36, X, 370; Torrens opposed to, VIII, 82–3; attacked by Cobbett, VIII, 74 & n., IX, 176 & n.
ingots called 'Ricardoes', V, 368–9; few demanded, V, 76, 311–12; see also IX, 176 n.
not fairly tried, IV, 224–5, V, 165, 312, 518, IX, 123, 141
see also I, 356–61, II, 48–9, IV, 104, V, xix, xxxiii, 71, 73, 204, 516–17, VI, 165, 300–1, VII, 353, VIII, 5, 6, 134, 361, IX, 201
Inquiry into...the Nature of Demand, 1821 (anon.), IX, 27 & n.
Insurance, I, 263, III, 19, 71, 161, 183, VI, 284 & n., IX, 104 & n.
Intellectual attainments, demand and supply of, VII, 131
Interest, see Rate of interest
Interests:
of the individual and of the community, I, 133–4, 349–50 n., III, 56
of landlords, contrasted with those of farmers or manufacturers, I, 312–13, II, 199–200, V, 158 n., and with those of consumers, I, 335–6, II, 117–18, V, 87; opposed to interests of every other class, IV, 21, VII, 17, VIII, 182, 207–8, see also II, 198, V, 314
of master and workmen, opposite regarding machinery, I, 388, 392, IX, 194
see also V, 53
Interlaken, X, 253–4, 258
Inventions, destroy capital but this no reason for suppression, I, 271, IV, 33; see also V, 179, and under Machinery
Inverarity MS, VI, 159 n.
Ionian Islands, vote on, V, xxii
Ireland:
bank failures, V, 70, 99
Catholic emancipation, V, xxii-xxiii, VIII, 50, 350–1, 369, see also V, 329–30

Ireland (*cont.*)
corn imports from, IV, 259–60, V, 94, 108, 125, VIII, 369, IX, 158
currency, III, 398–9
curse of small farms, IX, 145–6, 153, 314, 372
indolence and low profits, II, 344–9, VII, 184 & n.
Insurrection bill, V, xxii
labouring poor, Ricardo member of committee on, V, xxvi–xxvii, 331 n., IX, 313 & n., 314, 316, 372
Lord-lieutenancy, motion for abolition of, V, xxii; see also IX, 145
Malthus's tour of, VII, 168, 174–6, 184
misrule in, IX, 153, 295–6, see also V, 99
potato famine in 1822, V, 234–5, IX, 231–2, 254
protecting duties, V, 57–8, 104, 218–19
remedies for evils of, I, 100 n., VII, 48, 334
taxation in, IX, 160 & n., 185 & n.
tithes composition bill, V, 304; see also IX, 153, 186
see also IV, 32 n., 408, V, 36, VI, 244, IX, 239–40, 274, Bank of Ireland and Exchange, Irish
Irving, John, M.P. for Bramber, V, 37 & n., 98
Isle of Wight, VII, 279, 283
Islington, VI, 49, 56, X, 25
Isola Bella, X, 291
Israel, early family name of the Ricardos, X, 18 & n. 4
Israel, Hannah, wife of Joseph Israel Ricardo, X, 19, XI, xxix
Italy, visit to, IX, 221–8, X, 291–339
Iveson, John, IV, 210–11, 260

Jackson, Randle, spokesman for Bank of England on Bullion report, III, 9 n., 145–53, 358–9
opposes increasing dividend, V, 466–7
on East India College, VII, 130 n., 131, 135–6, 138

Jackson, Sir T., & Co., loan contractors, X, 85
Jacob, William, witness before agricultural committee, V, xxiv, IX, 67, 87
Letter to Samuel Whitbread, 1815, I, 268 n., VI, 180, 186, 190
Jacobs, Mr, his piety, X, 389
Jamaica, I, 339, III, 350, X, 350 n.; see also Exchange
James, J. T., *Journal of a Tour in Germany*, 1816, X, 395
James, William, letter in Ricardo Papers, X, 388
Jannaccone, P., VIII, 375 n.
Jefferson, Thomas, on Ricardo's *Principles*, X, 372
Jeffrey, Francis, editor of *Edinburgh Review*:
articles by, X, 397; in *Scotsman*, VIII, 82
vetoes M^c^Culloch's reviewing of Malthus, VIII, 139, 189, 325
his 'mercenary troops', III, 9
see also VII, 353, VIII, 166, 205, 351, IX, 206 n., 218, 342, X, 50, 272
Jeffrey, Mrs (*née* Charlotte Wilkes), VIII, 205, X, 272 & n.
Jenks, L. H., *The Migration of British Capital to 1875*, X, 58 n.
Jenner, Dr, given the palm over Napoleon, X, 211
Jesus College, Cambridge, VI, xix, xx n.
Jew brokers, X, 22, 56–7, see also IX, 267 n.
Jewish Historical Society of England, *Transactions*, IX, 278 n.; *Miscellanies*, X, 22 n., 57 n., 60 n.
Jewish origin of Ricardo, X, 16–33, 37–9
Jews, letter on disabilities of, IX, 277–8
Jobbers, Stock-Exchange, X, 69–70; Ricardo a jobber, X, 70–3
Joel, Jacob de, X, 26
John Bull, newspaper, IX, 136, 204
Johnson, J. M., III, 432–3
Johnstone, A., *London Commercial Guide*, 1817, VI, 284 n.
Johnstone, A. Cochrane, and the Stock Exchange hoax, VI, 105–7
Johnstone, George, *Speech on Lord Stanhope's bill*, 1811, X, 400
Jonas, J., X, 383
Jonathan, D., X, 336 n.
Jones, Inigo, his work at Ford Abbey, VI, 125
Jungfrau, X, 254
Junius, VI, 10 n.

Kaltenbrunn, X, 239
Kay-Shuttleworth, Nina, see Hills, Mrs Eustace
Keelmen, strike of, VIII, 99
Kegan Paul, C., *William Godwin*, VIII, 114 n.
Kelly, Patrick, III, 168, 186
The Universal Cambist, IX, 183–4 & n.
Kemble, John Philip, X, 268–9
Kennington, Ricardo's homes at, X, 46, 110–11
Kensington Gardens, see Walks
Kent, Duke of, takes chair at meeting on Owen's plan, V, 467 & n.; persuades Ricardo to join committee, VIII, 45–6; see also VII, 346
Keynes, J. M., 'Robert Malthus', in *Essays in Biography*, VI, xiii, 35 n.
Keyser, Isaac (D.R.'s brother-in-law), VII, 15, 240, X, 56–7
Keyser, Rebecca (D.R.'s sister), see Ricardo, Rebecca
Kiddington, X, 36 n., 64
King, Lord:
demands his rents in gold, 1811, V, 316
scheme for resumption, V, 353
suggests stopping Bank dividends while gold at a premium, VII, 262–3
and *Principles*, VII, 250–1
see also V, 351, 354, 356, VI, 231, VII, 173, VIII, 19, 164, IX, 123 n.
Thoughts on the Restriction of Payments [1803], III, 4, 51, VI, 9, VII, 250 n.; Horner on, III, 73, 83
Thoughts on the Effects of the Bank Restrictions, 1804, III, 51, 173, VI, 9

King of Clubs, VI, 87 n., X, 50; see also VI, 91, 171, 180, 196, 198, 220, VII, 8, 18, 20, 136, 138, 262, 291 n., VIII, 18, IX, 151, 157
Kinnaird, Douglas, on East India College, VII, 131–2; see also IX, 41–2
Kinoshita, Akira, X, 385
Kirkcudbright, IX, 135 n., 302 & n.
Kirkland, Nugent, and Portarlington seat, V, xvi, VII, 216, 232, 346–7
Kirkpatrick & Co., III, 430
Knatchbull, Sir Edward, M.P. for Kent, V, 81, 86, 90
Knotty point on fixed value and changing profits (Malthus), IX, 65–6, 74–85, 90–101, 111–13; other knotty points, IX, 158 & n.
Knyvett, his concert, VI, 90; at Gatcomb, VIII, 282
Koch, Christian Friedrich, hock merchant at Frankfort, X, 223 & n., 226
Koe, John Herbert, Bentham's amanuensis, VI, 161 n., VII, 74, 336, 351
Koizumi, Shinzo, X, 384
Kolthammer, F. W., X, 365
Kotzebue, A., his play 'The Stranger', X, 199
Kunatt, Stanislaw, young Pole met on the Simplon, X, 289–90 & n., 301, see also IX, 223–4; translator of Ricardo, X, 379

Labour:
- demand for, not the same as supply of necessaries, VIII, 236, 248, 258 n.; depends on circulating, not on fixed, capital, II, 234 & n., see also I, 395–6 n.; diminished by taxation, I, 233, VIII, 177
- economy in the use of, I, 25–6, 36, 44, 51, 65 n., 80, 133; see also Machinery
- estimation of different qualities of, I, 20–2
- immediate and accumulated, IV, 379–80, 386, IX, 307, 338–9, 365, see also I, 34, 410, VII, 316 n., IX, 323, 343, 385

Labour (*cont.*)
- natural and market price of, I, 93–7, II, 227–8, 268; commodity price of, II, 371; see also Wages, natural price of
- quantity of, in a day's work, different in different countries, II, 87, IX, 305, 309–10, 319, 322, 337, 347–9
- quantity of, as measure of value, I, 12–13, 15, 17 & n., 85–6, 88, IV, 381–6, 397; not a perfect, but a tolerable one, II, 66–7, IV, 405
  - labour bestowed on a commodity (Ricardo), I, 13–14, 24–5, 37, 46–7, 73, II, 34–5, 101–2, IV, 387, IX, 348; and on machines, II, 87
  - labour commanded (Malthus), II, 29–30, 383, 410–11, IX, 348, see also I, 18–19, IX, 1–3
- see also Employment, Value, measure of, Wages

Labour of horses, I, 394, II, 335; of machines, VIII, 138, IX, 325 n., 369; of nature, I, 76 n.
Labourers:
- real condition of, II, 249–50
- their situation in a general glut, II, 308
- benefit from rise in value of money (Cobbett), IX, 166, and cp. IX, 40
- their taste for enjoyments should be stimulated, I, 100 & n., see also II, 373, VI, 147, VIII, 275

Labouring classes:
- cannot contribute to taxation, I, 159, 235, and cp. 347–8 & n.
- distress of, 1819–20, V, 47, 224–5, VIII, 103
- fully employed in agriculture and in manufactures, 1821, IX, 13, 40
- see also Classes, working, Manufacturing classes

Laing, John, VII, 244–5
- *Account of a Voyage to Spitzbergen*, VII, 245 n.

Lamb, George, M.P. for Dungarvan, V, 185, VII, 363 n.

Lamb, William, M.P. for Hertfordshire (afterwards Lord Melbourne), V, xiv, xxiii, 24, 185, 350
Lambeth, Ricardo's marriage at, X, 38; his homes in, 46
Lambton, John George, M.P. for Durham, motion for the reform of parliament, V, 112, VIII, 367 n.; see also X, 36
Lancaster, Joseph, educational reformer, letter in Ricardo Papers, X, 388; see also VI, 112 n., VII, 45 n., 155 n., X, 402
Lancaster, Joseph, stockbroker, *The Bank—The Stock Exchange... An Exposé* [anon.], 1821, X, 93–4 & notes, 95 n., 123–4 & n.
Lancey, Miss, governess, IX, 241, X, 177, 197–8, 209, 220, 235, 237–8, 305, 327
Land:
  appropriation of, and value of commodities, I, 23 n., 67, 77–8
  that pays no rent, I, 74, exists in every country, I, 328, not necessary for theory of rent, I, 412–13 n., VII, 372, 379, VIII, 4, 57, 149–50; see also I, 83 n., 113, 157, 181, 225, VI, 173
  supposition of fertile tract added to island, IV, 18, VI, 162, 217–18, 220–2, see also I, 15
  neat surplus from, defined, VIII, 311
  land as a machine, I, 408, II, 118, 185, IV, 24 n., 34, VIII, 208
  see also Diminishing returns, Fertility, Rent
Land tax redemption plan, V, 248, 250, 259–60
Landaff, Bishop of, see Watson, R.
Landed gentlemen, hostility to Ricardo, VIII, 147, IX, 262, 266, X, 349
Landlords:
  their interests opposed to those of every other class, I, 335–6, II, 116–17, 198
  their interest in protection permanent, that of manufacturers temporary, I, 312–13, II, 199–200
Landlords (*cont.*)
  relinquishing their rents would not lower price of corn, I, 74–5, II, 118, 182–3, IV, 21
  make the laws, VIII, 182, IX, 158, see also V, 81, 291, VIII, 158, 348, 350, IX, 37
  Ricardo misrepresented as enemy of, II, 117–19, VIII, 207–8
Lang, A., *Life of Lockhart,* VIII, 205 n.
Lang, L., X, 383
Langman, Lady, VI, xxxv, XI, xxvii
Langston, James Haughton, M.P. for Woodstock, V, 185
Language:
  new and unusual, accusations of, I, 19, II, 190–4, IX, 283
  meaning of terms, I, 47 n., II, 322–3, III, 228–9, 247–8, V, 166, VI, 22, 25–6, 34–7, 41–2, VII, 81, 145
  disputes about words, II, 35, 224–5, 250, 259, VIII, 121–2, 149, 228–9, 311, IX, 10
  Verbal Disputes in Political Economy, IX, 27 & n., 38
Lansdowne, Lady, V, 17 n.
Lansdowne, Marquis of, VII, 284 n.
  member of Lords' committee on resumption, V, 351, 354, 356, 364–5, VIII, 19–20, IX, 270
  Ricardo's visit to Bowood, VII, 198 n.
  see also VII, 284, 291, 356, X, 37 n., and under Petty, Lord Henry
Laputa: tailors, VII, 122; philosopher, VIII, 114
La Rochefoucauld, VII, 168
Larpent, George, VIII, 367 n.
Lasteyrie-Dusaillant, Comte de, IX, 231, 253, 273
Lauderdale, Earl of:
  on supply and demand, I, 384–5
  and monopoly of the home market, VI, 169–70
  gold and silver payments by the Bank, I, 371 n., VIII, 3
  silver as standard of value, VIII, 45 & n.

Lauderdale, Earl of (*cont.*)
member of committee on resumption, V, 351, 354, 365
see also VII, 142, 265, 267, VIII, 29 n.
Inquiry into...Public Wealth, 1804, I, 276, 384
The Depreciation of the Paper Currency, 1812, VI, 81
Letter on the Corn Laws, 1814, VI, 169–70, 186, 189, 192
Three Letters...of An Old Merchant, 1819, V, 17 & n., VIII, 45 n.
Laurence, Charles, stockbroker, VII, 14
Lausanne, IX, 218, X, 264, 268–9
Lauterbrunnen, X, 257
Lavater, Johann Kaspar, his tomb, X, 238
Laveno, X, 291–2
Law Merchant, committee on, 1823, Ricardo a member, V, xxvi, 293; Report, IV, 280
Law proceedings, tax on, V, 147
Leases, and improvements in agriculture, I, 269 n., II, 142–3, 202, VI, 140, 145, 174–5, 177
Le Bas, C. W., professor of mathematics at East India College, VII, 168, 253
Ledbury, IX, 121 n.
Leeves, E., biography of Huskisson, XI, xxix
Lefevre, John George Shaw, IX, 224, X, 289 & n.
Legacy duty, I, 153, V, 315
Legal tender: silver and gold as, I, 366–72; gold only, V, 16 & n., VIII, 3; bank notes as (1811), V, 316, VI, 45, 68
Leghorn, see Livorno
Leicester Fields, ground for school, VII, 190, 198, see also VI, xxix
Leonardo da Vinci, X, 301
Le Roy, Arnaud Jacques, see Saint-Arnaud, Comte de
Le Sage, A. R., *Gil Blas,* VII, 303, X, 290
Leser, Dr E., X, 378
Leslie, John, VIII, 28 & n.; his ice machine, IV, 249
Lethbridge, Sir Thomas Buckler, M.P. for Somerset:
on pressure of taxation, V, 101 n.
on 'the abominable theories of political economists', V, 169
on absentee residents abroad, V, 186
Russian tallow, V, 291, 294
see also V, 195, IX, 265–6
Letter to the King, by a Commoner, 1820, VIII, 144 n.
Letters to the Proprietors of Bank Stock, by an Old Proprietor, 1816, VI, 276, 278, 283, 288
Levi, guide at Haarlem, X, 204
Levick, George, IX, 181 n.
Levy, Harriet, wife of Jacob Ricardo, X, 58
Lewis, Thomas Frankland, M.P. for Beaumaris, V, 351, 354, 356, VIII, 19
Leycester, Ralph, M.P. for Shaftesbury, V, 198, 202
Leyden, IX, 211, X, 204
Liberal principles of trade, IV, 70–1, IX, 269, see also V, 44, VIII, 164, 381
Library, Ricardo's, X, 399–402
Liddes, X, 285–8
Liesse, André, *Un professeur d'Économie politique sous la restauration, J.-B. Say,* IX, 192 n.
Life annuities, see Annuities
Lille (Lisle), VII, 160, X, 185–6, 188
Limitation of currency, principle of, I, 353–4, II, 48, III, 357, 373, IV, 64–5, VII, 353, VIII, 186
Lincolnshire, Malthus's visits to, VI, 34–5 & n., 40–1, VII, 193, VIII, 226, 349; see also V, 304
Lindo, Esther, *née* Delvalle (D.R.'s aunt), X, 29, 106
Lindo, Isaac, X, 29
Lindo, Miriam, wife of Benjamin Ricardo, X, 59
Lindsay, Dr James, Unitarian minister, VIII, 84, X, 40–1; robbery at his house, X, 118 & n.; see also IX, 60

Linen, duties on, I, 317, V, 57–8, 104, 290; see also IV, 374
Lisbon, VI, 85
Littleton, Edward John, M.P. for Staffordshire, V, 74, 218, 351
Liverpool election, Ricardo declines standing for, V, xix, IX, 182–3, XI, xiv
Liverpool, 1st Earl of, *Treatise on the Coins of the Realm,* 1805, I, 369 n., III, 7, 30, 31 n., 32, 41–2, 65–7, 81, 176, 189 n., 203, VII, 21, X, 390
Liverpool, 2nd Earl of, First Lord of the Treasury:
  and resumption of cash payments, V, 351, 353, 365, VIII, 134, X, 90 n.
  wants Canning in his Cabinet, IX, 115
  see also IV, 251, V, 84 & n., VIII, 200 n., 287, 294, IX, 269–70, X, 78 n., 86, 88
Livorno, Ricardo's ancestors in, X, 18 & n.; visit to, X, 321; Horner's grave, IX, 227–8, X, 322; see also IX, 234, 242, X, 323
Lloyd, Lewis, on ingot plan, V, 357–8
Loans:
  method of issuing, X, 75–9; discount on prompt payment, V, 343–4
  whether in 3 or 5% stock, IV, 184–5, V, 67, VIII, 320, 332
  for Great Britain, table of, X, 80–1
  loans bid for by Ricardo, 1806–1819, X, 75–94, see also 57–8
    in 1807, X, 80; tribute from subscribers, X, 125–8
    in 1811, X, 80; anxiety of friends, VI, 48–9 & n., 52
    in 1815, X, 82–4; and Waterloo, VI, 229, 231 & n., 233, 237–8, 245, 249, 251, 262; Malthus sells too soon, VI, 231 & n.; see also VI, 230, X, 78 n.
    in 1819, X, 84–91; and sinking fund, IV, 173, V, 18–19, VIII, 30–1, 33; speech on, V, 21–2 & n.; see also X, 78 n.
    in 1820, speech on, V, 58–60
  Report on negotiation of loan, 1796, X, 75–8 notes
Loans and taxes for war compared, I, 244–7, IV, 185–90, VIII, 170, 172
Lobatto, Rehuel Cohen, X, 18
Lobb, Charlotte, wife of Ralph Ricardo, VIII, 22 n., X, 59
Locke, John:
  favours silver as the only standard, III, 65–6, 81, 202
  corn less variable than gold, V, 210–11
  his tolerant spirit, VII, 205–6
  see also VII, 227, 229
  Essay concerning Human Understanding, VII, 197, 205–6, 211–12
  The Reasonableness of Christianity, X, 395
  Some Considerations of...Raising the Value of Money, III, 65, 81, 188, 202
  Further Considerations, I, 369, X, 390
Lockhart, John Gibson, VIII, 204, 205 n.
  Life of Scott, IX, 136 n., 187 n.
  Peter's Letters to his Kinsfolk, 1819, VIII, 25 & n., 112, 134
Lockhart, John Ingram, M.P. for Oxford:
  on Ricardo's riddle, V, 83, 88–9
  on delay of agricultural report, V, 114
  Ricardo's propositions 'destructive', V, 173, though not intentionally so, 175–6, 180
Lombardy, plains of, X, 302
London Institution, VI, 281 & n., X, 49 & n.
Londonderry, Marquis of (up to 1821 see Castlereagh, Viscount):
  on sinking fund, V, 25
  concurs with Ricardo on taxation and agriculture, V, 127 n., 154, 155
  chairman of agricultural committee, 1822, IV, 203–5, prepares report, IX, 180
  on measures for the relief of agriculture, V, 155–9, 169, 182, 185–6, 195, 197
  Mallet on, V, xxv
  his suicide, IX, 214–15, X, 241, 243
  see also V, 124, 129, 145, 174, 335

Longman, T. N., publisher, IX, 116 & n.
Lotteries, IV, 147–8, V, 3
Louis XVIII, VI, 235
Lowenthal, E., X, 372
Lowless and Crosse, Ricardo's solicitors, X, 390. See also Bleasdale, Lowless and Cross
Lowndes, Mr, V, 476
Lowry, Rebecca, *née* Delvalle (D.R.'s aunt), X, 29
Lowry, Wilson, X, 29, 49
Lubbock & Forster, Ricardo's bankers, X, 55 n., 68
Lucca, X, 324
Lucerne, X, 249; Lake of, 245–8
Luddites, V, 302 n., VIII, 385
Luneville, VII, 167
Lungern, X, 251
Lushington, Stephen Rumbold, and balance-sheet form of accounts, V, 100, 145; see also VI, 149
Luxuries:
  whether taste for, essential for net revenue, VIII, 285, 300–1, 309, see also II, 312–15, III, 276, 278, VII, 70
  expenditure on, and employment, I, 392–4, II, 332–3
  fall in price of, does not affect rate of profits, I, 132
  spending on, distinguished from prodigality, III, 284–5
  of the labourer, V, 26, see also II, 347
  luxury of the Grand Duke of Baden's palaces, VII, 165
  taxes on, I, 205, 233, 235–6, 241–4, VIII, 177, 189–90, 195–6
Lyne, Charles, *Letter to George Rose,* 1810, X, 401
Lyons, IX, 229, X, 341–3
Lyttelton, William Henry, M.P. for Worcestershire, V, 3, 26–7

Maberly, John, M.P. for Abingdon, IX, 288 & n.
  motion on retrenchment, V, 79
  public accounts, V, 145
Maberly (*cont.*)
  redemption of land tax, V, 248, 250, 259
  malt and beer tax, V, 301
  see also V, 35, 143, 185
Mc Colluch, J., innkeeper, VII, 37 n.
Mc Culloch, John Ramsay, VI, xxi–xxiii, IX, 312
  adherence to Ricardo's doctrines, VI, xxii, VIII, 376 & n.; later modified, X, 370
  reviews *Principles,* VII, 282, 291, 296–7; alterations in ed. 2 due to: on taxation, I, 152, 242, VII, 280–1, 286, 334, 349, 353, on currency, I, 354, 356–61, VII, 353, VIII, 4–5, on corn trade, I, 267, 318, VII, 354; in ed. 3, VIII, 341–2
  and article 'Funding System', VIII, 137–8, 141
  and Notes on Malthus, VIII, 296–9, 312, 315, 318, 325, 333–4, 338–40, XI, xiii
  on Ricardo's concession that some prices rise with a rise of wages, VIII, 339–40, 343, 352
  early views on machinery, VIII, 171 n.; reverses his opinion, VIII, 366 n.; shocked by Ricardo's change of view, VIII, 381–6, 391–2, IX, 9, 13–14, 18–19
  accumulated profits regarded as labour, IX, 358, see also IV, 377–8, 410–11
  on 'labour of machines', IX, 369, see also VIII, 138, IX, 325 n., 343, 354 n., 358–9
  joins in discussions on absolute and exchangeable value, IX, 301–3, 309, 312–13, 353, 358, 363, 366–9, 375, 377, see also 324–5
  his measure of value, IV, 376–9, 410–12; goes further than Ricardo, IX, 178, 185. See also Value, measure of
  on tampering with the standard of currency, VIII, 392, 396, IX, 15

McCulloch, J. R. (*cont.*)
suggests reducing interest on national debt, I, 426 n., VII, 93; too violent for Ricardo, VII, 37–8, 102–6; later disowns, VII, 93 n.; suppresses Ricardo's revealing note, I, 426 n.; see also VIII, 378 n.
his proposal for paying off national debt, VIII, 157–8 & n., see also VII, 351–2, VIII, 4
attacks corn laws, IX, 160, 186, 197
disagrees with Blake on depreciation, IX, 271–2, 275–7, 284–7, 289, 302, 312
on Malthus as an economist, VIII, 139, 167, 312, 378; not allowed to review him in *Edinburgh Review,* VIII, 189, 325; meets him in London, IX, 312
holds private class in political economy, VIII, 365–6, IX, 134 & n., 155; his public course, IX, 272 & n., 277, 301; sends lectures to Ricardo for comment, IX, 134–5, 139, 178–9, 184–5, 192–4
visit to London, IX, 275, 284, 290–1, 301–2, 312
resents John Wilson's election as professor, VIII, 204–5 & n., IX, 205 n.
abused by Scottish tories, VIII, 205 n., IX, 205–6 & n.
Ricardo memorial lectures, IX, 301 n., 391 & n.
list of letters, IX, 394–5
see also II, viii–xi, 64 n., 353 n., 452 n., IV, 146, 375 n., VII, 245 n., 259, 307, 339, X, 35 n., 59, 372, 387

Articles in *Edinburgh Review*

1818: on Ricardo's *Principles,* VII, 179 n., 278–9, 280–2, 285–9, 291, 295–7, 309, 316 n., 319
on *Economical and Secure Currency,* IV, 47, VII, 353–4, 383, VIII, 1–2, 5–6, 10, 20, 23–4
1819: Trade with France, VIII, 82, 127

Articles in *Edinburgh Review* (*cont.*)
1820: Taxation and the Corn Laws, I, lviii, VIII, 164–6, 168–74, 176–7
Foreign Commerce, VIII, 190, 197
Tithes, VIII, 203, 214, 222, 229, 237, 262
1821: Effects of Machinery, I, lviii, VIII, 325, 338, 351–2, 366 & n., 373, 378, 383, IX, 9, 18
Degrading the Standard of Money, VII, 93 n., VIII, 392, 396, IX, 7 n., 15
1822: High and Low Taxes, IX, 160, 185
Corn Laws, IX, 186, 188, 192, 197
Ireland, IX, 186
1823: Funding System, VIII, 223
East and West India Sugars, IX, 273, 277
1824: Combination Laws, VIII, 313 n., 338
Rise and Fall of Profits, IX, 179 n.
East India Company, IX, 330
1827: Taxation, VIII, 238 n., IX, 342, 345, 362
1830: Commerce in Holland, IX, 135 n.

Articles in *Scotsman*

1818: on Ricardo's *Principles,* VII, 219–20, 222, 256
1819: Importation of Foreign Corn, VIII, 28
1820: Ricardo's plan for paying off national debt, VIII, 157
Merchants' Petition, VIII, 178 n.
Malthus's *Principles,* VIII, 178, 185
Corn Laws, VIII, 197
Translation of Say's *Traité,* VIII, 315, 374
1821: Reduction of the Standard, VIII, 378 & n., IX, 15
Agricultural Report, IX, 7–8
Evidence in Political Economy, IX, 162 n.
High and Low Taxation, IX, 185 n.

Articles in *Scotsman* (*cont.*)
1822: Money, V, 515, IX, 140 n.
Peel's bill, IX, 149 & n.
County Meetings, IX, 159 & n.
Standard of National Prosperity, IX, 179
Rate of Profit, IX, 179
Protection to Agriculture, IX, 183 n.
Cost of Production, IX, 206 n.
Progress of Commercial Science, IX, 187 n.
1823: Blake's *Observations on Expenditure,* IV, 326, IX, 284–5, 286 n., 289, 301 & n.
Combination Laws, VIII, 313 n.
Obituary of Ricardo, X, 369
1824: Exchangeable value, IX, 366 n.

Articles in *Supplement to Encyclopaedia Britannica*

Corn Laws and Trade, I, 267 n., 318 n., VII, 295, 337, 354, VIII, 22, 37, 159
Cottage System, VII, 295, 337, IX, 231
Exchange, VII, 384, VIII, 2–3, 37, 81, 85–93, 126, 128, 131, 139, 140–1
Interest, VIII, 313, 316, 338, 341, 345
Money, IX, 134, 140, 149, 157, 159
Political Economy, VIII, 189 n., IX, 187 n., 206, 271, 275, 330–1
Value, VIII, 189 & n., 203, 214, 226, 229, IX, 313 n., 334

Other Works

article on value in *Edinburgh Magazine,* 1818, IV, 307, VII, 315–16 n., 324, 326, 354, 362, 364, 376
Essay on a Reduction of the Interest on the National Debt, 1816, VII, 37–8, 93 n.; enlarged version, 1816, I, 426 n., VII, 93, 102–5, X, 399
Progress of Commercial Science, 1822, IX, 186–7 & n.
Rise of Political Economy, 1824, IX, 134 n., 162 n., 178 n.
Principles of Political Economy, 1825, IX, 275 n., 325 n.

McCulloch, Other Works (*cont.*)
Literature of Political Economy, 1845, II, xiv n., III, 6, VI, xxii, VII, 93 n., VIII, 337 n., IX, 135 n., 277 n.
Early English Tracts on Commerce, 1856, IX, 150 n.
Treatises and Essays, 1859, VI, xxii, X, 370
Note on Rent, IV, 6–7 & n.
his edition of Ricardo's *Works,* II, xiv, V, 488, VI, xxii, X, 368–70, see also VII, 93 n., X, 377, 381; table of corresponding pages in other editions of *Principles,* I, 443–7, of Pamphlets, III, 435–7, IV, 419–22
publishes Ricardo's papers on parliamentary reform, V, 489–90, 494, X, 368
Life and Writings of Ricardo, successive versions, X, 369–70, see also I, xix, II, xiv, III, 6 & n., IV, 8 n., 358, V, xx n., VI, xxii, X, 14, 29, 35 n., 38–9, 53, 375
Letters to David Ricardo, VI, xxiii
Macculloch, Dr John, geologist, VII, 309 & n., 319
McCulloch, William, Examiner of India Correspondence, VIII, 251 & n., 252, 254, 262–3; see also VIII, 241, IX, 333, 373
Macdonagh, Michael, *The Reporters' Gallery,* V, xxvii n., xxviii n., xxxi n.
Macdonald, Captain D., letter in Ricardo Papers, X, 388
McDonnell, Alexander, VIII, 57 & n., 62, 75, 152 n.
Machiavelli's tomb, X, 317
Machinery, I, 386–97
early view: beneficial to labourers, I, 386–8; raises wages, IV, 35; employs no less labour, II, 351–3, V, 30, 31 n., VII, 157–9, VIII, 171, 215; see also II, 365, VI, 228
transitional view, II, 234–9
later view, injurious to labourers, I, 388–92, V, 302–3; Barton's view found correct, I, 395–6 n.

Machinery (*cont.*)
Ricardo's change of view discussed, I, lvii–lx, 386, VIII, 373 & n.; earliest statement of, VIII, 377; McCulloch shocked, VIII, 381–6, 391–2, IX, 14–15, 18, answer to, VIII, 386–90, 398–400; labouring-class opinion, IX, 18 & n., and cp. VIII, 384–5; discussion at Political Economy Club, IX, 9 & n., 158 n., 159
increases net revenue, but may diminish gross, I, 389–92, VIII, 387, IX, 13, 14, 23, see also VI, 294
always the product of less labour than it displaces, I, 42, 62; in constant competition with labour, I, 395
effects of, on the relative value of commodities, I, 30–8, 59–63, II, 361–2, III, 303
adds to riches, not to value, I, 286 & n., 287, see also III, 334
and rate of profit, I, 131–3, 387, see also I, 62, II, 408
no cause of unequal distribution of property, IX, 243–4
difference with Malthus on, defined, VIII, 387, see also II, 361, 365
old countries impelled to employ, I, 41 n.
should not be discouraged, I, 396–7, V, 303
restrictions on export of, opposed, V, xx, 332
Cobbett defends use of, V, 302–3 & n.
manual weavers and, V, 68, 302–3
land as a machine, II, 118, 185, IV, 24 n., 34, VIII, 208
workmen regarded as (McCulloch), IX, 343
labour of (McCulloch's notion), VIII, 138, IX, 325 n., 369; questioned by Ricardo, IX, 358–9
employed in agriculture, I, 15, 82, II, 335 n.; in cotton manufacture, IV, 33, V, 68; in mining, I, 14, V, 93 n., 391 & n., 427, VIII, 3
wear and tear of, I, 39

Machinery (*cont.*)
see also I, 16, 25, 266, 271, V, 55, 290, 450, IX, 193, and under Capital, fixed, Steam engines, Thrashing machine
Machlup, Dr Fritz, X, 378–9
Mackenzie, Alexander, *Voyages from Montreal,* 1801, VII, 189, X, 394
Mackintosh, Sir James, M.P. for Knaresborough:
appointed to East India College, VII, 251 & n.
his eloquence, VIII, 148
on *Essay on Profits,* VI, 182
on *Principles,* VII, 280
on Reform, VII, 263 & n., VIII, 68 n., 327–8
unlucky article on eve of Waterloo, VI, 280
see also V, xxi, xxii, 128, 335, 351, VI, 87 n., VII, 111, 253–4, 284, VIII, 22, 25 n., 107, 375, X, 50
articles on Parliamentary Reform in *Edinburgh Review,* 1818, VII, 263 n., 1820, VIII, 327–8 & n.
Vindiciae Gallicae, 1791, X, 398
Letter to Pitt on his Apostacy from Reform (anon.), 1792, VIII, 63, 68, 77, 84, 148
MacMinn, N., and others, *Bibliography of J. S. Mill,* IV, 7 n., IX, 385 n.
McNiven, Mrs Charles, X, 272–3 & n.
Macon, X, 342
Macrae, and the Stock Exchange hoax, VI, 106
McVickar, John, *Outlines of Political Economy,* 1825, IV, 147 n.
Maggiore, Lake, X, 291
Mahomed Reza Khan, VII, 237
Maitland, Charles Fox, X, 139
Malines, X, 191
Mallet, Sir Bernard, I, xi
Mallet, John Lewis, diarist:
first meeting with Ricardo, VII, 50 n.
on Ricardo's physical appearance, X, 51; his personality, VIII, 152–3 n., X, 51; his Stock Exchange activity, X, 73

Mallet, J. L. (*cont.*)
and Moses Ricardo, X, 16–17
glimpse of the agricultural committee, V, xxv
impact of Ricardo's speech on resumption, V, 17 n.
Ricardo cheered by Ministers, V, 127 n.
Robert Owen incident, V, 331 n.
inner workings of resumption committees, V, 352–4, 365–6, VIII, 18 n., 19 n.
on plan to pay off national debt, VIII, 147 n.
on machinery, I, lix–lx
rotten boroughs, VII, 254 n.
on Huskisson, IX, 270 n.
on 'Silly Billy', X, 187 n.
visits to Gloucestershire, VII, 187 & n., 189, VIII, 157 n.
correspondence with, XI, xvii–xxi and cp. X, 389
see also VI, xxxv, VII, 220 n., 252, 275 n., VIII, 21 n., 367 n., X, 32 n., 67, 95, 314 n., 370
Mallet du Pan, XI, xvii n.
Mallory, Harriett, see Ricardo, Harriett
Mallory, Henry (Harriett's brother), X, 242–3, 254, 264–5, 318, 343
Mallory, Miss, X, 265, 344, 351
Mallory, Mrs, X, 264–5
Mallory, Robert Harvey, VIII, 284, X, 61
Malthus, Charles, VIII, 308 n., 318
Malthus, Henry, VI, xx n., 298 & n.
Malthus, Mrs, VI, 29, 60–1, 87, 298, VII, 175 n., 265, VIII, 107, 308
Malthus, Robert, I, xi, VI, xx
Malthus, Sydenham, brother of T. R. Malthus, VI, xx, 295, VIII, 308 n., 318
Malthus, Col. Sydenham, VI, xx
Malthus, Thomas Robert, VI, xviii–xxi
professor at East India College, VI, 77, 159, 240, 336, 341, 346, VII, 26, 51, 119, 130–2, 135–8, 213–14, IX, 251

Malthus (*cont.*)
his living at Walesby, VI, 35 n., 40–1, VII, 193, VIII, 226, 349; 'Parson Malthus', VIII, 74 n., VII, 212–13; tours Ireland, VII, 174–6, 184; visits Paris, VIII, 224–7
friendship with Ricardo, VIII, 41, 101, 178, 380, IX, 111–13, 382; Ricardo's visits to, VI, 322, 325, VIII, 173; visits to Ricardo, in London, VII, 24, 26–7, 29, 35, VIII, 47, 64, at Gatcomb, VII, 48, 51–2, 56, 361, 365, 368–9, 370–2, VIII, 314–15, 317–18, 331, 334, 336; bequest to, X, 105
loan of 1814, VI, 107–8, 110, 116, 119, 122; of 1815, sells on eve of Waterloo, VI, 229, 231 & n., 233, 235, X, 84
his library at Jesus College, Cambridge, VI, xx n.
location of his MSS, II, xiii, VI, xx, X, 386–7
list of letters, IX, 395–7, see also XI, x
other letters: to Horner, VI, 186–8, to Sismondi, VIII, 375–7; letters quoted, to Prévost, I, liv, to Horner, VI, 159 n., to Cadell and Davies, VI, 160 n.; see also, to Place, VII, 2 n., to Napier, IX, 302 n.

On Ricardo's Works

on Ricardo's *Principles,* VII, 176, 179; alterations due to him: in ed. 2, I, li, on rent, I, 412–13, VII, 282–3, on importation of corn, I, 428–9, VII, 271; in ed. 3, on effects of rise of wages, I, xliii–xliv, 35 n., 43 n., II, 64, IX, 178, on improvements in agriculture, I, 81 n., 335 n., II, 118, on cost and value, I, 47 n., II, 34, 101, on rent as proportion, I, 49 n., 83 n., 402, II, 196–8, on rent and fertility, I, 404 n., II, 121–3; see also I, 18–19
on *Economical and Secure Currency,* VI, 298–9, 300, 313, 315, VII, 10, 19–20

On Ricardo's Works (*cont.*)
on *Essay on Profits,* VI, 186, 188, 190–1, 216–18, 221–3

On Economic Subjects

accumulation, effective demand restricted by, VI, 142, 149; not true of France, VIII, 225–6; see also II, 310–11, 321, 325
arena for employment of capital, VI, 103–4 & n., see also II, 140, 293
on bounties, VI, 289, 314, 346, VII, 2, 68
foreign trade, whether profits from are clear gain, II, 401–2, 405–9, see also VI, 167–8, VIII, 182–3
machinery, II, 351–2, 357, 360–1; relation to Ricardo's views on, VIII, 382, 387, IX, 23
motives to produce, IX, 9–10, 13, 15–16, 19–21, 24–6
his measure of value, see Value, Malthus's measure of
population: wages the great regulator of, I, 218–20, VI, 155, see also II, 249
on corn raising demanders, I, 400, 405 n., II, 107–9, 142, VIII, 236; whether food or population precedes, VII, 201–2 & n.
and facility of producing food, VI, 140
artificial checks to, VII, 63, 218–19, VIII, 71, 80–1
price: natural, regulated by supply and demand, II, 46–7, 52–3, VII, 250–1, see also VIII, 201, 207; 'real price', I, 414–16, VII, 145, see also I, 413 n.
depressing effect of fall in, IV, 36–7
three causes of high price, I, 400–1
price of corn: regulated by last additions, VI, 195, 198, 200; regulates all prices, VI, 203, 212, VII, 105
startling conclusion that rise in price of, increases surplus, VI, 185,

On Economic Subjects (*cont.*)
187, 190–2, 194–6, 199; qualified, VI, 201–2, 207–8; controverted, VI, 189–90, 192–4, 196–8, 203–5, 209–10
advantages of high price, VI, 231, 236, 255, increases employment, VI, 200, 204; low price not advantageous to lower classes, IV, 35
profits: denies that profits of farmer regulate all profits, VI, 104, 117–18, 152–3, 155, 167, 182–3, 207, VII, 176
and facility of production, VI, 140, 224–6, 289–91, 296–7, 303–4, 318–19, VII, 52, 176, VIII, 194–5
and diminishing returns from the land, VI, 207, 209, 216–18, 220–3
and demand and supply, VII, 52, 68–9, 77, 80
public works, XI, x–xi
rent: his theory of, I, 398–429, see also I, 5–6, IV, 9–10
alters opinion on no-rent land, VII, 371–2, 379
supposes rent a creation of riches, I, 398, II, 116, 166, VI, 173–5, VII, 120, see also VIII, 209
misrepresents Ricardo on landlords, II, 117, VIII, 182, 184, 208, see also IV, 35
restrictions on importation of corn: effects of, IV, 27, 30, 32–3, 35–6, VI, 110, 116–17; throws off impartiality, VI, 177–8, 205; his dangerous heresy, VIII, 142
taxation of necessaries, IV, 33–4 n., VI, 173, 176; taxes as remedy for distress, II, 379, 432–3, VIII, 181
wages: real, II, 249–50, VII, 81 & n., 214
rise of, effect on prices, I, lxiii, 35 n., 43 n., II, 64
and rent, II, 132–3
and price of corn, II, 243–4

Opinions on him

always for merchant against consumer, VIII, 215, see also II, 409

Opinions on him (*cont.*)
a friend to moderate reform, VIII, 107; too moderate, VIII, 129; no real wish for, VII, 263, 266, 368–9; his reform no reform, VII, 372, 374, see also VII, 380
accused of inconsistency, II, 64–5, VI, 38–9, VIII, 209, 232–3, 331, IX, 329, 347, 350, 378; of fallacies, II, 96, VIII, 233–4, IX, 287; of using 'a new language', I, 19, IX, 283; his replies, VI, 202, IX, 365
aversion to controversy, VII, 247; socratic method used on, VII, 378
M[c]Culloch on his poisonous nostrums, VIII, 366; thinks him over-rated as an economist, VIII, 139; on his trick of book-making, VII, 383, VIII, 341
see also I, xlviii, l, lv, IV, 3, 349, VI, 249, 270 n., 274, VII, 15, 34 n., 177, 257, 264, 316 n., 357, VIII, 96–7, 99, 385, 391, IX, 30, 31, 155, 218, 242 n., 261, 265, 268, 342, X, 35, 50, 83, 90, 141, 179, 375–6, 405

Works

articles on Bullion in *Edinburgh Review:* Feb. 1811, III, 10–12, 99–123, VI, 21–30, 33–42, 47, 82, see also VI, xviii n.; Aug. 1811, VI, 47–8 & n., Ricardo's lost notes on, VI, 66 & n., references to the notes, VI, 73–8, 82–3, 87–92; see also III, 12, VI, 31 n., 41
review of Godwin on Population, 1821, IX, 84, 89–90, 154; keeps authorship secret, IX, 94, 101
Essay on Population, I, 398, VII, 126–8, 194, 201–3, 214, IX, 51–5, 62; ed. 1, 1798, VII, 2, 212 n.; ed. 2, 1803, VII, 2–3 & n.; ed. 3, 1806, I, 218–19; ed. 4, 1807, I, 106, 162; ed. 5, 1817, with Additions, VII, 123–4 & n., Sumner's review, VII, 247, Say on, VII, 168, IX, 36, alterations to meet Ricardo's objections, VI, 289, 314, 336, 346, VII,

Works (*cont.*)
2–3 & n., 26–7; French translation, X, 270 n.; see also VI, xix, 103 n., 295, 317, 341, VII, 8, 21, 24, 30, 46 & n., 68, 383 & n., VIII, 323, 341 n., 361–2, IX, 147, 232, X, 399 and under Godwin, *Reply to Malthus,* Place, *Reply to Godwin*
Grounds of an Opinion, 1815, IV, 4–5, VI, 176 n.; Ricardo on, I, 414–15, 419–20, 427, II, 61, IV, 9, 32–9, VI, 177–8; Torrens on, VI, 205 n.; see also I, 429, IV, 30, VI, 182, 186, 201 & n., 211
Inquiry into Rent, 1815, IV, 5, VI, 167, 172 n.; Ricardo on, I, 5, 398–429, IV, 9, 11–12, 15 n., 38, VI, 172–3, 176–8, VII, 120; Malthus replies, VI, 174–6, VII, 123; see also I, 74, II, 71, 73, 118, IV, 22, 24, 27 n., 33, VI, 182, 183, 211, VII, 379, X, 382, 399
Measure of Value, 1823, II, xii, IX, 280 n., 280–3, 287, 309, 318–19; his table of the invariable value of labour, IX, 281 & n.; M[c]Culloch on, 290; Trower on, 292–3; reviewed by J. S. Mill, 385 n.; see also I, xxxix, IV, 358, IX, 302 n., 317, 334, 370, X, 392
Observations on the Corn Laws, 1814, VI, 109, 167 & n., 205; ed. 3, 1815, I, 408–9, 414, 416, IV, 32, VI, 167 & n., 177, VII, 120
Principles of Political Economy, ed. 1, 1820, II, vii–viii; planned as answer to Ricardo, II, 11–12, VII, 215, 221, 247, VIII, 65–6; Ricardo on, VII, 284, 371–2, 379–80, VIII, 79–80, 130, 132–3, 179–85; deserves rough handling (M[c]Culloch), VIII, 138–9, 167, 189; Trower on, VIII, 201, 218–20, 320–2; dull sales, VIII, 298, 312; reviewed by Torrens, VIII, 185, by M[c]Culloch, 178 & n., 185; revision for new ed., II, xii–xiv, VIII, 285, 298, 308, 341 & n., 373, 377–8, IX, 249; French translation, VIII,

Works (*cont.*)
225 n.; see also I, lvi, VII, 194, 257, 312, 329, 370, VIII, 22, 41, 47, 64, 74, 109, 142, 160 n., 173, 222, 261, 325, IX, 239, XI, xiii
Ricardo's *Notes,* see under Ricardo, David
Statements respecting the East India College, 1817, VII, 114, 119, 121, 136
proposed edition of *Wealth of Nations* forestalled, VI, 159 n.; notes for, VI, 159–60, 169
article on Malthus, by W. Empson, VI, xx, VII, 2 n., 201 n.
essay on, by J. M. Keynes, VI, xiii, 35 n.
Malvern, visits to, VII, 66, 70, 84, VIII, 231, IX, 90, 104, 108
Man, Isle of, corn shipments through by fraud, V, 78
Manchester massacre, 1819, VIII, 54 n., 56–8, 66, 70, 80, 107, 111–12 & n., 129, see also V, xxii
Manicheism, VII, 196, 206 & n., 212
Manning William, M.P. for Lymington, Bank director, V, 8, 14, 201, 351, 365
Mansfield, Sir James, IV, 112–13
Mansfield, John, M.P. for Leicester, V, 20
Manufacturers:
greatest gainers from cheap corn, IV, 35–6
distress of, V, 133, 492 n., see also V, 315
Manufactures:
improvements in, I, 141, IV, 374, VI, 194, VIII, 171–2
protecting duties on, opposed, IV, 250–2
manufactured necessaries, I, 224–5; taxes on, I, 243
see also II, 291, V, 184 and under Inventions, Machinery
Manufactures and agriculture:
comparative advantages of, VII, 270–1, 279; whether either is more productive, VIII, 102–3
Manufactures, agriculture (*cont.*)
transfer of capital between, I, 306–7, V, 83
prices of, move in opposite directions, VIII, 232–3
proportions of wages and profits in, V, 177–8, see also II, 380
profits of manufacturers and farmers compared, I, 110–17, 122
Manufacturing classes, V, 296, VII, 220
Manufacturing country:
England as, V, 180
population of, better informed than agricultural, IX, 192–3, and cp. IX, 67
see also V, 408–9
Manuscripts, Ricardo's, X, 386–98
Marcet, Dr Alexander, V, 352, VIII, 19 n., X, 49
Marcet, Mrs (Jane), V, 353, VIII, 56 n., 163, X, 172
Conversations on Political Economy, 1816, advice for second edition, VII, 140 & n.; ed. 4, 1821, IX, 122; see also IX, 118, X, 270 n.
Marengo, plain of, IX, 222, X, 335
Marginal contents, Mill on, VI, 324, 329 & n., VII, 7, 97, 107, X, 391
Marginal theory, IV, 6 n. 3
Marjoribanks, Stewart, M.P., V, 185
Mark Lane, quantities of corn sold in, IV, 261, IX, 181, see also table IV, 270
Market, extending the, I, 93, 132, II, 360–3, 420, VI, 93, 104–5, 225, 228–9
Market price, I, 88–92; see also Natural and market price
Marks, Jeanette, *The Family of the Barrett,* X, 267 n., 350 n.
Marlow, Bucks., VI, xvi, IX, 5, 11, 41, 43, 48
Marnell, Mr, VII, 254–5
Marryat, Joseph, M.P. for Sandwich, on price of bullion and foreign exchange, VI, 7; see also III, 80 n., V, 102 n., 111, 144, 298, 301

Marshall, Alfred, *Principles of Economics,* I, xx, lii
Martigny, IX, 220–1, X, 283–4, 288
Martin, Richard, M.P. for Galway ('Humanity Martin'), V, 122; on the 'member for Portarlington', V, 289
Martinique sugar, V, 298, VI, 93
Marx, Karl, *Theorien über den Mehrwort,* I, xxii n., IV, 306, IX, 27 n.
Mary Ann, Miss, letter to, X, 164–6; see Bayley, Mary Ann
Mass of commodities, I, 128, 132, 134, 274, 278, 421 n., 423, II, 371, 373, 383, 390; money value of, IV, 39; rent estimated in, II, 137; as measure of value, IV, 59, VI, 22, 170–1, of absolute value, IV, 374, 400; see also VI, 42, 153, 163, IX, 361, 363
Mass: of corn, VI, 191, of gold and silver, III, 303, of prices (Bentham), III, 299, 301, of revenue, III, 281, of wealth, III, 332; general mass of circulation, III, 328, of production, I, 179
Massani, Tommaso, valet de place, X, 321
Masses, the, VIII, 111; the mass of the people, IX, 126
Matthews, William, *Historical Sketch of the Origin of Gas-lighting,* 1827, X, 56 n.
Maunoir, Dr Jean-Pierre and Mrs, X, 272 & n.
Maximum price, for corn, VIII, 158–9, for provisions, VII, 203 & n.
Maxwell, Captain and Mrs, X, 264, 266–8, 334
Maxwell, John, M.P. for Renfrewshire, on handweavers, V, 68; see also V, 56 n., 158 n.
Maxwell, Sir Murray, VII, 270 n., 273 & n., 357
May, Thomas Erskine, *Constitutional History of England,* V, xiv n., xxi n.
Mayence, VII, 165, X, 221
Mayor, Mr, Brook Street house bought from, VII, 17
Meade, Catherine, wife of Mortimer Ricardo, X, 64
Meade, Gen. Robert, X, 64
Mechanics Institute, Chichester, VII, 155 n.
Meetings of the people in 1819, VIII, 57, 59, 80, 110–11, 133, 146–7, 328; right to hold, V, 28–9, VII, 368; see also Manchester massacre
Meetings, county, see County meetings
Meilen, X, 243
Meillerie, Rocks of, IX, 220, X, 282
Meiringen (Meyringen), X, 252
Melbourne, Lord, see Lamb, William
Mellish, William, M.P. for Middlesex, Governor of the Bank, IV, 86–8 & n., 138–41, V, 20, 26, 464–5, VI, 276, 305
Melon, J. F., *Essai politique sur le commerce,* 1761, I, 244
Melville, Hon. R. S. L., X, 136, 138–40
Melville, Lord, VIII, 204
Memel, V, 182
Menial servants, see Servants
Mer de Glace, IX, 216, X, 275
Mercantile system, I, 316–17, III, 111, 118, V, 219, VIII, 164
Mercator's letters on bullion in *Morning Chronicle,* III, 27 & n.
Merchant vessels apprenticeship, V, 273–4, 276–7, 282–3
Merchants:
  loans to, IV, 278–81
  profits of, II, 393–4, 401
  Malthus always for, II, 409, VIII, 215
  see also II, 26–7, 376–7, X, 163
Merchants' petitions:
  on commercial distress, 1819, V, 37
  for free trade, 1820, V, 42–6, VIII, 164, 178, 183 & n.
  protest against Reports of 1819, VIII, 29 n.
Merle, William, III, 345, 351
Mestre, X, 310
Methodism, V, 330 n., VIII, 118
Metternich, Prince, III, 432 n., 433
Michelangelo's tomb, X, 317

Middle class, see Classes
Middleton, Conyers, *Examination of the Bishop of London's Discourses,* 1750, X, 398
Midleton, Lord, VII, 23
Mieville, V. A., VI, 112 n.
Miklashevsky, A., X, 382
Milan, visit to, X, 298–301; Bonaparte's unfinished gate, IX, 221–2, X, 300; see also IX, 228
Mildmay, Lady, X, 333–4
Mile End, Ricardo's house at, VI, xix, 47, 53 & n., X, 47, 118
Mill, Henry (son of James), VIII, 211 n.
Mill, James, VI, xv–xviii
- educated to be a priest, VII, 213 & n.; his large family, VI, 137; and Sir John Stuart, VIII, 105 & n.; and John Black, IX, 201 & n.
- dependence on Bentham, VI, 136, VII, 181–2 & n.; Chrestomathic school, VI, xxix, xxxi, 112 & n., VII, 182 n., VIII, 197–9; at Ford Abbey, VI, 124–6, 254, 309–10, 322, VII, 169, 181–2; proposed radical review, VIII, 16–17 & n.
- appointment at East India House, VIII, 40 & n., 47, 51, 72, 162, IX, 180; promotion, IX, 280 & n.
- friendship with Ricardo, VII, 73–4, 246, X, 8–10; walks with, VI, xxxiv, VII, 263, 266, 268, 273, 275, VIII, 7–8, 10, 162, X, 264; Ricardo's 'schoolmaster', VI, 321, 324, 329–30, 338–40, VII, 7, 59–60, 66, 73, 107, 111, 196, 199, 205, 301–2, 317–18, VIII, 58, 60
- visits Ricardo, at Mile-end, VI, 47, at Brighton, VIII, 211–12, at Gatcomb, VI, 137, VII, 277, 285, 292, 299, 302–3, 305–6, VIII, 51, 229, 231–2, 241–2, IX, 329, 332–4, 377; reckoned 'immoderate' by Mrs Ricardo, VII, 303
- arranges visit to Bentham, VI, 156–7, 160, 161 & n.
- urges Ricardo to enter parliament, V, xiii–xvii, VI, 138, 252, VII, 85–6, 110, see also IX, 182 n.

Mill, James (*cont.*)
- suggests travel journal, IX, 208, 209, X, 178–9, 190, 198
- on Ricardo's last illness, IX, 390–1
- bequest to, X, 105
- and *Economical Currency,* IV, 46–7, 93, VI, 313, 320–1, 324–5, 329–32, 335, 337–8, VII, 4–5
- and *Essay on Profits,* IV, 8, VI, 249, 338–9
- and *Funding System,* IV, 145–8, VIII, 54–5, 57–61, 66–7, 78, 83, 105–6; on payment for, VIII, 240, 242–3 & n.; see also VIII, 72–3, 123, 141
- and *Notes on Malthus,* II, ix–xii, xvi, VIII, 292–3, 296, 333, 346
- and *Plan for a National Bank,* IV, 274, 359, XI, xxvi
- and *Principles,* I, xiii–xxvi, l, lii, liii, comments on draft, VII, 60, 66, 86–8, 97–101, 106–8, 111–12; see also X, 10
- and Ricardo's posthumous works, XI, xxvi
- and Bentham's *Alarm,* III, 261, 263, 265–6, VI, 13–14, 18–20
- on Godwin's answer to Malthus, VIII, 291–2, 307, see also 323; on Place's reply to Godwin, IX, 47–8, 59, 103, 115–16
- on Say's notes on *Principles,* VII, 375, VIII, 5, 10
- his measure of value, quantity of labour worked up, IV, 375–6; 'labour of machines' included, IX, 325 n.
- supply can never exceed demand, IV, 178, VI, 56, 132, 134, 141–2, 148, 149, see also II, 311
- year as turnover period, I, xlii
- parliamentary reform, V, 113 n., VI, 252–4, 308–9, VII, 198, 238, 301, 303, VIII, 52–3, 58–9, 291; on Ricardo's discourses, VII, 373–4, VIII, 8–10, 68
- on Whiggery, VIII, 8–9, 68, 106, 327–9
- on education, VII, 196–7, 313–14, 317–18, 356–7 & n.

Mill, James (*cont.*)
on 'fashionable life', VI, 59, VII, 364
Horner on, III, 9–10 & notes; Wakefield on, VII, 182 n.; Mill on himself, VII, 181–2
list of letters, IX, 397–9; letters quoted: to Place, VI, 157 n., VIII, 105 n., to Dumont, VIII, 40 n., to Napier, VIII, 59–60 n., 68 n., 243 n., IX, 6 n., 150 n.
see also VI, 46 n., 51, 102, 270, 274, VII, 14, 28–9, 36, 132, 179, 180, 255, XI, ix n.

WORKS

articles: in *Edinburgh Review* on Th. Smith's *Theory of Money*, III, 9 n.; in *The Philanthropist*, VI, 313
articles in *Supplement to Encyclopaedia Britannica:* Colonies, VII, 183, 195, IX, 56
Government, V, 113 n., VIII, 211, 213, 240, 291, IX, 102, 148, 154 & n., 213
Jurisprudence, VIII, 290–1, 296, IX, 5, 154
Liberty of the Press, IX, 5, 6 n., 11, 41, 44, 102–3, 154 & n.
Prison discipline, IX, 280
see also VII, 329
Analysis of the Human Mind, 1829, IX, 332–3 & n., 374
Commerce Defended, 1808, II, 360, n., IV, 178, VI, xv, 132
Elements of Political Economy, 1821, IX, 114–15; Ricardo's notes on, I, xliv, IX, 125–33; a school book, VIII, 327, 331, IX, 117–18; steers clear of value, VIII, 296–7, 336–7; see also I, xlii, VIII, 229, 262, 283, 362, 368–9, 375, 395, IX, 6 n., 69, 87, 103, 122, 147, 154, 159; ed. 2, IX, 325 n.
History of British India, 1817: writing of, VI, 309, VII, 75–6, 182–3, 195; publication, VII, 197, 204, 207, 210 & n.; Ricardo on, VII, 222–3, 227–8, 231, 236–44, 249; reviewed

Mill, James (*cont.*)
in *Edinburgh Review*, VIII, 10 & n.; see also I, xxi, xxiii, VI, xvi, 309, 313, 317, VII, 111, 113, 186, 221, 252, 253, 257, VIII, 50, 106
lost paper on bullion, 1811, VI, 49–50, 53–9, 60–2
James Mill, by A. Bain, IX, 390 n.; see Bain
'Life of', by John Morley, VI, xxxvi n.
Mill, John Stuart:
Ricardo's early interest in, VI, xvii, IX, 44, 48, 60, 104, 115, 117; his paper on the measure of value, IX, 385–7
his education, VI, xxxi, 329 n.; attends lectures at Bagshot, VII, 313, astonishes professors, VII, 314, 326; account of studies, VII, 313 n., VIII, 198, XI, xxvii; classes at Montpellier, VIII, 293, returns grown up, IX, 43–4, 332
appointment at India House, IX, 280 & n.
his library, IV, 326; his copy of Ricardo's *Principles*, VI, xviii n.
see also III, 265, VI, 124, VII, 165, VIII, 297, IX, 107, 331 n.
review of Malthus's *Measure of Value*, IX, 385 n.
Autobiography, I, xix, VI, xvii, xxxiii n., 329 n., VII, 212 n., 213 n., 292 n., VIII, 17, 186 n., 293 n., IX, 107 n., 201 n., 280 n., 332 n.
Dissertation on Rent, 1827, IV, 7 & n.
Principles of Political Economy, VI, xv
Bibliography of, by N. MacMinn and others, IV, 7 n.
J. S. Mill, A Criticism, by A. Bain, VII, 313 n.; see Bain
Mill, Mary, IX, 334 n.
Mill, Mrs James, VI, 51, 53, 60, VII, 55, 62, 314–15, 326, VIII, 210–11, IX, 334
Mill–Ricardo papers, VI, xliii, X, 386; contents of, X, 391–2; found in Ireland, I, ix–x

Millar, John:
Historical View of the English Government, 1787, VII, 197, 382, ed. 1803, X, 397
Origin of the Distinction of Ranks, 3rd ed. 1781, VII, 197 n., X, 399
Milligan, Joseph, publisher, X, 371–2
Mills, William, VII, 313 n.
Milton, Viscount, M.P., V, 42, 47
Minchinhampton: Ricardo's purchase of Manor of, X, 95–6, 105; schools established at, VII, 45 & n., IX, 328–9, X, 169; celebrations for the Queen, VIII, 296; coaches to, VII, 277, VIII, 310; see also X, 168, and under Gatcomb Park
Mines:
rent of, I, 85–7, 329–32; mines that pay no rent, I, 87, 192, 332
discovery of mines, and value of currency, III, 54, 269–70, 303, 362, 376–7, 391
tax on gold, effect on mining country, I, 195–9
improvements in machinery for mining silver, V, 93 n., 390–1 & n., 427, VIII, 3, see also I, 14, 146
see also Coal mines
Minimum wage regulation, VII, 142
Minster, Ricardo's estate at, X, 98, 105
Mitchell, Mr, VIII, 214, IX, 1
Mocatta and Goldsmid, bullion brokers, VI, 85, IX, 278 n.
Moerdyk ferry, X, 195, 197
Moggridge, Mr, V, 515–16, 519–20
Mombert, Paul, X, 378
Monarchy, VII, 380–1
Monbrion, M., *Principales banques de l'Europe,* 1805, III, 175 n.
Money, William Taylor, M.P. for St Michael, on Owen's disbelief in a future state, V, 330, 331 n.
Money, I, 352–72, III, 13–127, IV, 43–114
alterations in value of, I, 48, 141–5,
effect on wages, I, 63–4, on foreign trade, I, 168–72, 228–9, 310–11, II, 154–6
no effect on relative prices, II, 396,

Money (*cont.*)
or on rate of profits, I, 50–1, 65, VII, 156, 159
gains and losses from alterations: fundholders, IV, 64, 229–30, V, 252–3, 320–1, 314, VII, 37–8, VIII, 396–8, IX, 39, landlords, III, 137, IV, 230–1, V, 313–14, farmers and manufacturers, III, 136–7, IV, 229–31, IX, 72–3, workers, IV, 257, IX, 166; see also V, 315–16
is not capital, III, 390, see also III, 92–3, 286–7; proportions between capital and money, III, 54
circulation of, admits of indefinite enlargement, III, 150, can never overflow, I, 352–3, is never saturated, III, 381–2, see also V, 71
circulation of notes and coin in 1822 estimated, IX, 201
money considered as a commodity, III, 103–4, 142, V, 346, VI, 24–5, 203; demand for, I, 193–4
as dead stock, I, 229, 232
degradation in the value of, I, 148, 310, V, 527, see also I, 228
depreciation of, see Depreciation
distribution of, through the world, I, 140, III, 87, VI, 74–5; world stock estimated, V, 209
economy in the use of, III, 86, 90, VI, 26, 93, between nations, III, 112–13, 242 n.; see also V, 420
an equivalent, not a pledge or security, VIII, 104
importance of, exaggerated in political economy, IX, 100, see also II, 180
perfect currency defined, I, 361, IV, 55, 66, V, 379
prices determined by quantity of, I, 105, III, 193 & n., 215–16, 230, VI, 93–4, by proportion between commodities and, III, 90, 106, 118, 311
whether prices raised by taxation require more money, I, 169 & n., 213–14 & n., III, 242–3, 385, IV, 321–2, discussed at Political Economy Club, IX, 158–9

Money (*cont.*)
principle of limitation of quantity, I, 353
quantity of, required to circulate commodities, III, 140–1, 238–9, 356–7, V, 417–18, IX, 101; reduced by density of population, V, 421
increase in quantity, lowers rate of interest temporarily, I, 298, V, 445, but not permanently, III, 374–6; can augment riches only at expense of wages, III, 318–19, VI, 16–17, see also III, 302, 334
relative price and relative value of, VI, 79
rise in value of, distinguished from fall in price of commodities, I, 47–51, 63–4, VII, 203 & n.
money and wealth distinguished, III, 108, 145
see also Bank notes, Circulating medium, Coin, Currency, Gold, Paper money, Rapidity of circulation, Silver
Money, standard of:
no invariable standard exists, I, 149, III, 65 n., 391, IV, 54–5, V, 209, VII, 42–3
gold the best standard, IV, 62–3, V, 388, 390–1, VII, 42–3; assumed to be invariable, I, xlii, 27–8, 46–7, 110 n., IV, 236, VI, 348–9; produced by same quantity of unassisted labour (ed. 1), I, 55, 63, 87 n.; by average proportions of fixed and circulating capitals (ed. 3), I, 45–6, 87, IV, 371, IX, 347
whether value of standard can be judged by the mass of commodities, IV, 59–61, V, 374, see also I, 377, III, 104–5
money without a standard, IV, 59, 62, 64, see also I, 354
Moneyed men, I, 89, III, 136, and cp. I, 123
Moniteur Universel, III, 179 n., X, 374
Monk, John Berkeley, M.P. for Reading, on sinking fund, V, 266
Monmouth, meeting at, V, 515, IX, 119, 121, 141 & n.; see also VII, 277
Monopoly:
natural monopolies, I, 404–5 & n.
and land, VI, 169–70, 175, 177; partial monopoly of land, I, 284, II, 114, VIII, 215, IX, 171, see also II, 104–5
of colony trade, I, 340–6
monopoly price, I, 249–51, 253, 384–5, II, 48–9, IX, 97–8, 100, see also I, 194, 197–8, 316–17 n.
see also I, 277, II, 260–1, 291, 409, V, 47, 88, 104, 111, 219, 301, VII, 202, VIII, 353
Montanvert, IX, 216, 235, X, 275
Mont Blanc, IX, 216, X, 257, 273, 275
Mont Cenis, X, 339; road, 340
Montesquieu: *Esprit des lois,* IV, 307 n., V, 288–9, VI, 308, 311, 332, VII, 383, X, 397; *Reflections on the...Roman Empire,* X, 398
Monthly Magazine, IV, 415–16
Monthly Review, on *Principles,* I, xxi
Monti, Vincenzo, Brougham reading the Italian poets with, VII, 74
Montrose Academy, VI, 138 n.
Moore, Daniel, VII, 254–5
Moore, Peter, M.P. for Coventry, V, xxvi, VIII, 324
Moore, Thomas, *Memoirs:* on Ricardo's quitting the Jewish faith, X, 37 n.; on Harriet Ricardo, X, 61
Morat, X, 263
Moravians, X, 213
Morellet, André, *Mémoires,* 1821, IX, 274
Morgan, John, loan contractor, X, 78
Morgan, William, F.R.S., the 'ingenious calculator', IV, 415–18, see also III, 358 n., IV, 99, 279, VI, 275
article on the finances of the Bank, 1797, IV, 415–16
View of the Public Finances, 1801, X, 78 n.
Morley, John, on Richard Sharp, VI, xxxvi n.

Morning Chronicle:
Ricardo's contributions to, III, 3–46, 129–53; see also III, 82 n., 88 n., X, 7, 14
Trower's letters to, III, 4, 22, 28, 81, 88
Mercator's letters to, III, 27 & n.
scale of discounts published in, IV, 416–18
parliamentary reports, V, xxvii–xxviii, 9, 49, 52, 138, 196–7, 250, 269, 293, 463 n., VI, 106, 335–6, IX, 291 n.
see also VI, 11 n., 78, VII, 218, 303, VIII, 221, IX, 201, 385 n.
Morning Herald, V, 121 n.
Morning Post, V, 463 n.
Morris, Dr, pseudonym of J. G. Lockhart, VIII, 25 n., 112
Morritt, Mr, IX, 232, 240
Mortimer, Thomas:
Every Man his own Broker, 1761, X, 77 n.
The Nefarious Practice of Stock-jobbing, 1810, X, 77 n.
Moselle, X, 219–21
Mr ——, a Continental merchant: evidence before bullion committee, III, 163, 168 n., 185, 288, 352–6; identified as John Parish, jun., III, 427–34
Mullion, Hugh, pseudonym of John Wilson, skit on McCulloch in *Blackwood's Magazine,* 1819, IX, 205–6 n.
Mullion, Mordecai, pseudonym of John Wilson, *Illustrations of Mr McCulloch's Political Economy,* 1826, VIII, 205 n., see also IX, 205 n.
Murray, John, Ricardo's publisher, VI, xxxv
Principles, ed. 1, I, xix; ed. 2, VII, 162, 333, 337; ed. 3, VIII, 315, 341 n.
rejects Place's book, IX, 47–8, 57–9, 61, 64, 115–16; lukewarm on Torrens, VII, 141
knocked down by ruffians, VI, 230
records of firm, X, 87, 355–6, 358, 360, 368
Murray, John (*cont.*)
list of letters, IX, 399
see also IV, 273, VI, 211, VII, 1, 4, 8, 16, 24, 120, 207, 361, 364, 370, 375, 379, VIII, 4, 152 n., 298 n., IX, 107 & n., 183, XI, xxvi
Murray, Sir John, I, xi, IV, 273, VI, xxxv, X, x
Murray, John Archibald, reprint of Dudley North's *Discourses upon Trade,* IX, 150–1, 157; see also III, 10 n.
Mushet, Robert: evidence on Resumption, V, 13; letters in Ricardo Papers, X, 388; see also VI, 88, 91, VIII, 367 n.
Enquiry into the Effects produced by the Bank Restriction Bill, 1810, III, 116, 248 n., VI, 8–9, 14, 89, Ricardo's copy, X, 402; ed. 2, III, 166–70, 174–5, 185, 204, V, 426–7, VI, 9 n., 14 n.; ed. 3, III, 169 n., VII, 384, VIII, 3 & n.
Series of Tables exhibiting the Gain and Loss to the Fundholder, 1821, VII, 93 n., VIII, 390–1 & n., 392, 396–8; ed. 2, V, 138 n., 252–3, 314, VIII, 398 & n., IX, 7, 39, 133

Nabarro, J. N., X, x, 17 n., 19 n., 20 n., 24 n.
Namur, VII, 160, 167
Napier, Macvey, editor of *Supplement to the Encyclopaedia Britannica,* VIII, 188 n.
and Ricardo's article 'Funding System', VIII, 54, 58–60 & n., 72–3, 75–6, 78, 83, 144, 188; payment for, VIII, 240, 242–3; see also IV, 145–7, VIII, 64, 69, 137, 141
see also VIII, 189, IX, 5, 41, 150 n., 302 n.
Selections from the Correspondence of, VIII, 60 n., IX, 6 n.
Naples, revolution in 1821, V, xxii, VIII, 363 & n.
Napoleon, VI, 199 n., IX, 247 n., X, 211, 324, 335, 345–7, 374. See Bonaparte

Napoleon III, X, 325 n.
Nasmith, James, *The Duties of Overseers of the Poor,* 1797, VII, 289 n.
National debt:
evils of, V, 33, 38, 54
whether cheap corn lightens burden of, IV, 39–40, VII, 104–5
management of, by Bank of England, IV, 51–4, 81–95, 98; table of charges, IV, 115–41; see also V, 100, VI, 275, 283–5, 333, 347–8
commissioners for, proposed, VI, 268, and cp. IV, 289–91
effects of annihilating, II, 451–2, on rate of interest, VIII, 145, on landowners and salary- and wage-earners, VIII, 238–9, on the middle classes, II, 444–5
M[c]Culloch's early suggestion for reducing interest on, VII, 37–8, 103–5, 351–3, VIII, 4; later disowned, I, 426 & n., VII, 93 n.; see also VIII, 157–8, 378 n.
see also Dividends, Sinking fund
National debt, Ricardo's plan to pay off: by tax on capital, V, 38, 271, on 'mercantile, landed and funded property', V, 187, 472; to be paid off at market price (1819), V, 34–5, VIII, 144, 147, 157, at par (1822), IX, 173–4; first outlined in *Principles* (1817), I, 247–8, then in *Sinking Fund* (1820), IV, 146–7, 196–7
special checks to be issued, V, 39, or particular paper money, VIII, 239
criticised by Brougham, V, xxxiii, 40–1 & n., 268–9, by Baring, V, 270; Grenfell on 'Ricardo's crotchet', V, 270–1; opposed by both stockholders and landowners, VIII, 147; 'a wild sort of notion', VIII, 147 n.; an 'adjustment of property', V, 266
objections to plan answered, IV, 197, VIII, 238–9
similar proposals, I, 248 & n., V, 37 & n.; Hutcheson's and Watson's, V, 40–1 & n., Heathfield's,
National debt, R.'s plan (*cont.*) VIII, 143–5, Sinclair's, VIII, 187, Trower's, IX, 174
see also V, xx, 20–1, 55, 86, 90, VI, 345, VIII, 33, 78–9, 152 n., 166 & n., 223, X, 187 n.
Natural agents, add to riches, not to value, I, 285–7; M[c]Culloch on, IX, 342–3
Natural and market price, I, 88–92, 119, 191, 196, 217, 312–13, 317 n., 340–3, II, 83, 299, VIII, 255–6
of corn, I, 301–3, 312–13, 374–5, II, 227–8
of labour, I, 93–6, II, 228
Natural price, or cost of production, I, 385, II, 34–5, 38–9, 46–9, 224, VIII, 207, see also VII, 250–1; or money cost of production, I, 383; or real cost of production, I, 301; or necessary price, I, 120, 302, II, 52; synonymous with value, II, 35
natural price of corn, I, 120, 374–5, IV, 241, VI, 198, or necessary price, I, 415; and restrictions on importation of corn, II, 154–5
Natural value: defined, II, 35; or necessary value, I, 415; and exchangeable value, IV, 375; and absolute (Malthus), IX, 307–11, 364
Nature, gifts of, I, 76–7 n.
whether rent due to bounty of, (Malthus) or niggardliness of, (Ricardo), II, 210–12
see also I, 69, 75, 85, 126, 134, 159, II, 123
Navigation laws, V, 190, 197; and Navy, V, 305, IX, 269 n.; see also V, 51, 478, IX, 342
Navy bills, I, 297, III, 291–2, IV, 102, V, 140–1
Neat: produce, VIII, 311, revenue, II, 381, VIII, 285, 300, surplus from the land, II, 164, VIII, 309, 311. See Net
Necessaries:
price of, relation to wages, I, 93, 95, 118, 161, 165, IV, 236, see also I, 296, IV, 179, VII, 57, 72, 81; rises as population increases, I, 101

Necessaries (*cont.*)
demand for, limited, for luxuries unlimited, I, 292–4, 387, VIII, 272, IX, 19
whether demand for labour is the same as supply of necessaries, VIII, 220, 236, 245, 248, 258, 270, see also II, 426
the labourer's necessaries, I, 20, 97, 104, 224, 234, 275, 306, 406, VIII, 275
manufactured necessaries, I, 243
see also Corn, Food, Provisions, Raw produce, Taxes on necessaries
Necker, Jacques, X, 269, 279–80
Net revenue, and happiness of human beings, I, 348–9 & notes, II, 381–2, VII, 378–9; see also under Revenue
Net surplus from land, II, 164–5; Malthus says impossible without taste for luxuries, VIII, 285, 300–1, 309; his ambiguous use of term, VIII, 311
Netherlands, IX, 309, X, 188
Neuss, IX, 211, X, 213
New Edinburgh Magazine, VII, 332. See *Edinburgh Magazine*
New Gravel Pit Unitarian Chapel, X, 40
New Grove, Ricardo's home at Mile End, VI, 51, 53 & n., X, 47, 118
New Lanark, V, 218, 468
New Monthly Magazine, VIII, 249
New Times, The, V, xxvii n., 3, VIII, 29 n.
Newcastle, Duke of, IX, 105
Newland, Abraham, Principal Cashier at the Bank of England, III, 188–90, V, 462, X, 76 n.
Newnham, Glos., VIII, 231–2
Newport, Sir John, M.P. for Waterford, V, 138, 185, 281, 335, 351, 354, IX, 160–1, 163, 185, 194, X, 99
Newspaper stamp duties bill, VIII, 148
Newton, Rev. Benjamin, *Diary, 1816–1818,* VII, 56 n.; MS diary, VIII, 334 n., X, 62 & n.
Newton, Isaac, on gold and silver coins, III, 203
Nicholas de Flue, Saint, X, 252–3
Nicholl, Sir John, M.P. for Great Bedwin, V, 351, 365–6
Nicoll, Walter, *The Planter's Kalendar,* 1812, VI, 237
Nimeguen, IX, 209, X, 213
No-rent land, see Land, that pays no rent
'No Trafficker', letters on bullion in *The Pilot,* III, 27 & n.
Noel, Sir Gerald, M.P., VIII, 324 & n.
Nominal, or money price, II, 67, 280; and real price, II, 250
Nominal value, II, 26–7
Nominal wages, see Wages, nominal and real
Norfolk County meeting (1823), Cobbett takes over, IX, 265 & n.
Norman, George Warde, X, 277 & n., 301; see also VIII, 367 n., IX, 218–19, 223, 288 n., 301
North, Dudley, *Discourses upon Trade,* 1691, IX, 150–1, 157
North, John Henry, IX, 274
Norwood, R. P., *History of Kiddington,* X, 64 n.
Nugent, Lord, V, 475
Nuncomar, VII, 237
Nunes, Abraham, X, 29
Nunes, Sarah, *née* Delvalle (D.R.'s aunt), X, 29, 106

Obata, Shigeo, X, 385
O'Connell, Daniel, V, xvii n.
O'Connor, Irma, *Edward Gibbon Wakefield,* VII, 216 n.
O'Connor, M. J. L., *Origin of Academic Economics in the United States,* X, 372
Old Proprietor's *Letters to Proprietors of Bank Stock,* 1816, VI, 276 n., 278, 283, 288
O'Meara, B. E., *Napoleon in Exile,* 1822, IX, 247

Omnium (scrip of government loans), X, 77 & n.; rising (1811), VI, 42, 48–9, rickety, 52; thriving (1812), 85 & n.; falling (1814), VI, 108, 110, 116, 119, a strange and sad business, 122, 128; rises with victory, VI, 231 & n., 233, 237; see also VI, 106, X, 80–4, 86, 89

Onslow, Arthur, Serjeant-at-law, M.P. for Guildford, moves repeal of usury laws, V, 109, 323, 335–7, VII, 46 n., VIII, 17 n.; see also VIII, 250

Oracle, Ricardo as the, V, 40 & n.

Orange, Prince of, *Proposals for... Trade,* 1751, IX, 135 n.

Ordnance bills, III, 292

Otaheite, VI, 290, 292–4, 296, 301

Otter, William, his edition of Malthus's *Political Economy,* 1836, II, xii, xiv

Overplus, proportion of, to capital, I, 91. See Surplus produce

Overstone Library (originally J. R. McCulloch's), IX, 302, X, 401

Overtrading, V, 397–8, 446–7

Owen, Robert:

- plan for employment of the poor, VII, 150 & n.; parliamentary committee to inquire into, V, xxvii, speech on, V, 30–1, VIII, 46 n.
  - Duke of Kent's committee on, Ricardo a member, V, 467–8, VIII, 42–3, 45–7
  - Torrens's speech on, VIII, 82, and article on, VIII, 82 n., 159 n., 164, 376 n.
  - see also V, 7, IX, 50
- his model villages, VII, 177 & n., and cp. IV, 222
- provision system at his shop at New Lanark, V, 218
- infant school, VII, 356, see also VI, 112 n.
- his irreligion, V, 328, VII, 177 & n., VIII, 153 n.; complains of Ricardo's allusion to, V, 330–1 & n.
- and birth control, VIII, 71–2 & n., IX, 62
- see also VII, 247
- *Life of,* written by himself, V, 468

Oxen, in Germany, X, 231, in Lombardy, X, 302

Oxford, Lord, VII, 217, 232

Oxley, Charles, VII, 162

Padua, X, 310

Page, Richard, his evidence in 1819, V, 361

- *Letters of Daniel Hardcastle,* 1819, V, 361 n., VIII, 3 n.

Paget, Thomas, *Letter to David Ricardo on the Depreciation in the Currency,* 1822, IX, 250 & n.

Paine, Thomas, *The Age of Reason,* V, 325; *An Appendix to the Theological Works of Thomas Paine,* V, 277; see also X, 395

Paley, Dr, his test for a theorem, III, 251–2; his spirit of toleration, V, 324–5

Palma, painter, IX, 222

Palmella, Count, VII, 276

Palmer, Charles, *Speech on the State of the Nation,* 1832, VIII, 143 n.

Palmer, Mr, of India, VII, 110

Palmer, Mr, of Monmouth, on Ricardo and Peel's bill, V, 515–17, 519–20

Palmer, Mr, Trower's adoptive father, VI, xxiii

Palmerston, Viscount, M.P. for Cambridge University, V, xxvi

Pamphleteer, The, 1817, VII, 32 n., 151 n., 260 n.; 1823, V, xxi n.

Panics: banks have no security against, IV, 68, V, 394, 409–10, 456; panic of 1797, III, 364–5, V, 15, 400, VI, 44; on the Stock Exchange, 1819, VIII, 32 & n.

Paper money:

- provides a cheap currency, IV, 234, 276, 298, VII, 42, VIII, 295; other advantages of, IV, 57–8
- perfect currency consists wholly of, I, 361, V, 387, VII, 151, but exchangeable for bullion, I, 356, VI, 69, VIII, 186, ought to conform to value of gold, I, 105, 195, and cp. VII, 37

Paper money (*cont.*)
value maintained by limitation of quantity, I, 353–4, see also III, 138–9, 269–70
Bank of England's rule for issuing, IV, 68 & n., see also III, 363–4, V, 255
made legal tender in 1811, V, 316, VI, 45 & n., see also VI, 68
should be issued only by the State, I, 362–3; Ricardo's plan for independent commissioners, IV, 114, 282–97, VI, 268, IX, 329
see also III, 332–5, and under Bank notes, Depreciation, Money
Paper Money System, III, 135, VIII, 153 n.
Paraira, M. C., and da Silva, J. S., *Gendenkenschrift 300-jarig bestaan Ets Haïm,* X, 31 n.
Paris: proposed visit to, in 1803, X, 117; visit in 1817, VII, 160, 164, 167, 178, 224, 231; with family in 1822, IX, 234, 236, 244–5, 248, X, 346–52; see also V, 186, VI, xxv, 247, 250, IX, 233
Paris, Peace of, 1814, V, 350, VI, 119 & n.
Parish & Co., Hamburg merchants, III, 430–1
Parish, Charles, III, 431
Parish, John, III, 431
Parish, John, jun., 'Mr. —' of the Bullion Report, III, 427–34. See also Mr. —
Parish, Richard, III, 431
Parish relief, I, 108, VII, 304, XI, xv–xvi; see also Poor, the
Park, Mr and Mrs, X, 309
Park, Mungo, *Journal of a Mission to the Interior of Africa,* 1815, VI, 244–5 n.
Parliament:
a narrow oligarchy, VII, 273, 290; controlled by interested men, V, 288, 478, VII, 299, and country gentlemen, IX, 180, 194, 246, 249; aristocratical influence, V, 284, 286, 496; few enlightened commercial men, VIII, 163; not moving in sympathy with the people, V, 269, 470, VIII, 330; an instrument of misgovernment (Mill), VI, 252, VIII, 329
Ricardo's seat in, V, xiii–xix, X, 11; Mill presses for, VI, 138, 252, 263, VII, 85–6, 110, 113, 190, 198, 300–2, 317, 349–50, 358, 364; search for uncontested seat, VII, 101–2, 110, 252, 254, 260, 264, 269, 272; settles for Portarlington, VII, 216–17, 232–3, 292–3, 300, 304–8, 311, 346–8, 355, 359, 362–3, 373, 382, VIII, 7, 10; takes his seat, VIII, 17 & n., 18–19, 21; re-elected 1820, VIII, 156, 162; tenure extended, VIII, 326–7, 330; refuses to contest Gloucestershire, VIII, 156, 162, or Liverpool, IX, 182–3, XI, xiv
price of a seat, V, xiv n., VII, 216, 254 n., 276
see also House of Commons, Reform of parliament
Parliamentary History and Debates, VIII, 61. See Hansard
Parnell, Sir Henry, M.P. for Queen's County, VII, 346 n.
arranges for Ricardo's seat in parliament, V, xiv–xvii, VII, 232, 300, 327, 346–8, 359, 363, VIII, 10, 17
on timber duties, V, 102, 104
sinking fund plan, V, 270–2, IX, 175
see also V, 86, 98, 335
Parr, Dr Samuel, VIII, 84, 106
Parsimony:
transfers, does not diminish, demand, II, 309, 326–7, X, 408
country enriched by, I, 278; Malthus denies this, IX, 19–20, see also II, 317, IX, 26
motives for, and effects of, distinguished, II, 9
see also Saving
Patten, Simon N., 'The Interpretation of Ricardo', I, xxi, IV, 8 n.
Patteson, Elizabeth, see Wilkinson, Elizabeth

Patteson, Sarah, see Wilkinson, Sarah
Pattle, Eliza, VII, 216 n.
Pauntley Court, Ricardo's estate, VII, 299 n., VIII, 48, X, 97–8, 105
Paupers: education bill, VIII, 25; literacy among, VII, 303–4, 306; Owen's workhouse for, VIII, 46; 'a million of' (1819), VIII, 139; Horton's plan for emigration of, XI, xv–xvi
Payerne, X, 263
Payne, Mr, V, 463 n.
Peacock & Co., III, 430
Peacock, Thomas Love, IX, 279 & n.
Pearse, John, Governor of Bank of England, M.P. for Devizes:
  submits paper to bullion committee, III, 113–19, 140; evidence, III, 356–61, 364–9, 419
  defends the Bank against Ricardo, V, 18, 143, and against Grenfell, V, 62
  see also V, 461–2
Pearson, Karl, and Morant, G. M., 'The Wilkinson head of Oliver Cromwell', X, 167
Peel, Sir Robert, M.P. for Tamworth, V, 365, VIII, 29 n.
Peel, Robert, M.P. for Oxford University:
  Chairman of committee on resumption of cash payments, V, 2, 7, 134–5, 350–4, 364–8
  replies to Attwood's attack, V, 186
  see also V, 18, 23, 200, 321, 371, 401, VIII, 20, 350–1, IX, 124, 146, X, 370
Peel's bill for resumption of cash payments (1819), V, 2–3, 7–8, 202, 368, VIII, 31 & n.
  and ingot plan, IV, 47–8, V, 135, 200, 351, 518, VIII, 20
  and increased value of currency, IV, 228–31, V, 310
  effects on price of corn, IV, 222, 228
  not fully acted on, V, 134, 206–7, 254
  Cobbett on, IX, 123 n., 140–1 & n.
Peel's bill (*cont.*)
  Ricardo blamed for ill-effects, VIII, 360 & n., IX, 122; defends himself, V, 515–21
  Western's motion for amendment, V, 198, 210, 218, 522–3, IX, 202
  and loan of 1819, X, 84–5
  see also V, 18, 186, IX, 165 n., 266–7 and under Resumption
Pemberton, Thomas, *Increase of the Number of Poor,* 1811, X, 402
Penny Cyclopaedia, article on Ricardo, X, 37 n.
Pensions, plan for spreading burden, V, 160–1, 191–5, 281–2, see also V, 156, 248–9, 265, 267, IX, 198 n. 3
People, the: their good sense, VIII, 59; on the side of good government, V, 498, VII, 261; an effectual check to government, V, 496–7, VII, 273, 322, VIII, 133; must in the end prevail (Mill), IX, 42; see also V, 500–1, VIII, 303, 336
Pepe, E., X, 355
Peploe, Samuel and Mrs, X, 314 n., 315, 317, 320
Perceval, Spencer, Prime Minister and Chancellor of the Exchequer, VI, 43 n.
  his bargain with the Bank in 1808, IV, 51, 53–4, 77, 81–3, 88–90, VI, 261, 283, 333, 337, 347
  Ricardo's ingot plan first submitted to, VI, 43–6, 70, VIII, 54, X, 10, 93
  see also III, 413 n., IV, 157–8, 193
Perkins family, X, 267, 276
Permanent versus temporary effects, VII, 120, 121–2; see also Short period
Perry, James, editor of *Morning Chronicle:* publishes Ricardo's first paper, III, 3–4 & notes, X, 7; Cobbett on, V, 41 n.; see also V, xxvii, VIII, 294 & n.
Pestalozzi, Swiss officer, X, 248
Peter the Great's house at Saardam, X, 208
Peterloo, VIII, 54 n. See Manchester massacre

Petty, Lord Henry, Chancellor of the Exchequer, 1806–7, VII, 284 n.
sinking fund plan, IV, 154–7, 175–7, 180, 193
see also IV, 416, VIII, 319, and under Lansdowne, Marquis of
Phelps, John Delafield, VII, 189, 191, VIII, 334 n.
Philalethes, *The Policy of a Restriction on the Importation of Corn,* 1815, VI, 201 n.
Philanthropist, The, VI, 313
Philips, George, M.P. for Wootton Bassett: on benefits of machinery, V, 302, 303; on Ricardo, V, 185; see also V, 352, VI, xxxvi, VIII, 70
Philips, Mr, VII, 316 n.
Phillips, George R., M.P. for Horsham, XI, xi–xii & n.
Phillips, Mr, his lectures on chemistry, VII, 313 & n.
Phillips, Thomas, R. A., portrait of Ricardo, IX, facing p. 1, X, 51–3
Phillips, William, geologist, VI, 180, 215
Physiocrats, VIII, 162. See also Économistes
Picciotto, J., *Sketches of Anglo-Jewish History,* X, 24 n.
Piedmont, revolution in 1821, VIII, 363 & n.
Piggott, Sir Arthur, X, 42–3 & n.
Pilot, The, newspaper, III, 27
Pinkerton, John, *Modern Geography,* 1802, VII, 189–90
Pinsent, Joseph, X, 389
Pisa, IX, 225, 227, X, 322–3
Pissevache, X, 283
Pitt, Joseph, X, 97
Pitt, William:
his sinking fund, IV, 41, 151–4, 158–9, 161–7, 174, 190–4, V, 118–20, 262, 265, VIII, 120
and Bank in 1795, III, 77 n.; renewal of Bank charter, IV, 91–3
views on poor law, I, 107 n.
friend of reform, V, 288; his apostasy, VIII, 63, 77
Pitt (*cont.*)
see also III, 188–9, V, 248, VI, 258, VII, 249, VIII, 61, 319, X, 75 n.
Speeches of, 1806, IV, 159
Place, Francis, VI, xxxv–xxxvi
and chrestomathic school, VI, xxix–xxxi, 112 n., VII, 198, VIII, 198, 212
and Say's visit, VI, 156–7 notes, 160, 161 n.
translates Say, VI, xxvi–xxvii, 160 n.
annotates *Principles,* VII, 183 & n., 189, 235
sends books on sinking fund, VIII, 66 n., 69, 77; comments on 'Funding System', VIII, 83 & n., 105–6, 118–25
and Thomas Evans, VII, 307–8
Westminster election, VII, 357 & n.
list of letters, IX, 399; other letters quoted: to Mill, VI, 161 n., to Bentham, VIII, 113–14 n.
see also VI, xxv, xxxviii, 158 n., VII, 182, 316 n., VIII, 115, 294 n., IX, 173, 288 n.
Illustrations and Proofs of the Principles of Population, 1822, IX, 49 n.; Ricardo reads MS, IX, 47–8, his comments, IX, 49–57, 59, 61–2, recommends publication, IX, 58, 64, 115–16; see also IX, 94, 101, 103, 120
Playfair, John, VIII, 58, 82
Playne, A. T., *History of Minchinhampton,* VIII, 283 n., X, 96 n.
Playne, William, VIII, 283 & n., 293
Pliniana, Villa, X, 296
Plough, I, 82; ploughing in the Netherlands, X, 188, with oxen in Germany, X, 231
Plowden, Francis, *Historical Review of the State of Ireland,* 1801, VIII, 49, 52
Plummer, A., article 'Sir Edward West', VII, 298 n.
Plunket, William Conyngham, M.P. for Dublin University, V, xxii–xxiii, VIII, 148, 350–1 & n., 362 n., IX, 274

Podmore, Charles, stockbroker, VI, 113 n.
Podmore, F., *Robert Owen,* VII, 177 n.
Podmore, Robert, stockbroker, VI, 112 n., X, 123–4
Podmore, Robert, jun., stockbroker, VI, 113 n.
Poland, corn production in, I, 15, 134, 144–5, IV, 265, VIII, 369, 374; see also I, 100 n., 378
Pole, Charles, Deputy-Governor of the Bank, V, 353
Pole, William Wellesley, M.P. for Queen's County, V, 350
Poles, two young, met on the Simplon, IX, 223, X, 289–90 & n., 301. See also Kunatt, Stanislaw
Police bill, Edinburgh, IX, 161–3, 179, see also 137
Police of the Metropolis, report on, 1816, VII, 150 & n.
Political economists, their 'abominable theories' (Lethbridge), V, 169; see also IV, 409, VI, 178, and under Economists, Theories
Political economy:
  object of, I, 5, VII, 122, VIII, 270, 278, 286
  whether a science, V, 162, 296, VIII, 152–3 n., 331, see also VIII, 100
  a guide to taxation, VIII, 79, 132–3, see also V, 44, VIII, 71
  true principles of, V, 296, 298, VIII, 207, daily gaining ground, VIII, 163–4
  makes progress in parliament, VIII, 150, IX, 166; Brougham 'lectures' the House on, IX, 164, 167, 207; Ricardo is read a lesson in, V, 178
  little knowledge of, on Stock Exchange, VI, 150
  fashionable with ladies, VIII, 56 n., X, 172
  French government prejudiced against, VIII, 225, 228
  attacks on, V, 248, 295, 306–7, VIII, 382, 387, IX, 155 & n.
Political Economy Club, X, 50–1; foundation, VIII, 367 & n., 381
  subjects discussed: glut, IX, 9–10; machinery, 9 n., 158 n., 159; Say's letters, IX, 36 & n., 158, 172–3 & n.; tax on all goods, and prices, IV, 320, IX, 158–9; riches and value, IX, 312 & n.; national bank, IV, 273; see also IX, 112–13, 116, 120, 264–5
  meetings attended by Ricardo, IX, 9–10 & n., 36 n., 172–3 & n., see also IV, 320
  Political Economy Club, Centenary Volume, I, lx, VII, 50, 187, VIII, 157, X, 35, 52, 67, 73, 370
  Minutes of Proceedings, 1821–1882, IV, 273 n., 320 n., VIII, 367 n., IX, 9 n., 116 n., 159 n., 173 n., 191 n., 265 n., 312 n., X, 51 n.
Poor, the:
  sufferings of, in 1816, VII, 61–2, 66–7, 87, 95, 209
  public provision for, objections to, VII, 248; sinks price of labour, II, 49, VII, 142
  parish relief and savings banks depositors, VII, 12, 63–4 & n., 96, 117, 125–6, 128–9
  education of children of the poor supported, VII, 45 & n., but not school feeding, VII, 359–60, 363; see also Education
Poor laws:
  report on, 1817, I, 107 n., VII, 150 n., 209, 219, 248–9; committee on, 1819, Ricardo a member, V, xxiv; Sturges Bourne's bill, V, 1, 6–7, VIII, 25, 74–5 n.; settlement bill, VIII, 30, 32; amendment bill, 1821, speech on, V, 113–14; see also IX, 198 n.
  pernicious tendency of, I, 105–9, 162, VII, 133–5, 360; ought to be abolished, I, 107, VII, 124–5, see also IX, 54–5, XI, xv–xvi
  proper object of, VII, 248
  effect of, on quantity of food, VII, 3, 202
  see also Parish relief, Public Works

Poor rates, I, 257–62, IV, 217–18, V, 45
Pope, Alexander, *Essay on Man,* VI, 327
Population, I, 78, 98–100, 159, II, 115
increases faster than capital, VII, 72, VIII, 368; alternately take the lead, IV, 22–3, see also II, 277, 321, VIII, 150–1 & n.
and fund for maintenance of labour, I, 78, 108–9, 164, 219, 289, 292–3; and wages, I, 125, 406–7, VIII, 273
and cheap food, I, 373, 409, IV, 19 n., VI, 140, VIII, 255, IX, 239, see also I, 292, VII, 360, X, 408–9
effect on rent, I, 70–2, 77, 102, 334, see also II, 133–4, VIII, 182
checks to: prudential, II, 220–1, 262, V, 303, VII, 218–19, VIII, 25, 183–4, IX, 55; artificial, VII, 63, VIII, 71 & n., 80–1, IX, 62 & n.; other restraints on, I, 100, II, 115, VII, 125
population in Ireland, I, 100 n., VII, 48
Malthus's principle of, I, 406–7, II, 111, 234, 262, 303, 341, VI, 140, 192, 195–6, 199, 318, see also II, 243, VI, 224, 301, VIII, 195, IX, 323
comments on Place's book on, IX, 49–57
see also Demanders, Happiness
Portarlington, Ricardo's constituency, V, xiv n., VII, 355, VIII, 17 n., 162; a 'quiet sort of borough', VII, 311; he 'never set foot in', V, 289
Portarlington, Earl of, V, xv n., xviii; negotiations with, for seat in parliament, VII, 216–17, 232, 293, 306, 308, 327, 346–8, 359, 382, VIII, 327, X, 99
Porter, George Richardson (D.R.'s brother-in-law), X, 60; bequest to, X, 105
article on Ricardo in *Penny Cyclopaedia,* X, 22 n., 37 & n.
Porter, Sarah (D.R.'s sister), see Ricardo, Sarah
Porteus, Dr Beilby, V, 325
Portions:
division of the whole produce of land and labour into three portions, I, 347, 411
portion of produce paid to landlords for rent, VII, 81; was previously a portion of the profits obtained from the land, IV, 18 & n., 20
portions distinguished from proportions (Malthus), II, 195 n.; rent not governed by proportions, II, 196 n.
see also Proportions
Portugal, I, 137–41, 377–8, III, 190, VI, 86, VII, 276 n.
Positive value, VIII, 394, IX, 1–2, 29, 339, 351
Potato:
Malthean objections to, IX, 232, 239, see also II, 215
potato question in Ireland, V, 225, 234, VII, 175–6, IX, 230–2, 237–9, 252–5, 257–61
see also I, 97, 332–3, V, 528, IX, 56
Potato flour: speculation proposed by Say, VII, 166, 224–6, 230; Lasteyrie's process for, IX, 231, 253, 259, 273
Power-loom, V, 68
Practical men, III, 163, 188, 190, 227, 239, 256, 362, IV, 240; Ricardo too theoretical, Malthus too practical, VI, 295; *Principles* not intended to be a practical book, VIII, 184
Pratt, J. T., *History of Savings Banks,* 1830, VII, 23, 187 n.
Precious metals, see Gold and silver
Press, the:
free press as check on government, V, 486, 497, VII, 298, 323, 368, IX, 102, XI, xxii, see also VIII, 53, IX, 55
in Scotland, VIII, 167 & n., IX, 136 & n., 142
parliamentary reporting, V, xxvii–xxxi
Hazlitt on periodical press, VII, 28 n., VIII, 185–6; Mill on liberty of the press, IX, 154 n.

Preston, Mr, VIII, 46
Prévost, Pierre, professor of physics at Geneva, IX, 219–20, X, 270 & n., 281, see also I, liv, II, vii, xii
Price:
puzzled to find law of, VI, 348, VII, 71–2, 83–4
early view that price of corn regulates all prices, III, 270, VI, 108, 114; found erroneous, I, 302, 307–8, 315, IV, 21 n., 35–6, 216, VI, 221, 269, VII, 105; Adam Smith's original error, VII, 100
rise in raw produce leaves all other prices unchanged, IV, 20, 236–7, VII, 24; this qualified for raw material contained, I, 117–18, IV, 20 n., VI, 179, 348–9
prices of all commodities cannot be raised by rise of wages, I, 104–5, 126, 303, 307–8, 315, IV, 213–16, 236; none rise, but some fall (ed. 1), I, 61–3, 66; some rise, some fall (ed. 3), I, 34–5, II, 60–4, according to proportion of fixed capital used, I, 46, 239, II, 274, VII, 82–3, VIII, 179–80, 193, and to durability of capital, I, 39–43
regulated by quantity of labour necessary for production, I, 110, 118, II, 34–5; by facility or difficulty of production, IX, 239, see also I, 191, VII, 3, 250; finally settled by competition of sellers, II, 38, VIII, 277
and value distinguished, IV, 60, 236, VII, 288, 297, see also II, 242, III, 360, IV, 373, VI, 54–5, and cp. I, 110 n.
natural and market, I, 88–92, 191, 196, II, 83, 299, VIII, 256–7, 271–2, see also I, 119, 217, 312–13, 317 n., 340–3
natural price regulated by cost of production, I, 301–2, 344, 382–5, 397, II, 34–5, 38–9, 46–9, 52–3, V, 300, VI, 177, 189, VII, 250–1, VIII, 201, 207, see also II, 40–1, 390, IV, 211
Price (*cont.*)
market price regulated by demand and supply, I, 382–5, II, 45, 47, VI, 148 & n., VIII, 272, 286, 302, see also I, 119–20
monopoly price, I, 249–51, 384–5, II, 48–9
absolute price, I, 63; permanent price, VII, 250–1; real price, I, 12, 410, 413 n., 414–16, II, 292, VII, 145, and nominal price, I, 274–5 n., II, 250; relative price, I, 12
relation of price to quantity supplied, I, 104–5, 384–5, V, 171, VI, 90–2, 163; small excess of corn, large effect on price, IV, 28–9, 219–21, 259, 266, V, 108, 318–19
four causes of high price of raw produce, I, 161, VI, 146, 154
distinction between alterations in value of money and in value of commodities, I, 47–51, 63–4, VI, 348, VII, 203
rise or fall in price, due to change in value of money or to difficulty of production, I, 417, II, 412, VI, 233
magic effect of rise in, on industry, IV, 36
price of labour, I, 46, 95–6, 315, II, 60, 248, 368, V, 38, 244, VI, 145, 234, VII, 8, 10, 199
price of wages, I, li–lii, 94 n., 95 n., 96 notes, 111 n., 118, 145, 303 n., II, 63, 231 n., 411, IV, 22, VI, 223, 241, and cp. IX, 325
price of production, VI, 146, 148, 155
prices: determined by mass of commodities on one side and amount of money multiplied by rapidity of circulation on the other, III, 311
of home commodities, how affected by rise in price of imported corn, VI, 206, 212–13
prices of the mass of commodities, I, 423; mass of prices (Bentham), III, 299, 301, 311; general price of goods, I, 169 & n., 228 n.
Bosanquet's opinion on rise of prices considered, III, 236–44

Price (*cont.*)
fall of prices in 1815, VI, 303–4, 328, 343–5; in 1816, V, 419–20, VII, 38; in 1821–2, V, 72–3, 108, 232, 241, IX, 152
resistance to reducing, VII, 67
see also Corn, price of, Remunerating price, Value
Price, R., M.P. for Herefordshire, V, 472, IX, 119, 121
Price, Dr Richard, IV, 151, 184
An Appeal to the Public, 1772, VIII, 64, 66, 320, 332
Price, Uvedale, *Essay on the Picturesque,* 1794, IX, 121
Principal and factor, Law of, V, 292–3
Prinsep, C. R., translates Say into English, VIII, 315 & n., 374 n.
Prisons:
Ricardo's visits to: as sheriff, VII, 276; in Amsterdam, X, 206; in Bologna, X, 312; dungeons in Venice, X, 308
county gaols, VII, 173, bill relating to, 1822, IX, 198
see also IX, 89, 280
Produce, gross and net, I, 178, 421 n.
net, increased by machinery, gross diminished, I, 388–92; McCulloch disagrees, VIII, 383–4, 387–8, 391–2, 399–400, IX, 13; see also VIII, 377
savings and net produce, IX, 131
see also Income, Revenue
Production:
regulates demand, I, 290–2, IV, 178, V, 434–5, VI, 163–4, VIII, 159, 181, 216, 236–7, 258, 273
quantity of productions, not value of, increased by trade, I, 128, 319
decreasing rate of, I, 98–9
whether discouraged by falling prices, VI, 303–5
bounties on, I, 321–6
Malthus on motives for, IX, 10, 13, 15–16, 19–21, 24–6, and cp. VI, 121
see also Cost of production
Productive powers: of labour, I, 98, VI, 191, of the land, I, 126, II, 321, 336
Productive services, Say's doctrine of, VIII, 228, 277, 379–80, IX, 34–5, 170–2 & n.; Ricardo objects to lumping them together, IX, 172 & n., 188 n.
Productiveness:
of labour, on last land cultivated, II, 276, 336; on the land and in manufactures, IV, 38; increased, and profits, II, 373
of capital, VI, 195; of the last capital employed on the land, IV, 347
of industry, and productiveness of capital, VI, 290–1, 294, 297, 320, 323
Professors, their reward regulated by demand and supply, IV, 189
Professorship of moral philosophy in Edinburgh, VIII, 204–5 & n., 215, IX, 205–6
Profits, I, 110–27, 289–93, IV, 3–41
beginnings of theory, IV, 3–4 & n., VI, xxi; corn-ratio theory, I, xxxi-xxxii, xlviii–xlix, VI, 108, 117
fall with growth of capital and population, I, 120, VI, 148–9, 152; Adam Smith's error, I, 289–90, VIII, 380
fall checked by cheap food, I, 132, II, 221–2, IV, 22, 25–6, 37, VI, 94–5, 104, VIII, 208–9; by improvements in agriculture, II, 157, 276, IV, 11 n., 19 n., 346
regulated by difficulty or facility of procuring food, I, 296, IV, 13 n., VI, 144–5, VIII, 194–5, on no-rent land, I, 126, II, 132, 276–7, 285, 363, IV, 347, VII, 78, X, 409; discussed in relation to Otaheite, VI, 289–90, 292–4, 296, 301–2
depend on low price of corn, I, 112–14, II, 125, VI, 168, 194, 205, 291; different effect if low price due to bounty, I, 323–4; difficulty in case of America, IX, 99–100

Profits (*cont.*)
profits of farmer regulate profits of all other trades, IV, 23–4, VI, 104, 133, 170, 194; Malthus disagrees, VI, 117–18, 139–40, 152, 167, 182, 207
lowered by tax on corn, I, 159–60, 166–7, 205, 233, 239, by restrictions on imports of corn, IV, 237–8, V, 33, 38, VI, 108, 110, 113–14, 116, 203; raised by free imports, IV, 35–6, VIII, 357–8
vary inversely with wages, I, 110, 118, 143, 292–3, II, 165, 264–8, 327, 393, 446–7, VI, 226, VII, 57, 155–6, IX, 99, 179; temporary exception, VII, 199; profits and wages always constitute the same value, I, 115, 403–4 & n., 411, IV, 349; rise of wages the only cause for fall of profits, I, 296, VI, 162
depend on proportions, not quantity, II, 345; on proportion of labour needed to support the labourers, I, 48–9, 125–6, II, 217 & n. 7, 258–9, 266–7, 290, VI, 108, 121, VII, 80–1, VIII, 73, 130, who work on no-rent land, II, 278–9, 284, 336, VIII, 194–5; on proportions of net to gross produce, VI, 204
high when capital scanty, VI, 131, 133
table of rent and profit, IV, 17; discussed, I, xxxii & n., VI, 187, 191, 194, 217, 220, 222
all rent a transfer from profits, II, 123, 157, 186–8, IV, 18, VI, 173, VII, 282–3; profits always rise when rents fall, IV, 14, 21, 35, 38–9
four causes of rise in price of raw produce, different effects on profits, VI, 146, 148–9, 154, and cp. I, 161
taxes on profits, I, 205–14; tax on wages wholly a tax on profits, I, 215, 226–7
also a cause of value, VIII, 194, but an insignificant one, VIII, 279. See also Value
difference with Malthus explained to Trower, VI, 103–5, and cp. 102; further discussions with Malthus, VI, 108–23, 128–34, 139–42, 144–9, 152–5, 162–3, 167–8, 170–2, 174–5
depend upon the arena for the employment of capital (Malthus), VI, 103 & n., 104, and cp. II, 140, 293
the mighty hinge (Trower), VIII, 267, 273
as 'wages of a particular kind of labour' (J. S. Mill), IX, 385–7
see also Distribution
Profits, rate of:
and rate of interest, I, 297, IV, 233, VII, 199
not altered by variations in value of money, I, 50–1, 65, VII, 156, 159
not affected by foreign trade, I, 133, IV, 25–6, nor by colonial trade, I, 345, VII, 202
tendency to equality of, I, 72, 88–9, 119, 129, 307, 416, VIII, 259, 270, 275, IX, 354 n., 358–9; different in different countries, I, 134, II, 86, VII, 176, 186
depends on ratio of production to necessary consumption, VI, 108, 204
diminishes with cultivation of poorer land, IV, 7 & n., 13–17, VI, 209–10, 213–14
see also Rate of interest
Progress: natural tendency towards, I, 265; uniform progress denied by Malthus, VII, 122; see also VII, 24
Progress of society: value of manufactures falls, of raw produce rises, I, 97, VI, 294; rise in value of corn, IV, 212, 235; rise in price of necessaries and rent, I, 70, 225, 334, VIII, 209, and of labour, I, 93–4, 120; see also Society, state of
Promissory notes, III, 415
Property:
sacredness of, I, 204, V, 69, 501–2; the people not hostile to, V, 500–1, VII, 273, 370, VIII, 59
unequal distribution of, IX, 243–4

Property (*cont.*)
effects of subdivision among children, II, 387, VIII, 225, 377
and alterations in value of money, III, 93, V, 107
pillage and destruction of, in 1816, VII, 45, 49
taxes on transfers of, I, 153–5, V, 291, 315
see also Tax on property
Proportions:
value measured by, II, 101, 138, 253, 267, VIII, 278–9, IX, 355–7
proportion of production to necessary consumption determines rate of profits, VI, 108, VIII, 130, see also I, 48–9, 125–6, II, 344–5
of immediate and accumulated labour in different commodities, IV, 379
of the whole produce distinguished from portions by Malthus, II, 195 n., 196–8 & n.
division of the whole produce by, see Distribution
Protecting duties:
justified in case of commodity subject to peculiar tax, IV, 217–19, V, 256–7, VIII, 158, 172–3, see also VI, 181
on corn, IV, 240–53; protection should be gradually withdrawn, IV, 263, V, 138, 173, VIII, 187, 357, IX, 8, 188, 195, see also V, 34, VIII, 103; fixed duty preferable to graduated, V, 83, 86, 88, 91, VIII, 158, 350, 359
Malthus throws off impartiality, VI, 177–8; his arguments for, answered, IV, 9, 27, 33
Irish protecting duties, V, 57–8, 104, 218–19
see also Corn laws, Countervailing duties, Import duties, Restrictions
Protection, arguments for, answered, V, 51
Corn law of 1815 the worst form of protection, IV, 242, 249, V, 173, 183–4
Protection to Agriculture, IV, 201–66
Providence, bounty of, IV, 31, 221. See also Nature, gifts of
Provident Institution at Bath, VII, 130 & n. See Savings banks
Provisions:
four causes of high price of, I, 161, 217–18, VI, 146–7, see also I, 400–1
advantages of cheap, II, 412–13, see also VI, 269
see also Necessaries
Prudential habits, among the labouring class, I, 106–7, II, 221, 262, V, 303, IX, 261
Public Characters of all Nations, 1823, X, 37 n., 38
Public deposits in Bank of England, IV, 51 & n., 99, VI, 334, 348
Public expenditure, second report from committee on, 1807, IV, 53, 78–81, 83–4, 88 n., 89, 91–4, 96–7, 98 n., 136, 139, VI, 282
Public opinion, as check on government, VI, 263, 311, VII, 238–9, 298–9, 322, 368, VIII, 211
Public works for relief of unemployment, V, 32, VII, 116 & n., 121 & n., XI, x–xi
Puget & Co., bankers, V, xvii n., VII, 347, 359, 363
Puller, Richard, XI, xxviii; see under Ravenstone, Piercy (his pseudonym)
Purves, George (pseudonym of Simon Gray), *All Classes Productive*, 1817, VIII, 38 n., 40; *Gray versus Malthus*, 1818, VIII, 38 n.

Quakers, VI, 180 n., VII, 26, 155 n., IX, 182 n.; Wilkinson family and, X, 36, 41–3, 45; birth of Ricardo's children registered with, X, 41–2 & n.
Quantity regulates value, V, 209, see also V, 170–1, VIII, 278, IX, 249, and under Price, relation to quantity
Quantity theory of money, III, 311. See Money

Quarterly Review:
1816: The Poor (Southey), *Records of the Creation* (Weyland), VII, 247
1817: *Essay on Population* (Summer), VII, 247
1821: Agricultural Report (Senior), IX, 109 & n., 122
Godwin's *Answer to Malthus,* IX, 147, 154
1822: State of the Currency (Coplestone), IX, 249
see also III, 428–9 n., VII, 173, 289 n., 297, VIII, 17 n., 44
Quatrelles L'Epine, *Le Maréchal de Saint-Arnaud,* X, 325 n.
Queen's trial, see Caroline, Queen
Quillacs hotel at Calais, X, 182–3

R.P. (Ricardo Papers), VI, xliii; contents of, X, 386–91; found in 1930, I, viii–ix
Radcliffe, John, VI, 240 & n.
Radicalism, VIII, 107, 129, 284, 314, 328, IX, 122, 148, 160, 292; radical reform, V, 29, VIII, 146; radical review projected, VIII, 16–17 & n.; see also V, xxii n., VII, 62–3 notes, 375
Rae, John, *Life of Adam Smith,* VI, xxxvii, 326
Rae, William, Lord Advocate, and *The Beacon* affair, IX, 136, 142, 187, 204–5, 207
Raguet, Condy, American free-trader, X, 389
Ramsay, George, *Essay on the Distribution of Wealth,* 1836, IV, 306
Ramsgate, Ricardo family at, 1812 and 1813, VI, 84, 85, 96, X, 136 & n.
Randall, Miss Fanny, X, 278–9
Raoul-Duval, Edgar, I, xi, VI, xxvi, xxvii, VII, 230
Raphael, X, 312, 316
Rapidity of circulation of money, and prices, III, 90, 276–7, 311; ratio of circulation (Trower), IV, 322
Rapperschwyl, X, 238, 243
Rate of interest:
not affected by quantity of money, III, 88–9, 92, 143, 150, 194 n., 341, 374–5, except temporarily, I, 298, V, 445
ultimately regulated by rate of profits, I, 110, 296–7, 300, 363, V, 12 n., 130, 346, VI, 108–9, VII, 199, see also II, 331, IV, 346, V, 269 n.
cannot be controlled by any bank, IV, 233
no criterion of over-issue of notes, III, 26, 88, V, 12
market and legal, I, 296–9, V, 338–47; Bank lends below market rate, I, 364
low rate foreshadows stationary state, IV, 234
fall of, in 1820, VIII, 260
Irish and English rates, V, xvii, VII, 216, 347, 355 & n., 363, 382
Ravenshaw, J. G., East India Director, VIII, 263 & n.
Ravenstone, Piercy (pseudonym of Richard Puller), *A Few Doubts as to...Some Opinions on...Political Economy,* 1821, IX, 45, 59–60, 62–4, XI, xxviii
Raw produce:
causes of rise in price of, I, 400–1, VI, 146, 154, VII, 120, 123, see also I, 93–4, 161, VI, 294; effects of rise, I, 115–18
price of, and manufacturing skill, I, 142, 145–6
taxes on, I, 156–75, 183, 252, VII, 115
farmer's capital consisting of, I, 117
see also Corn, Necessaries
Real, see under Exchange, foreign, Price, absolute, Rent, Value, Wages
Redesdale, Lord, V, 351
Redundancy of currency: use of term, III, 61, VI, 22, 25–6, 34–7 & n.; or cheapness of currency, VI, 36, 41–2
as cause of depreciation, III, 63, 74 n.; and of unfavourable exchange, III, 59–60, 107, 109–10, VI, 62–5, 74, 82, 87, see also VI, 27–8

Redundancy of population, I, 390, 394; and redundancy of capital, II, 277, 339, 426–7; redundancy of both together impossible, VIII, 181, 185, 278
Rees, Abraham, *The Cyclopaedia*, 1819, VIII, 61, 67
Reform of parliament:
speech on Lambton's motion for, V, 112–13, VIII, 367 n., on Lord John Russell's motion, V, 283–9, IX, 288, 292; other speeches on, V, 470, 473–5, 484–6, VIII, 330
discourses written as an exercise, V, 489–512, VII, 302, 317, 329, 332, 349–50, 358, 364, 376–7
correspondence with Trower on, VII, 260–1, 266–7, 272–4, 289–90, 298–9, 309–11, 319–24, 340–5, 365–70, 373–5, 381, VIII, 12–16, IX, 267–8, 292
discussions on, at Easton Grey, VIII, 56–9, 61–3, 68, 75, 129–30
reform and revolution, VIII, 49–50, 146
see also V, 26, 29, 493 n., VII, 270, 360, VIII, 152 n., and under Ballot, Borough system, Elections, Representation, Suffrage
Regent, Prince, V, xvii, 28, VII, 208, 372, 382. See also Wales, Prince of, and George IV
Reichenbach waterfall, X, 254, 257
Reid, Hugh G., *Biographical Notice of McCulloch*, VI, xxii, xxiii
Reid, Irving & Co., X, 85, 88, 89
Reid, Thomas, on perception of external objects, VII, 229, 235
Religious opinion, see Free discussion
Rembrandt, X, 206
Remunerating price, for corn, IV, 210–13, 218, V, 49–50, 84–5, 89, 152, 164–5, 182, 244; for provisions, X, 184
Rent, I, 67–84, IV, 9–10, 13–18
the payment for the original and indestructible powers of the soil, I, 67, IV, 18 n.; includes return from capital inseparable from land, I, 261–2 n., see also II, 202
and diminishing returns, I, 70–2, 74–5, 83–4, IV, 211–12
the difference between the produce of two equal capitals, I, 71, 413 n. 2, II, 134, see also I, 83
last portion of land cultivated pays no rent, I, 71, 74, VI, 173; not necessary for theory of rent, I, 412–13 n., VII, 372, 379, VIII, 4, 57, 149–50; last capital pays no rent, I, 72, 328–9, II, 73, 166–7, 172, IV, 240, VI, 177, 198
not a component part of price, I, 77–8, 329, II, 72–3, see also I, 22–3 n.; not part of cost of production, II, 42–5
a transfer, not a creation, of wealth, I, 197, 399–400, II, 116–17, IV, 18, VII, 120, 282–3, VIII, 182; transferred from profits, II, 123, 157, 186–8, VI, 173; Malthus's error in supposing it clear gain, I, 398, II, 166, 223
rise of, a symptom, never a cause of wealth, I, 77–8; rises with growth of wealth and population, I, 102–3, VI, 294; high rent a symptom of approach to stationary state, VII, 16–17
whether high because of difficulty (Ricardo) or of facility (Malthus) of production, VI, 290, 292–4, 296–7, 301–3, 318–19, see also I, 411
whether rent and fertility rise and fall together, I, 75–7, 402–4, II, 121–3, 211
effects of improvements in agriculture, I, 79–83, 412, II, 118, 134–5, 185, IV, 11 n., 19 n., 41, VI, 190, VIII, 182, 184, 208
rent the effect, not the cause of high price of corn, I, 74, II, 71, IV, 212, IX, 197, see also I, 427
tax on, falls wholly on the landlord, I, 173, 175

Rent (*cont.*)
fall in rent due to cheap imported corn not an evil, II, 161–2, 173, IV, 41
and quantity of capital employed, I, 78; no greater capital required by farmer who pays a higher rent, II, 75
as share of produce, I, 49 & n., 83–4 & notes, 334, 402–3 & notes, 411, II, 195–8, IV, 18 & n., IX, 40; not governed by proportions, II, 196 n.
as surplus produce, I, 75, II, 122–3, 128, 134, 210–12, IV, 11 n., VI, 204, VIII, 182, 209
origin of theory of, IV, 6–7; relation between profits and, IV, 14, 21, 38; table of rent and profit, IV, 17, VI, 187, 191, 194, 217–18, 220; theory explained in terms of Malthus's measure of value, II, 124–7
'getting rid of', simplifies theory of distribution, VIII, 194, and cp. IV, 7–8
corn rent and money rent, I, 82–4, 102–3, 157–8, 177, 210–12, 322, II, 128, VII, 92
real rent, I, 175, VIII, 209
building rent and ground rent, I, 201–4, see also I, 174
Adam Smith on, I, 327–37; Malthus's opinions on, I, 398–429
rent of mines, like rent of land, effect, not cause, of high value of product, I, 85; Adam Smith's contrary view criticised, I, 329–32
mine that pays no rent, I, 87 & n.
see also Distribution
Reply to Mr Say's Letters to Malthus (anon.), X, 405–10; see also Cazenove, John
Reporting, parliamentary, V, xxvii–xxxi; imperfections of, V, 49 n., 111 n., VIII, 196, 371, IX, 284; Ricardo misrepresented, V, 81 n., 92 n., 129 n., VIII, 356–9, IX, 164, 175; his own transcripts, V, xxx–xxxi, 231, 309, 332, XI, xxv; committee on, 1878, V, xxix n.; other reporting, V, 463 n., VI, 336
Reports of committees: see Agricultural committee, 1821, and 1822; Bank of England charter, 1832; Bank restriction act, 1797; Bullion Report, 1810; Children in manufactories, 1816; Corn laws, 1814; Education of the lower orders, 1816, 1818; Finance, 1819; Grain, 1814; Police of the Metropolis, 1816; Poor laws, 1817; Public expenditure, 1807; Resumption of cash payments, 1819; Roman Catholics, laws on, 1816
Representation of the people:
a necessary reform, V, 286–9, 470, 475, 484, 498–9, VII, 368; household suffrage sufficient, V, 473, 485, VII, 273 & n.; universal suffrage going too far, V, 29, 502, VII, 261, 270, 360, 369–70, VIII, 129
Whigs and, VIII, 62, 68, 335–6
see also VII, 321, VIII, 50, 52–3, 148, 227, and under Reform
Republican, The, Richard Carlile's paper, XI, xxi–xxiv
Restrictions:
on importation of corn: effect on profits, IV, 16 n., 237–8, VI, 108–10, 113–14, 116, 119, 146; effect on value of money, II, 154–6; conflicting interests of landlords and manufacturers, I, 312–13, II, 199–200; sudden removal ruinous to farmers, VIII, 103; see also Corn laws
on trade: justified to restore natural relation, VIII, 173; petition against, V, 42–6; see also VIII, 82, and Protecting duties
Resumption of cash payments:
Horner's motion for Committee, 1816, IV, 51
Peel's resolutions, 1819, V, 7–8, 18, 490; Ricardo's speech on, V, 9–17, VIII, 31–2 & n.
committees on, 1819, V, 350–70, see also IV, 226, V, 44, 522, VIII, 19–21, 23

Resumption of cash payments (*cont.*)
Ricardo's evidence to Commons' committee, V, 371–415, to Lords' committee, V, 416–57
Lords' reports, IV, 227, V, 13–14, 354, 356, 361–4, 367, 370, 403, VIII, 27, 36; Commons' reports, V, 9–10, 12, 14–15, 355–60, 366, 370, VIII, 21, 36–7, see also V, 151; Ricardo's speech on, V, 2–3; Bank directors on, IV, 267–70; merchants' petition against, VIII, 29 n.
cash payments bill (Peel's bill), V, 91; R.'s speeches on, V, 91–100, 105–8, 110; see also VIII, 368
Baring's loans to France and, V, 352 n., VII, 292 n.
attacks on: Cobbett's, VIII, 74 & n., IX, 106 & n., 123 & n., 140–1 & n., 153, 166–7, 176, 250, 267 n.; City opposed to, VIII, 29 & n., 31–2 & n.; Rothschild pressing for deferment, X, 89–90 & n.
Bank opposed to, VII, 292 & n., VIII, 20–1, 134–5 & n.; advised to reduce issues gradually and sell bullion, V, 13, 40, 61–2, 105, 206–7, 518; advice ignored, V, 76, 106, 110, 135–6, 165, 255, 312, 519; their mismanagement, IX, 15, 22, 140–1, 202; cash payments resumed too soon, V, 135, 140–1, 311–12
effect on prices: Ricardo estimates 3% if ingot plan adopted, V, 10–11, 16, 105, 527; 6 or 7% if coin used, 206, 255; later allows 5%, 94, 127, 134, 311, 385, and then 10%, IV, 228, 259 n., V, 142, 150, 165, 204, 255, VIII, 350, IX, 152; Baring says 25%, V, 45–6, 72, 77; Attwood, 30%, 105, 312; Palmer, 50%, 520, 527; others, up to 100%, 252; see also V, 94, 127, 134–6, 209, 312–13, 353, 385, VIII, 186
Resumption (*cont.*)
effect on price of corn, IV, 222–35, 262, on taxation, V, 386, 525
Western's motions: June, 1822, V, 198, 202, 210, 212–18, IX, 202, 207; July, 1822, V, 223–31, Ricardo's speech on, 231–45; in 1823, V, 309, R.'s speech on, 309–21, see also V, xxx & n.
'the Ricardo System', V, 92, VIII, 5, 20, 361
see also III, 427, VIII, 38, 150, and under Ingot plan, Peel's bill
Revenue:
gross and net, I, 347–51, 393–4
labour supported from gross, I, 388, 390, II, 236, but sometimes receives part of net, I, 348 n., 425, II, 381, VII, 378–9, VIII, 311; see also Wages
taxes paid from net, I, 421–4
proportion of, consumed and reproduced, III, 329
pecuniary and real, III, 280–3
capital and revenue, III, 281–2, VII, 121, VIII, 319–20, XI, xi
see also Income, Net revenue, Produce
Revolution:
Malthus's fears of, VIII, 107–8, 129
and Reform, V, 495, 497, VIII, 49–50, 146
revolution in Naples, V, xxii, VIII, 363
see French revolution
Revulsions of trade, I, 265–6; see also VIII, 275
Rhine, X, 215–22, 233–7; swim in, VII, 163
Riazanov, D., X, 382–3
Ricardo, Abigail (D.R.'s mother), *née* Delvalle, X, 24–8; drives David from home, 37–8; her children, 54–61
Ricardo, Abigail (D.R.'s sister), X, 58; visit to Gatcomb, VII, 55, 66; bequest to, X, 105; see also X, 133, 135

Ricardo, Abraham (D.R.'s father), X, 19–26; settles in England, X, 3, 20–1; on Stock Exchange, 3, 21, 23; naturalized, 22; obtains 'Jew brokership', 22; marriage and children, 24, 54–61; his homes, 24–5; sends David to Holland, 3, 31; estrangement from him, 37–8; reconciliation, 38; his will, 25–6; see also VI, 49 n., 56, X, 4–5, 53, 67, 75 n., 104

Ricardo, Abraham (D.R.'s brother), X, 55

Ricardo, Benjamin (D.R.'s brother), X, 59, 105

Ricardo, Birtha (D.R.'s daughter), X, 64; Maria Edgeworth on, X, 168, 170–1; goes on Continental tour, X, 177, 209, 222–3, 235, 237, 256–7, 284, 305, 327, 330–1, 352; see also VIII, 232, 284, IX, 45, 240, 296, X, 105

Ricardo, Daniel (D.R.'s brother), see Ricardo, Francis

Ricardo, David:

birth and childhood, X, 3–4, 29–30; at school in Holland, X, 30–3; employed on Stock Exchange at fourteen, X, 4; studies science with a friend, X, 6, 34–5; speaks Dutch, X, 194, 209, 214, and a little French, VII, 161, 165, IX, 213, X, 117, 181, 220, 255, 271, 333; his education 'neglected', VII, 190, 196, 305; difficulty of writing, VI, 314–15, 326, VII, 53, 65–6, 83, 305, 327, VIII, 55, 141; worst of memories, VIII, 7, 295, see also IX, 45

Jewish background, X, 16–32, 37–9; Unitarian connections, X, 39–41; doubts on taking sacrament as Sheriff, X, 42–3

marries at twenty-one, X, 5, 36–8; estranged from parents, X, 37–9; his children, X, 61–4; visits Osman at Cambridge, X, 136–40; opposes Fanny's marriage, VIII, 325, 334–5, X, 161–4; his fiftieth

Ricardo, David (*cont.*)

birthday, X, 164–5; his grandchildren, VII, 89, 177, 223, VIII, 329

homes in London: in childhood, X, 29–30, at Mile End, VI, xix, 47, 53 & n., X, 47, 118, Upper Brook Street, VI, facing p. 1, 52–3 & n., 59, 82, VII, 1, 13, 17–18, X, 48, 105, 336 n.; his counting-house, VI, 19, X, 74; country house, see Gatcomb Park

Clubs, X, 49–51; Geological Society, VI, xxx, 205–6, X, 6, 144; King of Clubs, VI, 87 & n., 220, VIII, 18, IX, 151; Brooks's, VIII, 28 & n., 163; Political Economy Club, VIII, 381, IX, 9–10, 36 n., 113, 158–9 & n., 172–3 & n., 264–5, 312

early visits to Holland, X, 33, 205, 207, see also IX, 210; relatives there, X, 201–2 & n.; proposed visit to Paris in 1803, X, 117; visit to Continent in 1817, VII, 160–5, 167–9; tour with family in 1822, IX, 209–29, 234–51, X, 175–352; a bad traveller, VII, 170, X, 247, 345

on the Stock Exchange, X, 6, 67–74, 123–4; loan contractor, X, 75–91; presentation from subscribers, X, 125–8. See also Loans

landed property, X, 95–9, see also V, 167, VII, 187 n., 230, VIII, 238, IX, 263; other investments, X, 99–102, see also VIII, 35, IX, 203–4; total estate, X, 102–4; coat-of-arms, VI, xli, 20 n., X, 54

Sheriff of Gloucestershire (1818), VII, 221, 223–4, 251–2, 255–6, 258–9, 276–8, 283 & n., 296, 372, VIII, 134, X, 42–3, XI, xii

speaks at Bank Court, V, 461–7, VI, 335–6, 341, 343, 346, VII, 19 & n.; enjoys attacks on the Bank, VI, 268–9

speaks at East India Company meetings, V, 475–8; refuses directorship, VIII, 250–4, 262–3, 281–2, 292

Ricardo, David (*cont.*)
enters parliament, V, xiii–xix, X, 11. See Parliament, seat in
finds speaking in public difficult, VI, 335, 343, 346, VII, 11, 381–2, VIII, 21, 38–9, 47 n., 142, 357, IX, 198, X, 51; but not in conversation, VII, 65, IX, 230, X, 168–9, 170; defect of hearing, VIII, 253, X, 299
his modesty, I, xix, VI, 241, 331, VII, 190, VIII, 60 n., X, 13; shyness, IX, 235, X, 140; no romance in his composition, X, 282; 'imposed upon by everyone', X, 244, 343, see also X, 117
alleged interested motives, V, 81–2, 87, 471, VIII, 147–8, see also VII, 5; Western's insinuations answered, V, 317–18, 526–7
his candour and liberality, VIII, 346, IX, 230; perfect sincerity and love of truth, II, 12, and cp. X, 169; no affectation or pretension, V, xxxii
his principles of toleration, IX, 278; supports Catholic emancipation, VIII, 350–1, 369, and free religious discussion, V, 280, 324–31, XI, xxii; opposed to Six Acts, VIII, 146–7; deplores persecution of the Queen, VIII, 299, 303–4; votes for liberal causes, V, xxii; arouses hostile feelings in County, VIII, 156–7 n. See also Reform of parliament
supports Chrestomathic School, VI, xxix–xxxi, 112–13, VII, 184, 190, 198, VIII, 191, 197–9, and Brougham's Infant school, but not school feeding, VII, 359–60, 363, 371; establishes school for the poor in Minchinhampton, VII, 45 & n., IX, 328–9
and Savings banks: Tetbury, VII, 26, 187 n., 220, City of London, VII, 34 & n., 46, 49–50 & n., Westminster, VII, 47, 49–50
views on public and private charity, I, 73 & n., VII, 248–9, see also I, 107, IX, 223

Ricardo, David (*cont.*)
on shooting as a sport, VII, 318–19, see also VI, 300, VII, 309; 'the barbarities of fishing and hunting', V, 122
his cautious driving, X, 168, and cp. VII, 361, VIII, 231–2; his horses too well fed and too little worked, VII, 365
not a particle of a farmer, VII, 207, see also VI, 150; as a gentleman does not reduce wages, VIII, 307
first reads *Wealth of Nations,* VII, 246, X, 7, 35–6; re-reads, VII, 88–9, 100, 111, 115; see also VII, 2
walks with Mill, VI, xxxiv, VII, 263, 266, 277, VIII, 7, 8, 10, IX, 210, X, 264; with Trower, VII, 147, 268, 273, 275; with Bentham, VII, 277, VIII, 191
his Benthamite principles, V, xix, VI, xxviii, IX, 52, 239, 259
'the Ricardo school', Sismondi on, VIII, 376–7 & notes
his 'peculiar opinions', VI, 178–9, 188, VII, 203, 214; 'paradoxical', II, 60, VII, 215, 222; 'new and unusual language', I, 19, II, 191–2, 194, see also II, 64, 117, 119, 126, 166, 331, VIII, 331, IX, 283
'abundantly theoretical', V, xxxiii, IV, 352, V, xxv, 93, 128 n., 270, see also V, 46, 109, 266, XI, xv; too theoretical, Malthus too practical, VI, 295; 'a visionary', VIII, 197; imagines strong cases, VIII, 184, 235, and cp. I, 121, IV, 312; 'dropped from another planet', V, 56, 85; 'the Oracle', V, 40, IX, 123 n., 141 n.
his library, X, 399–402; reads Bayle's *Dictionary,* VII, 190, 196, VIII, 49, Berkeley, VII, 277–8, Clarendon, IX, 45, History of Ireland, VIII, 49, Locke and Hume, VII, 197, 205–6, 229, books of travel, VII, 189, 259, IX, 218, Turgot and Montesquieu, VII, 382–3, Warburton and Beattie, VII, 277–8

Ricardo, David (*cont.*)
portraits and appearance, X, 51–3, frontispieces to vols. V, VIII, IX
illness and death, IX, 388–92, X, 12; his will, X, 104–6; his tomb, X, 12
Brougham's sketch, V, xxxii–xxxiv; Cobbett on, V, 40–1 n., VIII, 74–5 n.; Mrs Grote on, IX, 288 n.; J. Hume and Huskisson on, V, 332; Mallet's sketch, VIII, 152 n., X, 51–2; Malthus on, II, 12; Sismondi on, IX, 244 n.
obituaries and biographies: *Annual Biography and Obituary* (Moses Ricardo), X, 1–15; *Encyclopaedia Britannica* (McCulloch), X, 370; *General Biographical Dictionary* (John Gorton), X, 38, 39 n.; *Gentleman's Magazine,* X, 103; *Globe and Traveller,* IV, 7; *A Centenary Estimate* (Hollander), X, 17 n., 18 & n., 20, 37 n., 81 n.; *Memoir* (McCulloch), in successive versions, X, 369–70, 375; *Penny Encyclopaedia* (G. R. Porter), X, 37 n.; *Public Characters,* X, 37 n.; *Scotsman* (McCulloch), X, 369; *Sunday Times,* X, 37 n., 40, 51; *Tablettes Universelles* (Say), X, 57 n., 103 n.; *The Times,* X, 20; *Windsor Express* (James Hitchings), VI, xxxv n.

WORKS

Absolute Value and Exchangeable Value, 1823, IV, 357–412; see also IV, 308, X, 392 n.
Defence of the Plan of Voting by Ballot, 1824, V, 487–94, 504–12; see also VII, 302 n., 327 n., X, 368
Economical and Secure Currency, 1816, IV, 43–141. See below, *Proposals for an Economical and Secure Currency*
Essay on the Influence of a low Price of Corn on the Profits of Stock ('Essay on Profits'), 1815, IV, 1–41, VI, 178–9 & n.

Works, *Essay* (*cont.*)
relation to *Principles,* I, xiii, xxx–xxxiv, lvi n., 69 n., 81 n., 271 n., IV, 8, see also I, lvii, 268 n., VI, 242 n., 249
draft shown to Trower, VI, 102, 103–4, 183–4; Malthus sees MS, VI, 176, 182–3, 187, 216
Mackintosh on, VI, 182; Mill and Say think it obscure, VI, 249, 270, 338–9; McCulloch on, VII, 105 n.
West's pamphlet and, IV, 4–6, VI, 179–80
editions and translations, IV, 8, X, 360–1, 371, 375–6, 378, 380, 381–5; table of corresponding pages, IV, 419
see also IV, 14 n., 26 n., X, 400
Fragments on Torrens, 1818, IV, 303–18; see also VII, 316 n., 372, 376–7, X, 392 n., 397
Funding System, article in *Supplement to Encyclopaedia Britannica,* 1820, IV, 143–200
invitation to contribute, VIII, 54, 72, 78; instructions from Mill, VIII, 57–61, 66–7, 83, 105–6; writing of, VIII, 75–9, 141, 144, 188; correspondence with Place on, VIII, 83 & n., 118–25; McCulloch on, VIII, 137–8; Trower on, VIII, 319–20, 332; question of payment, VIII, 240, 242–3 & n.
editions and translations, X, 368, 375–6, 378, 381; table of corresponding pages, IV, 421
see also VI, xxxv, xxxvi, VIII, 69, 81, 127, 131, 238, 262, 307, X, 355
High Price of Bullion, The, 1810, III, 47–127, note on, III, 5–12
reviewed by Malthus, III, 11, 99 n., VI, 24 n.; Bosanquet on, III, 207, 215, 229 n., 248; sent to Perceval, VI, 43 n.
ed. 3 with Additions, III, 8; ed. 4 with Appendix, III, 11, V, 351; editions and translations, X, 356–9, 368, 371, 374–6, 378, 380–5; table of corresponding pages, III, 435–6

Works, *High Price* (*cont.*)
see also III, 176 n., 248 n., VI, xxxiv–xxxv, 4, 6, 7, 11, 22, 41, 165, 203, VII, 31 n., X, 390, 400
Journal of a Tour on the Continent, X, 175–352; see also VI, xviii, IX, 208, 209 & n., X, 371
Letters to McCulloch, ed. Hollander, X, 372–3; see also I, xxxvii, VI, xx n., xxiii, VII, 37 n., 93 n., VIII, 173 n., IX, 320 n., 345 n., X, 387
Letters to Malthus, ed. Bonar, X, 370, 383; letters misdated, IV, 3 n., VI, xxi & n., 226 n., VII, 135, 148; see also VI, xx, VII, 201 n.
Letters to Trower, ed. Bonar and Hollander, X, 371; see also I, vii, III, 36 n., 406, V, 142 n., VI, xxiv–xxv, IX, 71 n., 166 n., 174 n., 278 n.
Letters written during a Tour on the Continent, 1891, X, 180, 371. See *Journal of a Tour*
Minor Papers on the Currency Question, ed. Hollander, X, 373–4; see also III, 9 n., 345, 380 n., 413, IV, 274 n., 308, 326, VI, xvii n., 1, IX, 31 n., 168 n., 331 n., 358, X, 387, 389, 401, XI, xvii n.
Note on Prices and Taxation, 1821, IV, 319–22; see also I, 214 n.
Notes on Bentham's *Sur les Prix,* 1810–11, III, 259–341; see also III, 427, IV, 7 n., VI, xxviii n., 14–20
Notes on Blake's *Observations on the Expenditure of Government,* 1823, IV, 323–52, see also X, 400; review of Blake's *Observations,* IV, 325–6, 353–6, see also X, 392 n.
Notes on the Bullion Report, 1810, III, 343–78, see also III, 10 n., 427, X, 387
Notes on McCulloch's article 'Exchange', VIII, 85–93
Notes on Malthus's 'Principles of Political Economy', II, 1–463
first reading of Malthus, VIII, 179–85, annotated, VIII, 207–9, 212, 215–17, 228–30, 283, 296, 301; two notes sent to Trower, VIII, 304–7, 323; MS sent to McCulloch, VIII, 298–9, 318, 325, 333–4, 338–40; seen by Malthus, VIII, 308, 314–15, 334, 336, 349, 373, by Trower, VIII, 393, again by McCulloch, IX, 135, 138, 148
publication advised by Mill, VIII, 292–3, 296, 333, by Trower, VIII, 320–1, 345–6, 395; his own doubts, VIII, 297–8, 305, 342, and McCulloch's, VIII, 340, XI, xiii
discovery of MS, II, xv–xvi, X, 387; first publication, II, xv–xviii, 118 n., 231 n., X, 373
see also I, liii, lv, lvii, lix, 49 n., 83 n., 87 n., 349 n., VIII, 312, 352, 363, 382, IX, 1
Notes on Trotter's *Principles of Currency and Exchange,* 1810, III, 379–403; see also X, 387
Observations on...an Article in the 'Edinburgh Review', 1811, III, 99 n., 99–127; see also X, 358–9
Observations on Parliamentary Reform, V, 487–503; see also VII, 302 n., 332 & n., 336, 376, X, 368, 375, 391
Observations on Trower's Notes on Trotter, 1811, III, 405–9
Observations on Vansittart's Propositions respecting Money, 1811, III, 411–23; see also X, 387
Plan for a National Bank, 1824, IV, 271–300
first outlined in 1815, IV, 45–6, 114; written in 1823, IX, 325–6, 329, 331, 334; published posthumously in 1824, IV, 272, XI, xxvi; MS of, IV, 274, X, 391; editions and translations, X, 367; pirated edition, XI, xxix; table of corresponding pages, IV, 422; see also I, 361–3, IV, 359–60, 415, VI, 165–6, X, 15, 402
The Price of Gold (*Morning Chronicle,* 1809), III, 13–46; note on, III, 3–6; editions, X, 373, 385; see also III, 82 n., 88 n., X, 7–8, 355, 390

Works (*cont.*)
Principles of Political Economy, 1817: writing of, I, xiii–xix; first stages, VI, 262–3, 309, 315–16, 321; instructions from Mill, 330, 339–40, VII, 60; expects to be stopped by theory of price, VI, 348–9; problem of value, VII, 20, 71–2, 82–4; work suspended, VII, 36, 53, resumed, 65–6; MS of first part of *Principles* sent to Mill, 73, 82, 85–6; writing the section on taxation, VII, 84, 87–8, 91–2, 115 & n., Mill's comments, 106–8; re-reads Adam Smith, Say and Malthus, VII, 88–9, 100–1, 115, 120; last section sent to Mill, 111–12, and one chapter to Malthus, 137, 139–40, 145, 176, 179
arrangement and division into chapters, I, xxii–xxx, see also X, 403–4; printing, VII, 140, 147; cancels, X, 403–4, XI, xxx; publication, I, xix, VII, 148
Malthus's first comments, VII, 176, 312
reviews: M^c^Culloch in *Edinburgh Review,* VII, 278–82, 285–6, 288, 289 n., 291, 295, 296–7, gets off first edition, VII, 312, 337, 351, VIII, 152 n., see also VI, xxi, VII, 319; *Scotsman,* VII, 219–20 n.; *British Review,* I, 60–1 n., VII, 219–20 & n., 222, 231, 235, 256, 259, 289 n.; *Blackwood's Magazine,* VII, 316 & n., 326, 332, 362
Torrens' 'Strictures' on, in *Edinburgh Magazine,* VII, 179 & n., 315–16 & notes, 338, answered by M^c^Culloch, VII, 315–16 & n.; Ricardo's lost reply, VII, 316 n., 364, 376, see also IV, 305–8, 315–18
notes on, by Place, VII, 179 n., 183 & n., 189; Say's notes on, see below, French translation
see also II, 171 n., VI, xviii n., xxi, VII, 144 n., 155 n., 227, VIII, 173 n.

Works, *Principles* (*cont.*)
ed. 2, I, xlix–liii, VII, 162, 327–9, 370, 383 & n., VIII, 11; changes: in chapter on value, I, xxxvii–xliii, VII, 331, 333, on corn importation, I, 267, 318, 428–9, VII, 271, 354, on currency, I, 353–4, 356–61, VII, 353, on durabilities of capitals, I, 31, 53, 58, 60–1, VII, 338, 377, on the Irish labourer, I, 100 n., VII, 334, on no-rent land, I, 413 n., VII, 371–2, 379, on rent, I, 412–13, VII, 282–3, on taxation, I, 152, 242, VII, 280–1, 286, 334, 337–8, 353, on Torrens, I, 96–7 n., 271, VII, 179–80; see also VII, 358 n., VIII, 10, 37, 150, 221, 237, X, 377
ed. 3, I, liii–lx, VIII, 315, see also, 333, 346; M^c^Culloch's suggestions, VIII, 341; rewriting of chapter on value, I, xxxvii–xlix, VIII, 194, 229, 261, 279–80, 283–4, 344; alterations in: due to Malthus, I, 35 n., 43 n., 47 n., 49 n., 81 n., 83 n., 335, 404, II, 64, 118, 121–3, 197 n., IX, 178, due to Say, I, 249 n., 264 n., 279–85, 287–8 n., 348 n., 349 n., II, 382, VII, 378–9, VIII, 301 & n., 315, see also 344–5; new chapter on machinery, I, lvii–lx, 386–97, VIII, 373 & n., 377, 381–92
printing, VIII, 333, 342; publication delayed, I, liv, VIII, 341 & n., 379; Say on, IX, 31
'becoming a text-book', VII, 309, VIII, 82; read by few (Mallet), VIII, 152 n.; not many converts, VIII, 227, 376, 377 n.; not understood in France, VIII, 224 & n.
list of editions and translations, X, 362–5, 368, 371–2, 374–8, 379–85, see also 355–6; table of corresponding pages, I, 443–7
see also I, 426 n., II, vii, IV, 146, 203 n., 272, 320, V, 362, VII, 8 n., 228 n., VIII, 71, 94, 320, IX, 46, 223

Works, *Principles* (*cont.*)
French translation by F. S. Constancio, with Notes by J. B. Say, VII, 361 & n., 362, 364, 370–1, 375, 378–9, VIII, 4, 136; sales of, VIII, 225, 227; see also I, l, 348–9, 413, II, x, 382, VIII, 5, X, 374–6, XI, xxix
Proposals for an Economical and Secure Currency, 1816, IV, 43–141
Grenfell suggests writing, VI, 241–2, sends books and papers, 257–61, 265–7, 275–8, 281–5, 288; reads MS, 285–7, urges publication, 305, 313
doubts whether to publish, VI, 294–5, 312–13; Malthus comments on MS, VI, 298–303, 315; Mill's advice, VI, 324, 329–34, 337–8, VII, 4–5, 7
MS revised, VI, 335, 343, 347–8; publication, VII, 10, 13–15, 16, 19; ed. 2, VII, 24–5; payment for, VI, xxxv, VII, 14; reviewed by McCulloch, VII, 353–4, VIII, 1–3, 5, 10, 20, 23–4
passages quoted, in *Principles*, I, 356–61, VII, 353, VIII, 4–5, 20, in speech, V, 205–6
list of editions and translations, X, 361–2, 367–8, 371, 375–6, 378, 380–1, 383–5; table of corresponding pages, IV, 420
see also III, 11, IV, 272, 415, V, 351, 355, 364, 390, 463 n., 465 n., VI, xxxiii, 342, VII, 39, 42, VIII, 36
Protection to Agriculture, 1822, IV, 201–70
a sort of minority report, IV, 203, welcomed by the government, IV, 204–5, V, 155; attacked by Attwood, V, 162–4; reviewed in *Scotsman*, IX, 183
editions and translations, IV, 205, X, 365–6, 378, 381, 383, 385; table of corresponding pages, IV, 421–2
see also IV, 326 n., 361, V, xxv, IX, 166 n., 181 n., 203 n., X, 118

Works (*cont.*)
Reply to Mr. Bosanquet, 1811, III, 155–256, note on, III, 10–12
reviewed by Malthus, III, 11, 99 n.; Mushet on, III, 169 n.
editions and translations, X, 359–60, 368, 371, 375–6, 380, 381, 385; table of corresponding pages, III, 436–7
see also III, 169 n., 427, IV, 320, V, 371–2, VI, 14, VII, 384, VIII, 91 n., 126, 140, 340, X, 358, 400
Speech on Mr. Western's Motion, 1822, V, 198 n., X, 366–7
Three Letters on the Bullion Report (*Morning Chronicle* 1810), III, 129–53, note on, III, 8–9; editions, X, 373; see also X, 355
Two Papers on Parliamentary Reform, V, 487–512
letter to a newspaper on Peel's bill (1821–2), V, 515–21, X, 392 n.
commonplace books, X, 393–8; see also IV, 307 & n., 308, 315
lost notes and papers: on Grey's speech on reform, VIII, 6 & n., 8–9; importation of corn, VIII, 199; price of gold, III, 33–4 & n; profits, VI, 102–4, see also I, xxxi, IV, 3–4; reply to Torrens on value, VII, 316 n., 360, 364, 372, 376–8, VIII, 8, see also IV, 307–8; on Say's *Letters to Malthus*, VIII, 284, 292, 298, 301 & n., 315, 341 & n., 344–5, see also VIII, 305, X, 405
mistaken attributions to, VIII, 165 n., 173 n.
Ricardo's books and pamphlets, numbers printed, X, 356–75
Ricardo Memorial lectures, 1824, VI, xxii, IX, 301 n., 391 & n., X, 370
Ricardo Papers (*R.P.*), VI, xliii; contents of, X, 386–91; discovery of, I, viii–ix
Ricardo Tracts, in Goldsmiths' Library, X, 400, 402

Ricardo, David (D.R.'s son), X, 62–3; at Cambridge, VIII, 284, 293, 297, IX, 44, X, 136; inherits Gatcomb Park, X, 105; see also VI, 128, 239–40, 243, 255, VII, 52, VIII, 241–2, X, 50, 118, 242, 259, 265

Ricardo, David Israel (D.R.'s uncle), X, 19 & n., 30

Ricardo, Esther (D.R.'s sister), first wife of W. A. Wilkinson, X, 59–60; visits Gatcomb, VII, 61, 66; her marriage, VII, 325, 330; death, IX, 279, 296–7; letter from, X, 133–5; see also VI, 264, 349, VII, 6–7, 55, X, 44, 105

Ricardo, Fanny (D.R.'s daughter), wife of Edward Austin, X, 62; her marriage, VII, 324–5, X, 161–4, Ricardo opposed to, VII, 330, 334–5, 350; her death, VIII, 183 & n.; bequest to, X, 105 n.; see also VII, 55, 107, 136, X, 54

Ricardo, Fanny, wife of Moses, D.R.'s brother, *née* Wilkinson, X, 44, 56; leaves her father's home, X, 121–2; bequest to, X, 106; see also VI, 323, 332, VII, 7, X, 111, 209, 225, 336

Ricardo, Francis or Daniel (D.R.'s brother), X, 58–9; as Ricardo's clerk, X, 74; executor of his will, 106; bequest to, 105; see also VI, 112 n., VII, 14, IX, 45, X, 115–17, 336, 347

Ricardo, Frank (D.R.'s grandson), X, ix, 61, 64

Ricardo, Frank, jun. (D.R.'s great-grandson), discovers Ricardo papers, I, viii, xi, II, xv, VI, xx, xxiii, X, 64, 386–7; see also X, 17 n., 52 n., 54 n., 127

Ricardo, Hannah (D.R.'s grandmother), *née* Abaz, X, 19, XI, xxix

Ricardo, Hannah (D.R.'s sister), wife of David Samuda, X, 56; visits Gatcomb, VII, 66, IX, 306; death of her two children, VII, 239–40; bequest to, X, 105

Ricardo, Hannah (D.R.'s cousin), X, 106

Ricardo, Harriett (D.R.'s daughter-in-law), wife of Osman, *née* Mallory, VII, 144 n., 186 & n., X, 61; Ricardo's 'own dear child', X, 348–9, 352; death of infant, VII, 268–9, 279, 284; loses her mother, IX, 263, X, 264–5, 268, 335, 355; Maria Edgeworth on, IX, 230, X, 168, 171; Mill's affection for, VII, 182, 318, 330, 335, VIII, 11, 50–2, 263, IX, 114–15 & n., 118, 120; see also VII, 306, 328, VIII, 48–9, 183, 284, IX, 125, 209, X, 179

Ricardo, Henrietta (D.R.'s daughter), wife of Thomas Clutterbuck, X, 62, VI, 100; her children, VII, 89, 101, 109, 113, 116, 307, 315, VIII, 329, IX, 234, X, 259, 280; moves from Bath to Hardenhuish, IX, 296, 328, X, 315; bequest to, X, 105; see also VI, 49, 51, 125, 219, 312, 324, VII, 15, 92, 136, 262, VIII, 56, 183, 213, 332, 400 n., IX, 14, 44, 144, 250, 262, 264, X, 136, 209–10, 219, 253

Ricardo, Henry David (D.R.'s grandson), X, 63

Ricardo, Lt.-Col. Henry George (D.R.'s great-grandson), of Gatcomb, X, 63; see also X, ix, 50, 53 n., 54 n., 399, 400 n.

Ricardo, Isaac (D.R.'s brother), X, 56

Ricardo, Jacob (D.R.'s brother), X, 57–8; and French Rentes, X, 101; letters, 129–32; bequest to, 105; see also VI, 112 n., X, 23, 25 n., 242, 390

Ricardo, John Lewis (D.R.'s nephew), X, 58; *Anatomy of the Navigation Laws,* X, 58; see also IV, 147

Ricardo, Joseph (D.R.'s brother), X, 54–5; bequest to, X, 105; see also VII, 15, X, 25 n.

Ricardo, Joseph (son of David Israel), X, 32

Ricardo, Joseph (D.R.'s cousin), X, 106
Ricardo, Joseph Israel (D.R.'s grandfather), X, 19, XI, xxix
Ricardo, Mary (D.R.'s daughter), X, 63; studies political economy, IX, 114, 118, 125, 331; Maria Edgeworth on, X, 168, 170–1; on the Continental tour, X, 177, 182, 189, 194, 196, 198, 200–1, 205, 209, 211–12, 217–18, 231, 234, 237, 240, 249, 251, 255–6, 262, 264, 269, 284, 286, 293, 295–7, 305, 318, 327, 331, 352; bequest to, X, 105; see also VIII, 232, 284, IX, 45, 219, 240, 296
Ricardo, Mortimer (D.R.'s son), X, 63–4; at Eton, X, 267, 389; at Cambridge, X, 136; estates left to, X, 105; see also VI, 240, IX, 44–5, 296, X, 164, 229, 242, 266, 336
Ricardo, Moses (D.R.'s brother), X, 56
  at school in Holland, X, 33
  as doctor, VII, 294, 330, 350, 357, 360, 376, 382, IX, 279, X, 44, 47, 118
  visits Gatcomb, IX, 375–6
  his ill-health, VII, 294, 296, 305, 309, X, 225, 229, 315, 336, 342
  bequest to, X, 105–6
  author of *Memoir of David Ricardo,* III, 3, X, 14–15; intended to write a fuller biography, X, 16; publishes *National Bank,* IV, 273, 275 n.
  see also VI, 84, VII, 14, 80, 302, 315, VIII, 10, 84, IX, 391, X, 35 n., 51
Ricardo, Moses Israel (D.R.'s uncle), X, 19, 30, 32
Ricardo, Osman (D.R.'s son), X, 61; at Cambridge, X, 136–40; his marriage, VII, 144 n.; at Hyde, VII, 182 & n., 186 & n., 190–1; moves to Bromesberrow Place, VIII, 48–9; letters to, IX, 209, X, 179, 198; in D.R.'s will, X, 104–5, 106, 127; and Ricardo Tracts, X, 400–1; see also VI, 10 n., 13, 219,
Ricardo, O. (*cont.*)
  VII, 55, 262, 293, 299 n., 303, 361, VIII, 263, 332, 400 n., IX, 13–14, 44, 103, 122 n., 296, X, 97, 109, 112, 118, 168, 259–60, 344, 386
Ricardo, Percy (D.R.'s grandson), X, 24 n., 54, 59
Ricardo, Peter W., X, ix, 53, 400 n.
Ricardo, Priscilla Ann (D.R.'s wife), *née* Wilkinson, X, 36 & n.
  marriage displeases relations, X, 38
  her father's legacy, 45, 118
  attends Quaker meetings, 41–2, 45–6
  her child noticed by Princess, 112
  insists on move to West End, VI, 52, 93, X, 48
  school at Minchinhampton, X, 169
  'her warmth and energy on trifling occasions', X, 115–17
  her kindness, VII, 7–8, X, 168
  thinks Ricardo always imposed on, X, 343
  reckons Mill immoderate, VII, 303
  her letters from the Continent, X, 209–10, 241–2
  carried over a mountain, X, 249, 251, 283–6, 326
  portrait by Heaphy, X, facing p. 1, 53
  Ricardo's bequest to, X, 105, and cp. 46
  see also VI, 47, 90, 115–16, 118, 323, VII, 17, 72, 84, 89, 186, 190, 201, 324–5, 332, VIII, 58, 183, 308, 310, 400, IX, 116, 213, 230, 233, 296, 326–8, 379, 391, X, 61, 64, 147–8, 188, 198, 214, 234, 237, 258–9, 295–6, 299, 324, 328–9, 340–1, 344, 346
Ricardo, Priscilla (Sylla), D.R.'s daughter, wife of Anthony Austin, X, 62; her marriage, VII, 12–13 & n., 19–30, X, 163; her children, VII, 136–7, 139, VIII, 329, 400 n.; her cheerful spirits, IX, 264, 296, 376; bequest to, X, 105; see also VI, 113, 115–16, VII, 7, 54, 56, 61, 70, 72, 113, 187 n., 262, 325 n., IX, 124 n., 250, 262, 389, X, 266, 348

Ricardo, Rachel (D.R.'s sister), second wife of W. A. Wilkinson, X, 59; visits Gatcomb, VII, 328, 336, VIII, 284; bequest to, X, 105; see also X, 133
Ricardo, Raphael or Ralph (D.R.'s brother), X, 59
  and Mill, VI, 251, VII, 61, 315, IX, 219
  visits Gatcomb, VII, 55, 66, 326
  on the continent with D.R. in 1817, VII, 160, 165, X, 220
  introduced to Say, VI, 250, 273, 312
  marriage, VIII, 22 & n., 25, 240
  bequest to, X, 105
  see also VI, 112 n., 151, VII, 14, 167, 295, 339, VIII, 10, 143, 214, 223, X, 74
Ricardo, Rebecca (D.R.'s sister), wife of Isaac Keyser, X, 56–7; see also VII, 240, X, 105
Ricardo, Rebecca (D.R.'s cousin), Mrs Da Costa, X, 206 n.; visit to, in Amsterdam, X, 206–7, 211–12; see also X, 19, 30
Ricardo, Rebecca Israel, X, 18 n.
Ricardo, Miss S., X, 18 n.
Ricardo, Sabethaz, X, 202 n.
Ricardo, Samson (D.R.'s brother), X, 60–1
  and foreign loans, X, 57–8, 101, 351, 390
  visits Gatcomb, VII, 66
  republishes *Plan for a National Bank,* IV, 273, X, 367
  bequest to, X, 105
  letter quoted, VIII, 298 n.
  see also X, 51, 347
  Observations on the pamphlet of J. H. Palmer, X, 60; *A National Bank,* IV, 273, X, 60
Ricardo, Samuel Israel (D.R.'s uncle), X, 19, 30
Ricardo, Sarah (Sally), D.R.'s sister, educational writer, wife of G. R. Porter, X, 60, 105; declines a present, 133–5; see also VI, 264, 309, 311, 322, 349, VII, 6
Ricardo, Solomon (D.R.'s brother), X, 61
'Ricardoes' (gold ingots), V, 368–9. See Ingot plan
Rich and poor countries, I, 266, 373–8, VI, 141
Rich class, see Classes
Richardson, Overend, and Co., discount brokers, IV, 280 & n.
Richardson, Thomas, evidence to the bullion committee, III, 377–8, to law merchant committee, IV, 280–1 & n.
Riches:
  case in which real riches are augmented by increase of money, III, 318–19, VI, 16–17
  imaginary, pleasure derived from, VIII, 187
  see also II, 235, and under Wealth
Riches and value, I, 273–88
  Say's definition criticised, I, 279–81, 287–8 n., VI, 271–4, VIII, 299, 379, IX, 169–71, 188–91
  see also I, 429, II, 192–3, 203, 207
Rio de Janeiro, VIII, 92
Rive, Charles-Gaspar de la, professor of chemistry at Geneva, X, 270–1 & n., 272, 281, see also IX, 218–20
Roads:
  as relief works, V, 32, VII, 116 & n., 121, VIII, 155, 283
  road construction in Holland, IX, 209–10, X, 213–14; under the Prussians, X, 222; in Italy, IX, 225–6, X, 326–31, 335
  excellence of Simplon road, IX, 221, 226, X, 288–9
  want of streets in Venice, IX, 222
  see also II, 368–9
Robarts, M.P. for Worcester, VII, 101
Robarts, Curtis & Co., bankers, X, 68 n., 80
Robarts, Lubbock & Co., bankers, X, 68 n.
Robertson, Alexander, M.P. for Grampound, on East and West India sugars, V, 297, 476–7, 479–83

Robertson, W., *History of Scotland,* X, 398
Robins, John, X, 81 n.
Robinson, Frederick John (President of the Board of Trade till 1823; thereafter see under Chancellor of the Exchequer):
his liberal principles, V, 42, 44–5, 146, 248, IX, 269
on scope of agricultural committee, V, 48, 81
on corn laws, V, 51, 78
see also V, xx, 68, 86, 188, 218, 250 n., 335, 350, 492 n., IX, 270 n., 273, 274
Robinson, Sir George, M.P. for Northampton, V, 185
Rocca, son of Madame de Staël, X, 279
Rockingham, Lady, VII, 264 n.
'Rodborough Simplon', X, 168
Rogers Ruding library, IX, 150 n.
Rogers, Samuel, VIII, 152 n.
Roget, Peter Mark, VII, 191 & n., 193
Roman Catholics:
Plunkett's motion for claims of, V, xxii–xxiii; franchise bill, 1823, V, 329 n., 330 n.; report on laws relating to, 1816, VII, 146 & n.
Catholic emancipation, V, xv, xxii & n., xxiii & n., VIII, 50, 350–1, 362–3, 369, see also VIII, 289, 304
Rome, IX, 227, X, 319–20
Romilly, Lady, VII, 198, 206, 328 & n.
Romilly, Sir Samuel, M.P.:
elected for Westminster, VII, 269, 270 n.
his system of reform, VII, 273
his suicide, VII, 328 & n., 345–6, 357 n., 370, and moving will, VII, 376, 383
see also V, 335, VII, 198, 285, 305, X, 42, 50, 281
Memoirs of, VII, 189 n., 250 n.
Romilly, William, IX, 220, X, 281–2
Rose, George, M.P., his bill for Savings banks, VII, 33, 45, 63, 128, 133, 141, 152–3, 173, 209; see also III, 63 n., 429
Rosenhagen, A., VI, 46 & n.
Ross-on-Wye, VIII, 231, IX, 27, 113
Rosser, Henry Blanch, young friend of Bentham, VIII, 113–17; *The Question of Population,* 1821, VIII, 114 n.
Rossi, Pellegrino, X, 270, 270–1 n.; see also IX, 219, 245, X, 375–6
Rothschild, Nathan Meyer: opposed to ingot plan, V, 357; loan of 1819, X, 85–90, see also V, 21 n., 58 n., VIII, 30 n.; French loan of 1823, X, 57; see also III, 427–8
Rotten boroughs, VII, 110. See Borough system
Rotterdam, merchants' houses fit for princes, X, 195–6; see also IX, 211, 241
Rousseau, Jean Jacques: *Confessions,* VII, 60; *Émile ou de l'éducation,* VIII, 11; *Nouvelle Héloïse,* VII, 303, 306, 318, 328, 330, 336, IX, 220, X, 61, 282, 394 n., 395–6
Royal Military College, Bagshot, J. S. Mill attends lectures at, VII, 313–14, 326; Torrens's son at, VII, 315
Rubens, VII, 160, 163
Rulikowski, IX, 223, X, 290–1 n.
Rumbold, Charles Edmund, M.P. for Great Yarmouth, V, 185
Run on Bank for gold, witnessed by Ricardo in 1797, III, 365, see also 98; danger of, under Ingot plan, V, 455–6. See also Panics
Rush, Richard, VII, 285
Russell, Lord John:
contempt for political economy, IX, 155 & n.
motion on reform of parliament, V, xix, 283–9, 488–90
on taxation as cause of distress, IV, 257–8 & n.
on the Queen's trial, VIII, 220–1
Russell family, X, 173
Russia: imports of corn from, VIII, 369, IX, 155 n., of tallow, V, 291, 294; see also III, 290, IV, 28, V, 77, 103, 110–11, 404–5, VI, xxxvii, 79 & n., 80

Rutherford, A. W., *Hints from Holland*, 1811, annotated, X, 401 & n.
Ruxton, Mrs, IX, 256, 257, X, 32 n., 172

Saardam, X, 208
Sachseln, X, 252–3
St Andrews University, adopts *Principles* as text-book, VIII, 82
Saint-Arnaud, Comte de, later Marshal of France, X, 325 n.; young officer met on the Continent, X, 324–5, 327, 330, 332–3, 340–2, 345; story of his ancestry and wealth, X, 337–8; 'not what he represented himself to be', 351; see also X, 178, 334, 339
St Germains, Earl of, V, 351
St James's Park, walks in, VI, xxxiv
St Martin, X, 273, 276
St Maurice, IX, 220, X, 283
St Michel, X, 340
St Quintin, Catherine, wife of Ricardo's son David, X, 63
St Quintin, William Thomas, X, 63
Salisbury, VI, 124
Salmon, W. W., X, 96 n.
Salvador, Mr, X, 201
Samuda, David (D.R.'s brother-in-law), X, 56; visits Gatcomb, VII, 66, IX, 327–8, 335; executor of Ricardo's will, X, 25 n., 105; see also VII, 14
Samuda, Hannah (D.R.'s sister), see Ricardo, Hannah
San Carlos, Duke of, X, 273
Sargans, X, 240
Sarnen, good-humoured host at, X, 250
Sarzana, X, 324–5
Saunders, Dr, VII, 110
Savile, Mrs, VII, 109–10, 113
Saving:
- and accumulation of capital, I, 131, 151 n., 166–7, II, 8–9, 383, 390–3, 402, III, 281–2, V, 438, VI, 16
- power of saving increased by machinery, I, 390, 396
- motive for, I, 133, IX, 25, 131

Saving (*cont.*)
- can only be from unproductive expenditure, II, 417; only from net revenue, I, 347–8
- saving is spending, II, 449, VIII, 181, X, 409
- cannot be a cause of stagnation, disagreement with Malthus, II, 325, IX, 24, 26–7; see also VII, 121
- see also Parsimony

Savings Banks:
- Rose's bill, VII, 33–4, 45, 63 & n., 116–17, 125–6, 128–9, 133, 141, 152–5, 173, 209, VIII, 202, 210
- parish relief to depositors, VII, 12, 63–4, 96, 117–18, 125–6, 129–30, 133–5, 141–2, 149, 248
- plan for life-annuities through, V, 121 & n., 128–9
- investment of deposits, VII, 152–4
- correspondence with Mallet on, XI, xvii–xxi
- Bath, VII, 23, 153; Chichester, VII, 155 n.; City of London, VII, 49–50 & n., 153–4, 180; Godalming, VII, 12, 23 & n., 34, 46, 96, 209, VIII, 202; Hertfordshire, VII, 174; Southampton Row, XI, xviii; Southwark, VII, 26; Tetbury, VII, 26, 187 n., 220–1; Westminster, VII, 34 & n., 47 n., 49

Say, Jean-Baptiste, VI, xxv–xxvii
- meetings with, VI, 156–7, 160–1, 275, in Paris, VII, 168, 231, IX, 244
- Professor of industrial economy, VIII, 291; his lectures, VIII, 225, 291, IX, 191–2, 223; see also X, 290
- difficulty in conversation, VI, 161, 219, IX, 244–5 & n., 248; reasons by exclamations, VIII, 260–1; his profound thinking and egregious blunders, VIII, 302; does not understand the new doctrines, VIII, 374, IX, 244, 249
- his golden maxim, I, 242, VII, 334, 338
- misunderstands distinction between quantity of, and value of, labour, VIII, 149, 161

Say, Jean-Baptiste (*cont.*)
confuses utility, value and riches, I, 279–88, VI, 247–8, 271, VIII, 280–1, 298–9, 379, IX, 168–71; defends his views, IX, 32–6, 63, 188–91; see also VIII, 276, 312, IX, 64
misunderstands no-rent land, I, 413 n., VIII, 4, 57, 149–50, see also VII, 372
on gross and net revenue, I, 347 n., VII, 378–9
on stagnation and counter-commodities, VIII, 227–9, 260–1
demand limited only by production, I, 290, IV, 178, VI, 163–4, 168, VIII, 258–9, IX, 13, see also II, 311, VII, 121
doctrine of productive services, VIII, 228, 260, 277, 379–80, IX, 34–5
on price of corn regulating all prices, VII, 105
his currency plan, VI, 165–6 & n., see also IV, 272
and Ricardo's *Principles:* on ed. 1, VII, 178, ed. 3, IX, 31–6, 46, 63–4, 154, 158, 168; his 'Notes' in French edition, I, 348–9 notes, 413 n., II, 382, VII, 178, 361, 364, 370–1, 375, 378–9, VIII, 4–5, 7, 10, 136–7, 149–50, IX, 244, X, 374–6, 379–80, see also X, 374–6, 379–80; alterations due to, in ed. 2, I, 413 n., VII, 372, 379, VIII, 4–5, 7, in ed. 3, I, 249 n., 264 n., 279–85, 287–8 n., 348 n., 349 n., II, 382, VII, 378–9, VIII, 301 & n., 315, see also VIII, 341 n., 344–5, IX, 46
letter read to Political Economy club, IX, 36 & n., 158 n., 172–3; elected to, IX, 173 n., 191 & n.
speculation in potato-flour, VI, xxv, VII, 166, 168, 224–6, 230, see also X, 95 n.
list of letters, IX, 399
see also I, 5, IV, 343, VI, 250, 273, 312, 336, VII, 186, 201 n., VIII, 22, 212, 270, 275, 331, IX, 187, 195, X, 57–8, XI, xi

Works

Catéchisme d'Économie politique, 1815, VI, 245 & n., Ricardo on, I, 287–8 n., VI, 247–9, 264–5, 269, Say's reply, VI, 271–4; ed. 2, 1821, IX, 169, 173 & n., 188–90; see also VI, 255
Cours complet, 1828–9, IX, 32 & n.
Lettres à M. Malthus, 1820, VIII, 227 & n., 280–1; Ricardo on, VIII, 227–8, 276–8, 284, 379–80, IX, 170–2, his 'Notes' on, I, lvii, VIII, 292, 298, 301–2 & n., 305, 315, 341 n., 344–5; Malthus on, VIII, 259–61; McCulloch on, VIII, 313; Say complains of misunderstandings, IX, 36; translation in *New Monthly,* VIII, 249; Cazenove's *Reply,* X, 401 n., XI, xxx, Ricardo's 'Notes' on the *Reply,* X, 405–10; see also II, 338, VIII, 225, 229, 249, 285
Mélanges et correspondance, 1833, VI, xxvii, 273, IX, 31 n., 188 n.
Œuvres diverses, 1848, VI, xxvi, xxvii, 165 n., 273, VIII, 291 n., IX, 31 n., 244 n.
Traité d'Économie politique:
ed. 1, 1803, IV, 178, VI, xxv, VIII, 7
ed. 2, 1814, I, 6–7, 69 n., 73–4 n., 155, 186–90, 227 n., 235–8, 242–4, 254–6, 264 n., 275 n., 279–80 n., 285–8, 290, 299–300 n., 307 n., 316–20, 344, 347, 349–50 n., 352 n., 355 n., 372 n., 379, 383, IV, 71, VI, xxv, 156, 160–1, 163–4, 168, VII, 89, 101, 105, 108, 112, 115, 121
ed. 3, 1817, VI, 270, 321, VII, 166 & n., 168, 178 & n., 219, 222, 231, 235, X, 399
ed. 4, 1819, I, lvii, 279–84, 421 n., II, 14, 311, VII, 227, VIII, 136, 149, 225, 228, 298–9, 312–13, 315, 341 n., IX, 32, 46, 171, 190, X, 399
ed. 5, 1826, I, 249 n.

Say, Jean-Baptiste, *Traité* (*cont.*)
Ricardo reads, VI, 163–4, re-reads while writing *Principles,* VII, 89, 101, 112, 115, comments on, VIII, 228, 298–9, IX, 46, 171; alterations to meet Ricardo's objections, VI, 321, VII, 166, 178, 227, VIII, 136, 315; McCulloch on, VIII, 312–13; reviewed with R.'s *Principles* in *British Review,* VII, 219, 222, 231, 235, see also VI, 255
intended translation by Place, VI, 160 & n.; Prinsep's translation, 1821, VIII, 315 & n., reviewed in *Scotsman,* VIII, 374
obituary of Ricardo in *Tablettes Universelles,* 1823, X, 57 n.; 'Notice sur Ricardo', X, 103 n.
articles, 'De l'Angleterre', 1815, VII, 94; 'De la crise commerciale de l'Angleterre', 1826, X, 58 n.
unpublished letters to Francis Place, VI, xxvi n.
Un professeur d'Économie politique, by A. Liesse, IX, 192 n.
Say, Louis, VII, 226 & n.; *Considérations sur l'industrie et la législation,* 1822, IX, 245, 248–9
Scale of discounts, 1782–97, IV, 415–18, see also III, 358 n., IV, 279
Scarce books, I, 12
Scarcity, as source of value, I, 12, 194, 250, 276–7, II, 204; see also III, 309–10
Scarlett, James, M.P. for Peterborough: Poor-law bill, V, 113; superabundance no cause of agricultural distress, V, 141; see also V, 185, IX, 198
Schaffhausen, X, 235–8
Scheveling, X, 203
Schmidt, C. A., X, 376
Schneider's hotel, Florence, X, 314, 319–20
Schools: Brougham's Infant School, VII, 356–7, 359–60, 363, 371; Charterhouse, VI, 129, X, 61–3; Dissenting Academy, Daventry, VII, 171 n.; Eton, VII, 138, X, 63, 267, 389; Ets Haïm, Amsterdam, X, 31–2; Fellenberg's, Hofwyl, X, 262; Haileybury, see East-India College; Harrow, VII, 138, X, 267; Lancasterian system, VI, 112 n., VII, 45 n., 155 n., X, 402; Minchinhampton, Ricardo's schools at, VII, 45 & n., IX, 328–9, X, 169; Owen's Infant School, VII, 150; Talmud Tora, Amsterdam, X, 31–2; Westminster, VII, 138; see also VI, 126, and Chrestomathic School
Schwediaur, Francis Xavier, VII, 167 & n.
Schwetzingen, X, 228–9
Schwyz, X, 245
Scotland:
banks, III, 228, 235, 399
burgh system, VIII, 326
cash accounts, I, 365–6
juries, VIII, 167, IX, 136, 142
long farm leases, VI, 174–5, 177, 297
press, VIII, 167, IX, 136, 142
Say's visit to, IX, 187
Scotch linen laws petition, V, 290
see also I, 256, 351, III, 286–7, VIII, 400
Scotsman, The, McCulloch's newspaper, VI, xxii, VII, 291, VIII, 167 & n., IX, 204–5
Ricardo subscribes to, VIII, 28, 142–3, 157
his papers on reform published posthumously in, V, 489, 494
Principles reviewed in, VII, 219–20 & n., 222
Malthus's *Principles* reviewed in, VIII, 178 & n., 185
articles: on agricultural distress, 1821, VIII, 337, 341; corn laws, VIII, 197 & n.; Edinburgh police, IX, 137
see also V, 515, VII, 259, VIII, 25 n., 82, 139, 205 n., 223, 239–40, 319, 359 n., 390–1, IX, 140 n., 142, 155, 277, 301 and under McCulloch, J. R., articles in *Scotsman*

Scott, Mr, surgeon, VI, 349
Scott, Sir Walter, Maria Edgeworth's visit to, IX, 259 & n.; see also VIII, 58, 204, IX, 136 n., 232
Ivanhoe, VIII, 152 n., 155–6; *New Tales of my Landlord,* VIII, 37 & n., 40, 44; *Quentin Durward,* IX, 294; *The Heart of Midlothian,* X, 169
Scrope, George Poulett, X, 63
Sebright, Sir John, M.P., IX, 148
Secheron, X, 264, 269, 270, 282
Sedgwick, actor, X, 112
Seditious Meetings Prevention bill, speech on, V, 28–9
Seignorage on coinage: principles of, III, 222–6; no objection to a moderate one, I, 371–2, V, 362; necessary if gold coinage retained under ingot plan, V, 401–7, 431; in France, III, 179; see also IV, 114, VII, 265, IX, 331
Selection of Speeches at County Meetings, 1822, V, 469 n.
Seligman, E. R. A., 'On some neglected British Economists', IX, 27 n.
Senior, Nassau William, meets Ricardo at Political Economy Club, IX, 312 n.; article on agriculture in *Quarterly Review,* 1821, IX, 109 & n., 122; *Conversations with... Distinguished Persons,* 1878, III, 261 n.
Sens, X, 346
Sentinel, The, newspaper, IX, 187 & n.
Seoane, J. A., X, 355
Sequeira, Rebecca Henriques de (D.R.'s grandmother), wife of Abraham Delvalle, X, 27
Serbelloni, Villa, X, 294, 296
Servants in Ricardo's household:
Mrs Cleaver, on Continental tour, X, 177, 182, 197, 235, 237, 297, 313, 328, 343–4
Darby, gamekeeper, X, 159–60, 265 & n., and cp. VII, 319
Thomas Darby, X, 159–61
John Drysdale, footman, X, 104 n., see also IX, 208
Servants (*cont.*)
Catherine Harrison, maid, her adventure, X, 144–59
Pamela, maid, X, 111
William Pike, butler, X, 104 n.
William Primmer, coachman, X, 26
Mary Rundle, X, 26
Thomas, X, 110, and cp. 350
Servants, menial: whether preferred to commodities, VII, 70, VIII, 102; see also I, 392–3, 395, 424, VI, 155, 164, VIII, 184
Services productifs, see Productive services
Servoz, X, 274
Seymour, Lady, *The Pope of Holland House* (John Whishaw), IV, 204 n., V, 128 n., VI, 66, 87, 135 n., 139 n., VII, 54 n., 144 n., 185 n., 251 n., 270 n., 291 n., IX, 109 n., X, 50 n.
Sewers, Ricardo member of committee on, V, xxvi, IX, 284 & n.
Sharp, Richard (Conversation Sharp), VI, xxxvi–xxxvii
Ricardo succeeds him as member for Portarlington, V, xv, xvi, xviii, VII, 311, VIII, 17–18
his travel hints, X, 179, 246, 296, 298 n., 301 n.
letters, VII, 291, VIII, 17
see also V, 352, VI, xix, 28–9, 31, 48, 59, 66–7, 71–2, 77, 82, 87, 90, 244, VII, 252, 263, VIII, 70, 152 n., 163, 204, 214, X, 49, 50, XI, xxvii
Shchepkin, M., X, 381
Sheet-anchor, Ricardo's, the invariability of precious metals, VI, 348
Sheffield Telegraph, XI, xxviii
Shepherd, Henry John, M.P., VIII, 56
Shepherd, Lady Mary, visits Gatcomb, VIII, 56 & n.; Maria Edgeworth on, X, 172
Shepherd, William, stockbroker, X, 126–8
Sheppard, Edward, X, 96
Sheppard, Phillip, Ricardo buys Gatcomb from, X, 95–6; dispute with, about a servant, X, 159–61
Sherborne, Lord, V, 469–70, VIII, 330

Sheriff, office of, VII, 255–6, 258–9, VIII, 113, 134, 148, 164; in Scotland, IX, 136; see also under Ricardo, Trower

Shitabroy, Rajah, VII, 237

Short period, VI, 170, see also VI, 153

Short time work prevents mobility of labour, VIII, 316

Shuman, courier on Continental tour, IX, 213–14, X, 177, 182–3, 185, 187, 191, 200, 204, 215–16, 221, 234, 244, 248, 263, 274, 297–8, 310–11, 342

Sicily, vote on, in 1821, V, xxii

Sidmouth, Lord (Henry Addington), IV, 153–4, 165, VI, 261

Sieber, N., X, 381

Sieveking, Heinrich, *Karl Sieveking,* III, 434 & n.

Sieveking, Karl, 'Geschichte des Pfund Sterlings' (MS), III, 434 & n.

Silberling, Norman J., 'Ricardo and the Bullion Report', III, 6–7, X, 91–4

Silberner, E., III, 266

Silk manufacture Acts, see Spitalfields

Silk trade with Bengal, IV, 251, V, 197, 478

Silver:

- whether gold or, the standard, III, 28–33, 36–46, 84–5 & n., VI, 4–6; silver the main currency under William III, I, 370–1; still the standard (Lauderdale), VIII, 45 & n.; preferable to gold as standard, IV, 63, 67 n., V, 428, 432, VI, 301, change of opinion, V, 390–1, 427; preferred by Malthus, VI, 299, and by Locke, III, 65–6; the currency of Hamburg, III, 180
- silver picked up on the sea-shore in a day, II, 81, IV, 406, VIII, 179; see Value, measure of, Malthus's
- price of, III, 29–32, 44, 85, VIII, 45; under the mint price in 1816, VII, 28–9; low price from forced abundance, I, 229
- exports to East Indies, III, 171–2, 249

Silver (*cont.*)

- law against coining, III, 36–7, 68–9; legal tender of coins limited, III, 42, 46, 66, 85; checks against excessive circulation of, I, 371 n.; debasement of, III, 30, 37–9, 70; recoinage (1816), V, 386–7, see also X, 201
- see also America, Spanish; Gold and Silver

Simond, Louis, met in Geneva, X, 270–3 & n., 281–2, IX, 218–20; his book on Switzerland, X, 239 & n., 246, 255 n.; articles on Fellenberg's school, X, 262 n.

Simonde, J. C. L. (later Sismondi, *q.v.*), *De la richesse commerciale,* 1803, I, 380–1 & n., 399, II, 105, X, 399

Simplon road, IX, 221–2, 226, 234, X, 288–9, see also X, 168

Sims, Miss, VIII, 308, 310

Sinclair, Sir John, VI, xxxvii

- his currency plan, VIII, 186, 386
- plan to reduce national debt, VIII, 187
- list of letters, IX, 400
- *Correspondence of,* 1831, VI, xxxvii, 143 n., 150 n., 151 n., VIII, 186, 386; *Memoirs of,* by his son, VI, xxxvii
- *Address to the Owners...of Land,* 1822, IX, 156
- *History of the Public Revenue,* ed. 3, 1803–4, VIII, 66
- *Observations on the Report of the Bullion Committee,* 1810, III, 139–45, 359, 428 n.
- *On...the National Calamity,* 1817, VII, 151 & n.
- *Code of Health,* 1807, *of Agriculture,* 1817, *of Finance* (never written), VI, 143

Sinking fund, IV, 149–67

- when real and when a delusion, IV, 172–84, VIII, 118–23; real in origin, V, 267, VIII, 67; has become a delusion, IV, 194, V, 20, 26, 62, 79–80, 194, 243, 265, VII, 94 & n.; ought to be abolished, IV, 99, VIII, 78, IX, 180

Sinking fund (*cont.*)
conditions for efficiency, I, 248–9, V, 262–5, VIII, 122
the savings bank of the nation, VII, 17; injustice of inroads on, IV, 40–1, VII, 105–6
not a cause of glut, IV, 178–80
whether it turns revenue into capital, IV, 183–4, VIII, 319–20
cannot be used both to annoy an enemy and to pay a debt, IV, 198, V, 25, 251, 268–9
application of, to reduction of borrowing, IV, 171–3; recommended by Ricardo, V, 4–5, X, 81–2, 85, see also V, 21–2 & n.
and land-tax, V, 259–61; and pensions plan, V, 160–1, 194–5, 248–9, 267
Stanhope's, IV, 149; Pitt's, IV, 151–3, 191–2, 194, V, 118–20, 262; Addington's, IV, 153–4; Petty's, 154–7; Perceval's, 157–8; Vansittart's, 158–67, V, 118–20, 262–3, VI, 91 & n.; Parnell's plan, V, 270–3, IX, 175 & n.
commissioners of, I, 362–3, IV, 182–3, 191, 194–5, V, 120 n., 194
speeches on, V, 4–6, 20–2, 24–5, 64–7, 115–20, 248–51, 259–65, 266–73, see also 129–30
article on, for *Encyclopaedia,* VIII, 54, 72, 75–8; see Ricardo, David, *Funding System*
see also III, 272–3, V, 101, 147, VI, 178, VII, 38, 260, VIII, 33, 110, 135, 147, IX, 269
Siordet, I. M., *Letter to Sir John Sinclair,* 1811, X, 401
Sirven affair, IX, 374
Sismondi, J. C. L. Simonde de, VIII, 22
discussions with, IX, 218, 220, 235–6, 243–4 & n., 248, X, 270, 278, 281
views on rent, I, 399–400
on unequal distribution of property, IX, 243–4 & n.
Ricardo's twenty-five readers, VIII, 376–7 n.
Sismondi (*cont.*)
too sentimental for McCulloch, VIII, 24–5
Malthus's letter to, VIII, 375–7
see also I, lv, 5, VIII, 224 n., 366, 382, IX, 219, X, 279, 322, 375–6, 409
Nouveaux principes d'économie politique, 1819, VIII, 22 & n., Ricardo on, VIII, 57, 80, McCulloch on, VIII, 24–5, 38, 40, 383, Torrens on, VIII, 376–7 & n.; ed. 2, 1827, IX, 244 n.; see also VIII, 109, X, 399
Études sur l'économie politique, 1837, IX, 244 n.
articles: on power of consuming and power of producing, VIII, 376, see also 224 n.; 'Sur la balance des consommations avec les productions', IX, 244 n.; on J. Barton, IX, 245 & n.
see also Simonde
Six Acts, Ricardo votes against, V, xxii, 28–9, VIII, 146; see also VIII, 110, 133
Skarbek, Count Frederick, X, 290 n.
Slater, James Henry, VIII, 323, IX, 144, 383
Slavery, in the West Indies, V, 483, in the East Indies, V, 297, 300
Smaler, Richard, VI, 113 n.
Smart, William, *Economic Annals 1801–1820,* VII, 116 n.; *1821–1830,* V, xxiv n.
Smiles, S., *A Publisher and his Friends, Memoir of John Murray,* IX, 107 n.
Smith, Adam, *Wealth of Nations:*
first reading of, X, 7, 35–6, VII, 246; re-read, VII, 88–9, 100, 107–8, 111–12, 115, 246, see also III, 7, VII, 2, X, 390–1, 399; *Principles* patterned on, I, xxiii–xxv
on greater productivity of labour in agriculture, II, 20, IV, 37, VI, 178, see also IX, 193; confines labour of nature to agriculture, I, 76–7 n.
compares banks with highways, III, 55
on bullion and foreign exchanges, III, 112

Smith, Adam (*cont.*)
colonial trade, I, 340, VII, 100
consumption as sole end of production, V, 219
his authority quoted by country gentlemen for high duties on importation of corn, I, 317
demand for necessaries limited, for luxuries unlimited, I, 293, 295–6, IX, 19; effects of demand on prices, VI, 148 & n.
depreciation of coinage through excess of paper, I, 354–5, III, 148–51; depreciation of colony currency, I, 356; observations on debased coinage apply to depreciated paper, III, 96–7, see also 76–7
effectual demand, power and will to purchase, VI, 58, 142, and cp. 56
and export of surplus goods, I, 291 n.
his free trade principles, I, 338, V, 43
on gold and silver, I, 366, III, 52–3
on value of gold, corn, and labour, I, 373–8, see also 18–19
overrates advantages of gross revenue, I, 347–9, II, 382, VII, 379
on labour as standard of value, I, 416, IV, 409, IX, 363, 380; alternates between standards, I, 13–14
legacy duty, I, 153–4
theory of money, III, 220, 327–8; paper money and taxation, III, 236–7
natural price, II, 38, 46, 52, VIII, 202, IX, 65, see also I, 375–6; real and nominal price, I, 274–5 n.
difficulty of estimating rate of profits, I, 296–7; profits in different employments, IV, 12 n.
rate of interest not regulated by quantity of money, III, 25–6, 88–9, 143–4, 150, 194 n., V, 12 & n.
on rent of land, I, 327–37; strict and popular senses of rent, I, 67–8; building rent and ground rent, I, 201–4; rent of mines, I, 329–32
effects of restrictions on export of precious metals, I, 228–9, 310

Smith, Adam (*cont.*)
on seignorage, III, 179–81, 222
low value of silver in Spain, I, 228–9
his maxims of taxation, and the land-tax, I, 181–6, see also I, 204, 235; taxes on raw produce fall on rent, I, 183–4, 252, IV, 33–4 n., 239, see also I, 199; but malt tax falls on consumer of beer, I, 252–3; taxes on wages, I, 215–16, fall on landholders and consumers, I, 222–8, 232–6
on value, I, 11–23, 309, see also III, 284, IX, 2, 190; his original error, I, xxxv–xxxvi, 22–3 n., VII, 100, 377, regards rent as component of price, I, 77–8, 329, II, 42–5, see also IV, 315–17
value and riches, I, 273, 276–8, 286 n., 429; criticised by Say, I, 285–7
real value of wages, I, 19–20
on evaluating different kinds of work, I, 21 n.
worshipped in Edinburgh, VII, 295
his errors: on bounties on exportation, I, 304–5 & n., 310–17, VII, 100, 107–8; on capital employed in foreign trade, I, 350–1, see also 129; on carrying trade being not of choice, but of necessity, I, 294; on colonial trade raising profits, I, 344–5, VII, 100, 202; on the peculiar nature of corn, I, 313, 413–14 & n.; on corn being always of the same value, I, 374, V, 210–12; identifies low value of money with high value of corn, I, 336–7; supposes price of corn regulates all other prices, I, 302, 307–8, IV, 21 n., VII, 105; food production always yields rent, I, 327–9, 332–3; thinks profits depend on accumulation without reference to population, I, 289–91, VIII, 380; rise of wages raises price of all commodities, I, 46
Cobbett on, IX, 267 n.

Smith, Adam (*cont.*)
David Hume's supposed notes on, I, vii, XI, xxvii
Louis Say's notes on, IX, 245, 248
Buchanan's ed. with Notes, 1814, VI, 159 & n.; see also I, 77 n., 216–20, 251–2, 254, 314–15, 334, 355–6, 370, VII, 101, IX, 206, X, 399
Cannan's ed., 1904, I, lxii
McCulloch's ed., IV, 6–7 & n.
proposed edition with notes by Malthus, VI, 159–60 n., 169; Malthus's questions to his pupils on, VI, 159 n.
see also I, 151 n., 365, II, 26–7, III, 58, 81, 145, 163, 188, 253, IV, 7, VI, xxxvii, 34, 95, 120, 272, 316, VII, 40, 98, 106, 180, 219, VIII, 24–5, 189, 225, 286, IX, 22, 164, 187, 210, X, 21, 53
Theory of Moral Sentiments, X, 399
Smith, Sir Charles, X, 277
Smith, George, M.P., V, 185
Smith, John, M.P. for Midhurst, banker: on inroad of machinery upon labour, V, 30 & n.; supports ingot plan, V, 359; see also V, xxvi, 37, 292, VII, 356, VIII, 45
Smith, J. B., Barclay & Co., III, 430
Smith, Joseph, *Catalogue of Friends' Books,* X, 43 n.
Smith, Kenneth, *The Malthusian Controversy,* XI, xxviii n.
Smith, M. F. L., *Tijd-affaires in effecten aan de Amsterdamsche Beurs,* X, 19 n.
Smith, Robert (father of Sydney Smith), IX, 60, 89 n., 108 & n.
Smith, Robert, M.P. for Lincoln, V, 277
Smith, Sydney, IX, 89 n.
visits Gatcomb, IX, 46, 63, 89–90
tolerates all religions but not atheists, IX, 60
on Ricardo's driving, X, 168
cousin of Trower, VI, xxiii, IX, 108
letter quoted, VII, 251 n.
articles by, IX, 89, 108
see also V, 352, X, 50
Smith, Thomas, accountant: his evidence on ingot plan, V, 360; *Essay on the Theory of Money,* 1807, III, 9 n.; *Reply to Mr. Ricardo's Proposals,* 1816, V, 360 & n.
Smith, Thomas, of Easton Grey, Ricardo's country neighbour, VI, 135 & n., VII, 187 & n.; Unitarian, VII, 171 n., X, 40, 169, 350 n.; first meeting at Malthus's, VI, 164; visits from, VII, 54, 56, VIII, 276, 282, X, 169–71; visits to, VII, 171, VIII, 56, 61–3, 75, 334 n., IX, 263–4; his collection of pamphlets, VIII, 62–3, 77, 84, 106; his death, IX, 232 n., 328; letters quoted, VII, 54 n., 186 n., X, 50, 298, 389; see also V, 128, VI, xxxii, 66 n., 244, 295, VII, 15, 35, 61, 90, 114, 144 n., 185, 191–2, 206, 223, 275, VIII, 107, XI, xii n.
Smith, Mrs Thomas (Elizabeth Chandler), VI, 135 & n.; her autograph collection, VI, 139 n., 164–5, 169; is widowed, IX, 232–3, 240, 251, 262–4, X, 337, 349; see also VII, 35, 189, X, 32, 389
Smith, William, geologist, VII, 119 n.
Smith, William, M.P. for Norwich, V, 296, X, 77 n., 285
Smithies, Rev., on the 'calculating economy of Mr Ricardo', IX, 267 n.
Smollett, Tobias, his tomb at Leghorn, X, 322
Smuggling, I, 378, II, 452, III, 183, V, 268, VII, 303, IX, 147, X, 169–70, 189, see also IV, 190
Smyth, Professor William, VI, 72, 196, 215, 219, 220, 240, 243, VII, 223, 252, 311, VIII, 114
Soap, as one of necessaries of labourer, I, 20, 224, 234, 275, IV, 257
Society for Mutual Improvement, VIII, 115, 117
Society for the Suppression of Vice, V, 277–8
Society, state of, stationary, retrograde, and progressive, I, 176–7, III, 274,

Society (*cont.*)
IV, 22–3; see also I, 108–9, IV, 234, VII, 16–17, and under Progress of society
Soetbeer, A., *Die Hamburger Bank,* III, 176 n.
Solly, Edward, merchant, V, xxiv, 174, 181–2, 185, VIII, 374
Somerset, Lord R. E. H., M.P. for Gloucestershire, VII, 272 n., VIII, 156 n.
South Sea Company, IV, 83, 149, VI, 276, IX, 198 & n.
Southey, Robert, his reveries on political economy, VII, 247 & n.
Spade husbandry, II, 238–9, V, 31, 35, IX, 56
Spain:
rate of exchange with her colonies, III, 171, VIII, 126, 141, see also I, 195–8
drain of gold to, VI, 122, 298
value of silver in, I, 228
war in, IX, 268–9, 274, 294, 315, 372, 378–9; sympathy with the Spanish people, V, 274 & n., IX, 213, X, 57
see also VIII, 294 & n.
Spanish America, see America, Spanish
Spanish and Portuguese ancestry of Ricardo, X, 17–19
Spanish funds, IX, 256, 262, 372, 379
Specie payments: Horner's motion on, 1816, IV, 51 & n., 65, VII, 28, 30 & n.; under Peel's bill, VIII, 32, 35–6, 39. See Resumption of cash payments
Speculation, V, 131, 141, 341–2, 449, VII, 16, 352, VIII, 39, see also III, 122; excess of, leading to stagnation, V, 385; see also Overtrading, Potato flour
Speculators, and real capitalists, III, 134–5; speculators in corn, IV, 253–4, V, 85, 90
Spence, William, II, 360 & n., IV, 178, VI, 132
Spenceans (followers of Thomas Spence), VII, 307 n.
Spezia, X, 326
Spicer, John, stockbroker, VI, 112, X, 126–8
Spicer, John William, VIII, 347
Spinoza, X, 31–2
Spitalfields silk manufacture Acts, V, 220, 292, 295–7, 306–9, IX, 318
Spring-Rice, Thomas, M.P. for Limerick, V, xxvi
Staël, Baron de, IX, 236, 242, 248, X, 351
Staël, Madame de, IX, 218, 242, X, 269, 278 n., 279; *Considérations sur la révolution française,* 1818, VII, 274, X, 397
Stafford, VII, 264
Stagnation:
and glut, IX, 10, 25
caused by produce not being adapted to wants, II, 415–16
cannot arise from saving, IX, 26–7
increase of consumption no remedy for, IX, 16, and cp. II, 307
and counter-commodities, VIII, 227–8, 260
commerce more liable to, than agriculture, IV, 254–5, see also VIII, 159
in 1815–16, VI, 328, 345, VII, 49, see also II, 441, VII, 192
in 1819, V, 384–5, 398–9
in 1821, IX, 16, 21–2, 26–7
abroad in 1817, VII, 161, 164
correspondence with Malthus on, IX, 9–11, 15–17, 19–27
see also Glut
Stamp duties: on bank notes, IV, 73, 94–5, 120–34, 295, VI, 258–61, 265–8; on transference of property, I, 204; see also V, 315
Standard of currency:
necessity of a fixed standard, V, 254; perfect currency defined in terms of, IV, 55
standard inevitably variable, III, 391, IV, 62–3, V, 205–6, 209, 442; gold the least variable, I, 45–6, III, 65 n., V, 388, 427, VII, 42–3

Standard of currency (*cont.*)
'commodities generally' as, IV, 61, V, 374, mass of commodities, IV, 59
corn as (Western), V, 210–11, 238–9, 313
currency without a standard, IV, 59, 62, 64, see also III, 255, V, 519
bank notes the standard in 1809, III, 79; ancient standard restored in 1819, V, 232
value of, altered by Bank's gold purchases in 1819, V, 312
when currency was depreciated 30%, R. would have lowered the standard, IX, 73–4; but not in 1819, when only 5%, V, 43, 73, 208
see also Double standard, Gold standard, Money, standard of, Silver
Stanhope, first Earl of, plan for a sinking fund, IV, 149
Stanhope, third Earl of: his Bank-notes Act, VI, 45, 88, V, 316; on gold, as standard of currency, VI, 54, as circulating medium, 54 n.
Star, The, newspaper, V, 57, 58, 464
Stationery, Ricardo member of committee on, V, xxvi
Staubbach waterfall, X, 257
Steam-engines, I, 31, 32, 53, 69, II, 74, 87, 361, IV, 33, 87 n., 393, V, 179, 500, VII, 157–9, VIII, 171, 192, 384, 389–90, IX, 193
Steam-packet, IX, 241, X, 181–2, 196
Steers, James, Ricardo's partner as loan-contractor, VI, 112 n., X, 79–82, 123–4, 125 n.
Stephens, Mr, X, 169
Steuart, Sir James, *Inquiry into the Principles of Political Oeconomy,* 1767, III, 33 n.; on pound and guinea, III, 32–3; on measurement, III, 72–3; currency without a standard, IV, 59 & n.; see also I, 5, III, 7, 81, VI, 34, 40, VII, 202, X, 390
Stewart, Dugald, VI, 156, VII, 211, 229, 235, 312, VIII, 58, IX, 5
Stirling, A. M. W., *Coke of Norfolk,* IX, 265
Stock Exchange:
Ricardo as jobber, X, 67–74; loans and, 79–94, 125–8; see also V, 338, VI, xxiii, 84, 112 n., 116, 143, 149–50, 340, 345, VII, 14, X, 3–6, 129
fraud on, in 1803, X, 123–4; hoax in 1814, VI, 105–7, see also X, 124
Waterloo and, VI, 231 n., 233, X, 83–4
'List of members', VI, xxiv n.
Stockholders, see Fundholders
Stock Jobbing, The Art of (1819), X, 69 n.
Stock notes, Vansittart's project, VII, 260 & n.
Stocks, price of, relation to rate of interest, V, 266, 269 n., 344–5. See also Annuities, Bank post bills, Bank of England, stock of, East India stock, Exchequer bills, French funds, India bonds, Navy bills, Omnium, Ordnance bills, South Sea Company, Spanish funds, Treasury bills
Stoke Newington, X, 25
Stokes, Charles, stockbroker, VI, 270 n., VII, 14
Stokes, John, X, 97
Stones, duties on, IX, 284, 291 & n.
Storer, H. S., *Delineations of the County of Gloucester,* picture of Gatcomb Park, VII, ix, 1
Stourton, Lord, *Letters on...Agriculture,* 1821, IX, 68, 87
Strachey, Mr and Miss, X, 169
Street, John, stockbroker, X, 126–8
Strickland, Mr and Mrs, IX, 232
Strike of keelmen at Newcastle, VIII, 99
Stroud, coach for Gatcomb, VII, 277, 331, VIII, 310; see also VIII, 295, X, 63
Stuart, Lady Jane, VII, 213 n.
Stuart, Mr, petition against duties on stones, IX, 291 & n.
Stuart, Sir John, friend of James Mill, VIII, 105 & n.; see also VII, 213 n.
Stuart-Wortley, James Archibald, M.P. for Yorkshire, singular argument for low bank-rate, IV, 234 & n.; see also V, 57 n., 86, 129, 148, 351

Stuckey, Vincent, country banker, supports ingot plan, V, 359; see also III, 234–5, 385

Sturge, Charlotte, *Family Records,* character of Mrs Ricardo, X, 45–6

Suasso, Abraham Lopes, X, 201–2 & n.

Suasso, B. L., X, 201–2 & n.

Subsidy, foreign, effect on exchanges, VI, 39, 41, 64–5, 73–8, 83, 89, VII, 43, on wages, VIII, 174, 177, 195; see also VI, 236, 241, 255–6

Sudbury silk weavers, V, 295

Suffrage, household, V, 473, 485, VII, 273 & n.; universal, V, 29, 485, 502, VII, 270, 360, 369–70; see also Ballot, Reform

Sugar:
- East and West India, V, 188–90, 297–301, 477, 479–81, IX, 273, 277
- as necessary of labourer, I, 20, 104, 306, 406
- sugar from beetroot, 'absurd scheme of Buonaparte', V, 51, 90–1, VIII, 356; see also IV, 248, V, 153

Sumner, Mrs Charles Richard, *née* Maunoir, X, 272–3 & n.

Sumner, George Holme, M.P. for Surrey, V, 48, 86; his *Life of C. R. Sumner,* X, 273 n.

Sumner, John Bird, later Archbishop of Canterbury: gives up political economy for theology, VII, 247–8; reviews Malthus on Population, VII, 247 & n. 2; *Treatise on the Records of the Creation,* 1816, VII, 247 & n. 4

Sun, The, newspaper, VII, 28 & n., 30

Sunday Times, Obituary of Ricardo, X, 40 n., 51

Sunninghill, VI, 240 n.

Supply, regulates value, VIII, 279; follows close on heels of demand, VIII, 302. See Demand and supply

Surplus produce:
- both rent and profits come out of, II, 128, 134
- yielded by land in form of rent not an advantage, I, 75, VIII, 182, 209

Surplus produce (*cont.*)
- and rent, distinguished by Ricardo, II, 122–3, 213, VIII, 182, 209, identified by Malthus, II, 122–3, 128, 223, IV, 11 n.; 'by the laws of nature terminates in rent' (Malthus), II, 123, 210
- limited by fertility, II, 130
- transmission of, to descendants, II, 319–20
- increased by rise in price of corn, Malthus's notion, VI, 185, 187, 190–2, 194–6, 199, qualified, 201, 207–8; controverted, 189, 192–4, 196–8, 203–5, 209–10
- wages as, II, 218
- see also Net surplus, Rent as surplus produce

Surrey County meetings: for the Queen (1821), VIII, 348 & n.; Trower shouted down (1822), IX, 165 & n.; see also IX, 268

Susa (Suze), IX, 228, X, 337–40

Suspension of cash payments, 1797, III, 169, 376, IV, 99, 283, V, 208–9, 216, 236–7, 350. See also Bank Restriction Act, Resumption

Sutherland, L. Stuart, III, 427 n.

Sutton, Mr, X, 83

Swatman, Edward, X, 136, 138

Sweden, III, 183–4

Sweden, Crown Prince of, X, 319–20

Swift, Jonathan, XI, xxx, see also VII, 122, VIII, 114

Sykes, Daniel, M.P. for Kingston-upon-Hull, V, 102, 147, 277

Takabatake, Motoyuki, X, 384

Talbot, Mr, VI, 93–4

Ta-li Kuo, X, 385

Tallow and candles, duties on, V, 146–7, 291, 294, see also V, 219, VIII, 372

Tarn, A. W., and Byles, C. E., *Guardian Assurance Company,* IX, 105 n.

Taste, influence on value, I, 194, see also I, 89–90, VI, 119, and under Wants and tastes

Tattlock, Thomas, III, 430
Taunton, Mrs, IX, 18
Tavistock, Marquis of, M.P. for Bedfordshire, V, 23, 26
Taxation, I, 150–5; a difficult subject, IV, 15 n., VIII, 132–3; neglected by economists, VIII, 71, 79–80, 130–1, IX, 69, 87
tends to diminish accumulation, I, 152 & n., 222, VII, 171, VIII, 168, 170, and production, I, 185, VIII, 154–5; an incentive to send capital abroad, V, 33, 38; a choice of evils, I, 167, 185; injurious to all classes, V, 137, 154, 168
and prices, I, 168–72, 228, III, 240–2, 328, V, 54, 74; whether tax on all commodities can raise prices with same quantity of money, IV, 320–2: it can (early view), III, 238, 242–3, it cannot, I, 168–9, 213, early view revived, I, 169 n., 213–14 n., IX, 158–9
ability to pay taxes, and cheap corn, I, 8, IV, 39–40, V, 83, 88–9, VII, 104
tax on bread: raises price of all commodities (early view), III, 270, see also III, 243; raises price of bread only, I, 254; does not diminish consumption of bread, I, 237 n.
tax on corn: raises price of corn twice (early view), VI, 206; falls on consumers of corn, I, 159, V, 258; lowers rate of profit, I, 166, 205, 239
tax on gold, I, 191–200
on ground rents, I, 203–4
on houses, I, 201–4, III, 138
on income, see Income tax
land-tax, I, 181–90; different effects if levied in proportion to rent or to produce, I, 181–3; does not fall on landlord, VIII, 79; Adam Smith on, I, 183–4; Say's view of, I, 186–90; sinking fund and, V, 259–61
tax on law proceedings, V, 147
on leather, V, 124–5, 127

Taxation (*cont.*)
on luxuries, I, 241–4, VIII, 177, 189–90, 195–6, see also I, 204, 233
on malt, I, 252–4, V, 26, 52, 101 & n., 294–5, 301–2, IX, 147
taxes on necessaries: shifted from the poor to the rich, I, 235–6; paid by consumer, not landlord, IV, 33–4 n., VI, 173; effects on comforts of labourers, V, 26–7, VIII, 168–71, 174, 176–7, 189–90, 195–6
tax on profits: effects on prices of different commodities, I, 205–10, VIII, 153–4; leaves corn rent unaltered, I, 211–12, VII, 91–2
tax on property, IV, 122 n., 155, V, 20–1, 23, 187, VII, 27, VIII, 190; on transfer of property from the dead, I, 153, landed interest exempt, V, 291; on sale of land, I, 154–5; see also IV, 86 n.
taxes on raw produce, I, 156–72; paid by consumer, I, 157, 159, 160, 196, 257, IV, 240, 255–6, VI, 173, VII, 38, 115; Adam Smith's incorrect view, I, 183–4, 252; affect corn rent but leave money rent unaltered, I, 157–8, 212, 322, VII, 92
taxes on rent cannot be shifted, I, 173, 175
taxes on revenue do not diminish demand, I, 237
tax on salt, I, 237, IV, 257, V, 84, 89, 147, 192, 194–5
special commodities proper for taxation, I, 240
tax on wages: compared with tax on necessaries, I, 215; diminishes rate of profits, I, 214, 226–7; Adam Smith's error on effects of, I, 222–5, 232–3; Buchanan's view criticised, I, 216, 218–22, VII, 108
war taxes, I, 244–8, IV, 155–7, 185–90, VIII, 170, 174–7
M[c]Culloch accuses Ricardo of encouraging ministers to taxation, VII, 281, 286, 349; passages altered in *Principles,* ed. 2, I, 152 n., 242 n., VII, 334, 337–8, 353

Taxation (*cont.*)
Adam Smith's maxims, I, 181–2, 204, 235
taxation and agricultural distress, IV, 255–9, V, 84, 89, 91, 124, 131–2
Tax on capital to pay off national debt, Ricardo's proposal, V, 38, 187, 271, 472. See National debt, Ricardo's plan to pay off
Taylor, C. W., M.P., IX, 147
Tea:
tax on, I, 240, V, 23, 189; as labourer's necessary, I, 20, 104, 306, VIII, 275
tea-trade, V, 481
a Dutch tea, X, 211
Teixeira, Mr, X, 211–12
Temple, Earl, M.P. for Buckinghamshire, V, 47
Teniers, VII, 163
Tennant, Smithson, VI, 90 & n., 135; Whishaw's *Account* of, VI, 244 & n.
Terry, Christopher, VI, 277, VII, 15
Tetbury, savings bank, VII, 187 n.; see also VIII, 295
Thanet, Earl of, V, 369
The Times:
reporter does not understand Ricardo, V, 129 n., IX, 164
breach with Owen, VII, 177 & n.
Hardcastle's letters to, VIII, 3 & n.
parliamentary reports, V, 67, 92, 95, 98, 100–3, 111, 114, 117–18, 121, 157, 223, 352, 368
see also VII, 131, VIII, 6, 36, 59, XI, xxviii
Theories: age of, V, 109; abominable theories of political economists (Lethbridge), V, 169; wild dreams of theorists, III, 195, and cp. V, 371; fanciful and impracticable theories (Lord Liverpool), IX, 269 n.; see also V, 143
Theorist, Ricardo accused of being a, IV, 352, V, xxv, 93 & n., 128 n., VIII, 347; 'abundantly theoretical', V, xxxiii; 'disregards experience', VIII, 152 n.; *Principles* not intended to be practical, VII, 378
Theory of Money (anon.), 1811, X, 400
Thiele, Ottomar, X, 378
Thistlewood, Arthur, VIII, 163 n.
Thompson, Thomas, country banker, III, 228
Thompson, William, M.P. for Callington, V, 185
Thomson's *Annals of Philosophy*, VI, 244 & n.
Thornton & Power, merchants, III, 431
Thornton, Edward, Minister at Hamburg, III, 430–1
Thornton, Henry, VI, 87–8
joint author of Bullion Report, III, 413–14 & n.
on unfavourable balance of trade, III, 59–61; unfavourable exchange, 75–7; export of gold coin, 58–9, 81
Enquiry into Paper Credit, 1802, III, 4, 58–62, 64 n., 75–7, 79–81, 83, 95, 100, 208, 365, X, 390
Substance of Two Speeches…on the Report of the Bullion Committee, 1811, III, 84 n.
see also III, 364 n., VI, 42, VII, 109, X, 49
Thornton, John, IX, 104 & n. 3
Thornton, Samuel, Governor of the Bank of England:
evidence on public expenditure, IV, 77–8, 91–4, V, 12 n.
on profits of the Bank, IV, 97 & n., 102–3, VI, 276, 283
on stamp duties, VI, 258
supports Ingot plan, V, 14, 363
see also VI, 288
Thornton, Stephen, Brothers & Co., Russia merchants, VI, xxxvii, IX, 104 n.
Thorpe, Mr, V, 353
Thoun (Thun), X, 258–61
Thrashing machine, burned to the ground, VII, 45; see also I, 82, 251, V, 90, 211, 525, VI, 187

Tierney, George, M.P., Whig leader, VI, 67 n.
on resumption of cash payments, V, 2, 8, 10, 14–15; member of the committee, 350, 354, 365
letter to, on bullion payments plan, VI, 67–71, see also V, 351
on the surplus profits of the Bank, IV, 102
see also IV, 166, VI, 306, VII, 252, 260, 305, VIII, 146, X, 93, 396
Tillotson, John, D.D., *Works,* 1712, V, 327 & n., see also 325
Timber duties, V, 102–4, 110–11, 306, VIII, 371
Time, as cause of variation in relative value, IV, 370, 381–3, 403, VIII, 193
owing to different proportions of fixed and circulating capital, I, 31, II, 58
or to different durabilities of fixed capital, I, 38–9, 43, 58–9, and of circulating capital, I, 31, 53 n., 61 n.
or to different times taken to bring to market, I, 34, 37, VIII, 142, 344
profits as compensation for time, IV, 375; denied by M^c^Culloch, IX, 366–8
Time bargains, and continuation, whether illegal, V, 338–45; see also X, 19 n.
Tintoretto, IX, 222
Tithes, I, 176–80
fall wholly on the consumer, I, 176, IV, 255
justify countervailing duties, IV, 217–18, 243, V, 45
like other taxes hinder production, VIII, 155
M^c^Culloch on, VIII, 203–4, 222, 229; extension of tithes to exempted lands, VIII, 237–8
valuation of, IX, 31, 39–40, 70, 88–9
see also I, 188, V, 304, VIII, 214, IX, 146, 199
Titian, IX, 222, X, 304, 307, 309
Tobacco, I, 406, VIII, 275; tax on, V, 23
Token currency:
silver as, V, 16; coined by the Bank, IV, 102; see also V, 14, VI, 86
gold tokens, Baring's proposal, V, 92, 96, see also V, 403 n.
Tooke, Horne, VIII, 152 n.
Tooke, Thomas, VI, xxxvii–xxxviii, IX, 250
evidence on agriculture, IV, 221, 228, 231, 259, V, xxiv, 214, 520, VIII, 366–7 & n., 370–1 & n., 373–4, IX, 67, 86, 106, 108
on resumption of cash payments, V, 361–2
draws up merchants' petition, V, 42 n.
Mallet on, VIII, 152 n.; Cobbett on, IX, 106 & n.
and Political Economy Club, IX, 158–9 n.
visit to Gatcomb, IX, 5, 14, 18, 27, 41, 105
letters from, VIII, 366, 371, IX, 104, XI, xxvi
see also V, 369 n., VI, xxvii n., IX, 46, 219, 224, 229, 266, 301, 345, 362
On High and Low Prices, 1823, IX, 250 & n., 314, 370
Letter to Lord Grenville, 1829, IV, 418
Some Account of the Free Trade Movement (anon.), 1853, V, 42 n.
Tooke and Newmarch, *History of Prices,* III, 8 n., V, 42 n., 369 n., IX, 106 n., 202 n.
Tooke, William Eyton, IX, 107 & n.
Tories, V, xx, VI, xxii, VII, 260, VIII, 25, 163 n., 205
Torrens, Robert:
first meeting with, VI, 215, 219
alterations due to, in *Principles,* ed. 2, on unequal durability of capitals, I, 31, 53, 58, 61, VII, 338; other additions to placate him, I, 96–7 n., 271, VII, 179–80, 333, 349; his intended review of *Principles,* IV, 305, VII, 179 & n., 180, 288, 309, 316 n.

Torrens, Robert (*cont.*)
controversy with, on value and capital, IV, 305–18, VII, 253, 315–16 & n., 338, 354, 364, 372, 376–7; his measure of value (quantity of capital employed), IV, 375, 393–5, IX, 355–7, 359; his lost paper on value, VIII, 128, 138 & n., 142
early view that price of corn regulates all prices, VI, 212–14, 269; later adopts Ricardo's views, VII, 24, 35–6, see also VIII, 163–4, IX, 120
his error on glut and counter-commodities, VIII, 227, 260
'labour of capital', IX, 369
opposed to ingot plan, VIII, 83
disagrees with Malthus on depreciation, VI, 205 & n., 215, 218–19; criticises his *Political Economy*, VIII, 185–6 & n., 226, 261–2
meets M^c^Culloch in Edinburgh, VII, 315–16 & n., 354
and election of 1818, XI, xi–xii, of 1820, VIII, 156–7 & n.
interest in *The Traveller*, IV, 7, VIII, 185–6 & n., 226, 261–2, 316, and *The Champion*, IX, 114 & n., 120, 122
letter to, XI, xi; lost correspondence with, VII, 180
his letters to Place quoted, VII, 179 n., 316 n.
see also IV, 320, VII, 31–2, 34 n., 177, VIII, 29 n., 143, 190, 229, 313, 367 & n., 373, 378, 381, IX, 159, 207, 312, 334
Comparative Estimate...with Strictures on Mr. Ricardo's Proposal, 1819, VIII, 83 & n.
Essay on the External Corn Trade, 1815, IV, 5, VI, 185 n.; few sold, VII, 141; Ricardo on, I, 96–7 n., VI, 188, 205–6, 212–13, VII, 179–80; Malthus on, VI, 185–6, 201–2, 211–12, 223–4; ed. 2, VIII, 164; see also I, li, 93 n., 271 n., VI, 269, VII, 31 n., VIII, 82, X, 399

Torrens (*cont.*)
Essay on Money, 1812, VI, 215, 219 & n., VII, 31 n., X, 399
Essay on the Production of Wealth, 1821, IV, 393–5, VII, 35, 141, 251, 316 n., VIII, 22, 47, IX, 46, 66, 68, 77, 113, 293; Malthus on, IX, 79–80, 87, 112; see also IV, 308
Letter to the Earl of Liverpool, 1816, VII, 24
Letters to the Earl of Lauderdale in *The Sun*, 1816, VII, 28, 30
'Strictures' on Ricardo's theory of value in *Edinburgh Magazine*, 1818, IV, 306–8, VII, 179 n., 315–16 & n., 324, 326, 332, 338, 360, 362, 364, 376; M^c^Culloch's reply, VII, 354; Ricardo's lost answer, VII, 360, 364, 372, 376–7, VIII, 8 & n.; see also X, 397
articles: on Owen in *Edinburgh Review*, 1819, VIII, 82 n., 159 n., 163–4, 227, 376 & n.; in *The Champion*, 1821, IX, 114, 120, 122
Tournay, X, 187
Towers, J. L., *Resumption of Cash-Payments*, 1811, X, 401
Townsend, John, letter from, XI, xxi
Trade:
increases enjoyments, not value, I, 319, II, 395, IV, 25–6
home and foreign, I, 133, 318–19
sudden changes in the channels of, I, 263–72
periods of prosperity and adversity (Malthus), VII, 122
see also Foreign trade
Tradesman, The, III, 9 n.
Tradesmen, V, 285
Trade Unions, see Combination of workmen
Traveller, The, Torrens's newspaper, V, xix, VIII, 185 & n., 316
articles on Malthus's *Political Economy*, VIII, 186 n., 226, 262
Treasury bills, IV, 282, 283 n.
Trevelyan, G. M., *British History in the Nineteenth Century*, X, 39 n.

Trinity College, Cambridge, Ricardo's sons at, X, 61–3; visit to, 136–40; see also VIII, 114
Tritton, John Henton, banker, III, 372–3
Trotter, Coutts, *Principles of Currency and Exchanges,* 1810, III, 115; 'Notes' on, III, 8 n., 379–403; 'Observations on Trower's Notes on', 405–8; see also X, 401
Trower, Hutches, VI, xxiii–xxv
'Friend to Bank Notes' controversy in 1809, III, 4–5, 21–46, 81 n., 88 n., X, 7–8
early chats on political economy, VII, 246; walks in Kensington Gardens, VII, 268, 273, 275; simple explanation to, on profits of capital, VI, 103–5, on value, IX, 1–3, 38, 87
advice from, on composition, VI, 326
correspondence with, on parliamentary reform, V, 490–3, VII, 266–8, 272–4, 289–90, 298–9, 309–10, 319–24, 326–7, 340–5, 360, 364, 366–71, 373–4, 381, VIII, 12–16
and Notes on Malthus, VIII, 201, 218–20, 320–2, 346, 395
and Savings Banks, VII, 12, 23 & n., 26, 33–4 & n., 96, 117–18, 128–9, 141–2, 149
on Loans, VI, 237–8, VIII, 30–1
on the management of the poor, VIII, 42–3
Sheriff of Surrey, VII, 255, VIII, 148, 164, 347, 348 n.; magistrate, VII, 96, 173, VIII, 70, 109, 131–2, IX, 312; East India proprietor, VI, 96 n., 343 n.
visit to, VIII, 162; never visited Gatcomb, IX, 377, 382–3, 338–9
list of letters IX, 400–1
see also VII, 15, 34 n., VIII, 130, X, 50, 78 n., 79, 103 n., 162, 177, 179
Christianity in India [1813], VI, 96; 'Note on prices and taxation', IV, 319–22; 'Notes on Trotter', III, 405–9
Trower, Mrs Hutches, VIII, 71, 80–1, 113
Trower, John, stockbroker, VI, xxiv, VII, 45, VIII, 35, 368, IX, 28, 40, 383, X, 82 & n., 85
Trower, Walter John, IX, 28 & n.
Tso-liang Chen, X, 385
Tucker, Mr, V, 483
Tudela, Abraham, VIII, 349 n.
Tunbridge Wells, VI, 92, 232
Turgot, A. R. J., I, 5, 238, 280 n.; his *Œuvres,* and *Life* by Condorcet, VII, 365 & n., 382, X, 399
Turin, VII, 216 n., IX, 227–8, X, 335, 338–9
Turkey, V, 495, IX, 39, X, 247
Turner, Dawson, V, xxx n.
Turner, Samuel, VII, 27 & n., VIII, 368; *Considerations upon Agriculture...and the pamphlet by David Ricardo,* 1820, V, 254, IX, 197 & n.; *Letter...to Robert Peel,* VIII, 42, 45
Turnip husbandry, I, 80–1
Turton, Sir Thomas, V, 466
Tuseany, Grand Duke of, X, 311–17, 320

Umbrellas in Milan, X, 298
Unemployed fixed capital, I, 265
Unemployed labourers, VII, 194. See under Employment of labour
Unitarians, Ricardo and, X, 39–41; see also VI, 135 n., VII, 171 n., VIII, 84 n.
Universal suffrage, would be going too far, V, 29, 485, 502, VII, 270, 360, 369–70; see also VIII, 99, 107
Upper Brook Street, Ricardo's house in, VI, facing p. 1, 52–3 & n., 82, VII, 1, 13, 17–18, X, 48, 105, 336 n.
Usury laws: Onslow's bill for repeal, V, 109–10, 323, 335–6; Ricardo's evidence, 1818, V, 337–47, VII, 305; report on, V, 336; see also I, 296–7, V, 97, 222, 511, VIII, 17 & n., 341 n.

Utility:
the foundation, not the measure of value, I, 11, 280 n., III, 284, VI, 247; dispute with Say on, I, 279–80 n., VI, 271, VIII, 276–7, 280, 299, 379, IX, 32–5, 168–71, 188–90, see also VIII, 260, IX, 64; Bentham on, III, 284
no standard for, in nature, VII, 242, see also VII, 302
iron and gold, utility and value contrasted, I, 283, IX, 33, 168
and riches, I, 281, VIII, 379, IX, 169
Utrecht, X, 212–13

Vagrant bill, IX, 181
Value:
chapter on, I, 11–51, first version, I, 52–66; absolute and exchangeable value, IV, 357–412; see also I, xxx–xlix
in early state of society, I, 12, 22–4, 26–7, 38 n., 42, 53–4, 58 n., 62 n., 112, IV, 315–18, IX, 2
regulated by quantity, not value, of labour, I, 11–20, 24–5, 46–7, 118, II, 34–5, 79, 100–2, IV, 397, VIII, 142, 149, 179
this not disturbed by rent, I, 67–78; but modified by accumulation of capital, I, 22–3 & notes, VII, 377–8, by the use of machinery, I, 30–8, 53, 56, II, 58, by different proportions of fixed and circulating capital, I, 66, IV, 318, by unequal durabilities of fixed capital, I, 38–9, 43 & n., 58–9, VIII, 339–40, or of circulating capital, I, 31, 53 n., 61 n., by the time taken to bring to market, I, 34, 37, IV, 404, VIII, 180, 192–4, 344, by the rise or fall of wages, I, 30, 33–6, 56–8, 60–3, IV, 317–18, 368, 384–5; all exceptions come under time, VIII, 193, IX, 356
profits also a part of value, IV, 373, 389, 392, VIII, 194, IX, 350–2, 356, 387, but an unimportant part, I, 36, II, 59, VIII, 279–80

Value (*cont.*)
discussion with Torrens on value, 1818–19, IV, 305–18, VII, 253, 315–16 & notes, 338–9, 354, VIII, 138, 142
value and price, early distinction, VI, 54–5; later, II, 242 & n., VII, 297, 378; latest, IV, 236, 373
puzzled by law of relative value, VII, 20, 71, 83–4
sheet-anchor the invariability of precious metals, VI, 348–9, of money, I, 47, 63, see also I, 87 n., II, 82–3
absolute value, IV, 361–412; letters on, IX, 297–300, 306–11, 341, 346, 352, 356, 364, 377–8, 383
distinguished from exchangeable value, IV, 398
measure of, a desideratum, IV, 395–6, mass of commodities as, IV, 400
see also I, xlvi–xlvii, 21, 43 n., 63, V, 209, VIII, 279, 339, 344
exchangeable value, defined, I, 92, IV, 398; papers on absolute and, IV, 361–412; value in exchange, I, 11
natural, IV, 375, or necessary, I, 415
positive, IX, 339, 351, and exchangeable, VIII, 394, IX, 1–2, 29
proportional, IV, 380
real, and exchangeable, II, 399, IX, 38, 68, 87, and nominal, II, 26–7, and relative, I, 42–3, IV, 394, and money price, IX, 83; real exchangeable value, II, 206 & n.
relative, II, 304, or exchangeable, VII, 20, and absolute, I, 21, VIII, 279, 339
value and cost, I, 47 n., II, 31, 34–5, 100–2
and riches, I, 273–9, II, 192–3, 203, 207
and utility, I, 279–80 n., 281–3, 287 n., see also I, 11, III, 284, and under Say, J.-B.
and wealth, II, 33–4, 375, VII, 312
value in use, I, 11. See Utility
definition of value, difference with Malthus, VIII, 229, 261, 278–9, see also IX, 352

Value (*cont.*)
simple explanation to Trower: on positive and exchangeable value, IX, 1–3, 38, 87, on differences with M^c^Culloch, IX, 377, and with Malthus, IX, 378
scarcity and, I, 12, see also I, 90, 119, 194, 209, II, 204
relative 'utility' of two definitions of value, VIII, 261, 278
see also Price

Value, measure or standard of:
earliest statement, III, 65 & n.
no invariable standard known, I, 17 n., 43, 275, II, 288, IV, 370, V, 217, IX, 346; no such thing in nature, IV, 404, IX, 387
variety of circumstances the difficulty, I, 44–5, IV, 368–9, 386–7, IX, 303–4, 319
search for an invariable standard, IV, 392, IX, 331, like measures of length and time, IV, 380, 391, 401, IX, 356, see also VII, 43
quantity of labour bestowed the least variable measure, I, 14, 46–7, II, 35, 66, VIII, 279, IX, 325, 344; doubtful whether for a day or a year, VIII, 344
medium between extremes preferred, VIII, 193, requiring both labour and capital, IV, 371–3, IX, 361, for a year, IV, 405; imperfections acknowledged, IX, 346–7, 352, 375
gold as a just mean, I, 45–6, 87 & n., IV, 389–90, 406, IX, 386; see also II, 82–3
M^c^Culloch's measure: quantity of labour, estimated by capital employed, IV, 376–9, 410–12, IX, 303, 330–1, 343–4, 354 n., 361; labour bestowed on agent of production, not on product, IX, 356, 359
cause of value different from measure of, IX, 344, 358, 377, see also IX, 178, 185

Value, measure of (*cont.*)
Malthus's measures discussed, II, 28–35, 66–7, 90–1, 94–102, 175–7, 206–7, 410–11, IV, 361–4, 371–3, 378–9, 390–3, 406–10, IX, 280–3, 297–300, 304–13, 318–25, 336–41, 345–66, 378, 380–2
(1) labour commanded, II, 28–35, 175–6, 410–11, IX, 280 & n., 322, 324, 348
(2) pay of a day's labour, IV, 361–4, 371, 392, 407, IX, 304, 319, 378
(3) mean between corn and labour, II, 95–9, 207, VIII, 233–4, 305–7, IX, 79, 84–5, 91–2, 100, abandoned, IX, 293
(4) silver (or gold) picked up in a day on the sea-shore, II, 81–2, IV, 365, 406, VIII, 179, 343, IX, 298, 305, 347–8, 354, 361, 363–4, 386; how profits are regulated in this case, VIII, 64–5, 73, 108
(5) the constant labour that produces the wages and profits in a commodity, IX, 280–3, 304–5, 307–10, 323–5, 338–40, 350–1, 382, intuitive proof, IX, 308
see also I, 18–19, II, 242, 281, VIII, 180–1, 193–4, IX, 290, 312, 334
Mill's: quantity of labour worked up, IV, 375–6; includes 'labour of machines', IX, 325 n., see also IX, 312
Say's: corn, I, 275 n.; quantity of things commanded, IX, 170
work done by natural agents and machines adds to value, I, 285–7
Adam Smith's: the toil and labour of acquiring, I, 12–13, 17, 309
the quantity of labour commanded, I, 14, 16–17
corn and labour, I, 18–19, 20, 377
Torrens's: quantity of capital employed in producing a commodity, IV, 375, 393–5, VII, 315 n., 354, IX, 355–6, 359, see also IV, 307

Value, measure of (*cont.*)
other measures discussed:
shrimps, result of immediate labour only, IV, 365, 367–71, 386, 388–90, 402–3, IX, 298, 347–8, 356, 361, 363–4, 381
oak-tree, result almost entirely of accumulated labour, IV, 377–8, 388, 410–11, IX, 303, 330–1, 343–4, 354 n., 359, 361; wine mellowed by age, IV, 369–70, 375–6, 387, 402–3, IX, 303, 330, 343, 359
cloth, mean between the extremes, IV, 369–71, 376, 382, 386–9, 403, IX, 298, 365
real measure of value, I, 21 n., II, 95, 206–7, IX, 81
Vandamme, General, X, 184–5
Vandyke, VII, 163
Van Lancken's collection of paintings in Antwerp, X, 191
Vansittart, Nicholas (see also Chancellor of the Exchequer):
Propositions on the Bullion Report, III, 411–23
his plan of finance, 1813, IV, 158–67, 198–200, V, 262–3, VI, 91–2 & n., 334, VIII, 120–2, see also IV, 175, 182, 193, VIII, 319
project of stock notes, VII, 260 & n.
in committee on Resumption, V, 350, 352 n., 354, 365
see also II, 433 n., III, 262, 429, VII, 252, 292 n., VIII, 350 n., IX, 6, 270, X, 82, 90 n., 189
Outlines of a Plan of Finance, 1813, IV, 40, 159 n.
Varese, X, 292
Velocity of circulation of money, see Rapidity
Venice, IX, 222, X, 306–10
Verbal Disputes, Observations on, 1821 (anon.), IX, 27 & n., 38
Verona, eve of the Congress, IX, 222, X, 302–6; Juliet's tomb, X, 305
Veronese, Paul, IX, 222, X, 304
Viner, Jacob, IV, 147 n., VI, xx n., IX, 61 n., 72 n.
Vizard, William, the Queen's Solicitor, VII, 264, 346, 355
Void in the currency, III, 24, 60, in the circulation, 61
Voltaire, correspondence with d'Alembert, IX, 335, 374–5; see also VI, 332, VII, 102
Volunteers, Ricardo as captain in the, X, 46–7, 118; see also X, 402, XI, ix
Bank Volunteers, IV, 97 n.

Wada, Saichiro, X, 384
Wade, R. W., stockbroker, VII, 14
Waentig, Heinrich, X, 378
Wages, I, 93–109
and proportion of capital to population, I, 98, 165, II, 252, 265, 302–4, 321, III, 389, IV, 22–3, V, 32, see also II, 8, VIII, 170–1, 258
corn wages fall, money wages rise, with growth of population, I, 101–4, II, 132–3, see also I, 305–6, II, 137, 259, VI, 189, VII, 202, 214 n.
increase in, implies full employment, II, 412
fall of, in 1816, VII, 75, 193, 199; in 1820, VIII, 290, 307; in 1822, V, 228; inadequacy of, for married men, V, 1, VII, 118, 124, 133
fall of, in 1821, without men out of work, IX, 20, 25, and cp. 40
should be sufficient to provide for periods out of work, VII, 248
bad system of Gloucestershire clothiers, VIII, 316
fixing of, opposed, V, 292, 296, 307, IX, 318; should be left to competition, I, 105, VIII, 316
petition of Spitalfields silk weavers, V, 292, 295, 306–8
and fund for maintenance of labour, I, 164–5, 196, 219–22, 225–6, 289, 292–3, 306, VIII, 258, IX, 24
and machinery, I, 16, 387–8, 392, IV, 35, VIII, 171 & n.
hand weavers' petition, V, 302–3

Wages (*cont.*)
market price of labour regulated by supply and demand, I, 94, 382, II, 268, see also I, 15, 96–8, 101, 104, 163–4, II, 413, V, 114, 303, VII, 57, 72, 78
natural price of labour regulated by price of food and necessaries, I, 93, 95, by difficulty or facility of producing food, I, 218, 296, VII, 57, 80–1; general rule modified, I, 160–6, 217, VI, 146; see also I, 118, 302, II, 78, 291, IV, 179, 236–7, 347, V, 33, 50, 241, VI, 108, VII, 72, 78, VIII, 234
natural price of wages different in different countries, I, 96–7, see also IX, 82, 282–3, 305
not part of net produce, I, 347–8, III, 283; opinion modified, I, 348 n., 425, II, 380–1, IV, 366, VIII, 257–8, 311; see also VII, 378–9 and under Revenue, gross and net
case of wages spent on unproductive consumption, IX, 16–17, 21, 24–6
nominal and real, disagreement with Malthus on, II, 249–50, 258–9, 278,
322–4, VII, 81 & n., 214, see also I, 19
and cheap parish labour, VII, 142, XI, xvi
poor-rates and, II, 49, V, 113–14
the great regulator of population (Malthus), VI, 155, (Ricardo), VIII, 169, see also I, 218–20, 292, 406–7
price of wages, I, li–lii, 94 n., 95 n. 3, 96 notes, 111 n., 118, 145, 303 n., 334 n., II, 63 n. 5, 231 n., 411, IV, 22, VI, 241, IX, 325; value of, II, 126
Adam Smith's view that rise of wages raises all prices refuted, I, 46, 61–3, 302–3, 307, 315, see also I, 104–5, 126, IV, 213–16, 236
curious effect of rise of wages: some prices lowered but none raised (*Principles,* ed. 1), I, 63, 66, VII, 82–3, 98; later view (ed. 3), some prices are raised, I, 35 & n., 43 & n., II, 62–4. See also Value, effect of rise of wages on
wages and profits: division by proportions, I, 125–6, 420–1, II, 61–2, 138, 194–5, 258–9, 266–7, 290, VII, 80–1, VIII, 194–5, on no-rent land, II, 196–7, 278, 284, 336
always constitute the same sum, I, 115, 120, 226, 404, 411; if wages rise profits fall, I, 205, 296, II, 266, VI, 162, VII, 57, 155–6, IX, 179; fall of, increases profits, I, 132, IV, 22, but not rent, IV, 11
provision system of, V, 218
real wages, II, 258–9, VII, 214, and nominal, II, 249, 322–4, VII, 81 & n., and money wages, VII, 81; real value of, I, 19, and nominal value of, I, 50, 65; real and nominal price of, I, 274–5 n.
in rich and poor countries, I, 373, 376, VI, 147; in a dearth, VII, 200–1, see also VII, 194
subsistence wages, I, 93, 159, 217, 305, 382, V, 50, IX, 17, 54
taxes on, I, 215–27, VIII, 169–70, are in effect taxes on profits, I, 226
raised by tax on raw produce, I, 159–61, 166, VIII, 195–6, and on other necessaries, I, 243; not affected by tax on luxuries, I, 243–4
raised by combination of workmen, VII, 203
see also Distribution, Labour
Wages fund, see Fund for the maintenance of labour
Wakefield, C. M., *Life of Thomas Attwood,* VIII, 370 n.
Wakefield, Edward, Ricardo's land agent, VI, xxxviii, X, 96–8
evidence on agriculture, IV, 211, 260, IX, 67
negotiations for seat in parliament, V, xiv–xvi, VII, 86, 216–17, 232–3, 254–5, 346–7, 355

Wakefield, Edward (*cont.*)
letters from, VII, 216, 232, 252, 346, see also X, 390; letter to Place quoted, VII, 182 n.
see also VII, 299 n., VIII, 48–9, X, 104 n., 267
Account of Ireland, 1812, V, xiv n., VI, xxxviii, VII, 347 n.
Address on Management of Landed Property, X, 96–7 n.
Wakefield, Edward Gibbon, VII, 216 & n., 217, 232–3, X, 53
Waldshut, X, 233–5
Waldstetter, Lake of, X, 245–8
Wales, Prince of, VII, 208, X, 111. See also Regent, and George IV
Wales, Princess of, X, 112. See Caroline, Queen
Walesby, Lincs., Malthus's living at, VI, 35 n.
Walker, Col. Alexander, VIII, 106 & n.
Walker, George, merchant, III, 430
Walks in London: Green Park, VIII, 191; Hyde Park, VI, xxviii n., VII, 277; Kensington Gardens, V, 490–1, VI, xxxiv, VII, 263, 266, 268, 273, 275, IX, 210, 345, X, 264; St James's Park, VI, xxxiv
Wallace, Professor at Sandhurst, VII, 292 n., 304 n.
Wallace, Thomas (Vice-President, then President, of the Board of Trade):
reduction of timber duties, V, 102, 110
navigation laws amendment bill, V, 190, 197
warehousing bill, V, 220, 275
Ricardo's tribute to, V, 246–7
see also V, xx, 335
Wallas, Graham, *Life of Francis Place*, IV, 145 n., VI, xxix, VII, 183 n., 357 n., 363 n., VIII, 105 n., 199 n., X, 34 n.
Wallenstadt, Lake of, X, 239–40
Walpole, Sir Robert, IV, 149, V, 118, 130
Walters, David, VI, 113 n.
Wants and tastes of mankind: effects on price, difference with Malthus, VI, 132, 134–5, 141, 147–8, 155, VII, 70, 122; see also I, 263, II, 24–5, 415 & n., IV, 343–4
War:
outbreak of, effects on commerce, I, 263, IV, 255, on agriculture, I, 266, 272
whether to be financed by taxes or by loans, I, 244–7, IV, 185–90, VIII, 147, 170
dependence on foreign supplies of food in time of, V, 54–5, see also IV, 264–6
increase of wealth and profits during (1813), VI, 93–4
termination of: effects on demand for labour, I, 265, 393–4, VII, 49, 67, on farmers, II, 110, on landholders, VI, 345, on rate of interest, VII, 199, on Bank, IV, 52, on price of gold and silver, VI, 119, 299, 318, 344, VII, 28; see also I, 90, II, 439
Warburton, Henry, F.R.S., VII, 275 n.
on price of seat in parliament, VII, 276
visits Gatcomb, VII, 56, 187, VIII, 276, 282–3
letter from, VII, 275
see also IV, 204, V, xv n., VI, 244, 295, VII, 28–9, 52, 54, 61, 139, 185, 206, 252, 361, IX, 107, 148, 312, X, 49, 216
Warburton, William, VII, 277
Ward, George, loan contractor, X, 85
Ward, William, Bank director, V, 354–5, VIII, 21 & n.
Warehousing system, V, 85, 90, 220, 275, see also IV, 29 n.
Warrender, Sir George, M.P., X, 187, 190
Washington, George, bust of, IX, 228
Waterloo, battle of:
effect on price of stock, V, 5, VI, 231–3, 235, 237–8 & n., X, 83
family visit to battlefield, X, 186, 188–91
Saint-Arnaud's views on, X, 333
see also V, xv n., VI, 239, 280, 316

Wathen, George, X, 265 n.
Watson, James, radical, VIII, 129
Watson, Richard, Bishop of Landaff:
Address to the People, 1798, anticipates plan for paying off national debt, V, 41
Apology for Christianity, 1776, X, 394
Apology for the Bible, 1796, X, 395
Anecdotes of the Life of, 1817, VII, 258 & n., 261, VIII, 323, 335
Watt, James, VIII, 82
Wealth:
real wealth, I, 425, III, 144; no difference to, whether products be exported or consumed at home, III, 330; Malthus's definition, II, 14–15
two ways in which it may be increased, I, 278–9; also increased by use of paper money, I, 361, and cp. III, 272
progress of: effects on profits, I, 120, IV, 11, 14, 18, 23, on rent, I, 77–8, VI, 181, 204, VII, 16–17, on wages, I, 94, 102, 112, see also I, 265, II, 414; impeded by corn-laws, IV, 32, 39, VII, 270–1. See also Progress of society
and value distinguished, I, 276, II, 33–4, 375, 420–1, see also VII, 312, IX, 248–9
distribution of circulating medium and, III, 120
see also Riches
Webb Hall, George, secretary of the Board of Agriculture, IV, 241 & n.; his reveries, IX, 153 & n., 165 n.
Weddle, Mrs, VII, 264 & n.
Wellesley, Marquis: his administration in India, VII, 241–4; Lord-Lieutenant of Ireland, IX, 124 n., 145, 153; see also VIII, 241
Wellington, Duke of:
battle of Waterloo, VI, 232, 235, 239, X, 190, 333
on Ricardo's speech, V, 17 n.
Wellington, Duke of (*cont.*)
in committee on resumption of cash payments, V, 351, 354, 365
see also X, 255, 259
Civil Correspondence, V, xiv
Werner, I., X, 381
Wesen, X, 239
West, Edward, *Essay on the Application of Capital to Land,* 1815, VII, 297–8 & notes; anticipates theory of rent and profits, I, 5, IV, 5–6, VI, 179–80 & notes; see also VII, 289, IX, 109 n., X, 400
West India Dock system, V, 104
West Indies: depressed state of property, X, 350 & n.; merchants, III, 429 n., V, 476, VI, xxxvi; planters, V, 153, 219; slavery, V, 483; see also III, 350 and under Jamaica, Sugar
Western, Charles Callis, M.P. for Essex:
motion for agricultural committee, 1816, V, 319 n., VII, 27, IX, 265
Ricardo's notes and speech on his resolutions on currency (1822), V, 223–45
motion on resumption of cash payments (1822), V, 198, 202, 210–18, IX, 202, 207; (1823), V, 309, 322, Ricardo's speech, V, 309–21, see also V, xxx, XI, xxv
imputes interested motives to Ricardo, V, 317, 320, 526–7, IX, 250, X, 103 & n.
see also V, 86, 101 n., 153, 155, 158 n., IX, 260, 293, X, 177, 185, 392 n.
Second Address to the Landowners, 1822, V, 317, 320, IX, 250 n., X, 402, XI, xxv; Ricardo's notes on, V, 522–8
Westminster election (1818), VII, 269–70 & n., 273 & n., 357–8 & n., 360, 363–4; *Authentic Narrative of,* VIII, 125 & n.; see also V, 474, 484, 486, 491, VIII, 57
Westminster Infant School, VII, 356–7 & n., 359–60, 363

Westminster Reform Dinner, Ricardo's speech at, 1822, V, 474–5; 1823, 484–6, see also IX, 288 n.
Westminster Reformers, VI, xxxv, VII, 357 & n.
Westminster Review, VIII, 17 n.
Westminster School, VII, 138
Weston, Ambrose, *Two Letters,* 1799, VII, 260 n.
Wetenhall, James, *The Course of Exchange,* VI, 79, 174, 176; tables of gold prices, III, 78 n., V, 462 n., VI, 85, 95
Weyland, John: *The Principles of Population and Production,* 1816, I, 99 n., VII, 46 n., 48, 63, 95; his review of J. B. Sumner's *Records of the Creation,* VII, 247
Wheatley, John, letter to, IX, 71–4
  Essay on the Theory of Money, 1807–1822, IX, 71–2 n., see also III, 7 n.
  Plan to Relieve the Country, 1821, IX, 72 n.
Whewell, William, X, 63–4
Whigs:
  Ricardo on, VIII, 6, 56, 62–3, 75, 206–7, 295, 316–17, 335–6, IX, 45; would be neither Whig nor Tory, VII, 260
  Mill on, VII, 373–4, VIII, 8–9, 58–9, 68, 106, 327–9, IX, 41–2
  and Tories in Scotland, VIII, 325, IX, 136 n., 187 n.
  see also VII, 270 n., 274, 357, VIII, 221, 294
Whishaw, John, VI, 66 n.
  on Ricardo's speech against Brougham, V, 128 n.
  visits Gatcomb, VIII, 107, 129
  discussions on reform, VIII, 61–3, 68, 75, 77
  letters to Ricardo, VI, 243, VII, 264; letters quoted, to Th. Smith, IV, 204, VII, 144 n., 270 n., IX, 109 n., to Horner, III, 9 n., VI, 159 n.
  see also VI, 87, 90, 196, 220, 240, 255, 295, VII, 14, 54–5, 57, 61, 90, 148, 169, 171, 174–5, 185, 188, 192, 206, 223, 250 & n., 252, 275, 280, 284, 295, 311, 355, 357, VIII, 57, 152, IX, 251, X, 50, 314 n.
  Life of Mungo Park, 1815, VI, 244–5 n.
  Some Account of Smithson Tennant, 1815, VI, 244 & n.
  see Seymour, Lady, *The Pope of Holland House* (John Whishaw)
Whitbread, Lady E., IX, 143
Whitbread, Samuel, M.P., VI, 232 & n.
White, Joseph, X, 98
White, William, X, 98
Whitehead, Rev. W. B., *Prosecution of Infidel Blasphemers, briefly vindicated in a letter to David Ricardo, Esq., M.P.,* XI, xxii n.
Whiteleaf Oak, Ricardo's estate, X, 104–5
Whiting, Mrs, X, 144, 156–7
Whitmore, John, Governor of the Bank of England, evidence to bullion committee, III, 193 n., 227–8, 356–61, 364–9
Whitmore, William Wolryche, M.P. for Bridgnorth:
  his system of duties on corn, V, 88; moves for lowering import price, 196, 256
  motion for equalisation of sugar duties, V, 297, 301, 479
  member of agricultural committee, 1822, V, 138, IX, 176–7
  see also V, 91, 185, 277, VIII, 357
  Letter on Agriculture, 1822, IX, 176–7 n.; ed. 2, 1823, IV, 326 n., X, 400
Wigram, William, chairman of East India Company, IX, 330, 373 n.
Wilberforce, William, M.P. for Bramber:
  on Ricardo as an economist, V, 40–1 n.
  attacks Ricardo on free discussion of religion, 280 n., 324–5, 328
  petition on slavery, V, 483
  see also VIII, 221 n.
  Life of, by his sons, V, 280 n.

Wilbraham, Edward Bootle, V, 369 n.
Wilderspin, S., *Educating the Infant Poor,* 1824, VII, 357
Wilkes, Charlotte (Mrs Jeffrey), VIII, 205, X, 272 n.
Wilkinson (family of D.R.'s wife), X, 43–6; crest, VI, 20 n.
Wilkinson, Alfred, X, 44
Wilkinson, Conrad, X, 60
Wilkinson, David, X, 59
Wilkinson, Edward, surgeon (D.R.'s father-in-law), X, 36, 43
  his 'detestable disposition', X, 111 & n.
  letter to, X, 119
  his death, X, 44
  his will, X, 45
Wilkinson, Edward, jun., X, 43–4
Wilkinson, Elizabeth (D.R.'s mother-in-law), *née* Patteson, X, 43, 45 n., 120
Wilkinson, Esther (D.R.'s sister), see Ricardo, Esther
Wilkinson, Fanny, see Ricardo, Fanny
Wilkinson, Horace, X, 60
Wilkinson, Canon Horace Ricardo, X, ix, 43 n., 60, 109, 117, 119
Wilkinson, Josiah Henry (D.R.'s brother-in-law), X, 44
  resentment against father, X, 44–5 & n., 121
  owns Oliver Cromwell's head, 'his real head', X, 173–4
  visits Gatcomb, VIII, 49, 51, 244
  correspondence with, X, 109–19, see also VIII, 46–7 n., X, 95, 317 n., 319–20
  bequest to, X, 105
Wilkinson, Norman, X, 118
Wilkinson, Priscilla Ann (D.R.'s wife), see Ricardo, Priscilla Ann
Wilkinson, Rachel (D.R.'s sister), see Ricardo, Rachel
Wilkinson, Robert, X, 45
Wilkinson, Sarah (D.R.'s sister-in-law), *née* Patteson, X, 44, 105, 109–11
Wilkinson, William Arthur (D.R.'s nephew), X, 44, 59–60
Wilkinson, W. A. (*cont.*)
  Ricardo's clerk on the Stock Exchange, X, 74, 115–17
  married Ricardo's sisters: Esther, VII, 325, X, 59, Rachel, X, 59
Wilkinson, William Ernest, X, 60
Wilkinson Papers, X, 386
Wilks, Mark, *Historical Sketches of... India,* 1810–1817, VII, 183, 195, 204
Will and power to purchase, II, 36–7, 307, 311–14, VI, 58, 131–3, 141, 155, 209. See also Demand
William, John, *Memoirs of T. Belsham,* VII, 171 n., VIII, 75 n.
Williams, Samuel, III, 183 n., 429 n.
Wilson, C. H., *Anglo-Dutch Commerce and Finance,* X, 21 n.
Wilson, John: contest for Edinburgh professorship, VIII, 204–5 & n., 215, IX, 205–6
  Works, ed. Ferrier, VIII, 205 n.
  Christopher North, A Memoir of John Wilson, by Mrs Gordon, VIII, 205 n.
  see also under Mullion, Hugh and Mordecai
Wilson, Sir Robert, dismissal from army, IX, 88, 110, 123–4
Wilson, Thomas, M.P. for London, V, 189, 192, 292, 351
Windham, William, speech against reform, 1809, VI, 307 & n.; see also VIII, 152 n.
Windsor Express, obituary of Ricardo, VI, xxxv n.
Wine:
  fall in price, V, 72 & n.
  committee on wine trade, VIII, 204 & n., 214 & n.
  letter to a wine merchant, X, 141–3
  wine from a wreck, X, 169–70
  see also II, 358, VI, 129, VII, 164, IX, 97, X, 163
Wisdom of our ancestors, V, 176, 178–9, 283, 475
Wodehouse, Edmond, M.P. for Norfolk, on Ricardo's good character but bad economics, V, 321–2; see also V, 86, 196, IX, 177, 265

Wollaston, William Hyde, F.R.S., VII, 185 & n.; see also V, 352, IX, 148
Wood, Colonel Thomas, M.P. for Norfolk, V, 269 n.
Wood End, Ricardo's property, X, 97
Woodfall, William, parliamentary reporter, V, xxvii
Woodrow, John, plan for savings banks, V, 121, XI, xxi; pamphlets on, V, 128 n.; his petition, 128
Woodward, H. B., *History of the Geological Society*, VI, 206 n., VII, 119 n., X, 29 n., 35 n., 49 n., 144 n.
Wooler, Thomas Jonathan, VIII, 329
Woollen manufacturers, I, 90–1, IV, 71 n., 251, V, 57
Wootton Bassett, V, xvi n., VII, 264
Worcester: Ricardo declines standing for, VII, 101–2, 110; music-week at, IX, 101; see also VII, 66, 71, 74, IX, 104, X, 61, 351
Working classes, see Classes
Wotton-under-Edge, VII, 187 n., VIII, 295, 400 n., X, 62
Wright, John, editor of *Hansard*, correspondence with, V, xxix–xxx, XI, xxv
  volume of MS Speeches, V, xxx n.
Wright (*cont.*)
  biography of Huskisson, IX, 270 n., but see XI, xxix
Wynn, Charles Watkin Williams, V, xxiii n.
Wynne, Henry, VII, 175, 265
Wynne, Mrs (Malthus's sister-in-law), VII, 175 n., 265
Wyvill, Marmaduke, M.P. for York, V, 277

Yamamoto, Toyokichi, X, 384
Ya-nan Wang, X, 385
Yate, Walter Honeywood, X, 97, 105 n.
Year, assumed as period of production and consumption, I, xlii & n., xlv, 59, 61, 150, II, 64–5; as mean period for measure of value, IV, 405, see also IV, 364, 389, IX, 386
Yonge, C. D., *Life of Lord Liverpool*, X, 90 n.
York, Duke of, VII, 208 & n.
Yoshida, Hideo, X, 385

Zinke, G. W., I, liv n., II, vii n., IX, 49 n.
Zug, X, 245, 253
Zurich, X, 236–8, 242–4
Zyst, Moravian establishment, X, 213